# National Parks for a
# New Generation

Independent analysis, mediation, the development of new ideas—
these are the hallmarks of The Conservation Foundation, a nonprofit environmental research group based in Washington, D.C.
Since its founding in 1948, The Conservation Foundation has been
dedicated to improving the quality of the environment and to promoting wise use of the earth's resources. The Foundation does not
have members. Nor does it lobby, litigate, or buy and sell land. It
does emphasize action-oriented research to influence policy.

# National Parks for a New Generation
## Visions, Realities, Prospects

**A Report from The Conservation Foundation**
**Sponsored by the Richard King Mellon Foundation**

Washington, D.C.

**National Parks for a New Generation:**
**Visions, Realities, Prospects**

Photographs by Janet Mendelsohn
Cover design by Sally A. Janin
Typography and interior design by Rings-Leighton, Ltd., Washington, D.C.
Printed by R. R. Donnelley & Sons Company, Harrisonburg, Virginia

**The Conservation Foundation**
Washington, D.C.

**Library of Congress Cataloging in Publication Data**
Conservation Foundation.
   National parks for a new generation.
   Includes index.
   1. National parks and reserves—United States.    2. National parks and
reserves—Government policy—United States.    3. United States. National
Park Service. I. Title.

SB482.A4C67  1985             333.78′3′0973             85-10948

ISBN 0-89164-090-8

We are deeply grateful for the support of the Richard King Mellon Foundation, the Burlington Northern Foundation, and the donors of unrestricted funds to The Conservation Foundation. Without them, this book would not have been possible.

**Project Staff**

John H. Noble
Michael Mantell
Phyllis Myers
Christopher J. Duerksen
William E. Shands
Richard A. Liroff
Christine Reid

**Photographs**

Janet Mendelsohn

**Senior Editor**

Robert J. McCoy

# Contents

# Acknowledgments

This book is the product of more than three years work by an inter-disciplinary project team made up of a land-use and public land planner, an urban specialist, a social scientist, and attorneys. In preparing it, the team visited more than 60 national parks and interviewed several hundred people. A number of outside experts generously reviewed and commented on chapter drafts.

Staff members of the National Park Service assisted the project almost daily. Hundreds of park service people in Washington, in regional offices and special units, and in the parks gave unstintingly of their time and shared their insights and information with us. Particular thanks go to the cultural and natural resource offices and the concessions and land resources divisions in Washington. Although this book calls for some changes in the park service, the dedication of park service people has conveyed a message that has informed our efforts.

We also talked with many others: landowners, citizen activists, business interests, officials of other federal agencies and state and local governments, and the staffs of conservation organizations, concessioners, and nonprofit groups doing business in the parks. They, like the officials of the park service, cannot be named individually because of space limitations. Generous help from the National Parks and Conservation Association and the Wilderness Society is particularly appreciated.

Outside reviewers included: Randall Biallis, Richard Briceland, Warren Brown, John Bryant, Robert Cahn, David N. Cole, Derrick Crandall, Andrew B. Dixon, Maureen Finnerty, David Gackenbach, Marshall Gingery, Destry Jarvis, Willis P. Kriz, William Leinesch, William Penn Mott, Jr., Ray Murray, Clay Peters, Paul Pritchard, Jerry Rogers, Joseph Sax, William Supernaugh, James Teer, and Roland Wauer. The park profiles were reviewed by personnel from each of the four parks—Yellowstone, Fredericksburg, Cape Cod,

and Santa Monica—who demonstrated uncommon patience in
fielding question after question after question. We are grateful for
the contributions of all these reviewers. None of them, of course,
bears responsibility for the contents of the book.

At The Conservation Foundation, the work of the project staff
was supplemented and supported by contributions of a number of
colleagues. In the final months of the project, Editor Bradley B.
Rymph tamed and refined the manuscript and guided it through
a hectic production schedule; free-lance editor Bethany Brown contributed to the editing; Bart Brown composed the index. Librarian
Barbara Rodes helped ferret out publications. Several former Foundation staff members and interns contributed as well: Virginia Coull,
Kate Dreyfus, William Heinemann-Ethier, Greg Lalley, Daniel
Miller, and Cindy Studer-Herleikson. Jenny Billet coordinated administrative support with the continuing assistance of Gwen Harley
and Tony Brown. Jody Appleton, Lori Baldwin, Fannie Mae Keller,
and Marsha White also helped.

The challenge of an extremely tight production schedule was then
met by Rings–Leighton, Ltd., of Washington, D.C., typographers,
and R.R. Donnelley & Sons Company of Harrisonburg, Virginia,
printers.

# The Photographs

Millions of photographs have been taken in our national parks. The photographs reproduced in books about the parks generally attempt to evoke the splendor of the nation's treasury of natural and cultural resources, reminding even those people who have never actually seen these resources how very important it is to safeguard them. In this book, we show the human face of the parks, reminding readers that ultimately *they* are the guardians of the national estate; it is theirs to enjoy or destroy. Our photographer visited seven national park units: Yellowstone, Yosemite, Death Valley, Fredericksburg, Cape Cod, Golden Gate, and Santa Monica Mountains. A rich mix of parks. A rich mix of people.

**On the cover:** *Yellowstone, August 1984. Artist Point, The Dietrich family and friends (Rexburg, Idaho).*

# Overview

The National Park System has entered an era for which its traditions and policies have not prepared it. After two decades that saw rapid, unprecedented expansion in the system, virtually no new parks are now being created. Efforts to extend park stewardship to special landscapes throughout the country have come to a standstill. Moreover, pressures on park resources continue to mount, and the need for more effective measures of protection goes unfilled. The cumulative impacts of heavy visitor use and deferred maintenance of resources, together with threats posed from activities originating outside park boundaries, will seriously damage the parks unless checked, at least in part, by an infusion of fix-up funds and by new, imaginative responses. Yet, in this time of uneasy transition for the parks, when modernization must be a top priority for the National Park Service, more emphasis has been placed on reducing federal expenditures than on enhancing the quality of park stewardship.

No consensus exists today on the fundamental questions facing the system of the future. Should the system be expanded to protect more of America's special places? How can the pressures on existing park resources be alleviated? To face these challenges, the National Park Service must look outward to form partnerships with conservationists, park neighbors, including other federal agencies, and state and local governments.

The position of the parks is very different from the one they enjoyed a dozen years ago, when The Conservation Foundation released *National Parks for the Future*. The needs of the parks themselves changed in the intervening years; the system has grown in size and complexity.

More profound change has stemmed from a shift in national priorities, evident since 1980, which has reshaped the opportunities to respond to park needs. The 1980s are not a time of great expectations for the management innovations that the parks require. They are a time of retrenchment, of cutbacks in domestic spending, of diminished confidence in federal initiatives as responses to national needs. They are a time, too, of reluctance to "lock up" the nation's resources, of preference for the market as a determinant of resource use rather than the commitment to preservation and public enjoyment that the parks represent.

The destiny of the parks in this emerging context has not yet been established; the balance between realistic acceptance of the times and insistence on timeless values is still being struck. The country's response to the challenges facing the parks will affect the integrity of resources already in the system and opportunities to expand the system to protect additional special places. At stake is no less than the future of the national estate.

## TIMELESS RESOURCES ENTER A NEW ERA

In our national parks, resources of unsurpassed significance are permanently protected, in Stephen Mather's words, "as close to what God made them as possible." The parks celebrate the nation, both the wonders of nature and the achievements of our people. They commemorate the cradle of liberty and the sites of fraternal bloodshed. Honored not only by millions who visit them each year but also by citizens proud of the national values that created them, the parks are one of America's great success stories.

National Parks for a New Generation: Visions, Realities, Prospects responds to the needs and opportunities of our time. Severe constraints on nonmilitary spending create today a policy context in which some recommendations made by The Conservation Foundation a dozen years ago appear anachronistic: a proposal to float a $100 billion federal bond issue to "buy back America," for example. Far from contemplating billions for new parks, the accession of Interior Secretary James Watt in 1981 spurred initiatives (and rumors of initiatives) that threatened the parks: there was talk of drumming some of the newer parks out of the system, of opening up more public lands to development, of increasing commercialism in providing visitor services, of paying paramount attention to park facilities rather than park resources, and of appropriating no funds at all for buying new parkland.

The ensuing period of acrimonious debate demonstrated the power of public and congressional devotion to the parks. Nothing has been drummed out of the system. Secretary Watt had to keep making clear that rhetoric about mineral extraction from public lands did not apply to the parks. The concessioners' role has not been significantly enlarged. Determined congressional action has provided funds to continue buying private lands inside the boundaries of parks already established, and appropriations for park operation and maintenance have more than kept pace with inflation. The renovation of park facilities initiated by Secretary Watt was unquestionably needed, and some funds were spent on stabilizing and restoring resources. Secretary Watt's successor, William Clark, calmed the waters, but there remain concerns that quieter initiatives may yet harm the parks where Mr. Watt's flamboyance actually rallied park defenders. Paradoxically, as controversies over park policies become muted and the parks are no longer in the news, the parks constituency will be more difficult to inform and mobilize.

Yet the parks have needs that arise regardless of current national priorities. No matter who had been chosen president in 1980, expansion of the system in 1985 would be proceeding more cautiously than at the end of the 1970s. For warnings about the consequences of rapid expansion by that time were coming from park advocacy groups, federal watchdog agencies, Congress, and some park service officials. So, too, would there be demands for administrative and management reforms of the National Park Service. The increased scale and diversity of the park system pose a challenge to the service's traditional operating style, a challenge compounded by today's higher public expectations and increased scientific understanding of the pressures that threaten to degrade park resources.

Within the arena of park debate, other issues, too, call for the continuing attention of officials: how best to assure that natural systems remain natural in the face of large numbers of visitors; how to elevate cultural and historic resource stewardship in a system that has viewed natural resources as its central concern; how to accommodate the needs of visitors for services with the recognition that commercialism is a particular enemy of the parks.

## WE TILT TOWARD PROTECTION

Any attempt to suggest priorities for the national parks must begin by directly confronting the conflicting directives that govern park policy and are embodied in the parks' statutory charter: to preserve the parks free from degradation, and to foster public enjoyment.

These two purposes have always been in some tension. The tension was less in the early years when the protection mission was itself best served by an aggressive policy of promotion and public relations, to ensure that a constituency for the parks was informed and enlarged to lobby for park creation and expansion against development interests. The parks' very survival once depended on increasing the number of satisfied and supportive visitors to whom Congress would listen.

The parks are indeed for people. Again and again our project staff has been reminded of that reality. Millions of children, the elderly, the handicapped and time-constrained, the sedentary who have ventured timidly into the outdoors for a glimpse of spectacular nature, all of these use, enjoy, are inspired and uplifted by the parks. They no less than hikers and climbers, backpackers and whitewater rafters and lovers of wilderness, are fully entitled to share in the parks experience. All derive pleasure and sustenance from the parks, many in different ways, in different parts of the parks, with varying levels of services and accommodations. This report, like the parks themselves, is for all of them.

Any excessively restrictive policy on use and access could not long survive, for the most committed advocates for the parks are people who have been to them. Yet there is no real danger of an excessively protectionist policy. Quite the opposite is true: growing impacts of visitors, increased development, commercialization, incompatible and polluting activities around park boundaries—these are the real problems confronting today's parks. And for that reason in this report we strongly favor more active protection of the parks. Protection against threats to park resources must have unprecedented priority for the national park system and its friends if public use and enjoyment is to remain meaningful in the years ahead. For want of adequate protection policies, the nation could lose the parks in all their splendor.

## THE CHALLENGE TO PROTECT PARK RESOURCES: PRESERVATION '95

No longer are most parks the remote wonders they typically were early in the history of the National Park System. More visitors and encroaching urban and energy development testify to greater accessibility and leave impacts such as the loss of vegetation, soil, and wildlife, along with the pollution of once-pristine air and water.

Pressures on park resources, more intense today than a decade ago, will intensify even further in the next decade and the next century. To protect park resources today and prepare them for the greater pressures to come, measures to defend these resources need greater prominence than they have so far received.

We recommend a 10-year program to institutionalize resource protection more firmly among the highest priorities of the National Park Service. The program would have several elements: staff hiring and training to provide specialized resource protection skills to more of the parks that need them, better planning to identify protection and restoration needs, and funding for projects to restore damaged resources that have already been identified.

At the core of this program, which we call Preservation '95, is a heightened commitment to the defense of the parks. Perhaps because degradation is gradual, its evidence readily overlooked amid the magnificence of park resources, public support for protective measures is often difficult to muster. To the visitor awed by the clarity of Crater Lake, the park defender who warns that clarity has declined since the good old days can seem to be carping about what is wrong with resources that are obviously wonderful. So it is perhaps not surprising that, despite some encouraging additional attention by the park service to resource protection, some badly needed defensive measures have lost out in competition with other park needs.

Preservation '95 would put those measures in place. Funding of $50 million annually for this program, spread over a 10-year period, would be substantially less than that required for the recently completed program to improve visitor facilities in the parks. It is a wise long-term investment, modest in terms of the needs, and will ultimately save costs. It makes sense even in a time of unprecedented budget deficits.

## THE SPECIAL CHALLENGE OF EXTERNAL THREATS

For more than a decade, conservation groups have been warning that threats to park resources arise not only from activities within the parks but also from activities outside park boundaries. Today, there can be no doubt that these activities are doing great harm—marring scenic vistas with intrusive development, polluting streams before they flow through parks, clouding the air over distinctive natural settings, marring the visitor's experience with the noise of logging and mining, and reducing wildlife habitat.

External pressures require attention at their sources, sometimes on private land, often on land managed by other federal agencies. Neither the park service nor Congress has been eager to effectively address the conflicts that arise when the parks and their neighbors clash. Yet there is precedent for measures that would go at least part of the way toward correcting these problems.

Thus, another broad initiative recommended by this report calls for laws, administrative arrangements, cooperative ventures, to defend the parks against external pressures. The initial emphasis should be on measures to reconcile management conflicts among adjoining federal agencies, using the kinds of conciliation measures that are already being applied under the Endangered Species Act, the Coastal Zone Management Act, and other federal legislation. In addition, there should be more experimental cooperative efforts among the park service, private landowners, and state and local governments, seeking to fashion solutions to cross-boundary problems that vary greatly from park to park and region to region.

There is no call here for simply subordinating the needs of neighbors to the wishes of the park service; any such effort would fail. Rather, the call is to recognize the coming of a new era in which the parks are no longer isolated fiefdoms, in which the defense of park resources depends on recognizing that the parks are increasingly becoming parts of larger communities.

No longer can the nation rely on the remoteness of its premier environments to protect them from degradation. A variety of partnerships among the park service, park support groups, neighbors and private citizens, state and local governments, and other federal agencies will be an essential feature of the new era. The Save Our Everglades Program initiated in Florida by Governor Bob Graham is one recent example of such an effort. Recent changes in service policy, which restrict participation by field personnel in local government deliberations, amount to a retreat from the needs of the parks and must give way to policies fostering cooperation.

## THE CHALLENGE TO RESTORE PARK CREATION TO THE NATIONAL AGENDA

External pressures on park resources are only one reason why partnerships are critical to the future of the system. The other reason is the presence *inside* parks of extensive lands that will continue to be owned by private citizens and by state and local governments. Privately owned lands are already incorporated in such "greenline" units as Cape Cod National Seashore and Cuyahoga Valley and Santa Monica Mountains national recreation areas. The accommodation of permanently nonfederal lands within park boundaries is critical for further expansion of the system.

For the past five years, system expansion has not been high on the national agenda. Creating new parks has been at a virtual standstill while Congress and the park service have coped with huge, uncompleted additions to the system that were initiated in 1978 and 1980. Only determined action by Congress has provided funds even to begin to address this backlog.

In fact, although the half-billion dollar cost (so far) of Redwood National Park reminds us of an era that has indeed passed, there are opportunities to create national parks and affiliated units to protect additional places—the Florida Keys, Tallgrass Prairie, Big Sur, and Lake Tahoe, among many others. These places belong in the National Park System. The longer the nation delays in putting them there, the greater the cost and the larger the risk of degradation, particularly at Tahoe and the Keys. The third major initiative recommended in this report calls for a series of measures to get the process moving again—measures that include assessing the backlog of unacquired land and opportunities to protect it more cheaply, reauthorization of the Land and Water Conservation Fund to provide essential funding, improvements in the ways new park sites are selected and parklands acquired or otherwise protected.

During the current period of budget stringency, greenline parks appear to represent the most important opportunity to extend the park system on a significant scale. If the resulting protection is less secure than in a park that is wholly federally owned, it is still greater than the only realistic alternative in many cases: leaving the areas unprotected.

The inclusion of private lands in parks, however, is not simply a way of avoiding the high costs of acquisition. The guiding vision is the protection of landscapes where people live and work in ways that are compatible with conserving the area's important and distinctive qualities. To protect more of the special places in an increasingly developed country, the greenline approach, long used in France, Britain, and other countries, must be made politically and administratively workable in the United States.

Greenline parks, like external threats, require the park service
to deal with private landowners on a continuing basis and on a
significant scale. The park service is still experimenting with
management methods for accomplishing this. In some units—
notably Cuyahoga and Upper Delaware—the efforts have been mired
in controversy. The park service in these places has been seen as
a heavy-handed intruder rather than a new partner in the community, and local governments have been unresponsive in passing compatible land-use measures. But when greenline parks work—in Cape
Cod, Lowell, and the Pinelands, for example—they provide splendid examples of building consensus and developing cooperative
relationships based on growing trust, mutual interest, and a mix
of conventional and novel land-protection measures. Both the park
service and elements of the parks constituency in Congress and in
conservation groups need to embrace a concept some have long
resisted. For an increasingly settled nation will need to find imaginative ways to protect far more land than it will ever be possible, or wise, to buy.

## PUTTING INITIATIVES IN PLACE:
## CHALLENGES FOR THE NATIONAL PARK SERVICE

None of the initiatives recommended in this report makes the task
ahead easy for the National Park Service. Preservation '95, with
its heightened priority for resource protection, will require some
reorganization as well as long-term commitment that the service
cannot provide without firm support from Congress, the conservation community, and the general public. No less difficult will be
the continuing transition to a style of management that is more open
to outsiders—inholders, neighbors, state and local governments,
other federal agencies—than was necessary when parks were
isolated. To be sure, a new style is emerging, not only at the innovative parks added in recent decades, but also at a number of
traditional parks. There remains, however, a long way to go.

Implementing such initiatives is only a small part of the challenge
that faces the leadership of the park service. Despite a tradition of
staff commitment that makes the service a national resource in its
own right, the service is in need of major administrative modernization. Having dug deeply into the park service's own records,
we know how flimsy some data are—even in such basic areas as
visitor use, not to mention reporting on resource deterioration. Thus,

time and again this report points to the need for better information to strengthen budget justifications during a time of fiscal stringency, to inform officials' decisions, to enable outsiders to participate more effectively in decision making. There is a need, too, to assure that career incentives reward the new breed of park manager and specialist in such areas as resource protection, land-use controls, scientific research, and citizen participation. Nor must a successful career be built only on service in the system's "crown jewels"— the Yellowstones and Grand Canyons. Parity must be ensured for stewardship of historic and cultural properties.

Seeking to modernize the service is not without risks; it could be disastrous if the modernizers were to focus their attention only on cost-effective schemes for delivering services. The key to wise modernization is to build on, not undercut, the institutional culture of the service. At the heart of that culture is the dedication of individual staff members at every level to the parks and to the people who visit them. Scarcely less central is the tradition of decentralization that leaves individual park superintendents a good deal of flexibility in responding to local differences in resources, pressures on those resources, visitor needs, and the like. Such local flexibility is accompanied by some looseness that impedes the work of the service—park plans insufficiently linked to systemwide priorities, for example, and a lack of accountability for resource protection. Yet the modern management techniques needed to improve efficiency and inform decision making must not be allowed to undermine a decentralization that is essential for wise management of a far-flung, diverse system.

Modernization will not be effective without continuity and imagination in park service leadership. While the "myth of Mather" still infuses the service with pride and purpose, there is a sense that the first park service director was in charge in a way that no one is today. Mather manipulated people, dollars, legislators, the press, to get what he knew he needed. Today, the park service director has become the short-term head of a bureaucracy, no longer the chief guardian of the nation's most treasured assets. The service in the heady days of the 1970s was a follower as conservationists and Congress pushed forcefully for expansion and innovation. A pattern of just responding, rather than leading, seems to have taken hold.

To deal with the challenges of the emerging era, the chief officials of the service must be allowed to lead and be expected to lead. In selecting future directors and also their chief lieutenants, there must be a search for individuals who bring not only imaginative leadership to their positions but who also represent the professionalism and the distinctive motivations traditional within the park service. The administration, Congress, and the conservation community need to join in providing the stimulus and support needed to bring this about.

## PUTTING INITIATIVES IN PLACE: CHALLENGES TO ORRRC

President Reagan recently appointed a Commission on Outdoor Recreation Resources Review, destined to be known as ORRRC II after its namesake of the early 1960s. Much has changed since the time when the deliberations of the original ORRRC provided the inspiration for vigorous federal involvement in resource protection and outdoor recreation. Some states have developed strong programs of their own, while other federal agencies have enlarged their visitor programs. The private recreation market is serving far greater numbers of Americans. Thinking has broadened about the value of natural and cultural resource protection and of varied recreational experiences. The experience gained from systems that grew out of the original ORRRC—wilderness, wild and scenic rivers, trails— needs to be assessed. The number of people enjoying our parks and other public lands has greatly increased.

Insofar as the park system is concerned, the chief task facing the commission is seeking consensus for park policy in Congress and the administration. The commission has a unique opportunity to address the broad needs facing the parks—in particular, recommending measures to protect natural and cultural resources more effectively and to expand the system in the future to incorporate other worthy areas. Among the particular initiatives needed are a thorough assessment of the dollar cost of clearing up the backlog of unprotected, unacquired parkland, coupled with a search for ways to complete the unfinished parks by less costly means. Finding a successor to the Land and Water Conservation Fund (LWCF) will prove no easy job. The fund has provided much of the wherewithal for the purchase of parkland not only by the federal government but also by state and local governments. If the commission is to succeed, it must find a way to reassert bipartisan support for the LWCF or its equivalent.

## FUTURE VISIONS: THE SPECIAL RESPONSIBILITY OF THE CONSERVATION COMMUNITY

Conservationists, in state and local as well as national groups, must assume new responsibilities in the years ahead. The era of cooperation, and particularly the more open decision making that it requires, could move park management closer to the conservationist vision of preserved resources—or, quite the opposite, could move the parks closer to commercialism and away from resource consciousness. The National Parks and Conservation Association, Wilderness Society, and Sierra Club as well as numerous state and local groups deserve added public support so they can pursue conservation goals.

If decisions are not to be excessively influenced by commercial interests and those who seek intensive recreation at the expense of resources, there must be considerably more active participation by conservation groups in the decision-making processes for individual parks. Often, that participation will be difficult, since the parks are far-flung, and citizens who benefit from preservation of park resources often live far away. Moreover, attention must be paid to what is achievable in a particular place and time, even if the ideal is unachievable.

Yet conservationists also have a responsibility to remind the country that today's politically feasible measures will not ultimately be sufficient to protect the parks. There is room for the visionary to urge that the wildlands of Alaska be even more strictly protected than is possible in wilderness in the rest of the country. There is room, too, to call the country's attention to France's treatment of the Lascaux caves, where people now view nearby replicas of priceless cave paintings that had been deteriorating under the impacts of visitors.

The conservation community is ultimately the guardian of another national asset: the special tradition of "park values." During the first years of the Reagan presidency, Secretary Watt symbolized for many a deliberate rejection of park values. He brought a different vision: of visitors as consumers of recreation services, of lean government and the private sector providing services in a cost-effective manner. That vision produced some decisions beneficial to the parks: the attention to repair and improvement of park facilities, in particular, was in many cases long overdue. Yet his vision rightly alienated park supporters, for it denied the highest meaning of the parks, somehow reducing park stewardship to the administration of federally owned recreational real estate.

The conservation community must never allow national leaders to lose sight of the feelings of transcendence that visitors experience on entering the Yosemite Valley or reliving the bloodshed of Gettysburg. These feelings and the resources that give rise to them will be cherished even more as society becomes increasingly crowded and commercialized.

After the experience of Secretary Watt, national leaders are perhaps less likely to reject the larger vision of the parks. There remain risks, however, that parks will be given short shrift in the drive for cost-effective management. There may be temptations, in particular, to cut back the interpretive services that are critical to visitors' understanding of park resources or to invite commercial development in an effort to provide additional funding. It is the responsibility of the conservation community to guard against such actions.

Leadership by the conservation community will be tested during the next generation as the country faces the need to extend the park tradition to land not owned by the federal government—to private lands, inside and outside park boundaries, that affect park resources and park visitors' experiences. The future of the parks will increasingly depend on these lands, to which "park values" have not previously been applied.

The tradition of park stewardship has stood as a notable exception to the mainstream of our national attitudes toward land. In the mainstream, the country has cherished the right of citizens to exercise dominion over land they own, subject perhaps to modest limitations, often grudgingly imposed, to protect resources or accommodate the exigencies of urban life. The sensitive stewardship traditions applied inside the national parks have not prevented "business as usual" outside—even adjacent to—park boundaries. The Gatlinburgs and West Yellowstones, tawdry gateways to some of our greatest natural parks, symbolize the contrasting traditions. As Roger Starr has pointed out, these communities exemplify a land-use tradition that is, in its way, every bit as American as the parks. Americans have accepted both traditions, using park boundaries to separate domains.

In the future, it will no longer be possible to reconcile the two traditions simply by fortifying boundaries. Park boundaries are not impermeable barriers that can isolate protected from unprotected lands. The world around the parks is changing, and parks—many of the older ones as well as those added more recently—depend more on what happens in that world.

The park system has not come to grips with the consequences of these pressures: if parks are to be protected, for use and enjoyment of future generations of Americans, the tradition of park stewardship must gradually be extended beyond park boundaries, to domains where mainstream attitudes about private property and freedom of action still prevail today. In some places, of course, the mainstream tradition is itself evolving, as citizens and their local governments recognize the links between sensitive land development, economic health, and the quality of life. Around many of the parks, however, the gulf between the values that govern the parks and mainstream land values is proving difficult to bridge.

To make feasible tomorrow what is impractical today, the conservation community must continue to further the evolution of the park ideal. Although many individuals in the park service share this vision, the service as an institution must balance the needs of tomorrow against the demands of constituents today. The conservation community is an advocate of values that transcend the demands of today. That is its particular vocation. And so it should continue to speak vigorously and faithfully for the next generation.

William K. Reilly
President
The Conservation Foundation
June 1985

# Executive Summary

For many of the last 25 years, America's national parks have been in the eye of controversy. For 20 of those 25 years, the park system expanded and innovated rapidly under the impetus of a powerful coalition of environmental, recreational, and urban interests. For almost 3 of those 25 years, the service answered to an extraordinarily controversial secretary of the interior whose actions were widely seen as aimed at changing policies with respect to acquisition of new areas, urban parks, concessioners, wilderness management, and mining and other resource-exploitation activities.

Today, the level of controversy is lower. Out of the eye of controversy, however, does not mean "back to normal." The park system and service face a challenging period of adjustment and continuing change, at a time when public funds are strained. The lower intensity of public debate reflects the kinds of issues—consolidation rather than heady expansion, improved administration, defense of protected resources against new and intensifed pressures—the nation must deal with in the years ahead. Yet this in no way diminishes the need for dynamic leadership to broaden public understanding and support for changing park policies, especially as public attention to the parks wanes in the absence of controversy.

Three concerns demand attention if the national parks are to retain in the future the distinctive place in American life they have today: improved stewardship of park resources; a new assessment of the role of the private sector in the parks; and innovative strategies for creating the park system of the future.

## STEWARDSHIP OF PARK RESOURCES

Despite the magnificence of the parks and the image of fine stewardship enjoyed by the park service, there is justifiable concern about pressures on park resources. The millions who visit the parks every year, and the facilities provided to serve them, leave undeniable impacts. Private activities such as grazing and mining, which exist in some units, often as a result of compromises when the unit was created, also leave their mark. So do the external pressures to which conservationists have been pointing for a decade or more: the disruption of wildlife habitat, pollution, visual intrusion originating on land the park service does not own. That these internal and external pressures are harming park resources is beyond doubt.

At the same time, public expectations of resource stewardship are rising. Growing understanding of ecosystems has brought more widespread appreciation of naturalness, of "letting nature manage nature." The conservationist vision of the parks as places for contemplative recreation, for experiences of transcendence rather than the mere satisfaction of recreation demands, has never been stronger. There is, too, growing appreciation of authenticity in the management and interpretation of cultural resources.

Paradoxically, naturalness and authenticity are achievable amid a developing society only by sophisticated management. The park service has, especially during the past decade, become increasingly adept at the measures needed to manage visitors—for example, requiring that reservations be made to visit some popular backcountry areas, barring camping near lakes and streams, educating visitors about the fragility of park resources. These measures fall far short of what will be needed in the decades ahead, however, and there has as yet been no comparable sophistication in responding to pressures from outside park boundaries.

Several steps have been taken to devote more attention to the condition of park resources. Since 1980, when a report on the *State of the Parks* documented numerous pressures on park resources, Congress has increased appropriations for resource management, and additional increases in budget and staff for this purpose have been provided under other programs. The National Park Service has identified hundreds of projects to prevent further degradation of natural and cultural resources and to repair or restore those already impaired. Some of these projects are being carried out with park base funding provided annually by Congress, or by special add-on money that Congress has appropriated. The Park Restoration and Improvement Program (PRIP), the $1 billion crash effort undertaken by the service between 1981 and 1985 to repair aging park facilities and infrastructure, protected some important resources as well. However, available funding has been insufficient to complete even those resource management projects that park staff feel are most urgent.

To preserve park resources and respond to rising public expectations, three broad initiatives are now needed: a comprehensive program to protect park resources; special attention to historic and cultural resources; and a campaign to combat external pressures on the parks.

## An Unprecedented Initiative to Protect Park Resources: Preservation '95

To assure that protection of park resources receives the attention it deserves, there is an immediate need for a 10-year program, Preservation '95, a resources counterpart to the facilities-oriented PRIP. For an additional annual expenditure of $50 million over a 10-year period, Preservation '95 would enable the service to address its most pressing problems in a pragmatic fashion, train a larger cadre of qualified resource specialists, and institutionalize resource management higher among park service priorities. The need for such an effort—which would be roughly half the cost of PRIP and spread over double the time—is beyond question; in less fiscally severe times, a larger program over a shorter period would be easily justifiable. Although even these costs seem high amid current budget constraints, delaying these initiatives would add significantly to the eventual costs—in those instances where delay did not prevent effective response altogether.

The program should include four elements:

- *Stabilization, repair, and restoration.* Building fences to control exotic animals, stabilizing eroding dunes, repairing damaged forts, restoring overgrown trenches at battlefields to their historic appearance are typical of the measures needed to restore damaged resources and provide protection against future damage. Hundreds of needed projects have already been identified.
- *Monitoring and research.* Resource management plans have also identified hundreds of other projects—for example, to monitor water quality, study the long-term effects of human activity on wildlife, conduct archaeological surveys—that would alert the service to emerging resource pressures and pro-

mote responses to them. More monitoring of visitor impacts is also needed.

- *Periodic, systemwide reports on resource conditions.* Since the *State of the Parks* report in 1980, the service has stressed the development of resource management plans for each park unit, and efforts have been made to link requests for funding to projects identified in the plans. The service has also increased its information and research capabilities. To keep up with intensifying pressures, however, a periodic, systemwide report of resource conditions should be prepared to aid in establishing systemwide priorities, enhance congressional oversight, and build public support for innovative, sometimes controversial, measures. The type of report needed is similar to the one called for in the National Park System Protection and Resources Management Act passed by the House of Representatives in 1983.
- *Staffing and training.* Although resource management staff has increased in recent years, staff skills and training need to be stepped up further and some qualified personnel reassigned to sites and positions where they can use their skills more effectively. The needs are acute in both natural and cultural resources management.

*Congress should consider financing some costs of Preservation '95 by earmarking user fees, including revenues from concessioner franchise fees.* While not a panacea, user fees could play an important role in providing funds for maintaining and restoring park resources, although a number of important technical issues—cost-effective collection methods, incentives to individual parks to collect the fees—would have to be resolved. Revenues from such fees, amounting to about $30 million a year, currently go to park land-acquisition efforts and to the repair of government-owned buildings.

## The Special Case of Historical and Cultural Resources

Managing the national parks' collection of historical and cultural resources, one of the largest in the world, presents distinctive problems. Natural forces, often the ally of natural resources, can be the enemy of cultural resources. As a result, cultural resource management raises distinctive questions of protection, and experts often differ on the answers. Which features are worthy of "Cadillac" restorations? What are less costly options? Which features are not worth repairing if damaged? Given cost constraints, how can intelligent decisions be made between funding stabilization and renovation of buildings and research for surveys, cataloging, park histories, and the like?

These distinctive issues deserve special attention and too seldom have received it. Cultural resource managers, whose training and methodology differ from those of natural resource managers, need more opportunities to cooperate and exchange information on policy matters with one another and with natural resource managers at the unit and regional levels. Also, closer ties are needed within the service between cultural resource managers and personnel who administer the service's historic preservation responsibilities outside the parks.

*The commitment of park service leaders to the management of cultural resources needs continued strengthening.* In a service whose perceived core responsibility has always been its natural areas, the responsibility for historical and cultural resources has too often been a stepchild. In units not set aside specifically as historic, for example, old buildings were long regarded as "intrusions" on the landscape, to be removed so that the land could be returned to nature. Despite improvements, the problem remains. Staff responsible for historical and cultural units have reported difficulty in competing for personnel and funds and have felt out of the mainstream in the competition for career advancement. The park service's persistent habit of treating cultural resources as inferior to natural wonders has prompted some observers to advocate a transfer of the historic sites and battlefield parks out of the park service, to the Smithsonian Institution, the National Endowment for the Arts, or to a new independent agency. We reject that approach for we see a deeper unity and coherence in the natural and cultural missions. The unique esprit and tradition of the park service should be challenged and stimulated, for it would be very difficult to duplicate. But a new commitment of park service leaders will be needed to right this imbalance and aid the service to become a model for the nation in managing cultural resources.

## A Campaign to Protect the Parks against External Pressures

The majority of reported threats to park resources—water and air pollution, visual and aesthetic intrusions, inadequate water supply, and so on—originate entirely or largely outside park boundaries.

Timber cutting and oil and gas leasing adjacent to Yellowstone limit grizzly habitat, for example; air pollution from distant sources obscures views at Grand Canyon; water pollution is a problem at Everglades and Mammoth Caves; commercial and residential development creates visual intrusions around Great Smoky Mountains, Grand Teton, and Gettysburg.

Protecting park resources against external pressures requires action outside park boundaries—sometimes miles away where pollution originates or park wildlife migrate. Yet efforts to assert park values on others' land—even land managed by other federal agencies—can cause the park service to be resented as a bossy neighbor.

As a practical matter, opportunities to protect against external activities vary, depending on who is responsible for them. In particular, activities located on federal land or dependent on federal funding can be addressed in ways not readily applied to other public and private activities.

### Protecting against Activities on Federal Land

As conservationists have repeatedly urged, *Congress should enact legislation to strengthen the voice of the service over threats to the parks that originate on nearby federal lands.* To be effective, the legislation should require coordination of activities and also of agency plans.

#### Activities

When proposed activities on federal land may harm a park, it is not enough simply to require the proposing agency to consult the park service and "consider" its objections. Neither, however, would it be satisfactory to give the service a veto over the other agency's proposal; other agencies have their own missions and constituencies to be considered.

*A process is needed that will provide incentives for the park service and its federal neighbors to work out mutually acceptable solutions. The Endangered Species Act provides an important model for the type of process needed.* It gives the Fish and Wildlife Service a strong say over federal activities that affect endangered species habitat, but it also sets up a negotiation process that prompts agencies to search for consensus on ways to reduce or avoid adverse impacts. If the parties cannot agree, a special statutory committee can exempt an activity from the requirements of the act. To avoid an all-or-nothing decision by the committee, agencies have a powerful incentive to work out a compromise. A similar provision is needed for review of activities that would affect national parks.

*Actions by other agencies within the Interior Department should be controlled by a directive from the secretary* that requires consultation with the park and moves the decision up to the regional offices of each agency, to the applicable assistant secretaries and finally to the secretary, if the parties cannot agree.

### Planning

Rather than waiting until potentially harmful activities are proposed, the park service should also work with other agencies as plans are prepared for land that may affect the parks. To facilitate this cooperation, *the service should, with funding from Congress and in consultation with affected agencies, identify "Areas of Critical Park Concern" outside park boundaries,* lands deemed critical to the future of a park: habitat or migration routes for wildlife, for example, or scenic viewsheds. The service should propose development policies, responsive to park needs, to guide federal activities in these areas.

*Legislation should require other federal agencies, in preparing their plans and activities for adjacent federal lands, to be as consistent as possible with any specific park service policies established for an area of critical park concern.* To handle disagreements, a negotiation process should be established comparable to the consistency negotiation process under the Coastal Zone Management Act.

### Protecting against Activities Receiving Federal Funds or Permits

Some activities that affect the parks, although they do not take place on federal land, do receive federal funding or permitting. Legislation should add park protection to the standards for evaluating these projects.

An appropriate model is the recently enacted Coastal Barrier Resources Act, which bars federal financial assistance or expenditures for projects (such as bridges and sewers) that would affect undeveloped coastal barrier areas. *Legislation should bar federal funding for incompatible projects in areas of critical park concern and, again following the model of the Endangered Species Act and other legislation, provide for a reconciliation process to balance park protection and competing interests.*

### Protecting against Other Activities

Many pressures on parks originate on private property, some outside park boundaries and some inside. Although statutes authorize the service to control the use of private property to protect park resources in a few places (for example, adjacent to Redwood National Park), the service generally has little authority over private properties.

The needs for additional protection against activities on non-federal lands vary from park to park. So do the local attitudes on land-use controls and participation by federal officials in local and state affairs. In practice, therefore, protective measures need to be highly localized.

*The most promising current opportunity to protect the parks against external threats from private lands lies in diverse cooperative mechanisms involving the park service and park neighbors.* These partnerships are needed to provide a forum where activities can be discussed, differences thrashed out, consensus developed. Park officials have helped form some local land trusts, for example, and have sometimes advised local coordinating councils and land-use agencies. *The park service should actively encourage its staff to cooperate in such partnerships and private initiatives. Present park service policies that impede such participation, apparently out of concern that it will unduly interfere in local affairs, are counterproductive and ought to be replaced by policies encouraging participation.*

*In addition, Congress should establish an experimental program in which the park service would take the lead in establishing partnerships at a few specified parks. Part of this program would involve designating formal park protection zones, adjacent to the selected units, within which special support would be made available, such as technical assistance or grants to pay for land-use planning. In addition, the service would be authorized to accept donations of lands and easements within these zones.*

The initiatives just recommended could improve the park service's capacity to preserve park resources and respond to higher public expectations. Yet these measures—which probably go about as far as the present political consensus will permit—would not, in themselves, save park resources from the many internal and external pressures that seem destined to increase in intensity.

Within the parks, degradation at some of the most popular sites could be eliminated only by discarding the central vision of preservation *and* access that is the genius of the system. So the parking lots and bleachers at Old Faithful, or something like them, probably must remain.

Outside park boundaries, measures to protect park resources conflict with goals of other land users and of states and local governments; compromise with these goals, too, is inevitable. In a country that relies on internal combustion engines and coal-fired power plants, for example, the haze at some of the western parks is unlikely to disappear soon.

Thus, despite the nation's best efforts, continuing pressures will produce some resource degradation—gradual, barely perceptible in many places, but degradation all the same. Some of this loss is the unavoidable cost of serving successive generations of visitors and of economic development outside park boundaries. The measures recommended in this report are essential to avoid still greater losses.

*In the long run, if preservation is to keep pace with intensifying pressures, the political consensus must itself shift so that protective measures unachievable today—to protect against the impacts of backcountry users and private landowners, for example—will become achievable tomorrow.* Increased understanding of resources can help provide the needed political support. So can enhanced awareness of the pressures on resources and of the measures needed to counteract them.

Preserving park resources more nearly unimpaired, however, may ultimately depend on more widespread respect, by an increasingly crowded and developed nation, for the visitor experiences that are less and less available outside the parks. For many, the vision of unspoiled nature exerts a moral claim that transcends management analyses of "user-days" and cost-benefit ratios. In communicating their experiences of awe, solitude, adventure, communion, repose, and reinvigoration to a wider audience, conservationists aid the continuing evolution of the park ideal in directions that can indeed help to preserve the parks for this and future generations.

## THE PRIVATE SECTOR IN THE PARKS

The private sector has been involved in national parks from the earliest days. Traditional concessions provide visitor services in about one-third of the parks. Recent decades have also brought a growing array of nonprofit organizations, volunteers, and contractors that not only provide food, maintenance, and interpretative services but also lease historic properties, raise funds for the parks, and help them in acquiring parklands.

Private activities sometimes provide cost-effective services and enrich park visitors' experiences in ways not otherwise achievable. Yet those activities can also impair resources, disrupt some kinds of visitor experiences, and influence the policies and capabilities of the park service. Thus, *there is a continuing need to reassess the role of the private sector in the parks.*

### Concessions

Concessioners operate in 111 of the 334 parks, providing lodging in 36 units, food services in about 70, as well as a variety of transportation and interpretative services—book and map sales, bus and boat tours, and burro rides, among others.

Many concessioners are small and of local origin; out of more than 500 concession contracts, only 113 produce gross sales of as much as $250,000 annually. Some of the largest operations, however, are run by subsidiaries of major corporations, such as TW Services, MCA, ARA Services, Greyhound, AMFAC, and Del Webb. In 1983, the largest 55 concessions generated 86 percent of total concession sales. Operations in only five parks—Glen Canyon, Grand Canyon, Lake Mead, Yellowstone, and Yosemite—account for nearly 60 percent of those sales. Some of the major installations, including several built decades ago in parks such as Yosemite, invite comparison to shopping malls or occupy particularly scenic spots where they seem incompatible with today's values.

Many of the major concession facilities would almost certainly not be permitted today if they did not already exist. Park service policy has for years favored the provision of new commercial services outside the parks wherever possible, not within them. Although facilities inside the parks could be a source of federal revenues and, if sensitively located, might be less obtrusive than some commercial establishments in gateway communities, there is too great a likelihood that new commercial installations would harm park resources and diminish the visitor's experience.

The major facilities that already exist raise continuing management issues. Not only do the facilities take up parkland, but some of their functions (for example, selling souvenirs) have been criticized as inappropriate to park areas. What most concerns critics is their perception that the concessioners' continual influence on the planning process within parks will result in a drive for more facilities and urbanlike services. Also, there are continuing suspicions (unprovable because the park service does not release information on profits) that some concessioners are profiteering.

*Although removal of many major installations remains an appropriate long-term goal, there is little likelihood that large-scale removal will occur soon.* A few facilities have become historic structures in their own right. Others are protected by long-term contractual guarantees that make buy-outs expensive. All serve large numbers of visitors, some of whom are likely to join with the concessioners in appealing to politics and custom in resisting removal.

Park service policy does call for concessioner facilities to be located where the least damage to park values will occur, and, in fact, some intrusive facilities have been replaced by new ones in more suitable locations. The opening of major new concessioner facilities in Yellowstone's Grant Village—located in an important grizzly bear habitat—creates some doubt, however, about the effectiveness of the policy.

In overseeing concessioner operations, the park service has moved in recent years toward a public utility model. The service determines not only the facilities and services to be provided by concessioners but the rates to be charged and the franchise fees paid for the privilege of operating in a national park.

*The public utility approach to overseeing concessions, coupled with ongoing efforts to enhance compatibility by removing structures from particularly unsuitable locations, establishes a realistic response to the unavoidable coexistence of established major facilities amid some of the nation's most magnificent resources.* Although the approach may not bring the mediocre services offered by some concessioners up to the high level achieved by a few, it nevertheless appears to be the only viable approach to protect the public in dealings with holders of monopoly rights. Three initiatives could make the regulatory process work better.

### Releasing Information on Profitability

The Concessions Policy Act, enacted in 1965, gives the park service broad discretion to write incentives and protections into concession contracts. The service also has broad discretion in determining the services, fees, and rates of concessioners. To enable it to apply the statutory standard entitling concessioners to a "reasonable opportunity . . . to make a profit," the service requires an annual financial report from each concessioner. One park service concession official noted that "the annual financial reports are used in everything we do; they are one of the best management tools we have." Such information, however, is withheld from the public, and an effort during the 1970s to obtain it under the Freedom of Information Act failed. The public must rely on inferences and estimates to evaluate entities that operate on public land, often under contracts of very long duration and with little or no competition.

*Release of financial information is essential to permit public oversight of the dealings, between concessioners and the park service, in which the concessioner's opportunity to make a profit is worked out.* Disclosure would permit more effective public scrutiny of the rates set and activities permitted by the park service as well as reduce opportunities for favoritism in establishing and administering contracts. This disclosure would also enlarge the opportunity for informed dialogue between concessioners and their critics, diminishing the stridency and suspicions of impropriety that are inevitable when the facts are kept secret. *The park service should reexamine its finding that such information is proprietary and thus exempt from the Freedom of Information Act. If necessary, Congress should enact legislation to assure that this information is made public.*

### Avoiding Excessive Protection in Concession Contracts

Many of the concession contracts in force today grant investor protections (monopoly rights, "possessory interests" in facilities, preferential rights to provide additional services) that have been traditional since the days of Stephen Mather and the creation of the park service. There is mounting evidence, however, that this array of protections is not necessary in all cases to secure needed investment or ensure good performance. These provisions may also stand in the way when the service tries to respond to changing conditions—for example, by moving facilities within a park or buying out a concessioner's interest.

*Although concessioners must have protections that will enable them to secure needed capital, the service should use every opportunity to avoid additional protections that impede long-term adaptation to changing conditions in the parks.* On the basis of the limited information available to the public, the following changes appear desirable:

- *New or revised concession contracts should, insofar as possible, require the service to pay only the unamortized book value of concessioner-built facilities it purchases, not the fair market value provided under the traditional "possessory interest" provision.* (A recent statute already makes this change when a concessioner is bought out because of unsatisfactory performance, and the service has instituted a similar policy when removing facilities altogether from a park.) Under the Concessions Policy Act, which allows greater contract flexibility than has often been recognized, the park service can determine the appropriate level of compensation for possessory interests.
- *Preferential rights to provide additional services in the parks should be granted only in the most unusual circumstances, if at all.*
- *The Concessions Policy Act should be amended to make another contract provision—the preferential right to contract renewal—discretionary rather than mandatory, as it now is when a concessioner has performed satisfactorily.* In several cases, this right has served less to secure needed investment or ensure good performance than to increase the value of the operation when the concessioner seeks to sell it to a third party.

## Improving Park Service Oversight

Since the 1970s, the park service has increased its administrative capabilities to oversee concessions. Today the service can, to quote one park service official, "deal with concessioners more on a business-like basis, rather than on just an environmental basis as we used to in the past." This effort should continue.

- The service should *expand periodic training programs for personnel who deal with concessions,* as well as for superintendents and managers who negotiate contracts and work daily with concessioners. Additional programs should be instituted for employees of concessioners (at the concessioner's expense) so they can better respond to the changing needs of the parks and visitors.

- To fight mediocrity, the service should *experiment with the use of incentives, such as pricing and fee reduction, to reward creativity and quality* beyond compliance with minimum standards. Some concessioners provide an exemplary quality of service with a fine appreciation of the special context of the parks. They should be recognized.
- The service should *take greater account of differences in concessioner size, services, and investments* so that the smaller concessioners are not overwhelmed by administrative burdens.
- The service should *facilitate more sensitive, informed public participation* in the formulation and application of concessions policies. Once background information is released, the service should encourage the constructive dialogue that has unfortunately not been a significant part of this process.

## New and Expanding Roles for the Private Sector

Unlike major concession operations, overall private sector activity in the parks seems likely to grow. Nonprofit organizations and volunteers, in particular, have become increasingly prominent during the past 25 years and seem destined to become more prominent still.

Several current efforts that promise to enlarge private sector involvement are the leasing of historic properties, permitting agricultural use of some parklands, and stimulating travel to lesser-used areas. In addition, Reagan administration efforts to decrease park costs and increase revenues have brought pressures on park officials to increase the role of the private sector in, for example, park maintenance and interpretation.

*Private sector activities in the parks are not ends in themselves, however; there should be no policy that private involvement either grow or shrink.* Rather, responsibility for park activities should be assigned after considering the full range of park values. *Efforts to reduce park costs, important as they are, should not be allowed to overshadow the needs to protect park resources and visitors' opportunities to enjoy them. The vitality of the park service must also* be protected. It is important for the service to continue to perform those functions that provide its traditional distinctiveness; the service must not be left to focus only on law enforcement and bureaucratic responsibilities.

Given the long history of experience with concessions, there are lessons that the service should now apply to other private sector activities. One is to anticipate the special influence that any private organization, whether profit or nonprofit, can come to have on park decision making. The other is to anticipate the need for flexibility, so that today's decision can be modified in the future if conditions and values change. Several steps are needed:

- *Open decision making.* Since suspicions of favoritism can undercut private sector contributions to the parks, park service decisions about future private sector activities should be open to public scrutiny and participation.

- *Reorganization within the National Park Service to improve administration of private sector relationships.* Virtually every type of private sector activity—concessions, cooperating associations, volunteers, leasing of historic properties, contracting —is overseen by a different office within the park service or on a park-by-park basis. A stronger organizational framework would allow more information and expertise to be exchanged within the service so that mistakes are not repeated, opportunities are not lost, and more consistency is achieved.

- *Avoidance of excessive legal protections.* Like concessioners, other private sector providers should not be granted excessive legal protections that make removal or change prohibitively expensive. The provision allowing leasing of historic properties for periods as long as 99 years, for example, should be closely reexamined from this perspective.

Particular attention should be paid to future private sector involvement in parks in Alaska. So remote from national population centers, largely pristine landscapes, these parks provide a unique opportunity both for innovative private sector activity that is responsive to the needs of place and for the service to avoid repeating earlier mistakes.

The challenge for the future is to shape and reshape private sector participation so that it enriches rather than detracts from the parks. On the basis of past experiences and present efforts, there is reason to hope that this challenge can be met successfully.

## CREATING THE PARK SYSTEM OF THE FUTURE

Following massive expansion in the 1960s and 1970s, the park system in 1981 entered a period of consolidation. Congress has appropriated $397 million since 1981 to acquire private lands within existing parks and has designated millions of acres of wilderness. Some acreage has been added to the system as a result of boundary adjustments, and the Illinois-Michigan Canal National Heritage Corridor has been established, although not formally included in the system. Only one new unit, the former home of President Harry S Truman, has actually been added (through donation).

Although park creation on the scale of the late 1970s cannot be expected in at least the near future, the system is unlikely to stand still. At minimum, the system of the future is likely to include some additional historic sites (birthplaces of presidents, for example) and a few additional carvings out of the public domain (although nothing remotely on the scale of the 1980 Alaska parks). Acquisition of some private land inside existing parks will continue. There will also be some protective acquisitions, following boundary adjustments, to defend existing parks against external pressures.

A more expansive vision would see today's parks as only the core of a future system providing preservation and public access to many more of America's special places. Some additional parks of substantial size would be formed, not only from the public domain but also, in at least a few cases, by acquiring private land. In the tradition of the 1960s and 1970s, both experimental parks responding to the priorities of their time and extensive "greenline" or cooperative parks in which protection and access would be provided in varied ways would also be established. The role of the park service might vary considerably from park to park; some parks might be formal elements of the system, while others—perhaps even the majority of future units—might be loosely affiliated like New Jersey's Pinelands and the Illinois-Michigan Canal.

*It is important to pursue the more expansive vision of the future. The United States still has many unprotected special places worthy of preservation and use in the national park tradition—among them, the Florida Keys, Tallgrass Prairie, Big Sur, and Columbia River Gorge. In addition, protective acquisitions, to defend existing parks, are increasingly needed.*

Adding new units to the park system is by no means the only suitable way to protect America's special places; state and local governments, private preservation groups, and other federal agencies also have served and will continue to serve as stewards of such places. But expansion of the park system was the approach used successfully during the 1960s and 1970s to protect some magnificent resources that would otherwise have been lost or degraded—Redwood, Lowell, and Voyageurs, to name a few. Although some lesser resources were protected as a means to serve urban populations and achieve other objectives, the expansion was accomplished without tarnishing the system's overall reputation for quality. The park service underwent some strains in coping with the expansion; yet experience at some newer units seems to be shedding light on how to solve problems that older parks, too, increasingly encounter. In sum, the expansion of the 1960s and 1970s was a wise long-term investment, adapted to the needs of a changing country.

The question today is how the dynamism that produced that expansion can best be rechanneled in the very different context of the 1980s. The special opportunity once represented by the public domain is largely (though not wholly) gone. Willingness to replace that opportunity by continued commitment of substantial funds for acquisition has not been demonstrated. The opportunity that may prove greatest in the long run—a broadened concept of parks to incorporate human settlements that remain partially under private, local, and state control—is still in the nascent stage. *To create a future system that builds on past successes as well as present realities, initiatives are needed in five areas—backlog land, the land protection process, greenline or cooperative parks, the park selection process, and funding.*

## Coping with the Backlog

First and most immediate, *a strategy must be devised to cope with the "backlog"—the private land, inside the boundaries of parks already established, that has neither been acquired by the service nor otherwise protected against incompatible development.* The backlog, roughly 307,000 acres, represents a formidable barrier to even thinking about system expansion. The $397 million appropriated for parkland acquisition since 1981 has gone almost entirely toward purchasing backlog land. No one knows the cost of buying the rest; additional spending of $550 million would hit the statutory ceilings authorized by Congress, but the actual cost would unquestionably be many millions more.*

*To put the backlog in perspective, two assessments must be made now.*

- *First, a thorough assessment of the dollar value of the lands in the backlog.* This will require that ongoing attention be paid not only to market prices of land but also to continuing changes made by Congress in unit boundaries and to changes made by the service in land protection plans. At present, no one keeps track of all these changes systemwide.
- *Second, an assessment of opportunities to reduce the backlog by completing unfinished parks in ways less costly than acquisition.* This will require examination of land protection plans to search out opportunities for use of alternatives to acquisition, including opportunities to get more effective cooperation from local and state governments in protecting parkland.

Because of the sensitivity of these assessments and the importance of performing them soon, they are appropriate tasks for the Presidential Commission on Outdoor Recreation Resources Review established by President Reagan in January 1985.

There are compelling reasons to continue reducing the backlog—not only to complete parks already authorized by law, but also to accommodate private landowners and to save costs before land values escalate further. There are also compelling reasons to look beyond the backlog in considering acquisition needs. Opportunities to protect a threatened resource, by adjusting the boundaries of an existing park or obtaining a choice site within a new one, are often now-or-never situations. *The backlog, though formidable, should not be allowed to prevent systematic evaluation of the full range of proposals for creating and expanding parks.*

---

*In addition to the backlog lands, there remain substantial costs for acquisition of Redwood National Park in California, which was expanded in 1978 by means of a "legislative taking" whereby the government condemned the land and left it for the courts to decide the amount owed the landowners. The government has deposited $352 million in court, but the final award is likely to be substantially higher. Redwood, the most costly park in the history of the system, is usually excluded from backlog calculations because the funds for it are not expected to come from the Land and Water Conservation Fund.

## Improving the Land Protection Process

When Congress creates a park that contains private land, that land must be protected, either by acquiring it in fee or through some supplementary measure such as an easement or a zoning regulation. Private grazing and mining rights within some parks also create a continuing need for park protection. Well-chosen protective measures not only enhance the overall effectiveness of efforts to preserve resources, but also reduce future administrative burdens faced by park superintendents and influence public perceptions of the service, whose dealings with landowners and state and local governments can enlarge or diminish future opportunities to create more parks.

*Several steps should be taken to improve the land protection process:*

- *The park service must complete land protection plans* for individual parks (over 125 have been approved) and update them periodically in consultation with landowners, local governments, and conservation groups to ensure that funds are spent where they are needed most.
- *Estimates of acquisition costs must be improved and updated* to avoid overruns and allocate funds more realistically.
- *Brief socioeconomic impact statements* for proposed new units can facilitate consideration, by Congress and the service, of the needs of residents and local governments.
- *The park service and Congress should assess opportunities to reduce the incompatibility of longstanding private grazing and mining rights in the parks.* The park service may be able to tighten the terms of grazing permits, for example. It needs more information about how extensive and legally valid claims are. Reducing or withdrawing subsidies for incompatible grazing activities within national parks should also be explored.
- *Congress should establish a revolving emergency fund of about $20 million* that the park service could draw on quickly, without additional congressional authorization, for land acquisition within parks under three circumstances: first, when the availability of a key parcel, designated for acquisition in a unit's land-protection plan, requires that action be taken immediately; second, when acquisition is the only feasible way to eliminate the threat of incompatible development on an inholding; and third, when the park service must condemn prop-

erty within units because private landowners have failed to comply with land-use controls.

## Making Greenline or Cooperative Parks Work

*Achieving an expansive vision for the system of the future depends in part on the success of greenline or cooperative parks that incorporate private property as well as state and local government lands within their boundaries.* The success of the greenline approach matters not only because several such parks are already in the system, but also because that approach is critical to establishing new parks in many of America's other special places where massive federal land acquisition would disrupt landowners and their communities. Greenlines also hold promise for avoiding the high costs of acquisition. Greenlines are not cost-free, however. Some land must often be acquired for inclusion in a park's core area for public access and educational facilities. The protective measures applied to private property (easements, tax incentives) also have costs—in forgone revenues, for example. Moreover, continued funding is essential to make credible the threat of condemnation that bolsters local zoning controls in greenline units such as Cape Cod and Fire Island; without funding, the protection of some private lands in those units would prove illusory.

*Greenlines will succeed only if protective measures (easements, zoning, incentives, assistance) can be established and then managed effectively over the long term. This requires continuing relationships with landowners and governments as well as sophisticated management methods. The park service must broaden its experience with, for example, monitoring and enforcement of land-use restrictions, cooperation with state and local governments through such mechanisms as voluntary coordinating councils, and the application of incentives and technical assistance to encourage cooperation and land stewardship.*

While park service experiments in managing greenline units are encouraging, they are so diverse and often so new that it is not yet possible to define the best models for such parks or to declare the approach an unqualified success. At Cape Cod, most of the land is owned by the federal government, while in Lowell, federal ownership is minuscule. In other greenline units, the appropriate mix of federal, state and local, and private ownership and management is still being worked out. One of the most promising future avenues—exemplified by the Pinelands National Reserve in New Jersey—may be park service cooperation with a state government acting as a pivotal partner in the arrangement.

*Several steps can be taken to increase the prospects of making greenline parks successful:*

- *The park service must continue to evaluate each greenline effort,* examining the effectiveness of resource protection together with dollar costs so that other units throughout the system, and future units as well, can learn from successes and failures.
- *National Park Service staff should be trained to work more effectively in greenline techniques,* with career paths and rewards offered for those who specialize in them.
- *The park service can foster closer cooperation with private, nonprofit land-conservation groups, especially land trusts,* by stimulating creation of such groups and providing them with technical assistance.
- *Congress can make tax incentives for land conservation more effective* by tying them to federal, state, or local criteria for identifying parcels and by limiting the opportunities for abuse.
- *In evaluating future park proposals, Congress should scrutinize proposed land-protection techniques. Particular attention should be given to assurances of state and local government cooperation* so that park objectives will not be undermined by, say, rezonings for inappropriate development. Wherever local governments are to participate in protecting parkland, their cooperation should be backed by the kinds of measures used in Cape Cod, where local zoning is to be in compliance with park service guidelines, or in Lowell and the Pinelands, where federal assistance is contingent on local cooperation and progress. *If state and local governments are not willing to accept a Cape Cod-type formula or a review process, new parks should be established only if acquisition will be the main protection tool.*

### Improving the Park Selection Process

*In the context of the 1980s, in a period of austere domestic spending, it is crucial that the process used to select new parks be respected as one that selects wisely.* The slower pace of expansion may permit the service, backed by the conservation community, to play a more influential role in that process than it did during the congressionally led expansion of the 1970s. *At a minimum, three elements are needed:*

- *A register, maintained by the service, for a broad spectrum of natural and cultural resources.* Not limited to sites suitable for park service management, this list should include a wide range of sites worthy of special management by somebody, somehow. Like the National Register for Historic Places, it should have a broad-based nomination process.
- *Targeted inventories by the service to bring potential park sites to public attention.* Two inventories warranted by current needs are an inventory of boundary expansions that would protect parks from external threats and an inventory of potential greenline park sites.
- *Periodic park opportunities reports by the service,* to call the attention of Congress and the public to the range of needs and opportunities for park creation.

## Funding

The Land and Water Conservation Fund (LWCF), which for two decades has been used to acquire private lands for parks, expires in 1989. Between 1965 and 1983, the park service spent $1.87 billion in LWCF money to acquire 1.46 million acres of parklands; the fund has also made possible the creation and expansion of state parks, the addition of acreage to the nation's wildlife refuge system, and the development of other outdoor recreation facilities on state and local parklands. *No other single decision will so fundamentally shape the National Park System of the future as the selection of a successor to the LWCF.*

*For national parks alone, even a minimal land-acquisition program will require a funding level approximating that of the last four years (roughly $100 million per year).* This will be needed for continuing acquisitions of land in the backlog (which is unlikely to have been cleaned up by 1989), for acquisitions essential to protect existing parks from external threats, and for creation of some new units, although not on the scale that characterized the 1970s. *A more expansive vision of the future park system, however, warrants a higher level of funding. An annual figure of $200 million for the next 10 years is needed to address the backlog, protect existing parks, and create new ones.*

Money for park acquisition is difficult to obtain even in good times, and funding levels for state and federal programs are erratic, making future park planning difficult. Advocates intended that the LWCF would overcome these problems by operating as a trust fund: providing a predictable, sizable flow of earmarked funds that would be insulated from year-to-year competition for appropriations.

In practice, the LWCF operates neither as a true trust fund nor as a simple authorization; it stands as a hybrid, midway between the two. There is a compelling moral logic that some revenues derived from depletion (or degradation) of natural resources should be invested in the nation's permanent estate. (The LWCF is derived principally from revenues for oil and gas leases in the outer continental shelf and, to a lesser extent, from user fees, motor boat fuel taxes, and the sale of surplus government property.) Yet it is difficult to argue for completely insulating park acquisition from the annual competition for funds before Congress, particularly when other domestic programs are being pared. *Overall, the LWCF has worked well over the years, and Congress could do far worse than to reauthorize it, thereby continuing to provide the psychological, albeit incomplete, insulation from politics that the LWCF has provided.*

*In examining the future of the LWCF, Congress should explore additional sources of revenue.* A trust fund composed of receipts from a recreational equipment excise tax, for example, might go far toward meeting acquisition needs. The Presidential Commission on Outdoor Recreation Resources Review should investigate alternative sources of future funding.

*Like the LWCF, its successor should continue to fund other organizations—state and local governments, federal agencies—that play an important role in land preservation and outdoor recreation.* Local and state parks accommodate significantly more recreation than national parks. Their visitation has been rising, and their important place in the larger parks network needs to be understood and supported. The national parks are but one element of a nationwide network of protected lands, and it is appropriate that a funding entity exists with a nationwide perspective.

## THE CHALLENGES AHEAD

Managing the 79.4 million acres in the National Park System today presents an extraordinary set of challenges. While the challenges demand responses from all Americans involved with the parks as visitors, advocates, policy makers, or partners in providing services, responses by the National Park Service itself will be most crucial in shaping the future of the system.

Changes over the last 25 years have conferred greater and more complex responsibilities on the service. Many parks, old as well as new, are now in the midst of development. More visitors come to the parks, and there are more historical and cultural resources. Parks have more private landowners inside their boundaries and resource pressures from outside. The service has grown larger and its "family" more heterogeneous.

*To address these and other challenges, the National Park Service must respond to a series of internal management deficiencies.* Among these are the lack of information adequate for well-reasoned decision making; failure to integrate planning with operations and budgeting; "ad hockery" in developing new policies; dissatisfaction in the service over such matters as recognition, career tracks, mobility, and the "caste system" between different types of parks; and the need to integrate specialists into a tradition of jack-of-all-trades rangers. The need for the service to look outward more than in the past, to cooperate more with landowners and other governments in the interest of park protection, will add to the complexity of the task ahead.

*In fashioning responses to the challenges, national leadership must keep in mind the Hippocratic dictum, "First, do no harm."* The service is enormously popular. There is evidence of successful innovation and institutional change within it over the past 25 years. There is also widespread evidence of remarkable individual dedication. In sum, regardless of its many problems with linking planning to budgets, determining priorities, and gathering data about hundreds of diverse units, the service works.

The key to minimizing harm is to recognize that the park service is at once a bureaucracy and much more than a bureaucracy. It has a proud institutional tradition and mystique that carry its people along beyond day-to-day dissatisfactions and that transcend issues like career tracks. The challenge of the future is to make the service function better as a bureaucracy in ways that build on its tradition rather than undercut it. Since many of the possible corrective measures, while desirable from a conventional bureaucratic standpoint, could undercut the tradition, this will not be easy. There is danger, for example, that the freedom of individual superintendents to respond to the remarkably wide range of problems that arise in their diverse units could be inappropriately curtailed, or that today's need for specialists could submerge the service's generalist traditions. Adaptation to contemporary challenges in managing and protecting resources and accommodating visitors is, however, essential.

The service's stance of "serving the American people" has created a broad base of support; it has also translated in recent years into reacting to changing values more than leading the way. The service, especially in recent years, has let long-standing friends in advocacy and constituency organizations carry the flag of controversy while it has tried to maintain the image of professional land steward carrying out the job defined by the political process.

The park service is not, of course, free to set its own course. It is subject to congressional appropriations and oversight. As an agency within the Department of the Interior, it comes under the discretion of presidential appointees and must constantly tack to the political winds. A distinctive combination of professional and political skills is needed for effectiveness as a park service director.

*The park service needs forceful central leadership to chart directions and manage the park system as a system. Park service leadership must advance a vision of the parks that is as broad and dynamic as today's system and the evolving values that have produced it.* If the challenges are to be addressed in ways that build on—rather than undercut—traditions, leadership of the service must be expected and enabled to function more forcefully.

Its legion of friends should ensure that the agency not be undermined by the pursuit of short-run objectives, whether to gain access to mineral resources or single-mindedly cut costs. We have a right to demand quality of the park service, and it has a right to our support in its efforts to achieve it.

# Chapter 1
# Preservation and Use: An Evolving Ideal

The National Park System contains the United States' highest mountain and largest geyser. It has active and dormant volcanoes, gorges and canyons, ice fields and glaciers, fjords and rivers, several hundred miles of shoreline, and thousands of acres of sand dunes and salt flats. It contains canals, trails, and parkways; forts, battlefields, and armories; factories and seaports; cliff dwellings, mounds, and villages of Indians; Spanish missions, homesteaders' cabins, ranch houses, mansions, and the residences of 12 presidents.[1] The Thaddeus Kosciuszko National Memorial in Philadelphia, occupying about one-sixteenth of a city block, is the National Park System's smallest unit;[2] the over 13-million-acre Wrangell-St. Elias National Park and Preserve in southeastern Alaska is the largest.[3] Every state except Delaware and nearly every U.S. possession contains at least one of the 334 units in the almost 80-million-acre National Park System.[4] Two out of three Americans have visited national parks; there were some 240 million park visits in 1983.

At the heart of the national park idea is a vision of distinctive places protected from impairment yet democratically accessible to all who wish to visit them. "National parks are the best idea we ever had," Wallace Stegner has written. "Absolutely American, absolutely democratic, they reflect us at our best rather than our worst."[5]

The national park idea responded to a unique opportunity: the presence in the vast public domain of great natural wonders. At a time when tens of millions of acres were being released from the public domain for exploitation, these special places were to be pre-

served for the enjoyment of present and future generations. Yellowstone (the first true national park) was established in 1872, followed
by such other spectacular sites as Yosemite, Sequoia, Mount Rainier,
Crater Lake, Mesa Verde, and Glacier.[6] The idea crystallized in 1916,
when 14 great scenic parks and 21 national monuments were put
together into a National Park System and the National Park Service
was created to care for it.[7]

The park idea soon moved beyond natural wonders and has never
stopped evolving. Now, there are parks with resources that are distinctive without being breathtaking, pristine, or remote and parks
that incorporate ecosystems and habitats, rather than "nature's
freaks." There are units established for distinctive manmade
features; 57 percent of the units in the system today are classified
as "historic." Park units once out of the path of civilization have
had development inch up to their boundaries; other park units have
been designated precisely because of their proximity to urban
populations. Some land within national park units is not owned
by the federal government, sometimes because of limited acquisition
funds, other times by design. And, as the national park idea has
broadened, the system has come to depend on management not by
the National Park Service alone but through partnerships with state
and local governments, private landowners, business interests, and
nonprofit groups.

The diversity of the system today reflects continued innovation
and experimentation—"a success story," observes Stegner, "the
steady advance of a splendid idea through more than a century."[8]
Still, through all the system's change, the purpose of the parks has
remained the same—in the language of the National Park Service
Act of 1916, which created the system and the service, to "conserve the scenery and the natural and historic objects and the wild
life therein and to provide for . . . enjoyment . . . in such manner
and by such means as will leave them unimpaired for the enjoyment of future generations."[9] Yet the meaning of this charge, with
its perpetual tension between preservation and use, has deepened
in response to new demands, pressures, and opportunities.

## PROTECTING RESOURCES

The idea of preserving resources for the enjoyment of future generations took hold in an America largely bent on conquering the seem-

*Yellowstone, August 1984. Upper Yellowstone Falls.*

ingly unlimited wilderness. The core concept is attributed to several 19th-century writers and thinkers, foremost among them the renowned landscape architect Frederick Law Olmsted, whose 1865 report to the California legislature on administrative and management policies for Yosemite Valley and the neighboring Mariposa Big Tree Grove was characterized by Olmsted's biographer as having "formulated a philosophic base for the creation of . . . national parks."[10]

In his report, Olmsted dwelt at length on the character of Yosemite's scenery: "the cliffs of awful height and rocks of vast magnitude . . . the tender foliage . . . the most placid pools . . . the most tranquil meadows . . . [the] variety of soft and peaceful pastoral beauty." He stressed that the value of what was being protected was "not in one part or one scene . . . or in any landscape that can be framed by itself, but all around and wherever the visitor goes."[11]

Government protection for public use of sizable tracts of extraordinary natural vistas and physical features remained the principal
motivation of the advocates of the 1916 act, which Olmsted's son
and namesake helped draft. In the meantime, however, the conservation movement had become far more complex. The older Olmsted's emphasis on the benefits that natural areas provided for people
was somewhat different from that of later conservationists, who
looked upon wilderness with a mystic fervor or saw the New
World's "wild country" as a "cultural and moral resource and a
basis for national self-esteem."[12] Still other advocates for conserving wild lands sought economic benefits. Some hoped that these
"monuments" could keep American travelers home.[13] Others, considering the rapid decimation of the magnificent virgin forests of
the Northeast and the consumption of the great pineries in the northern Lake States, sought yet another kind of conservation: resources
used in the production of goods needed to be managed carefully
and wisely. Only in the future did the idea take hold that protection
of all components of ecosystems was necessary to maintain elements
valued by visitors such as wildlife, or that conservation of resources
in a natural state might have intrinsic value or could be a source
of critical scientific information about natural processes.

The 1916 organic act provided little guidance about how the service's preservation mission was to be carried out. Debate during
its passage, for example, presaged strong pressures for using park
resources for economic purposes. "Lest the grass go to waste," the
legislation permitted grazing in all parks except Yellowstone. The
representative from Arizona supported the designation of Grand
Canyon as part of the system provided that "the water power and
mineral resources . . . can be made available for use without detract-
ing from its grandeur."[14] The act gave the secretary of the interior
the power to destroy such plant life and animals "as may be detrimental to the use of the parks" and to sell timber when "in his
judgement the cutting of such timber is required to control the
attacks of insects or diseases or otherwise conserve the scenery or
the natural or historic objects."[15] There was only nascent knowledge
about the natural processes that made the scenery.

By 1920, the park service's first director, Stephen T. Mather, could
list in a report numerous proposals to construct dams in Yellowstone
to tap the rich water resources of the region and to cut timber, graze,
and mine.[16] Mather adamantly opposed pressures he considered

inappropriate or unrelated to park objectives. Yet during his tenure, the service routinely killed predators to protect popular animals—a policy that eventually led to overpopulation, disease, and starvation, as well as to overgrazing of forage and erosion of the land.[17] Surplus animals were "reduced" by shooting them or sending them to zoos, and plant "pests" were destroyed, altering the balance of plant and animal life.

A different course was set at the start of the 1930s under Mather's successor, Horace Albright, when biologist George Wright surveyed wildlife in the parks and established and directed the Wildlife Division of the service's Branch of Research and Education. Park wildlife, said Wright, "face immediate danger of losing their original character and composition. . . . The vital significance of wild life to the whole national-park idea emphasizes the necessity for prompt action."[18] Wright's premature death in 1936 blunted the force of his innovations; nevertheless, he did, in a short time, "introduce a set of new management concepts into an old-line Federal organization, and recruit from all over the country a team of park-oriented biologists, most of them not long out of the graduate schools, to help carry out the new ideas."[19]

World War II created new resource problems for the parks, as commercial interests pressed for the use of park resources to support war efforts. The most publicized assault was aimed at the valuable groves of Douglas fir and Sitka spruce that clothed the rugged mountains and moist western valleys of Olympic National Park. Light, strong Sitka spruce was then a prime component in manufacturing aircraft. Park service Director Newton Drury and Interior Secretary Harold Ickes managed to fight off pressures from the timber industry by persuading Washington war officials that sufficient supplies of the wood could be acquired from outside park boundaries and Canada.[20]

In recent decades, growing ecological awareness has been accompanied by increased demands for resource protection. Seminal reports in the early 1960s on the importance of maintaining and restoring the functioning of natural systems in the parks were followed by a series of notable contributions by conservationists, scientists, and park advocacy groups expressing concern about the condition of park resources and the need for management reforms. This renewed emphasis on standards for managing traditional natural areas in the park system occurred as the park service was also being given responsibilities for managing additional, diverse areas with resources in a variety of conditions. In addition to relatively unspoiled natural and cultural areas, the units had small communities, farms and ranches, privately owned recreational developments, businesses, and so on. Many were in or near urban areas.

## ACCOMMODATING VISITORS

Democratizing access to America's scenic wealth was to Olmsted as powerful a motivation as protecting it. His Yosemite report emphasized that one of the unique features of America's parks was to be their "accessibility to all citizens for use and enjoyment." The report criticized Europe for preserving scenic areas only for the "governing classes" and well-to-do, generally denying use to that continent's ordinary citizens because they were considered incapable of genuinely enjoying natural scenery. America's parks were to be different, the report maintained, by being made open to all citizens, including the "humble toilers" and those "who suffer most from lack of recreation."[21]

As noted environmental lawyer Joseph Sax has observed, the national parks idea was an expression of the same democratic principles that underlay the distribution of the national estate to provide farms for American families. Parklands could not be sensibly divided into small holdings; instead, they were to be kept intact as "public places" for all Americans, now and in the future.[22]

Early in national park history, a natural alliance developed between the railroads, park supporters, and the park service to attract visitors. Grand hotels, such as El Tovar in the Grand Canyon, comfortable restaurants, and other services became integral parts of rail industry operations in many national parks.[23] Often, these facilities were sited in the most spectacular sections of the parks—commanding close-up views of Old Faithful and Yosemite Valley, for example—and were imposingly designed by talented architects in rustic styles deemed appropriate for the parks.[24] Construction was executed with considerable quality, drawing on natural materials available in the region. However, the architecture reflected the contemporary tastes of the nation's wealthy far more than Olmsted's idea that "artificial constructions" should be restricted within "the narrowest limits consistent with the necessary accommodation of visitors."[25] Although he favored the construction of unobtrusive roads, trails, and cabins in Yosemite, it is unclear whether those expensive, marvelously designed hotels would have upset Olmsted. For his life work involved designing, not preserving, landscapes and integrating often elegant architectural embellishments into natural settings.

When Mather took over the new park service, the federal areas were often referred to as the "nation's playgrounds," and Mather's efforts promoted that image. As he prodded Congress to establish new national parks, Mather also concentrated on attracting visitors to existing units. He hired writer-editor Robert Sterling Yard away from the *New York Herald* to work as the publicist, and Yard was soon pumping out books and articles about the parks. Prominent writers and officials were invited to visit the parks—a device Mather had used effectively in 1915 when rousing public interest in the creation of the system and the service. Travel posters urging Americans to explore their nation first often set the appeal against the backdrop of a familiar national park scene.

The hallmark of Mather's term was the development of roads, hotels, and campgrounds to make the parks accessible and visitors comfortable. He welcomed the automobile. "Our national parks are practically lying fallow," Mather said, "and only await proper development to bring them into their own."[26]

Disciples of the great naturalist and Sierra Club founder John Muir, although fierce advocates for wilderness values, joined in promoting park visitation. Threatened by the growing strength of the utilitarian school of conservation, which urged dams, reclamation, and sustained-yield forestry rather than scenic preservation, and by the continued unpopularity of the parks with hunting, mining, and grazing interests, the preservationists were eager to have the parks used by larger numbers of visitors. The damming of Hetch Hetchy Valley in Yosemite, authorized in 1913, in particular, reinforced their conviction that roads, hotels, and other facilities in the parks for visitors were preferable to dams or aqueducts.[27]

Spurred on by the automobile, visitation has increased far more than Mather could have anticipated. The impacts have become so visible in certain areas that instead of seeking to encourage park use by stimulating construction of visitor facilities and offering services, modern-day preservationists and park advocacy groups criticize such endeavors as being at odds with park purposes. In the 1940s, the Sierra Club changed the words in its general Declaration

Yosemite, February 1984. Linda Hansen, Maggie Donahue, and Beth Fuller
(San Francisco). "We usually camp out in the wilderness. This is luxury.
Staying in one of these cabins has been great. . . . The thing about Yosemite
is there's so much here. You can ski, you can swim, you can do day hiking,
you can do really extensive backcountry hikes. There's trout fishing here,
some of the best in California. Rock climbing. . . . I feel we can look at a
lot of the same things John Muir looked at. They haven't built an elevator
up to the top of El Capitan . . . yet. It still has the same grandeur that it had
when I imagine John Muir saw the valley and in the pictures Ansel Adams
has taken. We can see that with our own eyes. But I think it is much different here in the winter than it is in the summer. In the summer the valley
is really populated."

of Purpose from "To explore, enjoy and render accessible the mountains of the Sierra Nevada" to "To explore, enjoy, and
preserve. . . ."[28]

There has long been disagreement over how the parks could best
be enjoyed. Early entrepreneurs in the parks, and the park service
itself in some instances, offered programs aimed more at visitor
amusement than enlightenment. Yard split with Mather in the 1920s
because of the latter's penchant for encouraging or permitting what
Yard considered to be inappropriate development and activities,

including a jazz concert and "vulgar" entertainment for Yosemite visitors.[29]

The post-World War II explosion of leisure time and affluence, accompanied by the proliferation of automobiles and the construction of interstate highways, stepped up the controversy. The recreation equipment industry soared, bringing to national parks visitors equipped to wind sail, hang glide, ski, or ride snowmobiles along mountain roads. At the same time, more insistent demands arose for oases that offered freedom from technological hubbub and change and a contrast with urban pressures. Some enthusiasts desire a "wilderness experience" far more solitary and even more dangerous than early park creators envisioned. Similarly, a rising interest in historic and cultural sites puts in question the compatibility of such activities as sunbathing, kite flying, and ball playing at those types of units.

Yet millions of visitors continue to come to the parks much as they always have, happy to camp near hordes of other people, or to stop briefly on a vacation itinerary that provides only a couple of hours to "do" Grand Canyon. Many rely on the recreational vehicles decried by the purists. Other millions are more regular visitors to particular park system units near the towns or cities where they live. The demands those people make may be quite similar to those they would make on a local or regional park—to fish or hunt, to walk their dog, to "blow off steam" on a weekend.

## RECONCILING CONFLICTS

Tensions between preservation and use will continue as a major challenge for park managers. Because demands on the parks evolve in response to changes in society, the reconciliations made by one generation must always be reconsidered by the next. And satisfying some demands by preservationists or by visitors will diminish options for satisfying others' desires. Sometimes, there is debate over the effects of a policy, facility, or action on natural and cultural resources; at other times, however, it is more closely related to differing opinions about what the visitor experience in national parks should be.

In all likelihood, some earlier reconciliations will seem surprising—or clearly inappropriate—to later observers. People today may cringe, for example, on hearing that park service staff once entertained visitors by feeding grizzly bears in sight of the dining room in Yellowstone, knowing now that these practices endangered visitors and led to difficult management choices that have come to threaten the very survival of the grizzlies in the park. Or they may read Olmsted's prescient comment that Yosemite would attract millions of visitors and wonder how he would have reconciled his vision of narrow winding roads and simple cabins with the need to accommodate those crowds. The flagstone-rimmed road that entirely surrounds Crater Lake contrasts starkly with the more sensitive recent treatment of the world's tallest Redwood, where the visitor drives part of the way but approaches the tree on foot.

By the same token, some of today's responses to changing demands would have been unacceptable only a few years ago. Visits to the backcountry in some popular wilderness areas are limited and available by advance reservation, while fences have been built to prevent crowds of visitors from abusing coastal dunes.

During the 1960s, a consensus arising from the lessons of ecology began to alleviate the resource disruption that had previously resulted from some well-intentioned but inadequately informed interventions by park managers. Responding to increasingly sophisticated understanding and the pressures of resource scientists and conservationists, park service policy began to recognize that preservation of resources requires more respect for natural processes. Though often controversial in application, this standard represents another fundamental step in the evolution of the park ideal.

The urban parks movement of the 1960s and 1970s represented still another reconciliation of new demands for preservation and use, as some argued that a main criterion for designating national park units should be accessibility to populated areas. A powerful alliance of conservation, recreation, and civil rights groups forged a consensus that expanded the park system with several new units in and near urban areas. At the same time, the idea of a park was itself broadening: in so-called greenline parks, human settlements are viewed as integral to the landscape to be protected and interpreted, rather than as intrusions on the natural scene. In the future, the challenge will be to manage these parks sensitively so that they impart as much of the traditional national park experience as possible.

Today, preservation-versus-use dilemmas seem more difficult and pressing than ever before. The park service has been called on to protect incredibly diverse resources, while higher standards for protecting these holdings, including those with historic and cultural values, are advanced by stronger and more varied constituencies. The service is being asked to develop, as a major strategy, new forms of protection based on land-use partnerships and less-than-fee interests. Demands by would-be users have multiplied. The enlarging body of scientific knowledge informs, but sometimes confuses, the debates over the effects of use on preservation, while at the same time technological prowess can enhance the damage that wrong decisions provoke. Sophisticated management techniques have improved the service's ability to cope with growing use, but visitors

*Yellowstone, August 1984. Geyser Basin.*

are more willing and better equipped to penetrate remote park domains. Increased interest by the private sector in park activities
creates new opportunities for visitor enjoyment but raises old questions about the appropriateness of such involvement. Activities outside of lands owned and managed by the park service now influence
the capacity of the park service to keep its own lands "unimpaired."

Materialism, homogenization of places and attitudes, plasticity,
and technology now permeate society to an extent that might sur-
prise even the pessimistic Muir. National parks stand apart as special
places. Inevitably, performance in the national parks will continue
to fall short of the impossible ideal that would leave resources wholly "unimpaired"; the compromises made along the way will leave
their marks on the resources that the next generation inherits. Yet,
as has been the case since the park service was established almost
seven decades ago, the struggle to apply the charge to preserve and
enjoy continues to refine the park ideal.

# Profile
# Yellowstone
# National Park

Y ellowstone, the largest national park in the continental United
States at 2.2 million acres, is larger than the states of Rhode
Island and Delaware combined.[1] It is also the oldest national park.
Established on March 1, 1872, by an act of Congress that carved
a huge rectangle—almost a square—out of federal territory that
would not be organized into states for another 18 years, Yellowstone's monumental natural features and exotic wildlife have attracted generation after generation of Americans and travelers from
abroad enticed by descriptions of America's western grandeur. In
1983 alone, there were 2.3 million visits to the park. Each month,
2,000 people write to park staff about Yellowstone. Annually, over
500 articles extoll the park in travel and special-interest magazines.[2]
Jobs here are the most coveted in the National Park System: An an-
nouncement of a ranger opening will likely draw over 250 applicants, and more than 1,000 people vie for limited volunteer slots.

The mythology surrounding the creation of Yellowstone National
Park exemplifies legends about the early park system's evolution:
fantastic natural sights reported by occasional hunters and trappers
to a disbelieving public in the early to mid-19th century; expedi-
tions in 1869, 1870, and 1871 by influential persons, mainly
Easterners, to witness the sights and bring back scientific documentation and aesthetic depictions; campfire vows to reserve the lands
for the people and to ward off otherwise inevitable commercialization and despoliation.

In the background was Jay Cooke, the financier of the Northern
Pacific Railroad through Montana who provided support for lob-

bying Congress to create Yellowstone National Park.[3] The general idea was to protect "curiosities" and "wonders," although neither Cooke nor Congress quite knew what should, or should not, happen there.[3] As a result, Yellowstone, like other early parks, enclosed a lot of land to avoid missing scenic features in unexplored areas. According to historian John Ise, "boundaries ran up and down mountain ranges, across rivers and valleys, with no regard for the problems of administration and protection."[4]

From its establishment, many milestones in the struggles to define a national park have been laid in Yellowstone. At first, the park lacked congressional appropriations for staff or housing for year-round personnel. Nor did it have any authority to stop poachers and hunters. In fact, in the early days, Yellowstone's staff (including the first superintendent) hunted for sport and winter meals.[5] Park officials successfully fought proposals to build an elevator by Yellowstone Falls in the 1890s and to dam Yellowstone Lake in 1920.[6] A half century later, in 1970, a father's lawsuit, prompted by his son's fatal fall into the Old Faithful geyser, catalyzed debates over safety and visitor protection throughout the park system.[7] The contract buy-out in 1979 of General Host, one of Yellowstone's two major concessioners, for $19.9 million reiterated the primacy of public objectives in private businesses in national parks.[8] (See chapter 5 on The Private Sector in the Parks.) Today, the struggle to save Yellowstone's grizzly bears symbolizes the park service's strengthened commitment to resource protection and natural systems management.

The word *Yellowstone* derives from the Sioux *Mi tsi a-da-zi*, meaning Rock Yellow River, which French trappers, the first Europeans in the area, translated into *Roche Jaune* and *Pierre Jaune*. The terms undoubtedly refer to the marvelous profusion of sulfurous yellow-to-orange tones in the virtually vertical cliffs of the canyon through which the Yellowstone River flows.[9]

Before the Europeans arrived, the warlike Blackfoot and Nez Perce and the wandering Crow peoples roamed Yellowstone, although it seems that only one Native American tribe, the aboriginal Sheepeaters of the Shoshonean family, resided in it permanently. The paucity of American Indian settlement, despite trails crisscrossing the area, has been attributed both to awe (of the bizarre natural forms and emanations of smoke and fire) and to the harsh climate.

Awe remains a normal response to this natural wonderland. Here, says the park brochure, "two contrasting elements, fire and water, have combined to produce a land of natural wonders. It is a land born in the fires of thundering volcanoes and sculptured by glacial ice and running water."[10] The thermal basins, gigantic columns of boiling water, hissing steam vents, and volcanic ash testify to the comparatively recent flows of lava (about a hundred thousand years ago) and the still-changing landscape. Yet, though Yellowstone's terrain borders on the bizarre in many places, its vistas of mountains, valleys, rivers, and waterfalls and an abundance of wildlife give other spots the essence of pastoral serenity.

A great stone arch, built in 1903, marks the traditional entrance to the park from the north through the town of Gardiner in Montana. Visitors once passed through by horse and stage, having debarked at Cinnabar Station three miles away, and were then taken to the Mammoth Hot Springs Hotel, eight miles inside the park, where the hot springs—whose changing hues are the effects of limestone deposits—could be viewed from the window.

Today, on the five-mile drive from Mammoth south along the Gardiner River, a visitor will likely encounter freely roaming deer, antelope, and other wildlife. Closer to Old Faithful, the entire area along the Firehole and Gibbon rivers is filled with geysers and emerald-colored thermal pools. First-class trout streams are an angler's mecca. Some visitors take loop road tours and boardwalk trails to view Midway and Lower Geyser basins. But it is to Old Faithful that everyone—as many as 20,000 people a day during July and August—eventually heads. The height of the geyser (up to 130 feet) and the predictability of the eruption have given it century-old fame. The grand Old Faithful Inn (built in 1903), the cabins, the graveled path, the enormous parking lot, the gift shop, the gas station, and even bleachers and a sign showing the time of the next eruption represent different phases in the responses of the park service to Old Faithful's abiding popularity.

Throughout the park are other amazing "main features," usually adjacent to "visitor villages" and near numerous lookouts for motorists or hikers. Majestic Yellowstone Lake, over 7,000 feet above sea level, is immense, cold, stormy, and virtually unswimmable. Visitors can fish in the lake, under strict park service guidelines, and the more adventurous can take a boat trip across the lake's "arms" (see map) into Yellowstone's backcountry. The shore's more accessible constructed features include the Lake Yellowstone Inn,

Bridge Bay Marina for private boats, concessioner buildings for tours and fishing trips, cabins, and a campground. Nearby, Fishing Bridge, which is prime habitat for wildlife, including bears, hosts a recreational vehicle campground.

The road from the lake to the canyon and Yellowstone Falls follows the Yellowstone River as it winds through Hayden Valley. The smell of sulfur rises from the mud-volcano thermal area, and, farther along, bison cross the road or graze in the rolling hills; Artist and Inspiration points at the canyon itself bespeak scenic grandeur and discovery. (In the days before cameras, powerful paintings of Yellowstone Falls helped the campaign to create a national park.)

Yellowstone's roster of so many "must see" areas for visitors has for many years affected development of distinctive use patterns. Just as early residential and commercial development in old cities reflected the basic practice of walking to work, Yellowstone developed centers around its main features to accommodate stage-coach-ferried visitors who, because of physical and safety limitations, could not penetrate the park's topography. When visitation exploded with the automobile, these hubs, based on historic use, expanded. One visitor area established in the late 1960s, Grant Village, was at first limited to a campground, a marina, and park service buildings, but the village now has 300 modern motel-type units, opened in 1983 and 1984 as part of a planned $28-million development.[11]

Still these hubs are highly concentrated. The vast backcountry of Yellowstone remains a wonder of solitude. Hikers in the area above Yellowstone Canyon can trek five miles through diverse terrain, covered with old-growth forests, geothermal pools, marshland meadows, and a glistening lake, and see nary a soul in their half-day trek. But the parking lots from which the hikers set out are crowded and congested, and sights along the canyon drive are littered with backed-up carloads waiting excitedly to snap photos of the majestic scenes and wildlife.

Yellowstone's visitors usually come from a distance. Most arrive by car in the family groups that have been the mainstay of visitation in recent years. Lately, more visitors have used organized bus tours and commercial outfitters, and park guests have become more and more likely to hail from Canada, Europe, or Asia. Because, regionally, Yellowstone is part of a magnificent park system complex that includes Grand Teton National Park and the John D. Rockefeller, Jr., Memorial Parkway, a scenic 82-mile corridor connecting Yellowstone with the Tetons, visitors are including time in surrounding areas in their visit agendas.

After a sizable increase in the 1960s and early 1970s, the number of visits to Yellowstone has leveled off in the past decade. The park's distance from populated areas makes visitation sensitive to national trends: the annual number fell below 2 million after the 1973 oil crisis, climbed to 2.5 million during the Bicentennial, plummeted below 2 million again in recession-ridden 1979, and in 1982 and 1983 rose to 2.4 million.

In June, July, and August, capacity crowds stay overnight in the park's lodge rooms, cabins, and campsites and fill the accommodations in the gateway communities outside the park. The average stay inside the park is three days.[12] Yellowstone sets limits on the number of consecutive days one can spend in the backcountry (2 to 7, depending on location and season) and in campgrounds (14 days), on how many accommodations can be reserved by tour wholesalers (20 to 40 percent), and on how many "pillows," or beds, can be built inside the park (8,200). All campgrounds operate on a first-come, first-served basis; backcountry permits can be reserved, in person, 48 hours in advance.

One of Yellowstone's two current concessioners, TW Services, Inc. (formerly TWA Services), is aggressively marketing winter visitation as well as promoting the "shoulder" spring and fall seasons. Winter use is exploding; about 85,000 visitors per season brave temperatures that fall to 20 and 30 degrees below zero Fahrenheit to enjoy cross-country skiing over 40 miles of groomed trails, snowmobile and snowcoach rides over 200 miles of unplowed roadways, and the warmth of the fireplace at one of two lodges open year-round.[13] The region is also being heavily promoted by the Yellowstone-Teton Travel Association and state agencies in Wyoming, Montana, and Idaho.

Managing the intense visitation to a few extraordinarily sensitive areas and controlling its effects on the resources might well be enough of a challenge to park managers. But they must also deal with external influences—activities in the five adjacent national forests and on private lands outside the park. Yellowstone's vulnerability to off-site environmental pressures typifies the dilemma facing national parks today.[14]

*Yellowstone, August 1984. Thermal pools.*

The $11.9 million appropriated by the federal government to run Yellowstone National Park in 1983 paid the salaries of 740 staff, in peak season, who served visitors, managed resources, engaged in scientific research, supervised personnel, monitored the budget, and simply kept Yellowstone clean and its trails groomed. A core staff of 215 worked the full year. In many ways, managing Yellowstone is akin to managing a city. Planning documents prepared over the last decade for the park amount to a sizable collection, including a comprehensive master plan prepared in 1974 and detailed studies in response to new issues (winter use and increased demand for the backcountry), changing values (new attention to cultural resource management), and priorities set in Washington (more contracting out to the private sector).

The federal government has exclusive jurisdiction over roads, land-use planning, and law enforcement in the park. Park staff can decide in which of the three surrounding states—Wyoming, Montana, or Idaho—they want to register their cars. Poaching, a federal offense, carries stiff penalties. Yellowstone has its own jail, with a resident magistrate. (The park operates many reciprocal agreements with its three neighbor states, coordinating policies on drinking age, speed limits, and the like.)

Yellowstone is not run by government alone. Assistance by private citizens, nonprofit groups, and concessioners is essential. For the past two years, enthusiastic retirees, as well as college students, have come to the park to spend at least four weeks working on trails, giving out information, and repairing buildings while staying in park-supplied accommodations. Volunteer interest is high, even more than in parks close to large metropolitan areas, according to Park Superintendent Robert D. Barbee, who took over the coveted post at Yellowstone in January 1983 after the death of widely respected Superintendent John Townsley.[15] Yellowstone's nonprofit cooperating association, the Yellowstone Library and Museum Association, stocks and sells educational books and materials.

The largest contingent of non-park-staff persons working at Yellowstone are employed by the park's two concessioners. TW Services' multimillion-dollar business involves 2,200 hotel rooms, deluxe cabins, and rustic shelters; a 358-space fully serviced recreational vehicle campground at Fishing Bridge; fancy and fast-food restaurants serving 1.7 million meals annually; and the marina on Yellowstone Lake, a bus system, and three horse-rental centers. The company employs 2,300 persons in the summer and maintains a permanent year-round staff of about 100 persons, providing them with in-park dormitories, dining rooms, and pubs.

The park's other concessioner, Hamilton Stores, Inc., has been a family business since 1915 when Charles A. Hamilton bought a small store that Henry Klamer had opened in 1897.[16] Hamilton Stores now owns a string of shops in 12 heavily used areas, sells souvenirs and maps, photo and camper supplies, and counter snacks. With estimated gross earnings in 1983 of over $12 million, Hamilton employed about 750 people.[17]

In 1980, the adequacy of the budget and staff of Yellowstone and other traditional parks became a point of contention in the wake of a report by the U.S. comptroller general that water and sewer facilities and overnight accommodations in many parks were unsafe. Interior Secretary James Watt picked up the theme in 1981, arguing that rapid system expansion had diverted maintenance money from the great western parks. Whatever the reason, Yellowstone was pinched. With an operating budget of $9.1 million in

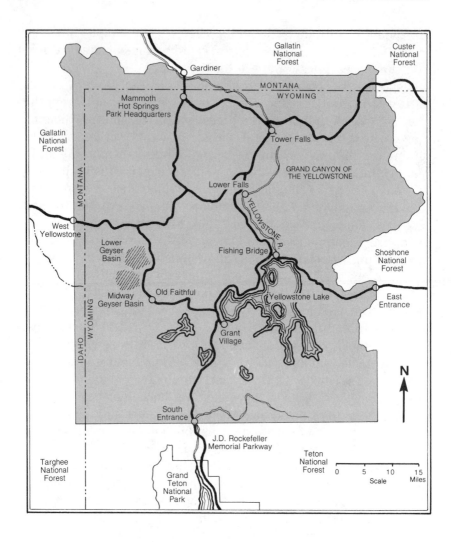

1980, the number of staff at peak season had fallen to 580 people, from around 700 in 1976.[18]

The recent emphasis throughout the park system on rehabilitation and maintenance has been visible in Yellowstone. Through 1983, the park spent $4.7 million in funds from the Park Restoration and Improvement Program (PRIP), a crash effort established to fix up facilities that had suffered from past neglect. The money went for a miscellany of projects, including upgrading water and sewer systems, repairing retaining walls and unsafe boardwalks at viewing sites, and rehabilitating historic structures. In addition,

$34.6 million of the park's regular construction budget is targeted for renovating, over a period of years, concessioner-operated facilities, including installing sprinkler systems and fire exits in the lodges, overhauling kitchens, and replacing roofs.[19]

In a novel arrangement for the park system, TW Services must reinvest 22 percent of its gross income annually for capital improvements and maintenance facilities. (This fund came to $4.5 million in 1983.) TW Services also invested about $13 million before its contract was fully negotiated and has loaned the service $7 million for additional construction and design.[20]*

Hamilton Stores, a more traditional concessioner that owns its buildings, has no contractual requirements for reinvestment other than the obligation to keep things in good repair. The park service is, however, negotiating a schedule of repairs and rehabilitation of Hamilton's facilities, including removal of certain structures from sensitive areas. Hamilton's annual concessioner fee is paid into a recently established Visitors Facilities Fund earmarked for rehabilitating government-owned buildings throughout the National Park System.

The park service has in recent years strengthened its management of concessioner activity, scientific research, and park planning in Yellowstone, but these are still relatively small budget items. The maintenance division accounts for three-quarters of the budget, with most of the remainder spent on visitor and resource protection—including law enforcement, administration, and interpretative activities. With so many demands for staff time, greater efficiency and productivity are current administrative buzzwords, referring to everything from saving energy to increasing reliance on tape-recorded automobile tours.

Tradition informs everything that happens at Yellowstone, but change—in activities inside and outside the park, in knowledge and values, and in the array of interests that want to influence policies in the park—is a constant challenge. While tradition provides the park system's "flagship park" with a distinctive mystique,

---

*The arrangements are structured legally so that funds generated in Yellowstone can remain in Yellowstone; formerly, the concessioner's franchise fee was paid into the U.S. Treasury. User fees for campgrounds operated by the park service and park entrance fees go to the Land and Water Conservation Fund.

it is also the source of inertia, according to Superintendent Barbee.

No issue highlights the tension between tradition and change at Yellowstone better than the fate of the grizzly bear. Before the turn of the century, 100,000 grizzlies roamed the West. Today, only two areas in the lower 48 states—Yellowstone and the Glacier National Park-Bob Marshall Wilderness Area in Montana—remain as major grizzly bear habitats. Experts say 200 to 300 grizzlies now roam Yellowstone,[21] and only some 30 cub-bearing females remain. Governmental and private studies have warned that the bears are on the verge of extinction in the United States outside of Alaska.

For many people, the visible bear in Yellowstone is the national park. In the late 1960s, the park service acknowledged that bears begging food from humans and foraging through garbage were antithetical to the national park concept of nature coexisting with civilization; moreover, such practices decreased the prospect of species survival. (In bear/visitor contacts, says Barbee, the bear "usually loses.")[22] In a controversial episode, the park service, after being advised by John and Frank Craighead—brothers who, as scientists, were monitoring bear density and behavior—to take corrective measures slowly, instead chose wholesale closing of major garbage dumps in the park.[23]

The service thought the bears would return to the forests, away from humans and their food, and lead free-ranging lives as an integral part of the ecosystem. That policy diverged markedly from earlier wildlife management practices. By the 1930s, for example, the park service had eliminated natural predators such as wolves, and, in the early 1960s, the service killed off thousands of elk to deal with a large herd of the animals. This triggered a seminal study of wildlife management in the parks by an advisory board chaired by A. Starker Leopold. That 1963 report urged the park service to cease manipulating nature and instead to retain parks in as natural a condition as possible.[24]

However, once a chain of natural relationships is broken, it is not easily reestablished. Bears that could not be "unhooked" from garbage were transported either to remote areas of the park or outside it. The animals sometimes died from the tranquilizers administered to prepare them for the journey, and those bears that persisted in returning to visitor areas were destroyed. Injuries to people increased. Some bears searched for garbage in the towns outside park boundaries, where they frightened people and were

Yellowstone, August 1984. The Standing family—Earl, Suzanne, Colby, and Cory—and Mr. and Mrs. John Roberts (Roy, Utah). Earl: "I would like to see more bears. It's disappointing to ride along the road and not see a bear. But I've seen too many people with their children too close to bears. They don't realize what they will do. We've even seen a woman trying to put a baby on a bear so she could take a picture. That's ridiculous. Some people say the bear is the problem and not the people. The first thing we ought to do is educate people."

vulnerable to poachers. Estimates of the numbers killed from 1968, when the dumps were closed, until 1973 range from 37, by the park service, to 189, by the Craighead brothers.[25]

Finally, a consensus was reached that saving the grizzly bears required more comprehensive measures by the park service in concert with other federal and state agencies. Together, those agencies revised and coordinated research and policies to help save the bears. In October 1982, the park service adopted a management plan emphasizing research, interagency cooperation, and selective visitor restrictions. An interagency study team—made up of representatives of the National Park Service, the U.S. Forest Service, the U.S. Fish and Wildlife Service, and the land-managing agencies of Montana, Idaho, and Wyoming—meets regularly to coordinate activities that affect the bears. The team works with adjacent communities to engage their cooperation in closing down dumps outside the park and developing standardized procedures for handling problem bears and poachers, for example.

One of the most controversial current issues in grizzly bear

*Yellowstone, August 1984.*

management is supplemental feedings. Advocates of these feedings say that, given the size of the current bear population, the service should enhance survival by providing food, primarily by dumping animal carcasses in the forests far away from people. This would also, it is claimed, help keep the bears within park boundaries, protected from poachers and other outside influences. Author Alston Chase, writing in *Atlantic Monthly* points out that Yellowstone is neither a zoo nor an unspoiled ecosystem. Development, roads, clear-cutting on adjacent national forests, and fire suppression, as well as a century of human feeding, have altered the ecosystem despite its appearance of naturalness. Chase believes that keeping the bear in Yellowstone is important; if this takes supplemental feedings, he argues, so be it.[26]

In early 1984, a subcommittee of scientists on the interagency team recommended against supplemental feeding. (The grizzly bear management plan reserves the possibility of providing some food "at times of crisis" in the future.) Superintendent Barbee agrees with the subcommittee, saying that reacting emotionally now with supplemental feeding is a throwback to the past ad hoc reactions of the park service. "There is a compelling argument for a hands-off approach," he argues, "and a lot we can do to achieve it. We have the mechanisms in place. Self-regulation should be the ideal we strive for even if it is not always possible to attain."

In a related issue, the park service's plan to shut down the fully serviced, concessioner-run Fishing Bridge campground for recreational vehicles and return the area to grizzly bears has raised vehement objections, although new overnight units would be placed elsewhere in the park. "Visitors have a lot of raw sentiment about how they expect to use the park," says the superintendent. "A tradition of use has developed which is difficult to change." The irony is that replacements for the overnight units removed from Fishing Bridge are being developed at Grant Village, a site officials now recognize as grizzly bear habitat, too.[27] At local public hearings in 1983 about the proposed Fishing Bridge phaseout, most who turned out opposed closing the campground. The issue has received wider attention as powerful recreational-vehicle and travel-interest groups have brought their case to congressional representatives in Washington, D.C., triggering a response from national conservation groups.

Barbee, who holds degrees in wildland management and zoology, believes that existing scientific data support the park service's position, although he admits that closing the campground is not "a trigger event." "It won't in itself save the grizzly," he says, "but it's part of a series of cumulative actions that over time will improve wildlife management here in Yellowstone." Following a summer marked by increased sightings of grizzly bears, and some maulings, one of which was fatal, Barbee called grizzly bears the park's "number one management problem."[28]

Barbee, who previously supervised a large team of scientists in California's Redwood National Park, describes Yellowstone's scientific staff as "lean." Its five professionals constitute a virtual doubling of staff in recent years, however. Reorganized, the team has identified research projects for park staff in forestry and water and mineral resources, as well as grizzly bears, and will try to promote research by private citizens and universities. The University of Wyoming, the University of California, and Utah State University already engage in cooperative research with the park.

Differing values, as well as conflicting and inadequate information, must be dealt with in resource management decisions. Park officials do not want to designate most of Yellowstone as wilderness, an idea studied for a decade. They argue that management already incorporates the wilderness perspective in most instances. Many environmental groups, however, feel that that perspective is not given enough emphasis. For example, motorboats are now permitted on Yellowstone Lake, although they operate at a crawl when they enter the lake's arms to bring visitors to the backcountry. Without motorboats, visitors would have to choose between a long boat ride by canoe or rowboat across the open lake, a dangerous prospect, or a rugged 20-mile hike from a parking area. Wilderness advocates argue that access to the backcountry should indeed be limited to those who can approach it "on its own terms."

The place of cultural resources in a great natural park is also a source of tension. For years, the cabins, the gas station, and the old Hamilton store around Old Faithful seemed "clutter" to many park service staff and visitors. The 1974 park plan provided a phaseout of the old cabins at Old Faithful, again by replacing them with new units at Grant Village.[29] But some argue that early lodging structures around Old Faithful are historically significant as a glimpse of what the first park tourists experienced. Indeed, the Warnock family, whose members have stayed at Old Faithful Inn for

*Yellowstone, August 1984. Buffalo herd.*

three generations, formed the Committee to Protect Our Yellowstone Heritage, and Wyoming's state historic preservation officer, who reviews decisions to demolish historic buildings in the park, is sympathetic. Old Faithful and its buildings, along with several other "villages," were nominated as historic districts in 1983.

"We have many resource considerations to balance," says Park Planner Dan Wenk. "How do we protect one type of resource without adversely affecting the other?" Argues Barbee, "In this park, nature is sovereign. We need to be sensitive to the past, and of course we'll keep Old Faithful Inn, but we don't have to fix cars or do laundry within 1,000 feet of the geyser, nor does the concessioner need to have its dormitories and pubs there."[30]

Yellowstone was once a remote fiefdom removed from many of the pressures of civilization. It is, however, only part of a distinctive ecosystem that encompasses an area the size of New England without Maine. Today, it is not large enough to sustain the grizzlies or to insulate the area's unique natural features from activities pursued beyond the park's borders.

Even the extensive buffering by adjacent national forests offers insufficient protection. In 1982, 70 individuals and corporations applied for geothermal leases on land in a national forest area west of the park. One site, only a quarter mile from a thermal area inside Yellowstone, raised widespread concern about the effect of geothermal drilling on Yellowstone's geysers, but no one really knew any answers. On the east, plans for oil and gas exploration raised fears about grizzly habitat. The national uproar over these plans has been stilled by recent changes in energy economics, which diminished commercial interest, but the threat remains. And a 1980 park service report detailed a host of other potential impacts on Yellowstone from sources outside its boundaries—for example, from acid rain, logging, housing development, and grazing.

Regional and national environmental groups joined forces to form the Greater Yellowstone Coalition to propose more coherent responses to threats to the park's resources. Arguing that Yellowstone is a "biological unit" with the Grand Teton National Park and adjacent national forests, the coalition is proposing measures to overcome "fragmented" management.[31] The individual chambers of commerce of the gateway communities have formed a Yellowstone/Teton Travel Association to strengthen their voice in the operations of Yellowstone, the lifeblood of the tourism that vies with agriculture as Wyoming's most important industry.[32]

All of these special interests, says Barbee, create a flood of demands for studies, planning reviews, and continuous consultation and coordination. "There are times when I despair, but I appreciate the need for checks and balances."

The small group of men who sat around a campfire over a century ago in the remote wilderness could hardly have foreseen the complexity, in modern times, of preserving Yellowstone's resources for people's enjoyment and benefit. Because they were able to see beyond the ideas and institutions of the day, Yellowstone remains a wonder. This vision, as much as an awesome physical place, is their legacy and continuing challenge.

# Chapter 2
# The Unsystematic System

What is the National Park System? Collectively, it consists of 334 units[1] designated by Congress or presidential proclamation, that preserve for public enjoyment many of the nation's best natural features and evidence of its geological past; a record of U.S. prehistory, settlement, military encounters, and social and cultural development; sites associated with national leaders and events in politics, sciences, the arts, and other fields; and outstanding areas for outdoor recreation (figure 2.1). The park system also includes many of the parks, parkways, forts, monuments, and historic and cultural sites in the Washington, D.C., metropolitan area.

Of the 334 units in the system, only 48 are formally designated as "national parks."[2] The others bear some 20 different titles, suggesting the impossibility of establishing neat categories for such varied holdings. "There have been occasional efforts to standardize the names . . . but . . . confusion over terminology continues," writes historian William C. Everhart.[3] Despite the different names, park service staff think of all the units as "parks."

Diversity—already evident at the system's formal creation in 1916 when several of the incorporated units were archaeological sites rather than unspoiled natural areas, and several were considered by some contemporary observers to be unworthy—remained a dominant force as the system enlarged in response to changing opportunities and priorities. Two periods of expansion stand out. In the 1930s and 1940s, the number of units more than tripled,[4] from 55 to 182, as, in addition to new natural areas in the West, the system added battlefield and military parks previously administered by

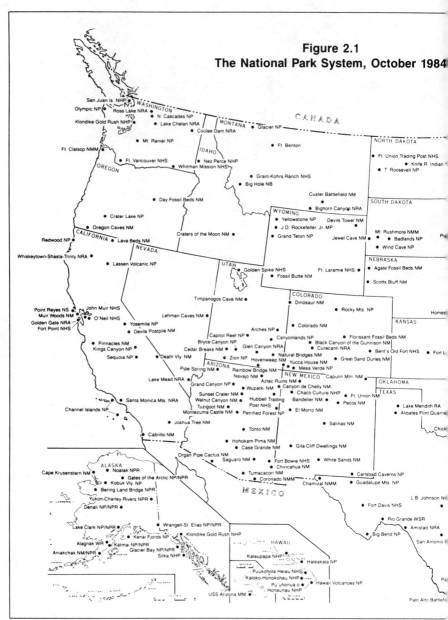

**Figure 2.1
The National Park System, October 1984**

*Reprinted by permission of the Sierra Club from "The National Park System," Sierra Club Information Services, San Francisco, California, October 1984.*

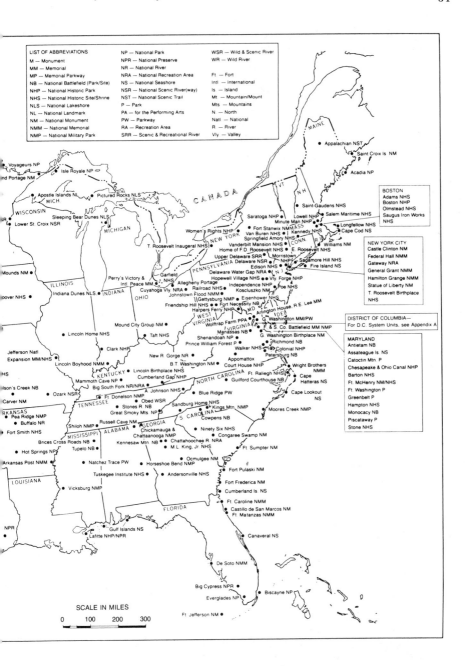

other federal agencies; numerous monuments and open spaces in the District of Columbia and its environs; new historical units; national recreation areas developed as part of the dam-building era; scenic parkways; and new parks in the East. In the 1960s and 1970s, the system expanded further, from 187 units in 1960 to a total of 333 units by 1980,[5] embracing a range of natural, scenic, recreational, cultural, and historical resources in response to the nation's growing environmental awareness and desire to serve urban residents more effectively.

These two periods enhanced diversity in several ways: they increased regional, urban, and recreational representation; historical and cultural preservation; and environmental protection. Parks were no longer concentrated in the West. Moreover, especially after 1960, the system allied itself with urban interests, significantly increasing the number of units relatively close to heavily populated urban regions. Preservation of distinctive aspects of American history and culture expanded so that, by 1983, 57 percent of the units in the system were classified as "historic."[6] Many of the newer natural units were less pristine or visually awesome than those previously included in the system, and a number were created to restore natural resources or end further degradation.

The debate continues over whether all this makes for too much diversity. For example, some critics propose that historical and cultural sites be spun off and administered separately. Others question recent so-called urban parks. To be sure, one can quarrel with individual units—the designation process has always mixed, in varying combinations, politics and advocacy with professional assessment. But the totality of the "unsystematic" system has deep national meaning. According to Yale historian Robin W. Winks, former chair of the National Park System Advisory Board:

> The national symbols people choose to preserve—the visible reminders of how a nation came to be what it is—serve as useful keys to understanding values. . . . Societies, after all, choose to protect the objects and emblems of their collective pride; great scenic wonders, natural preserves, and game parks do not survive by accident. . . . That they exist at all is a statement about the time in which they were established, and that they continue to survive is a clear indication that they are still regarded as having great public worth.[7]

## NATURAL AREAS

Most of the considerable acreage in the park system belongs to units established primarily to protect unique natural resources. The 48 areas designated as national parks today represent a minority of the total number of units in the National Park System, but they protect 47.9 million acres, or 60 percent of the system's total. Many of the 78 national monuments in the park system also are set aside because of their outstanding geological or scenic natural formations.[8]

### The Great Western Parks*

At the core of the system are the superlative national parks of the West, nearly all carved from the public domain. The first true national park, *Yellowstone* (see profile), was established in 1872, only two years after a party of explorers, determined to find out the truth of fantastic tales of steaming vents and bubbling lakes, agreed that "the sight of [Yellowstone] . . . ought to be as free as the air or water."†[9] That pattern repeated, as other adventurers sought out rumored geological wonders, discovered them in a primeval state, and saw the lands ultimately set aside from the public domain.

By the turn of the century, four more national parks had been created on the monumental model. Three were established in 1890, within days of one another and with remarkably little congressional debate. The most spectacular is *Yosemite National Park*, in California, the creation of which is a tribute to the tireless national campaigns of John Muir and *Century* editor Robert Underwood Johnson. The federal park protects the glacier-carved Sierra high

---

*The great western parks are sometimes called the "crown jewels" of the National Park System. Because the system as a whole might better be thought of as the "crown jewels" of the country, the term is generally avoided in this book.

†Two other contenders for the title "first national park" are *Hot Springs*, in Arkansas, and *Yosemite*, in California. Hot Springs was set aside as a national "reservation" in 1832 and designated a national park in 1921.[10] Experts consider it an aberration, however. Yosemite Valley was ceded to the state of California in 1864 and dedicated to "public use, resort, and recreation."[11] While some cite this as the origin of the national park concept, Yosemite Valley was not given national park status until 1905, when it was ceded back to the federal government and incorporated into Yosemite National Park.

country surrounding the magnificent Yosemite Valley and Mariposa Grove, both ceded to the state of California in 1864. Because of state mismanagement, the central portions were ceded back to the federal government in 1905 and added to the national park.

*Sequoia National Park* and the smaller *General Grant National Park*, both in California, were established to protect groves of giant sequoia that were being cut down wantonly by lumber interests. Sequoia wood, paradoxically, is unsuitable for most commercial purposes. The creation of Sequoia National Park, which also includes the glacier-incised spires of the Sierra Nevada range and Mount Whitney, the highest mountain peak in the country outside of Alaska, is credited mainly to Visalia, California, publisher and editor Colonel George Stewart.[12] General Grant National Park became part of *Kings Canyon National Park* when the latter was established in 1940.

Washington's Mount Rainier, with its icy-covered high peak rising impressively over surrounding dense forests and meadows of subalpine wildflowers, became the next great park. Although much of *Mount Rainier National Park*, created in 1899, was virtually inaccessible, a proposal to build a cog railroad to its summit raised fears about commercial exploitation.[13] The National Geographic Society, the Sierra Club, the Appalachian Mountain Club, and other organizations in the nascent conservation movement were important influences in Congress's decision to create the park.[14]

By the time the National Park System was formally put together in 1916, five more of today's great western parks had been established:

*Crater Lake National Park* was established in 1902 following unsuccessful efforts to set this natural wonder aside as an Oregon state park. Oregon Judge William Gladstone Steel, who had been mesmerized as a boy by the volcanic lake's incredible blue color, devoted his life to finding a way to preserve the lustrous lake for public benefit and served as the park's second superintendent.[15]

*Glacier National Park*, on the spine of the northern Rockies in Montana, was created in 1910. Its precipitous peaks, rising more than 10,000 feet, shelter lakes, streams, wildflowers, and wildlife. Explorer and scientist George Grinnell, allied with the Sierra Club and other conservationists, fought hard for congressional approval of the park; their cause was strengthened by the support of railroad interests seeking benefits from tourism.

In 1915, Stephen Mather arrived in Washington, D.C., to help
the secretary of the interior manage the national parks. (The following year, the National Park System and Service were created, and
Mather became the service's first director.)* Also in 1915, Congress
established *Rocky Mountain National Park* in Colorado. The park
includes 65 peaks higher than 10,000 feet[17] and a scenic richness
attributable to its unusual range of altitudes. The successful campaign to set aside this massive mountain system directly on the Continental Divide was primarily the work of Enos Mills, the "John
Muir of the Rockies," who attracted a national following through
articles he wrote for the *Saturday Evening Post*. Mills was supported
by the secretary of the interior, the U.S. Geological Survey, and
state interests that wanted to promote tourism.[18]

The next year, 1916, less than a month before the park service
was created, *Hawaii National Park*, encompassing active volcanoes,
dormant craters, and primeval ecosystems on the islands of Hawaii
and Maui, was established, following promotion by island busi-
nessmen. The Maui unit, designated as *Haleakala National Park*
in 1960 after the dormant crater that is its dominant feature, also
protects a unique and fragile tropical ecosystem, scenic pools, and
endangered wildlife. The Hawaii unit, renamed *Hawaii Volcanoes
National Park* in 1961, includes still-active Kilauea and Mauna
Loa.[19]

*Lassen Volcanic National Park* was created about the same time.
When Lassen Peak erupted and attracted wide public interest, a
California congressman promoted the elevation to national park
status.[20] (The peak and another area that became part of the park,
Cinder Cone, were already national monuments.[21]) Despite his interest in expanding the number of parks, Mather opposed Lassen
because of concessions made to commercial interests.[22] Later Mather
decided its beauty justified compromise. Fumaroles, mud pots, and
hot springs remind visitors of eruptions, although the volcano has
been dormant since 1917.

---

*The story about how Mather came to Washington is legendary: Interior
Secretary Franklin K. Lane replied to a letter Mather sent him complaining
of poor management in Yosemite and Sequoia national park by saying, "If
you don't like the way the national parks are being run, come on down to
Washington and run them yourself." Mather decided to accept the challenge,
working initially as Lane's chief assistant.[16]

Most of the national parks that became the National Park System in 1916 were linked by the "monumentalism" of their natural features—mountains, trees, glaciers, or lakes.*[23] This was not true of the entire group, however. Several other units in the group—*Wind Cave*, *Sullys Hill*, and *Platt*—were seen by contemporaries as of lesser quality than the others, and the basis for their inclusion was more political than scenic.[24]

The original system also included 21 national monuments,[25] among them *Devils Tower*, an 865-foot volcanic shaft in Wyoming; *Muir Woods*, the first example of a unit created by donation of private lands[26] and, until 1968, the only stand of California coastal redwoods in the system; *Pinnacles*, also in California, which has unusual, high rock-spire formations and caves; and the sandstone *Natural Bridges*, in Utah.

---

*Monumental natural features were not the only reason for inclusion in the original National Park System. *Mesa Verde National Park*, a member of the "founders" group, was singled out in 1906 to protect its spectacular pre-Columbian cliff dwellings. *Montezuma Castle*, an extremely well-preserved cliff house in Arizona, and Pueblo Indian ruins in New Mexico were included in the original system as national monuments.

*Yellowstone, August 1984.*

Varying degrees of conflict surrounded the creation of these national parks and monuments. Proposed parklands, according to historian Alfred Runte, had to be proven "worthless"—devoid of known minerals, good farmland, commercial timber.[27] The dominant mood in Congress and the country, of course, favored divestiture of federal territory to settle, expand, and exploit the land base. The archetypes of Runte's thesis are Yellowstone, with its hissing and steaming terrain, and Rainier, roadless, rocky, and icy.

Critics of the "worthless lands" thesis caution against taking the debates of the time too literally, because park advocates may have argued that splendid natural resources had no economic value just to convince Congress to withdraw these lands from commercial pressures.[28] Although it is difficult to reconstruct the truth now, apparently, for several decades, advocates for scenic protection were able to work with advocates for economic growth, agreeing on park boundaries that enclosed "features" and left outside lands believed to have economic value. Conflicts were present, of course, but on the whole those who shaped the park system worked to "find that compromise between altruism and materialism that best captures the public interest."[29]

Disputes among various interests became fiercer as more settlers pressed westward, railroads pierced the lands, surveyors mapped the mountains and deserts, and claims were staked. Park creation, more and more, was accompanied by qualifying language protecting mining claims, private property, and railroad rights.

As western states were brought into the Union, the question arose whether they, rather than the federal government, could take on the responsibility for protection. The example of Yosemite Valley's mismanagement by California,[30] as well as the still-formative conditions in many state governments, generally made these discussions short-lived. In most instances, the choice was either preservation in the federal domain or commercial development. There were notable exceptions, however, and superlative resources worthy of national park status were protected in some states, when local benefactors and political and economic interests found mutual advantage. California redwood groves, for example, were purchased by private philanthropists and donated to the state; wealthy local and summer residents in New Hampshire provided a good bit of the money to help buy the logged New Hampshire forests, and the state, along with the U.S. Forest Service, returned the lands to more natural condition.[31]

In the decade after the National Park System's creation, four more great western parks were established. Of the four, three had previously been set aside as national monuments. *Mount McKinley National Park* in Alaska, established in 1917, rivaled Yellowstone's size.[32] Although it includes the highest mountain—20,320 feet—in North America, in a dramatic natural setting, the national organizations that advocated federal park status (the Boone and Crockett Club, Campfire Club of America, and others) primarily wanted to protect the abundant mountain sheep, caribou, grizzly bear, and other wildlife. The park's size was expanded and its name changed to *Denali* in 1980.

Although the official birth of *Grand Canyon National Park* antedates World War I, its awesome scenery had inspired powerful advocacy for its protection much earlier. As mining, recreational, and preservation interests struggled, much of the mile-deep chasm[33] evolved from a forest reserve (in 1893) to a game preserve (in 1906) to a national monument (in 1908) and, finally, in 1919, to a national park.[34] The park was enlarged in 1975 to incorporate adjoining parts of the canyon.

Two extraordinary smaller natural parks were established at this time. *Zion National Park*, an amazingly colored canyon and mesa landscape incised by erosion in the Mukuntuweap Plateau of southern Utah, gained park status in 1919. Discovered and named by wandering Mormons, Zion was, according to John Ise, a "true national park with no concessions to commercial interests."[35] In an unusual move, Congress appropriated money to buy 80 acres of private land.[36] *Bryce Canyon National Park*, promoted by Mather, Horace M. Albright, and a Utah senator, was, again according to Ise, "easy to establish, because everyone who saw it recognized its superlative national park quality; it was small, and had little that commercial interests would fight for . . . only scenery."[37] Proclaimed a national monument in 1923, the horseshoe-shaped amphitheater with its jewel tones was authorized as a national park in 1924.

Other monumental units were still to come—*Grand Teton National Park*, in Wyoming, in 1929;* *Olympic National Park*, in

---

*Grand Teton National Park was expanded in 1950 to include about 203,000 acres in the Jackson Hole area.[36]

Washington State, in 1939; and *Kings Canyon*, in California, in 1940, for example. These were the culmination of decades-long struggles, although some controversies over boundary adjustments continued. All involved some lands transferred from the Forest Service. *Death Valley* and *Joshua Tree national monuments*, proclaimed in 1933 and 1936, respectively, in California, are equals of the great parks in scenery. There were also new western units exhibiting unique natural features, such as *Big Bend National Park* (1935), in Texas; *Carlsbad Caverns National Park* (1930),* in New Mexico; and a host of smaller units.

But a great era in the West had drawn to a close. The monumental "vestiges of primitive America" were all discovered, if not always protected. The creative alliance between capitalist expansion and conservation gave way as philosophical and economic differences made compromise less palatable. Commercial interests realized that apparently worthless lands often had great economic value. Conservationists, seeing protected resources in older parks suffer because of inadequate size and naively drawn boundaries, tried to adjust older boundaries and close "loopholes." They also sought transfer of high-quality resources managed for multiple uses by the Forest Service to the park system.

A new ethic—"complete conservation"—began to engage conservationists and park service leaders. Moving beyond the goal of simply protecting spectacular scenery, they began to think of protecting interrelated natural systems and living landscapes, including wildlife and flora and their habitats, and resources of ecological and scientific significance that had a more subtle appeal.[39] Achievement of such goals would require broad-based political support, Mather sensed, and setbacks in Congress already had demonstrated the vulnerability of the western-based system. The shift from monumentalism aided park service officials as they searched in the East for counterparts to the great western natural areas.

## National Parks in the East

One year after the close of World War I, the first national park in the East, *Acadia*, was added to the park system. The rugged Maine

---

*Carlsbad Caverns National Park was created from the existing Carlsbad Cave National Monument, which was proclaimed in 1923.

coast, with its spectacular cliffs, had clear parity with the great parklands of the West. The big difference was that land here was privately owned and costly. With rare exceptions, Congress had been ada-
mant in not appropriating money for buying land and, in fact, was
less than forthcoming in providing dollars to run the parks as well.

Like many of the western parks, Acadia was primarily a "one-
man crusade."[40] George B. Dorr and a group of influential and
wealthy seasonal residents, including John D. Rockefeller, Jr., at
first bought available properties in the area as a state-chartered, tax-
free public service corporation. They turned to the federal government in disenchantment after the Maine legislature threatened
annulment of their charter.

Sentiment for creating other eastern parks was growing. Spurred
by Mather, the secretary of the interior appointed a commission
to examine, firsthand, the merit of different locations.[41] Inevitably,
the commission used the language of the West—"topographic
features of great scenic value," "ruggedness," and "primeval
character"—in recommending specific areas.[42]

Support coalesced around the Great Smoky Mountains National
Park, in the Appalachians (North Carolina and Tennessee), and the
Shenandoah National Park, in the Blue Ridge (Virginia). Both were
authorized by Congress in 1926. Although the combination of scenery, wilderness, and botanical variety close to the western ideal was
most realized in Great Smoky, both were, in the eyes of park experts since then, "transition parks" in the progression to a new
sensibility about resource protection.[43] Shenandoah had noteworthy
cultural, as well as natural, qualities and, in fact, was rather intensively settled. Rough roads wound through mountain hollows to
cabins, farms, and cemeteries, and large parcels had already been
cleared and planted. Although most of Great Smoky was owned
by pulp and lumber companies, 1,200 tracts were farms and 5,000
were lots with summer homes.[44]

It took almost a decade after congressional authorization for both
Great Smoky and Shenandoah to be fully established. Congress
insisted that states and private interests donate a minimum acreage
before the parks became operational. Local resistance and problems
with inholders, problems that had arisen in the West but were now
to become more widespread as parks were carved out of lands once
in private ownership, also delayed the parks' establishment. Advocates organized local coalitions to scramble for public and private

*Death Valley, February 1984. Sunrise.*

dollars, and again John D. Rockefeller, Jr., came to the rescue. For
Great Smoky, a $5 million purchase fund was created by appropria-
tions from Tennessee and North Carolina and by donations and gifts
from local benefactors and school children. The additional $5
million needed for the estimated purchase cost was donated by the
Laura Spelman Rockeller Fund.[45] In Shenandoah, the state of
Virginia bought out residents and moved them to towns and communities outside the park.[46] Congressional reductions in the
minimum acreage needed to establish Shenandoah and a modest
Rockefeller donation added the final impetus for the park's realization. Over the years, the park service aided nature to restore the
Blue Ridge to forest.

   *Mammoth Cave National Park*, in Kentucky, the longest recorded
underground passage in the world, and *Isle Royale National Park*,
a forested wilderness island in Michigan's Lake Superior with a
pre-Columbian history, were authorized in 1926 and 1931, respectively. Private lands had to be acquired here, too, and Congress at
first would not give any money for acquisition. Later, some federal
funds from New Deal programs were made available. Questions
about whether these new parks met national park standards were
raised, especially when the authorization for Mammoth Cave was

passed by Congress with little debate despite the absence of the customary report by the secretary of the interior.[47]

The authorization of *Everglades National Park* in 1934 marked a significant departure for the park system. The Everglades park encompasses a large ecosystem, over 1 million acres, without "great mountains, deep canyons, tumbling waterfalls."[48] Preservationists saw a "river of grass"; others an ugly swamp.[49] A fragile subtropical wilderness, the Everglades contain incredibly abundant wildlife, including rare birds and amphibians, threatened by extinction because of extensive drainage and development. Distinguished scientists, the Audubon Society, and the Boone and Crockett Club gave their strong support to forming the park. The National Parks Association, at first skeptical, joined the advocates after conducting its own assessment. Granted the region differed from the "great scenes in our existing National Parks," the association's report said, but the Everglades area was "no less arresting, no less memorable."[50] The park was not established until 1947, however. Florida delayed acquisition, and land prices rose, especially after oil was discovered.

## New Natural Areas

During the past 25 years, important natural units have continued to enter the system. The public's increasing appreciation for wilderness, especially notable during this period, has influenced the selection of new natural units and the policies for managing them. This attitude has influenced management of established units as well.

In 1968, the park system's inner circle of spectacular, monumental national resources finally was joined by *Redwood National Park*. The delay in creating a federal park protecting coastal redwoods can be attributed both to the trees' high commercial value and the success of conservation groups, such as the Save-the-Redwoods League and the Sierra Club, in purchasing sizable tracts of redwoods in the late 19th and early 20th centuries and donating them to California as state parks.

After World War II, the Sierra Club, arguing that the state parks were islands cut off from the natural systems on which they depended, broke away from this accommodation between conservationists and industry and led the battle to protect the remaining old-growth redwoods. By 1960 only 10 percent of the original 2 million acres of redwood giants remained, a small percentage in state parks and the bulk owned by lumber corporations.[51] The Sierra Club pressed for a federal park of about 90,000 acres, to include logged forests, riverways, drainage basins, and buffer areas as well as the giant trees.[52] The 1968 boundaries, however, encompassed only 58,000 acres (including the 27,500 acres of state parks).[53] The most spectacular redwood grove along Redwood Creek was narrowly surrounded by parkland.

Visible evidence of these boundaries' inadequacy soon was provided by extensive storm damage near this grove, attributable in part to logging outside of the park.[54] In 1978, a congressional report concluded that the 1968 park was "not adequate to preserve a manageable drainage unit capable of ensuring the survival of a varied and self-perpetuating redwood forest," and 48,000 acres were added.[55]

In both 1968 and 1978, a "legislative taking" transferred ownership immediately to the federal government. Redwood's cost is expected to be the highest for any national park—somewhere near $1 billion—by the time all the settlement awards and interest are made.[56] The 1978 act also created a park protection zone, outside Redwood's boundaries, in which land could be purchased either from a willing seller or, if not acquiring the land would result in extensive damage to park resources, by condemnation.[57]

In 1971, *Voyageurs National Park* was established in the remote Minnesota forest and lakes where adventurous French Canadian trappers and fur traders traveled by canoe in the 17th and 18th centuries between Canada and the Pacific Northwest. Of the park's 218,000 acres, 80,000 are glacial lakes and streams.[58] Advocates of the park included those emphasizing its wilderness qualities and those hoping its creation would bring tourists to this sparsely settled, economically depressed part of Minnesota. Voyageurs still faces pressures by hunting interests, who object to restrictions on hunting and trapping; recreationists, who want to increase access to the park's interior; and wilderness buffs, who want to retain the diminishing opportunity to experience rarely visited wild areas.[59]

Finally, one of the country's most important land-use controversies was settled in 1980 with the passage of the *Alaska National Interest Lands Conservation Act.*[60] The battle over disposition of the largest expanse of undeveloped lands in public ownership—

Yosemite, February 1984. James R. "Pete" Peterson (far right) with family and friends (Fresno, California). "I like it with a lot of people here. The night before last my niece wanted to roast some marshmallows, so she and her little friend, who's eight, took their marshmallows over to someone else's campground. There were a couple of little kids over there, and they sat around and talked with them. It was great."

lands with great economic potential and majestic splendor—pitted conservationists, who argued that this was America's "last chance to do things right the first time,"[61] against native rights, access rights, and commercial development advocates. As congressional debate over the competing claims of native Alaskans, sport hunters and fishers, commercial mining and timber companies, and wilderness interests extended over several sessions, Alaska's governor and the state's congressional representatives tried to trim the acreage and strictness of federal protection.[62]

The final compromise set aside over 100 million acres, about one-third of the state, more than doubling the size of the National Park System and tripling the amount of land managed as wilderness.[63] Among other provisions, the act added 43.6 million acres to the system, expanding 3 parks and creating 10 new parks or preserves; 53.8 million acres to the National Wildlife Refuge System; and 6.6 million acres of National Forest, increasing the acreage of existing units by 3.4 million acres and establishing two new national monuments to be managed by the Forest Service. It also created a 1.2-million-acre national conservation area and a 1-million-acre national recreation area, in addition to adding segments of 26 rivers to the National Wild and Scenic Rivers System and designating 12 more as study sites.[64]

Each designation means something different for the way the resource can be managed and used. Sport hunting is allowed in the national preserves and wildlife refuges (although subsistence fishing and hunting can continue in designated zones in all the areas). No mineral development can take place in national parks, refuges, and wild and scenic rivers except where there are valid, preexisting claims.[65] Wildlife refuges are open to oil and gas leasing at the discretion of the secretary of the interior. National forests are, as elsewhere, managed under principles of multiple use and sustained yield.[66] The settlement, as part of a larger package, conveyed 44 million acres to Alaskan natives, in accord with the provisions of the Alaska Native Claims Settlement Act of 1971, and resolved issues raised when Alaska was designated as a state in 1958.

## CULTURAL AND HISTORICAL UNITS

The park system includes 190 units that Congress specifically set aside for their cultural and historical value. Approximately 50 more units were established primarily to protect other resources but also to contain significant cultural areas.[67] For almost two decades after the park system was created, these units, and there were few, consisted mainly of pre-Columbian Indian ruins; later, as the number increased, Congress differentiated them as national historic sites, national military parks, national battlefields and battlefield parks, and national memorials.*

As the names suggest, these cultural and historical units form an eclectic collection. In addition to American Indian ruins, they include sites of major events in the nation's history, and others of broad cultural, more than historical, significance. Some units honor the relatively intact birthplaces or former homes of the nation's great men and women; others commemorate an important theme in American history rather than preserve a noteworthy site itself. Some involved the complete rebuilding of a former structure, rather than its preservation, and some cannot really be classified. Many of the nation's most important historic sites, such as Mount Vernon and Monticello, are not within the system, and some lesser ones are.

The park system's role as federal guardian of historic sites dates from 1933, when President Roosevelt issued an executive order transferring all military historical areas, primarily Civil War sites, from the War and Agriculture departments to the National Park Service, dramatically increasing the number of units in the system.[69] At that time, federal ownership of nonmilitary historical sites was very limited—some Spanish missions, a Mormon fort, the house where Lincoln died, and the Custis-Lee Mansion.[70] (At the time, there was little interest in historic preservation in general anywhere in the country.)

Roosevelt had been carefully cultivated by Park Service Director Horace Albright.[71] Both shared a deep interest in history and sensed its spiritual value for a country deep in the Great Depression, as well as its material benefits in providing jobs for architects, engineers and other professionals, and unskilled young men. Moreover, the

---

*The distinctions among these categories are not always clear-cut. Many parks designated as historical and cultural units also have distinctive natural features, and others, created for their special natural resources, also have important cultural and historical values. Mesa Verde has wilderness areas, for example, and Yellowstone has historical districts.[68]

park service had, in the late 1920s, established its credentials by work in a cluster of colonial sites—George Washington's Virginia birthplace; Jamestown and Yorktown, near Williamsburg, Virginia; and Morristown, New Jersey, the 1779-80 winter headquarters of the Continental Army. Park service staff worked closely with their private sector counterparts at Colonial Williamsburg, exchanging ideas about research, exhibits, and ways to provide "popular, informative, correct, and noncontroversial" interpretation.[72]*

The 1935 Historic Sites Act made formal the directions Albright had pursued (he had by now resigned and been replaced by Arno B. Cammerer).[73] Guided by an expert Advisory Board of National Parks, Historic Sites, Buildings, and Monuments, the park service began a national survey to identify sites for inclusion in the federal system or for protection and management by states, local governments, and private citizens in cooperation with the federal government.[74]

As nascent policies were thrashed out, some envisioned a rather complete national system of excellence—eventually to include privately owned areas such as Colonial Williamsburg. Scholars argued that ruins should be kept "as is"; others argued for rebuilding places to enhance the drama of interpretation and attract many visitors. Local preservation groups often wanted money from the federal government without giving over their special properties; members of Congress deluged the park service with demands to establish federal units in their districts.[75]

Today, individually, the historical units are of varying significance, vulnerable to professional criticism that the collection reflects insufficient academic discipline and an excessive political influence. As a collection, however, there is a coherence: It reflects the comparatively late start in the United States in preserving buildings with historical value; the reliance on private and local initiative, to the extent possible; and the diversity of places capable of imparting significant messages about the past to this nation's pluralistic citizens. Efforts to increase the objectivity of the assessment process for new units continue.

---

*Williamsburg, the site of Virginia's colonial capital, has been restored and reconstructed by private benefactors.

## American Indian Ruins

The first broad theme that the park service uses to categorize historical and cultural units is "original inhabitants."* At *Mesa Verde National Park*, in southwestern Colorado, established in 1906, visitors climb ladders to view prehistoric cliff dwellings and hear about the aboriginal civilizations that once flourished and then mysteriously disappeared in many sites in the American Southwest. Mesa Verde's inclusion in the system was the result of pressure by educational and scientific groups, who, aroused by widespread looting at unguarded sites, called for federal protection of significant abandoned settlements. Just two weeks after establishing Mesa Verde, Congress passed the Act for the Preservation of American Antiquities, enabling the president to proclaim as national monuments "historic landmarks, historic or prehistoric structures, and other objects of historic or scientific interest" on federal land.[77]

Added soon after to the park system as national monuments were *Chaco Canyon*, now *Chaco Culture National Historical Park*, *Montezuma Castle, Navajo*, and *Salinas* (originally proclaimed as Gran Quivira), all in Arizona and New Mexico, where the largest concentration of aboriginal ruins exists. Other areas in these states, including *Walnut Canyon, Gila Cliff Dwellings*, and *Tonto*, were proclaimed as national monuments during this same period and were transferred from forest service jurisdiction to the park system in 1933. Additional southwestern sites with American Indian ruins continued to be added as national monuments in the 1920s and 1930s—for example, *Tuzigoot*, a large American Indian pueblo that flourished between 1100 and 1450 A.D.; *Wupatki*, a site with unusual red sandstone pueblos built about 1065 A.D.; and *Aztec Ruins*, containing the erroneously named remnants of a 12th century Pueblo Indian community.[78]

Indian ruins in the East and Midwest are also represented in the park system as national monuments. Indian burial mounds and ceremonial sites are protected in *Ocmulgee*, in Georgia; *Mound City Group*, in Ohio; and *Effigy Mounds*, in Iowa. *Pipestone*, in Minnesota, preserves a quarry used by native Americans for making cere-

---

*Beginning with the advisory board's first survey, the service has developed broad themes as an organizing context for additions to the system. This discussion of historical units generally follows the service's current themes, departing in some instances in the interest of compressing the material.[76]

monial pipes; *Russell Cave*, in Alabama, the archaeological record of nearly 9,000 years of human life; and *Knife River Indian Villages*, added to the system in 1974 as a National Historic Site, in North Dakota, the remains of historic and prehistoric Plains Indian villages.

In recent years, four parks relating to different aspects of early Hawaiian culture have been established—*Kaloko-Honokohau National Historical Park*, the Honolulu site of major settlements before the arrival of Europeans; *Pu'uhonua o Honaunau National Historical Park*, a sacred "safe harbor" formerly known as City of Refuge; *Puukohola Heiau National Historic Site*, King Kamehameha's temple; and *Kalaupapa*, once a leper colony on Molokai Island.

## Early Exploration and Colonization

Another major park service historical/cultural theme covers early New World exploration and colonization. Simple markers identify the approximate sites where *Ferdinand De Soto*, *Francisco Vasquez de Coronado*, and *Juan Rodriguez Cabrillo* first landed in the New World. In some units, forts and other structures endure.

Early English discovery and settlement are represented in *Fort Raleigh National Historic Site*, in North Carolina, site of the Lost Colony's ill-fated 16th-century venture into the New World; *Colonial National Historical Park*, at Jamestown, Virginia, the site of the first permanent English settlement in the New World; and *Fort Frederica National Monument*, Georgia, a British fort used to help contain the Spanish in Florida.

Several units have remains of early Spanish missions, while the *San Juan National Historic Site*, in Puerto Rico, preserves the massive 16th-century fort that guarded the Spanish gold trade. Various efforts by the French to establish permanent settlements are marked in national monuments in Florida, Maine, and Arkansas.

## Colonial Life

Some 18 units, most in the original 13 colonies, relate to the struggle for independence and the War of 1812. Preeminent, of course, is *Independence National Historical Park*, occupying some 37 acres in downtown Philadelphia. The central feature is the old Pennsylvania State House, or Independence Hall, where the Declaration of Independence was signed and where, in the hot, muggy sum-

mer of 1787, the Constitution was thrashed out. The federal park
as it stands today, including a number of significant buildings and
sites associated with the American Revolution and Benjamin Franklin, was authorized in 1948, but individual buildings had been protected earlier by governmental or private groups. Most of the
buildings including Independence Hall still are owned by
Philadelphia, although the federal government operates and maintains them through a cooperative agreement with the city. Federal
designation was accompanied by the creation of a green expanse
around the buildings on acreage cleared with federal funds (for Independence Park) and with city and state funds (for Independence
Mall).[79]

*Boston National Historical Park* also links historic buildings of
the Colonial period—Faneuil Hall, Bunker Hill, Old North Church,
Old State House, Old South Meeting House, the Paul Revere House,
Dorchester Heights, and the Charlestown Navy Yard, the berth of
the USS *Constitution*, "Old Ironsides." These buildings are scattered and no clearance was involved when the park was authorized in 1974.[80] As in Philadelphia, most sites are not owned by the
park service.

In Manhattan, *Federal Hall National Memorial* marks the site of
many famous events: here John Peter Zenger was tried in 1735 for
publishing articles opposed to the British, the Second Continental
Congress met in 1785, and George Washington took his oath as the
first president. The *Statue of Liberty National Monument* com-
memorates the alliance of the French and Americans in the
Revolution.

The influence of Williamsburg, Virginia, in recreating a time and
place through architectural restoration and reconstruction is especially evident in such park units as *Salem Maritime National
Historic Site*, in Massachusetts, with its ambience of a bustling 18th-
and 19th-century whaling and trading port, and *Hopewell Village
National Historic Site*, in Pennsylvania, a rural iron-making village
of the 1800s.

### Western Settlement

The nation's march westward, marked by exploration, trade, settlement, and conquest, is represented by a number of units in the
system. *The Chesapeake and Ohio National Historical Park* follows

the 184-mile-long Chesapeake and Ohio Canal built between 1828 and 1850 to move commerce between the eastern states and the Ohio Valley. *Allegheny Portage Railroad National Historic Site*, in Pennsylvania, has remnants of the canal's technological rival, the railroad, which traversed the Allegheny Mountains at this site, moving passengers and freight to the West. The lands that Daniel Boone crossed are now in *Cumberland Gap National Historical Park*, which is in Kentucky, Virginia, and Tennessee. Jefferson's vision of national expansion and the explorations of Lewis and Clark and others are memorialized in the *Jefferson National Expansion Memorial National Historic Site*, on St. Louis's Mississippi riverfront. Reflecting late 1930s' notions of urban revitalization,[81] creation of this park involved demolition of 40 blocks of old St. Louis and a good many structures that would today be considered architecturally and historically distinguished.[82] *Fort Clatsop National Memorial* preserves a Lewis and Clark campsite on the Oregon coast.

The important role of trappers and trading posts in the exploration and settlement of the frontier is recognized in such park units as *Bent's Old Fort National Historic Site*, *Fort Union Trading Post National Historic Site*, and *Voyageurs National Park*. *Fort Vancouver National Historic Site* in Washington State, on the Columbia River, was the Hudson Bay Company's fur-trading headquarters.

A number of sites mark places along the two major routes West, the Oregon Trail (with its California branch) and the Santa Fe Trail. *Scotts Bluff National Monument*, in Nebraska, preserves a prominent landmark for Oregon Trail travelers; *Fort Laramie National Historic Site*, in Wyoming, a military post on the trail; *Whitman Mission National Historic Site*, in Washington, the place where exhausted pioneers found medical assistance and supplies near the end of their arduous travels; and *El Morro National Monument*, in New Mexico, the "inscription rock" on which the pioneers scratched their initials alongside those of earlier Spanish explorers.

The vanquishing of the American Indians is marked in *Horseshoe Bend National Military Park*, in Alabama, and *Big Hole National Battlefield*, in Montana. *Lava Beds National Monument*, California, is the site of a natural fort used by the Modoc Indians in a fierce, futile battle. The Sioux and Cheyenne victory over the 7th U.S. Cavalry took place at *Custer Battlefield National Monument*, in Montana.

The final taming of the frontier is celebrated in such places as

*Fredericksburg, November 1984.*

*Golden Spike National Historic Site* at Promontory, Utah, where the Central Pacific and Union Pacific railroads joined in the first transcontinental railroad in 1869, and *Homestead National Monument of America*, in Nebraska, one of the first parcels of land claimed under the Homestead Act of 1862. *Grant-Kohrs Ranch National Historic Site*, in Montana, preserves a portion of one of the West's largest 19th-century cattle ranches.

## Homes of Famous Americans

Sites of importance in the lives of famous Americans—birthplaces or later residences of persons of influence in politics, the arts and sciences, or other areas of American society—comprise many units in the system.* Apart from their associations with these persons, these structures often provide a sense of the life of a particular social group at a particular time.

---

*Park officials successfully fought off many requests to include tombs of famous Americans, although some are parts of units designated as their birthplace or residence. However, the tomb of President Ulysses S. Grant, whose signature created Yellowstone, *General Grant National Memorial*, in New York City, is a unit in the system.

Places associated with presidents include the first home of *Abraham Lincoln* (with a symbolic truncated cabin), as well as the farm where he grew to adulthood and his home in Springfield, Illinois; the birthplace of *Theodore Roosevelt*, his North Dakota ranch (Elkhorn), and his New York estate and summer White House, (Sagamore Hill); and the homes of *John and John Quincy Adams, Martin Van Buren, Andrew Johnson, William Howard Taft, Herbert Hoover, Franklin D. Roosevelt, Harry S Truman, Dwight D. Eisenhower, John F. Kennedy,* and *Lyndon B. Johnson, in addition to the birthplace of George Washington.*

Other residences of notable Americans include the "Grange," home of Alexander Hamilton; *Arlington House,* the Custis and Lee families' mansion where General Robert E. Lee made his agonizing decision to fight for the Confederacy; "*Val-Kill,*" Eleanor Roosevelt's Hyde Park retreat; the 38-room Maryland residence of *Clara Barton,* founder of the American Red Cross; the Georgian mansion of *Thomas Stone,* a signer of the Declaration of Independence and delegate to the Continental Congress; and places lived in at one time or another by *Frederick Law Olmsted, Henry Wadsworth Longfellow, Albert Gallatin, Augustus Saint-Gaudens, Thomas Edison, Carl Sandburg, Edgar Allan Poe, John Muir,* and *Eugene O'Neill.*

## Cultural Diversity and the Struggle for Equality

The cultural and ethnic diversity of the United States and some of its most significant social struggles are remembered in several units. Sites of significance in black history include: *George Washington Carver National Monument,* in Missouri, the birthplace and boyhood home of the black agronomist, designated in 1943; *Booker T. Washington National Monument,* in Virginia, birthplace of the black educator, designated in 1956; and the *Frederick Douglass Home,* in Washington, D.C., designated in 1962. More recently, park units have been created at *Tuskegee Institute National Historic Site,* the college Booker T. Washington established in 1881 to educate freed blacks; *Maggie L. Walker National Historic Site,* the Virginia home of a former slave's daughter who became the first woman president of a U.S. financial institution; and *Martin Luther King, Jr., National Historic Site,* which includes King's birthplace, church, and grave, as well as 68 acres of the black community in which he lived and preached, now a historic district.

*Chamizal National Memorial*, an amphitheater and auditorium used by performing groups from both the United States and Mexico, was established in 1974 on the site where a treaty peacefully ending a 99-year dispute between the two nations was signed.

Two units associated with the women's movement were created in the past decade: *Sewell-Belmont House* in Washington, D.C., the headquarters of the National Women's Party since 1929; and *Women's Rights National Historical Park*, in Seneca Falls, New York, the site of the 1848 Women's Rights Convention and the homes and offices of several suffragettes.

*Ellis Island*, part of Statue of Liberty National Monument, marks the site where millions of immigrants entered the United States.

## Military Themes

A military park system, consisting primarily of 13 Civil War battle sites and cemeteries, forms the nucleus of the park system's collection of historical units. These sites of valor in the nation's epic civil struggle retain a special place in the system for visitors and park service staff alike. Today, the system includes 19 battle sites; including *Fort Sumter*, where the first shots were fired, *Manassas*, *Antietam*, *Gettysburg*, *Fredericksburg*, *Chancellorsville*, *Vicksburg*, and *Appomattox Court House*. Additional units where memorable events related to the Civil War occurred include *Harpers Ferry*, raided by abolitionist John Brown; *Andersonville*, the prison where thousands of Union prisoners of war were interned and more than 15,000 buried; *Ford's Theatre*, where President Lincoln was shot, and *Peterson House*, across the street, where he died; and *Fort Jefferson*, a federal military prison during and after the Civil War.

A number of units mark the sites of battles fought during the Revolution and the War of 1812, some well remembered—*Minute Man*, *Saratoga*, *Fort McHenry*—and others nearly forgotten. *Palo Alto Battlefield National Historic Site*, near what is now Brownsville, Texas, was the site of the first major encounter on American soil in the Mexican War.

World War II battles are represented by two units: the *Arizona Memorial*, built above the sunken hull of the battleship destroyed in the Japanese attack on Pearl Harbor, in Hawaii, and *War in the Pacific National Historic Park*, commemorating the U.S. capture of Guam.

Dedicated in 1982, the *Vietnam Veterans Memorial*, in Washington, D.C., honors the men and women who served in the Vietnam War, identifying by name those who died or who are missing in action.

## The National Capital Region

In a distinct category are the more than 300 sites, monuments, and open spaces in and around Washington, D.C., managed by the park service. These include the memorials to *Lincoln*, *Washington*, and *Jefferson*, an island park dedicated to *Theodore Roosevelt*, and a memorial grove to *Lyndon Johnson*; the *White House* and the *National Mall*; the *George Washington Memorial Parkway*; the *John F. Kennedy Center for the Performing Arts*, and the *Wolf Trap Farm Park for the Performing Arts*, and the newest addition, the *Nancy Hanks Center* in the renovated Old Post Office Building; and the city's extensive system of parks, parkways, and reservations. Individual sites are managed as part of park service administrative units within the region. Seven such units exist: the White House; National Capital East; National Capital Central Mall Operations (including the major monuments to Washington, Jefferson, and Lincoln); Rock Creek; C & O Canal; and George Washington Parkway (including Roosevelt Island and all sites accessible from the Virginia side of the Potomac River).[83]

## "Affiliated" Historical Units*

Almost all of the historical and cultural units in the National Park System are owned by the federal government and managed by the National Park Service. Some were donated by state or local governments or private interests. The federal government also, however, enters into cooperative agreements, under which the park service is "affiliated" with a unit but state governments and local groups continue to own and operate it. The service may provide technical assistance and a small initial grant. Diverse arrangements in this category have been worked out for such places as *Touro Synagogue*, in Newport, Rhode Island; the *Chicago Portage National Historic*

---

*"Affiliated" units include natural areas as well—for example, *Pinelands National Reserve*.

Site, in Cook County, Illinois; and *Jamestown National Historic Site*
and *Green Springs Historic District*, both in Virginia.

## INNOVATION CONTINUES: NEW TYPES OF UNITS

In the 1930s, the National Park System added parkways, reservoirs
as national recreation areas, and recreational demonstration areas.
Unlike historical and cultural units, which have continued to be
added to the system, these units clearly belong to the attitude of
a particular era. The 1960s and 1970s brought new types of areas
as well, namely seashores, lakeshores, and parks in or near major
metropolitan areas. These all leave a considerable legacy.

### Parkways

The *Blue Ridge Parkway*, a scenic corridor in Virginia and North
Carolina that skirts the crest of the Blue Ridge Mountains for almost
500 miles between the Shenandoah and Great Smoky national parks,
was the system's first entire unit to be authorized as a "parkway."
Construction began in 1933 to extend Skyline Drive, in Shenandoah, started one year earlier at the suggestion of Herbert Hoover.[84]
High in the mountains, Skyline Drive gave the conceptual model
for the more ambitious Blue Ridge Parkway.*

Parkways, or boulevards, were a powerful design influence in
the 1930s, with excellent examples already in place in innovative
states and cities. As envisioned by early landscape designers like
Olmsted, Vaux, and Eliot, the parkway was no mere road. Its function was to provide a "psychological carryover of the restful influence of one large park area to its echo in another, with little or
no interruption on the way."[85]

Building parkways also created many jobs, and federal relief
dollars provided startup funds for both Skyline Drive and the Blue
Ridge Parkway, built as a joint effort of the park service and the
Bureau of Public Roads, with states providing the rights-of-way.
Historian John Ise has noted that these costly undertakings were

---

*The *George Washington Memorial Parkway*, along the Virginia and Maryland shores of the Potomac River near Washington, D.C., linking historic landmarks in the life of George Washington with recreational and scenic areas,
could be considered the system's first parkway on the basis of its authorization
in 1930. But it was not transferred to the park system until 1933.

"splendidly built," with numerous overlooks, fine vistas, and picnic areas for "unhurried enjoyment" by numerous travelers.[86] A parkway, Natchez Trace, was authorized in 1934 along the historic Indian trail in Mississippi, Tennessee, and Alabama that Andrew Jackson followed to defeat the British at New Orleans. Lands adjoining the Blue Ridge and Natchez Trace parkways were intentionally kept as working farms, protected from change by scenic easements acquired by the state and then donated to the park service.[87]*

## National Recreation Areas

The first of a wave of national recreation areas, Lake Mead National Recreation Area, was established in 1936 to capitalize on the recreational benefits of the Nevada reservoir created by what was then Boulder Dam. Following recreational feasibility studies by the park service, usually at the request of the agency that was constructing the dams—namely the Army Corps of Engineers or Bureau of Reclamation[88]—eight more national recreation areas were designated to provide boating, fishing, and swimming in the reservoirs created by the massive federal investments for flood control, electricity generation, and irrigation: Coulee Dam, Lake Chelan, and Ross Lake in Washington State (the last two are virtually extensions of North Cascades National Park, but the lands were placed in separate units because they were associated with artifical impoundments); Curecanti, in Colorado; Bighorn Canyon, in Montana; Lake Meredith, in Texas; Glen Canyon, in Utah and Arizona; and Whiskeytown-Shasta-Trinity, in California (the U.S. Forest Service administers portions of this unit). In most cases, the park service operates recreational facilities and programs; ownership of the land and water remains with the agency that manages the dam.

## Recreational Demonstration Projects

Catoctin Mountain Park, in the Maryland Appalachians, and Prince William Forest Park, in Virginia, are the only recreational demonstration areas remaining in the federal system out of the 46

---

*In 1972, the John D. Rockefeller, Jr., Memorial Parkway, a scenic 82-mile link between Yellowstone and Grand Teton, commemorated the philanthropist's many contributions to national parks.

established in 24 states during the Depression.[89] Under this program, the government bought almost 400,000 acres of marginal
agricultural lands, mostly in the East (usually within 50 miles of
populated urban areas), with the purpose of reclaiming the land,
using armies of unemployed young men to construct group camping areas for recreational visits by urban dwellers, and eventually
turning them over to the states.[90] Responding to Franklin D.
Roosevelt's interest in a new federal responsibility for recreation,
the park service was simultaneously working vigorously with state,
county, and local officials to develop recreational facilities on
nonfederal parklands.[91] The effort was undertaken by Conrad L.
Wirth, a landscape architect who became director of the park service
in 1951.[92]

Such New Deal innovations involving land reclamation, job creation, and road, trail, and facility construction aroused concerns
among national park advocacy groups, such as the National Parks
Association and the Wilderness Society, that traditional parks and
protection of unspoiled distinctive natural resources were being
neglected.[93] Other innovations at this time, including the establishment of a natural sciences unit in the service under biologist George
Wright's direction, received wider conservationist support. (See
chapter 4 on Stewardship of Park Resources.)

## Seashores and Lakeshores

Although the addition of seashore units to the park system is a
phenomenon of the 1960s and 1970s, the groundwork was laid in
the 1930s, when the park service did an extensive reconnaissance
of the Atlantic and Gulf coasts to identify beaches suitable for public
use.[94] This was one of several studies undertaken by the park service as part of the New Deal effort to gather basic data about the
nation's resources to increase their productivity and public benefit.

Cape Hatteras National Seashore, in North Carolina, authorized
in 1937, was the only seashore unit created as the immediate result
of the seashore study. It took North Carolina 15 years to put together
the 100 square miles for the Cape Hatteras unit, because the lands
were almost all privately owned. Facing "sunset" provisions set
down by Congress, the Avalon and Old Dominion foundations provided sizable grants for acquisition, on condition that the grants
be matched by the state. Acquisition problems in Cape Hatteras and

the advent of war tabled the issue of additional seashore units for some 20 years.[95] In 1955, a second seashore study by the park service warned that private ownership and development were rapidly increasing.[96] Eventually, 4 lakeshores and 10 seashores were added to the system, ranging from a beach adjacent to steel plants in Indiana to an unspoiled barrier island in Georgia.[97]

The designation in 1961 of *Cape Cod National Seashore*, in Massachusetts near Boston, (see profile) initiated almost two decades of invention and unprecedented expansion in the National Park System. Cape Cod's Great Beach had been an acquisition priority in the park service's 1955 seashore study.[98] To be sure, the Cape Cod unit, like many earlier units, had spectacular natural features and abundant wildlife. It was not the first park in the East, or the first "national seashore," or the first to involve federal purchase of privately owned lands.* In Cape Cod, however, these threads came together in such a way that they set a new direction. Congress established a partnership between the Interior Department, local governments, and private landowners—the so-called Cape Cod formula—that lifted the federal power to condemn properties within the park if the towns in which they were located passed compatible zoning. Permitting hundreds of landowners to remain not only stilled local opposition but preserved vistas of natural resources and settlement in the distinctive Cape Cod landscape.

*Point Reyes National Seashore*, along the California coast, was authorized in 1962, although it was not established until a decade later. Like Cape Cod, Point Reyes had stretches of superlative undeveloped beach and distinctive plant, bird, and sea life. It was even closer to urban populations, in this case the San Francisco metropolitan area. The park's start-up problems included rapidly escalating land prices and local protests against the park service's $35 million plan to develop the park intensively for mass recrea-

---

*Direct purchase of private lands had occurred before, as noted earlier, in minor purchases and then by allocation of New Deal funds. The first example of significant congressional appropriation of purchase funds for acquisition was Minute Man, in 1959, involving over $10 million to purchase private lands in Concord, Massachusetts, to recreate the landscape of the battle that launched the American Revolution. Unlike Cape Cod, extensive clearance was involved in Minute Man to enhance the authenticity of the historical landscape.[99]

tion.[100] Eventually, Congress increased the funds for acquisition, and the park service adopted a visitor accommodations plan more in keeping with the natural setting.

Fire Island National Seashore, a roughly half-hour ferry ride from Long Island, was authorized in 1964.[101] Despite its proximity to the nation's most populous metropolitan area, New York City, the seashore (by virtue of being an island) had remained relatively unspoiled by civilization at the time of its designation as part of the park system. As at Point Reyes, however, that designation posed difficult issues of reconciling protection of natural beauty with the promise of serving millions of people.

Pictured Rocks National Lakeshore, the park system's first national lakeshore, was authorized by Congress in 1966; authorization for Indiana Dunes National Lakeshore followed later that year. Pictured Rocks is a relatively remote area, but Indiana Dunes, at the time of its establishment, was in the middle of a thriving industrial complex, an hour-and-a-half drive from Chicago and a half-hour from Gary, Indiana. Mather had first recommended Indiana Dunes for national park status shortly after becoming park service director; even though the region including the lakeshore had changed substantially since then, the local Save-the-Dunes Council had kept the issue of federal designation alive. (The state had set aside a limited area as a park in 1925.)

Statutory provisions for privately owned lands within the boundaries of both Fire Island and Indiana Dunes followed the Cape Cod model. Some homeowners were permitted to remain, either for an extended leaseback period after they sold their lands to the park service or permanently if local governments passed compatible local zoning.[102]

## Urban Initiatives

On October 27, 1972, a potent alliance of environmental and urban interest groups witnessed the creation of both Gateway National Recreation Area, in New York City, and Golden Gate National Recreation Area, in San Francisco. The Gateway Citizens Committee and the Regional Plan Association spearheaded the effort on the East Coast, while, on the West Coast, People for a Golden Gate National Recreation Area marshaled its forces under the leadership of Amy Meyer and the Sierra Club's Edgar Wayburn.[103] In Washington, support and drive came from George B. Hartzog, Jr., park service director from 1964 to 1972.

Together, these new units added over 60,000 acres of parkland within a couple of hours drive of more than 20 million people.[104] The two units continued the coastal emphasis in park designation, but they also represented the triumph of a growing "urban parks" movement, whose advocates identified numerous sites in and near populated areas with resources meriting protection as national parks.

Although location weighed heavily in the selection of potential sites for urban parks, these areas also had a legacy of significant natural and cultural resources, often threatened by suburban growth. Gateway's diverse resources, for example, include the Jamaica Bay Wildlife Refuge, Breezy Point, Sandy Hook, and the old Floyd Bennett Field. Golden Gate stretches along 60 miles of Pacific shoreline from just south of the Golden Gate Bridge to Point Reyes in the north.[105] It encompasses historic ships, Alcatraz Island, Fort Mason Center (now bustling with arts and community groups), Fort Point, and Lands End on the San Francisco side, and, across the bay, the Marin Headlands, Mt. Tamalpais State Park and Muir Woods National Monument, Stinson Beach, and the Olema Valley beef and dairy ranches (federally owned, but leased back to working ranchers).

In both of these urban parks, far more of the lands were already publicly owned than had been the case in the earlier seashore and lakeshore units. The unique availability of surplus military lands along the coast, paired with the inability of states and local governments to buy or maintain them, was a persuasive argument for creating the new units. Equally potent in the wake of the urban riots of 1968 was a commitment to provide recreation for the poor and minority groups. This commitment became reflected in innovative park programs to provide subsidized transportation from poor neighborhoods to the parks and environmental education for school groups.[106] Another significant innovation in Golden Gate permitted the park to retain—instead of return to the U.S. Treasury—any funds it received for leasing several renovated, historic buildings.[107]

*Cuyahoga Valley National Recreation Area*, established in 1975, is located along the scenic valley between Cleveland and Akron, Ohio. The remains of successive American Indian, Moravian, trading, and other settlements as well as the old Ohio and Erie Canal add cultural and historical interest to the area. When their efforts to enlist state aid to protect the valley's rural character from suburban encroachment foundered, advocates turned to Congress. An area resident, Congressman John Seiberling (D-Ohio), was a member of the House Committee on Interior and Insular Affairs.[108] Congress authorized $34.5 million to acquire property within park boundaries, providing for both conventional fee purchase and scenic easements. Compatible local zoning was encouraged, rather than required, as a condition for allowing residents to remain.[109] Unfortunately, a combination of circumstances, including park service opposition to the park's designation and misunderstanding of the park's objectives, aroused a good deal of local controversy in the early years of the park.

Continuing these urban initiatives, in 1978 Congress designated the *Chattahoochee River National Recreation Area*, near Atlanta; the *Lowell National Historical Park*, in Massachusetts; the *Jean Lafitte National Historical Park and Preserve*, in New Orleans; and the *Santa Monica Mountains National Recreation Area* (see profile), near Los Angeles. This rapid-fire designation of new units was notable not only for quantity but also for scale of innovation. Today, each of these parks addresses the protection of sizable urban landscapes and increasing public enjoyment somewhat differently. The strategies, shaped by landownership patterns, market conditions, local and national politics, and the availability of federal funds, are experimental models in the evolution of parks that are less dependent on complete federal ownership and more dependent on collaboration with other levels of government and the private sector.

In *Lowell National Historical Park*, for example, the "park" is in a real sense the downtown of Lowell, Massachusetts, an early site of the Industrial Revolution. Its idle, century-old mills, empty lofts, and low-rise commercial buildings illuminate a significant era in American technological progress. Outright federal acquisition has been intentionally minimal, and park officials instead work with the city and state and business and citizens groups to encourage the restoration and adaptive use of significant buildings. Educational programs are offered in a visitor center that exemplifies what the park preaches: located in a renovated old mill, it shares space with shops, housing for the elderly, and offices. A 15-member historical commission has broad authority to plan, restore, manage, and acquire property in Lowell's central area, now a historic district, and has administered a revolving loan fund to help property owners finance rehabilitation.[110] The secretary of the interior was given the authority to withhold funds unless Lowell passed local zoning consistent with park purposes.[111]

*Pinelands National Reserve*, in New Jersey, with over a million acres of low forests, bogs, and marshes, 56 municipalities, and 400,000 year-round residents is another innovative unit. Close to Philadelphia and densely populated areas in New Jersey, the reserve's huge underground reservoir of 17 trillion gallons of pure water, its varied agricultural uses, and unique recreational opportunities argue for special management. The plan for protecting the Pinelands is structured to retain state and local governments as primary land managers.[112] (Emphasizing the experimental nature of this relationship, the reserve is not an integral part of the park system but rather an "affiliated area.") The federal government has established a planning commission, representing all levels of government, to develop a comprehensive management plan for the entire area.[113] The plan, worked out in cooperation with the state, envisions that the reserve's central 368,000 acres will remain undeveloped as a "preservation area," while growth will take place in appropriately zoned spots on the perimeter. State law requires that county and municipal plans conform with the overall Pinelands management plan.[114]

### Twenty-Five Years of Change

The past 25 years have been a period of remarkable change for the parks. Five measures of the changes between 1960 and 1983 are compared in figure 2.2: the growth in the number of park units, amount of acreage, number of permanent staff, number of park visitors, and the amount spent in constant dollars for operations and maintenance.* Most changed since 1960 are the growth in visitation and the amount spent on operations and maintenance. Contrary to popular perceptions, increases in acreage are not particularly dramatic, if Alaska is excluded from consideration.[115]

A current statistical snapshot of how staff, funds, visitors, and acreage are allocated through the system today, following the pro-

---

*Each line in figure 2.2 represents an index of change for an indicator, with the base of 100 assigned to its level in 1960.

**Figure 2.2**
**National Park Trends, 1960–1983**

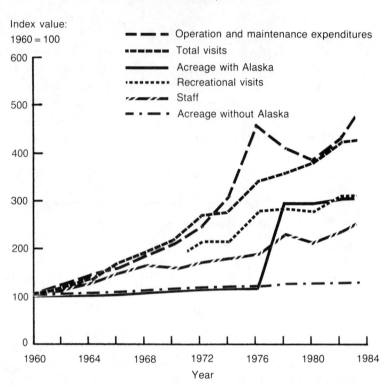

Note: For further explanation of categories, see References section.

Source: Ric Davidge, "Trends in the National Park System" (Washington, D.C.: U.S. Department of the Interior, Office of the Assistant Secretary for Fish and Wildlife and Parks, final draft, 1983); and U.S. Department of the Interior, National Park Service—"National Park Statistical Abstract, 1983" (Denver: Denver Service Center, Statistical Office); "Public Use of the National Parks: A Statistical Report, 1960–1971" and "1971–1980"; "Summary of Acreages Administered by the National Park Service," tables, 1960–1984; Budget Office, "Operation of the National Park System, Appropriations Fiscal Years 1960–1984," table, March 29, 1984; and information provided by Personnel Office, Staffing Branch, 1984.

found changes since 1960, appears in figure 2.2. As of 1984, parks in Alaska accounted for 70 percent of the total acreage in the system but less than 3 percent of either funds, staffing, or visitation—a situation that is sure to change in the future.[116] Parks in the three western regions (excluding Alaska) account for almost a quarter of the total acreage in the system, while visitation and number of units are both highest in the East.

## OTHER LAND MANAGEMENT SYSTEMS

The diversity of the National Park System has been enhanced by the creation of several systems for managing categories of public lands that involve all federal land managers and state and local governments. The park service has responsibility for administering areas within park system units designated in these categories by Congress.

The *National Wilderness Preservation System*, established in 1964, sets aside public lands to be managed for present and future Americans "in such manner as will leave them unimpaired for . . . use . . . as wilderness."[117] Lands set aside by Congress as wilderness are managed by four different agencies—the National Park Service, U.S. Forest Service, Fish and Wildlife Service, and Bureau of Land Management—depending on which agency administers the area included. Of the 88.8 million acres in the federal wilderness system, 36.7 million are in 37 National Park System units.[118] In the closing days of the 1984 session of the 98th Congress, President Reagan signed legislation approving the addition of almost 8.6 million wilderness acres. Most of the new wilderness is national forest land, but California's national parks gained more than 1.4 million wilderness acres and 850 acres were added to *Chiricahua National Monument* in Arizona.[119]

In designated wilderness areas, all permanent development, including roads, is excluded. Mechanical forms of transport—cars, vehicles, motorboats, and aircraft landings—are prohibited. Activities such as hiking, horseback riding, and primitive camping are generally allowed.[120] Although the term *wilderness* was part of the language and thinking that created national parks, this contemporary usage is quite different. "The laws creating National Parks and Monuments deliberately left the way open for the construction of roads and tourist accommodations," wilderness historian Roderick Nash has observed.[121] Large, rustic hotels were seen as "fitting in with nature," even when they blocked views of prime natural sites.[122]

Park officials have not been enthusiastic about formally designated wilderness.[123] They have, in recent years, developed new management approaches for "backcountry" areas—their preferred term— aimed at providing a more authentic experience in nature for the visitor and protecting sensitive and unique resources. Quotas and reservations are imposed at popular sites, and development of roads and visitors' accommodations in newer parks has been generally more restrained than in older parks.

The *Wild and Scenic Rivers System* and the *National Trail System* were established in 1968.[124] The Wild and Scenic Rivers System includes three categories of rivers—wild, scenic, and recreational—which are managed under plans approved by the secretary of the interior or the secretary of agriculture, depending on which department administers the land through which a river flows. A river may continue to be owned by state and local governments and, where appropriate, be managed in partnership with the federal government. Eight river system units were created in the 1968 legislation, including several in the park system. Twelve rivers in Alaska managed by the park service were added in 1980. In all, 62 rivers had been designated by 1982.[125]

The National Trail Systems Act encourages federal, state, and local agencies to work together to establish scenic trails, preserving their natural setting and protecting them from incompatible residential or commercial development.[126] Again, federal ownership is not mandated. One of the trail systems designated in 1968, the *Appalachian National Scenic Trail*, consisting of 2,100 miles from Maine to Georgia, is now a unit in the park system.[127] The trail is protected by a combination of federal and state acquisition, easements, and purchase by private land trusts and trail clubs until state or federal governments can acquire land interests. By mid-1984, 8 national scenic trails (about 14,500 miles) and 5 national historic trails (about 9,000 miles) had been designated. About 20 percent of these trail miles are available for public use.[128]

## THE FIRST CENTURY

The first century of the National Park System has involved continued experimentation and innovation to fashion new responses to changing public needs. The designation of Yellowstone in 1872 was no less an experiment than was the establishment of park units near cities in the 1960s and 1970s, or the setting aside of vast acreages of Alaska in 1980, or the creation of federal, state, and local partnerships for resource protection and use.

The system's diversity is a record of this experimentation. Expansion and growth reflect changing times, values, and opportunities. There have been struggles to add units—and to keep them out. The mere fact that individual units continue in the system reflects the continuing hold of tradition as the system adapts to change. Although not every unit has remained in the system once designated, or necessarily deserves to continue as part of it, the difficulty of de-designating a unit once it has become part of "the family" is appropriate to the concept of the National Park System.

Despite the system's considerable change over time, it is fundamentally a conservative institution. Its core values and mission have a timeless quality, frustrating at times to advocates who wish park service attention to new types of resources. Considerable credit for the evolution of the national system as a continuing experiment should, therefore, be given to citizens whose grass-roots advocacy has repeatedly made the difference in park system expansion.

*Golden Gate, February 1984.*

# Chapter 3
# The National
# Park Service

In the lore of national parks, Stephen T. Mather, the first director of the National Park Service, has become a figure of mythic proportions. But "the house that Mather built," to use biographer Robert Shankland's characterization, was originally quite small.[1] The 1916 National Park Service Act authorized, in the Washington office, a director at $4,500 a year, an assistant director at $2,500 a year, a chief clerk at $2,000, and some additional staff—for a grand total of $19,500.[2] By 1917, these staff members were responsible for managing a park system with 14 national parks and 21 national monuments[3] and for spending about half a million dollars on developing facilities for some 487,000 visits.[4] By 1983, the National Park Service employed over 18,000 men and women[5] in the central office in Washington, in 10 regional offices, plus two special centers, and in the 335 park units, which saw more than 240 million visits for recreation that year.[6]*

## BEGINNINGS

That the service's first director was not only dynamic but rich was fortuitous. Mather made his fortune in Chicago, manufacturing borax, and used it to build public support for the parks by promoting public awareness of the magnificent resources that had been set aside; by encouraging tourism; by meeting often with "movers and shakers" in the worlds of wealth, political influence, and resource conservation; and by lobbying for new units even though he could not be assured of Congress's support for those already in the fledgling system.[7]

Mather helped raise private funds and contributed his own money to buy and upgrade Yosemite's privately owned Tioga Road to make

---

*The 335th unit, Georgia O'Keeffe National Historic Site, in New Mexico, was deauthorized in 1984 at the request of Ms. O'Keeffe.

the park more accessible; eventually, the road was donated by Mather to the government.[8] Mather paid the salary of Robert Sterling Yard, the park service's first public affairs officer and subsidized a fancy park-promotion brochure. (The brochure also was financed, in part, by the railroads to attract affluent visitors.) Mather arranged conferences, Yellowstone campfires, and mountain trips for carefully selected groups and paid for a rustic "clubhouse" in Yosemite to house bachelor rangers.

Mather's "central purpose" was to develop a "smoothly running, well-coordinated system" to run the parks.[9] Before the establishment of the park service, the remote wilderness empire was loosely administered by other federal agencies as well as by the Department of the Interior. To establish an image of quality and efficiency for the new service, Mather handpicked park superintendents and rangers and fended off the civil service, so he could be "free to unload misfits and to shift his other men around."[10] Rangers became civil servants in 1925, as did superintendents in 1931, just over two years after the exhausted and ailing Mather retired.

By 1929, the symbols of the service were in place: the park superintendent, the ranger, and even the uniform. Together with Horace Albright, Mather's assistant from 1915 and successor as director, Mather shaped an operating style of visible, confident leadership; of shrewd orchestration of both the power elite's and the public's support; and of "old boy" network personnel policies.

Given both the remoteness of the parks and the poor communications of the day, much depended on selecting the right person to oversee a park. Often that person was Mather's friend or someone who knew someone he knew. Because the jobs were unprecedented, there was no specialized training. The qualifications were, as much as anything, those associated with Mather: love of the out-of-doors, "a strong, honest, and forthright personality," and an ability to inspire people to work their hardest.[11]

## THE SERVICE TODAY

As the park system expanded in size and in complexity, the park service, too, grew and diversified, responding to in-park growth and to social changes. Through the years, the service has performed admirably in warding off enormous pressures to tap parks' protected resources—water for hydropower in the Depression, timber for airplanes during wartime, and coal after the 1970s energy crisis. Polls reflect the public's acceptance of the service's stewardship and of its effectiveness as a bureaucracy. In a 1983 Roper poll, respondents ranked the National Park Service highest among 15 federal agencies.[12]

Observers of the park service see a level of enthusiasm and dedication among its employees rare in government. A 1982 study of staff attitudes, for example, found wide agreement with such statements as, "My job gives me a feeling of worthwhile accomplishment," "What happens to this organization is important to me," and "I enjoy working for the National Park Service." Almost all participants, say the study's directors, identify strongly with the organization and share "collective beliefs" in "the Mather family" and the park service's "tradition."[13]

Yet the staff respondents also demonstrate a good deal of individual dissatisfactions. The admiring public would undoubtedly be surprised to know that some employees believe the service's much-touted organizational pride and solidarity may be facing a serious test.[14] The contrast between collective pride and individual discontent is well expressed in the comment, "I work for the system, not the service."[15] For the park service, where much of the reward for employees derives from collective pride in public approval of the "park family," chinks in its organizational mystique are not to be taken lightly. The National Park Service is not a typical bureaucracy.

**Structure**

The National Park Service is one of 13 agencies in the Department of the Interior. With the equivalent of 16,282 full-time staff positions (FTEs) in 1984,[16] the agency accounted for roughly one-fifth of the department's total authorized workforce.* (See box on the data dilemma.) The service's entire budget in fiscal year 1984 amounted

---

*The number of positions is calculated in terms of "full-time equivalents," or FTEs, rather than the actual number of employees. In this method of counting staff positions, used throughout the civil service since 1982, the time worked by all personnel during a year—regardless of whether they are temporary, permanent, full or part time—is converted into a year-round average; for example, two half-time employees equal one FTE. The number of

## Visitation and the Data Dilemma

The National Park Service collects a wide variety of statistics—from the amount of acreage in the system, to the types of employees by region, to the number of search-and-rescue missions undertaken in each unit. These data are essential to establish management policies, budget requests, and land acquisition priorities. They are also regularly used by advocates of various philosophies to show that the park system or park service is suffering from an illness that their tonic will cure. Too often, the listener accepts these statistics as gospel, without knowing what they really measure or what their limitations are.

Information collected by the park service on visitation illustrates the need to look behind the figures. To begin with, what is a "visit"? Under the service's current definition, a visit is simply the entry of anyone (other than park service personnel or concessioners and their employees) onto the lands or waters it administers.[1] Visits may be "recreational" or "nonrecreational," with the latter including entries by persons going to and from inholdings, by ncn-concession-related tradespeople, by government personnel, and by through traffic.

In 1983, the park service recorded 335.8 million visits to areas within the system; in 1960, the figure had been only 79.2 million. However, that does not mean that four times as many people visited the parks in 1983 as in 1960; other factors influenced those numbers. For one, the definition of a visit changed during those 23 years. A change in the 1960s caused the official number of net visitors to suddenly increase 16 percent. And the introduction, in 1971, of the recreational/nonrecreational visitor categories also significantly increased visitation figures. For some parks, the change simply meant a breakdown of pre-1971 visits into recreational and nonrecrea-

tional categories. For others, however, it resulted in counting additional visits that had previously been excluded.

The rapid growth of the park system during the 1960s and 1970s also makes statistics on visitation trends misleading. For example, systemwide visitation totals for 1981 show a 55.2 percent increase over 1971 totals. But when visits to parks added during the 1970s are removed from the 1981 totals, the increase comes only to 20.1 percent,[2] meaning that over 60 percent of the park system's visitation increase over that period was due to the addition of new, predominantly urban-oriented parks rather than to increases in visitation at the older units of the system.

The park service uses a variety of methods to obtain visitation figures, from traffic counters (coupled with surveys of the average number of persons per car) to visual reports. A range of methods is necessary because the service must balance the need for accurate statistics against the cost of obtaining them. Some parks have several uncontrolled access points, while at others entry is restricted to one of several check-in points. As a result, great variation exists among units in the accuracy of visitation figures, making it difficult to compare statistics for individual parks.[3]

Another problem is that, because visits are categorized only as recreational or nonrecreational, very different experiences and uses of the parks— for example, an arduous hike to the top of Yosemite Falls and a quick drive through Yosemite Valley—end up being treated as equal. If, over time, the relative proportion of people hiking to people driving shifts substantially, this change is not reflected in the visitation figures.[4] Moreover, determining whether a visit is recreational or nonrecreational is not always easy. Take, for example, the case of parkways.

Since it is not possible to stop every car and inquire into its passengers' purpose, arbitrary methods must be used to estimate visitation. Natchez Trace, for example, simply declares that one-third of all its visits are non-recreational. The George Washington Memorial Parkway does not include automobile traffic in its figures but rather counts the number of visitors to particular structures within the unit.

In short, visitation figures are estimates and are not comparable over time due to changing conditions. They tell little about who is using a park, what they are doing there, how long they are staying, or what attracts them—all important considerations for the management of park units and the park service.[5]

to $994 million, or 15 percent of the department's total appropriated funds.[18] Responsible for 79.4 million acres of land, the park service is the third largest manager of public lands in the Interior Department, behind the Bureau of Land Management and the Fish and Wildlife Service.[19]

The park service is a hierarchical organization with lines of authority flowing from a headquarters office in Washington through regional offices to the park units. It is also highly decentralized, based on a powerful tradition that originated when parks were remote and communications poor but that has persisted as the system has diversified. The park service director, appointed by the secretary of the interior, reports to the Interior Department's assistant secretary for fish and wildlife and parks.

Although the secretary has ultimate responsibility for park policy, the assistant secretary oversees park policy and operations. In 1984, approximately 4.5 percent of the total staff, or 730 positions, were assigned to the headquarters office in Washington, D.C.[20] WASO (for WAShington Office, as headquarters is called by everyone in the service), is responsible for "the development of policies, programs, regulations, and procedures; and coordination and relationships with Congress, the Office of Management and Budget, the Department [of the Interior], and the public."[21] The Washington

---

employees in the service at any time differs from the FTE number because some work less than full time to accommodate the special seasonal needs of parks and because some authorized positions are vacant.[17] All references to "staff positions" in this chapter are to FTEs. References to numbers of personnel or employees, on the other hand, are to actual people employed by the service.

office prepares the budget each year, consolidating requests from the regions for transmittal to the secretary, and provides professional services to the regions and the parks. WASO also administers grant, technical assistance, and recreation and historic-preservation support programs.[22]

Reorganized in 1983, WASO has two assistant directors (one for personnel and administrative services and the other for financial and data systems) and four associate directors (one each for cultural resources, natural resources, park operations, and planning and development). The reorganization, one of many in recent years, tried to streamline central planning and strengthen policy making by transferring many positions from headquarters to the regions and field.[23]

Of the 16,282 staff positions in the service in 1984, 13,107, or 80.5 percent, were assigned to the parks, where, under the direction of superintendents or park managers, the work of directly protecting resources and accommodating visitors actually takes place.[24]*

Staff size varies greatly from park to park. Yellowstone, for example, had 412 staff positions in 1984, compared to 7 for the Edgar Allen Poe National Historic Site. Two of the newer urban units, Golden Gate and Gateway national recreation areas, had sizable staffs, with 196 and 380 positions, respectively, but others—Chattahoochee River, with 41 positions, and Santa Monica, with 64—did not.[25] Park staffs, of course, operate the parks day-to-day and prepare budgets, which are transmitted to the regional rung of the park service ladder.

The regions perform many of the same functions vis-à-vis parks as WASO does for the regions. There are 10 regional offices with 1,664 staff positions or 10.2 percent of the total.† The Rocky Mountain Regional Office, with 227 staff positions, is the largest; the smallest, the Alaska Regional Office, with 93 staff, is responsible for the largest amount of federally owned park acreage (figure 3.1).[26]

Each regional director wields considerable influence over park policies and programs by his or her authority to review park budgets,

---

*Superintendents have wide latitude in organizing their staffs, and similar titles in different parks do not necessarily entail the same duties.

†The service's 10 regional offices are: Boston; Philadelphia; Washington, D.C.; Atlanta; Omaha; Denver; Santa Fe; San Francisco; Seattle; and Anchorage.

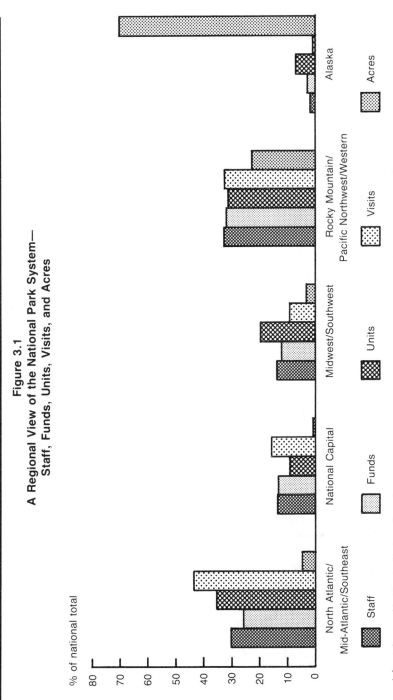

Figure 3.1
A Regional View of the National Park System—
Staff, Funds, Units, Visits, and Acres

% of national total

Staff  Funds  Units  Visits  Acres

North Atlantic/
Mid-Atlantic/Southeast

National Capital

Midwest/Southwest

Rocky Mountain/
Pacific Northwest/Western

Alaska

Source: Information provided by the National Park Service.

assign staff, fund specific programs, and determine priorities of requests from units for line-item appropriations by Congress. In addition, each regional director has wide latitude in organizing his or her staff. (Again, a similarity in the title of employees serving in different regional offices does not necessarily mean similar responsibilities.) The 10 regional directors meet formally with the park service director several times a year to consider policies, issues, and other matters and essentially function as an informal cabinet, even a quasi-board of directors, for the director.

Distinct from the regional offices are two technical assistance centers. The Denver Service Center in Colorado and the Harpers Ferry Center in West Virginia were established at the beginning of the 1970s to provide specialized professional and technical expertise to all the parks; they are assigned 569 and 188 FTEs, respectively, and account for just over 4 percent of the total park service staff.[27]

The Denver Service Center provides consultant architects, engineers, landscape architects, and others to parks for major planning and construction projects. In 1984, the Denver Service Center's construction budget totaled $107.6 million; another $100 million was earmarked for rehabilitation and repair on highways, and $14 million was tagged to help build the Cumberland Gap Tunnel.[28] Other specialists at the center work in diverse servicewide functions, including aircraft operation, acquisitions, concession management, and statistical analysis. The Denver Service Center's staff has shrunk somewhat in recent years, down from a peak of 819 employees in 1978, in part because more work is contracted out to private firms.

The Harpers Ferry Center was established to upgrade, through centralized operations and responsibility, the quality of exhibits, audiovisual presentations, and publications systemwide. Like the Denver Service Center, the Harpers Ferry Center is an independent unit that reports to an associate director in Washington. Employees at the center prepare and plan museums and wayside exhibits, TV films, slide tapes, and literature. The center's 1984 program budget of nearly $14 million[29] pays specialists that include a cinematographer, a sound engineer, cartographers, editors, and graphic designers.

Smaller centers and field offices established in response to regional and servicewide needs augment the natural and cultural resource capabilities of the park service. These units vary in organi-

*Death Valley, February 1984. Zabriskie Point.*

zational structure, regional or servicewide responsibilities, and place
in the hierarchy (some report to the region in which they are located
and some to the Washington headquarters office). Six cultural resource centers have been established at the regional level,[30] as have
three other units in Colorado specializing in natural resources
servicewide.[31] In addition, several land-acquisition offices are
located in the regions and the parks, and an Interagency Fire Center
is housed in Boise, Idaho. Nine regions also have cooperative agreements with 23 universities for studies, reports, and publications,
primarily on resource management issues.[32]

Finally, the park service operates two training centers, the Horace
M. Albright Training Center at Grand Canyon, Arizona, and the
Stephen T. Mather Training Center at Harpers Ferry; ranger skills
are emphasized at Albright, and interpretative skills at Mather. Other
courses are offered in natural resource management, basic management, and equal opportunity. The service's total training budget
of $3.2 million in 1984 was allocated among these two centers and

the Federal Law Enforcement Training Center at Glynco, Georgia.[33]
Each region also received money for mandatory training in equal
opportunity, new-employee orientation, law enforcement, and
safety.[34]

## Policy Setting

An informal system of power sharing governs much of the park
service's management. Although this undoubtedly slows the pace
of change within the service, in so doing it contributes to the stability
of an institution that might otherwise be overly vulnerable to the
whims of transient political appointees.

The park service is not, of course, free to set its own course. It is
subject to congressional appropriations and oversight. As an agency
within the Department of the Interior, the National Park Service
comes under the direction of presidential appointees—especially
the secretary and the assistant secretary for fish and wildlife and
parks—and must constantly tack to the political winds. Its budget
requests compete with those of other agencies within the department and with other departments in reviews by the Office of Management and Budget before reaching Congress. Superintendents'
requests for staffing and funding move up from the park to the region
and, then to headquarters in Washington.[35]

Officially, decisions among competing needs are based on objective professional judgments. Even at the park level, however, a
superintendent's requests, including requests for special cyclical
funding, reflect perceptions of current interests in headquarters and
in Congress. Even in lean budget years, a superintendent with a
direct ear in Congress can get congressional "add-ons" at the elev-
enth hour without going through the official priority-setting process.
Concessioners may ensure that money is spent on snowplowing
roads for spring visitors, even though important research projects
remain unfunded. Invisible lines of influence crisscrossing the hierarchical organization charts affect the actual flow of money, staff,
and organizational support for the activities and decisions that determine how well the park service mission is carried out.[36]

Power ebbs and flows among WASO and the regions and the
parks, depending on the current administration's policy, and the
personalities and working styles of the director and regional directors. The direct influence of the interior secretary and the assistant

secretary for fish and wildlife and parks varies with federal administrations. Ostensibly, these officials work through the park service
director. However, a secretary or assistant secretary often takes an
interest in a particular issue and, in effect, bypasses the chain of
command. Nathaniel Reed, assistant secretary for fish and wildlife
and parks under presidents Nixon and Ford, for example, was a
forceful park advocate, whereas changing the direction of national
park policy was a key issue on the departmental agenda of James G.
Watt, when he began, in 1981, a highly controversial term of service
as secretary of the interior.[37]

Until George Hartzog was fired from the position in 1972,[38] the
park service director was widely considered to be above party
politics. In the Mather tradition, directors survived changes of
presidents and parties and tried to emulate Mather's dual role as
the highest ranking professional and a forceful advocate of the parks
to Congress and the public. After Hartzog's departure, a series of
"revolving-door" appointments of directors, some of whom did not
have support from within the service, weakened the position; between 1973 and 1980, the park service had four directors.[39] Then,
in 1980, Russell Dickenson, a long-time park service employee, was
appointed by the Carter administration and continued to serve during the Reagan administration until 1985.

Superintendents of the high-status parks (for example,
Yellowstone, Grand Canyon, and Great Smoky Mountains) have
their own network of influence. They tend to be old hands, many
having served as rangers. A few have held high-level positions in
headquarters or as regional directors.[40] Because of their breadth of
experience and the force of their personalities, their views are
solicited by regional directors and even the director.

## Staff

On September 30, 1983, 18,097 people worked for the park service. Of these, 9,936 were permanent as full-time, part-time, and
part-year employees, a 55 percent increase since 1970. Another
8,161 worked in various temporary positions, up 34 percent since
1970.[41]* These positions included rangers, park superintendents,

---

*These numbers refer to actual staff, not FTEs. A "census" of park service
employees on board each September 30 is submitted to Congress annually
along with the budget.[42]

park technicians, various types of specialists, park police, and maintenance and clerical workers.

## Rangers

Former park service Director Horace Albright described rangers as "one of the most romantic figures in life."[43] In the popular mind, the ranger *is* the service. Most visitors use the term for all the people they see in uniform—the ones who distribute brochures, answer questions, collect campground fees, or give campfire talks.

To the people who work in the service, however, the title of ranger is far more restricted: it is, technically speaking, the title for about

*Yellowstone, August 1984. Bill Hape, maintenance supervisor. "There are a lot of people that are just prouder than heck to be park service. You rub shoulders with a lot of people from different walks of life, and they always have a comment. What I like about working in Yellowstone is doing the job and seeing the result of it. I'm addicted to the park service, to people, to the park. I'm not necessarily saying I like my job day after day. Much of it gets dumped on you. You get a paycheck out of it. But people appreciate a clean park, good roads. . . . People notice what's done here at the park level. I'm not knocking the regional offices, the Washington office, or anything. But here is where the action is, not at some desk a thousand miles away. The work that actually needs to be accomplished, you see it, you know it, you know what needs to be done."*

2,000 of the people in the coveted "025" park management classification. (This category also includes the approximately 500 superintendents, assistant superintendents, and manager assistants.) In January 1984, rangers comprised over 13 percent of the persons working for the park service.[44]

In the service's early days, rangers were generalists who were expected to do everything—attend to visitors' needs, take care of horses, arrest poachers, maintain trails, repair park buildings, even lay out campgrounds. Then rangers were "men who have worked their way up through the ranks without the benefit of education other than that which they . . . received in the mountains and the forests."[45]

Today a ranger typically has a college degree and is likely to be a specialist, by dint of experience and training, in law enforcement, interpretation, search and rescue, or fire management, for example.[46] Although the park service continues to group all rangers in the same general category, when parks advertise a ranger opening, they often specify "KSAs"—the knowledge, skill, and ability to perform a specific task—that an applicant must have. There are calls for rangers who are historical interpreters, rangers who have experience dealing with private inholders, and rangers who are resource managers. The ranger on the job, however, is still supposed to do whatever has to be done.

A ranger's job varies considerably as a consequence of many factors—some obvious, such as the type and size of park, the park's proximity to a metropolitan area, or the level of visitation, and others less obvious. A single person may be called on to know about forest diseases, fire control, historic preservation, riot control, campground management, and folk arts and crafts, as well as to collect statistical information, write reports, take water samples, analyze findings, make inspections, and speak to the public. Particularly in smaller park units, people who hold ranger positions must be extremely versatile and knowledgeable.

The ranger's knowledge, skills, and abilities are kept in tune with the service's existing and emerging needs through staff training and diverse park assignments. Although training courses are offered for all groups of personnel, many—beginning with a seven-and-a-half-week course in skills, values, and park lore for promising new rangers[47]—are directed to grooming the ranger for a vast array of responsibilities. The list of the park service courses is extensive, but the number of spaces is limited. Because access to these courses is highly desirable, and often provides rungs in the "career ladder," slots are eagerly sought. The courses reflect new needs, based on new knowledge and values—for example, concession administration, interpretation, equal opportunity, historic preservation, natural resource management, and maintenance.[48]

The most controversial response to a perceived training need is the congressionally mandated training in law enforcement.[49] In the early 1970s, reflecting changes in society outside the parks, rangers encountered many law enforcement issues inside the parks—a youth riot in Yosemite, marijuana growing in a few western units, weekend drinking in Whiskeytown-Shasta-Trinity, nude bathing in Cape Cod, and increasing robberies and car thefts.[50] In response, Congress passed legislation clarifying jurisdictional issues and the right of designated rangers to carry guns, make arrests, and issue warrants. Rangers with policing responsibilities are now required to take 200 hours of law enforcement training and to participate in a 40-hour refresher course each year.[51] Park advocacy groups question such extensive training compared with the lesser training available or required in other aspects of rangers' duties.

Rangers traditionally must hold jobs in many different parks if they expect to advance. Although there is no official policy, Associate Director Stanley Albright has called mobility "the foundation upon which [the] workforce has long been based. The employee who has benefitted from many types of work experiences in many different areas, served under many mentors along the way, and . . . developed the friendships . . . and networks is a basic component of what we call the park service family."[52]

In recent years, because of both employee choice and constraints on the agency's budget, mobility among the rank and file has slowed. Forces reducing staff interest in transfers have included the larger number of rangers with working spouses and the desire of many rangers to invest in a home and become part of a community.[53] From the agency's perspective, the high costs of relocation are an economic constraint to mobility.

Another influence on mobility has to do with transfers among historic/battlefield, natural, and urban/recreation park units. Retaining the strength and esprit of "one service" despite increasing diversity of park types is a challenge. Different types of parks make different demands. Employees whose only experience is in remote wilderness parks may find adjusting to work in urban parks difficult, and vice versa. Interpreters in urban parks do not have a "captive audience" every night, for example, and more outreach is needed to attract visitors to programs.

When an opening is available in a park, the superintendent reviewing applicants' resumes is, like any supervisor, attracted by related experience. Staff from urban or historical parks have perceived difficulties in transferring to natural parks because of an "old ranger" prejudice that the newer, innovative parks are not the "real" parks, although some feel that "crossover" between types of units is occurring more often.* Because the park service does not systematically record information on transfers, and official policies do stress the value of diverse experience, conjectures about the extent of crossover are difficult.

## Park Superintendents

If the ranger is the central symbol of the professional in the service, the park superintendent is the symbol of the manager. In a 1971 article, John McPhee wrote:

> The superintendent of Yosemite is a . . . strong-appearing man. . . .
> He wears a silver watchband with turquoise inlay and a large silver-and-turquoise shell-inlay ring. . . . He is Hartzog's idea of the park service personified—a man who does anything well and is ready to serve anywhere any time.[54]

This superintendent had been raised in a park where his father was a superintendent. Obviously, such characteristics and qualifications are not spelled out in civil service regulations. Despite the stereotype, superintendents are a diverse group, and are becoming more so.

There are 244 superintendents in the National Park System (some smaller units have "park managers," reporting to a regional superintendent).[55] The position of superintendent in each park is graded according to the complexity and responsibility of the job.†

---

*Several persons interviewed for this book had experience in both urban and natural parks.

† According to park service guidelines, a number of factors, such as park size and visitation, are considered in establishing a superintendent's grade. The guidelines recognize that such factors as environmental conflicts, the

The superintendents of the most complex and popular parks—
Yellowstone and Golden Gate, for example—are paid more than
their counterparts in smaller or less-visited parks. Among superintendents, 19 have the highest grade (GS 15), while 73 have the
lowest (GS 11). Most are graded in between.[57]

Since the days of Mather, superintendents have had a good deal
of autonomy.[58] Frequent transfers provided the breadth of needed
experience and forged common bonds among superintendents. But,
as the park system has expanded and units have become more
diverse, specialized training and distinctive personal qualities have
become essential. Today, parks are no longer remote, and concepts
of public participation have changed significantly. Superintendents
are now less likely to run their parks as fiefdoms and instead are
apt to work with a variety of interests whose activities influence
park management.

The role is especially challenging in newer parks established in
already settled areas. Says Lewis Albert, superintendent of Cuyahoga
Valley National Recreation Area, between Akron and Cleveland,
Ohio:

> I began working for the service in Yellowstone. I thought the superinten-
> dent had vice-regal authority. Here, hundreds of people can tell me what
> to do. We're dealing with politicians and others in the community who
> resent authority. They're not part of the club.[59]

Before being assigned to Cuyahoga in 1984, Albert had already
demonstrated his skill at dealing with local zoning and political
issues in his former position as superintendent of Lowell National
Historical Park, in Massachusetts.

In addition, superintendents are no longer invariably expected
to come up through the park service ranks. For example, the park
superintendent at Gateway National Recreation Area gained much
of his experience in another agency within the Interior Department,
but was judged to have the drive and innovative qualities needed
to run that unusual park at a difficult stage in its development.

Commenting on these trends, one superintendent says, "There
is less of a fraternity now among superintendents."[60]

---

need for restoring and rehabilitating resources, the presence of long visitor
seasons, and remoteness from populated areas may merit a higher grade. A
position that requires a superintendent to establish a new park area gets double
credit in the grade assessment. Superintendents' salary levels in 1984 ranged
from $25,366 to $65,327.[56]

Increased staff sizes have been accompanied by additional supervisory positions, including assistant superintendents, manager assistants, chief rangers, chiefs of interpretation, district naturalists, and maintenance foremen. There are now more than 120 assistant superintendents in the parks. A number of higher-grade supervisory slots were filled by transfers of staff from the disbanded Heritage Conservation and Recreation Service in 1981 and from the Washington office and the regions in 1983.[61] Although the transfers streamlined headquarters and regional offices, staff in the parks comment that the always narrow path to advancement is further impeded by the influx of higher-paid staff. A countervailing prospect is found in the service's estimate that 40 percent of the highest-rated ranger-park managers will be eligible to retire within five years.[62]

*Yosemite, February 1984. Jan Van Wagtendonk, research biologist. "You'll see a lot of people engaged in activities that have a resource orientation. A lot of cross-country skiers. . . . You'll also see people in high heels and stockings. But they are out there, and I have to give them credit. Pushing babies and carrying ice chests. They are bringing everything with them, but at least they are out there, and they are actually walking. They are under muscle power, and they are getting closer to the resource. . .. But if you get too many people enjoying it, all of a sudden the enjoyment starts dropping off. . ... The park belongs to the people. What we do as public servants to keep it for them, that's really the question."*

## Park Technicians

Aside from the more than 13 percent of the service in the ranger-park management track, another 2,462 persons, or 16 percent of the total staff, were park technicians in January 1984.[63] The public thinks of these technicians as rangers and, in the sense that many technicians do the same work as some rangers, this perception is not completely off base.

Park technicians were introduced into the service almost two decades ago to serve as paraprofessionals, like medics or legal aides, who would be recruited locally to perform the rangers' more routine chores for lower pay. Today, park technicians often complain that they do essentially the same work as many rangers, but for far less pay.[64] Many are college graduates, even with masters and doctoral degrees, who want to move up the management ladder. But most of them are in nonprofessional grades of the federal wage scale (with salaries ranging from $12,367 to $17,138), while most ranger-park managers are in professional grades (with salaries between $20,965 and $30,402).[65] The position of park technician does not lead to higher grades and greater responsibilities directly; rangers, in contrast, are on a professional track that can lead directly to the superintendency.[66]

Many park technicians who intend to remain in the service try to move into the ranger-park manager classification, but opportunities are limited. Until 1980, a technician's experience was not even recognized as a contributing qualification for a ranger position in some areas.[67] Access to the ranger training courses is also an issue. Even though many of these courses are open to both rangers and technicians, the limited slots are often assigned with an eye toward grooming rangers as future managers.[68]

One solution to the problem, debated at length, is to merge the ranger and park technician classifications. So far, however, the classifications remain separate.[69] Higher salary costs are one obstacle to change. So are concerns over diminishing the ranger's elite status—or, as it is more usually expressed, retaining "professionalism."

## Specialists

The parks have always needed specialized talents beyond those of the rangers and the superintendents. In the early days of the parks, hotel construction required such expertise. The system's first landscape engineer began work in Yellowstone in 1918, where he reviewed the planning and building of concessioner facilities, campgrounds, and roads and trails in western parks.[70]

But Mather, a strong advocate of the jack-of-all-trades, might well be dismayed by the two-inch thick list of specialist classifications in the park service today: equal opportunity assistant, communications specialist, computer clerk, biologist, exhibits specialist, outdoor recreation planner, accountant, nurse, pilot, deckhand, job coder (figure 3.2). Yet recent reports on natural and cultural resources have expressed concern over the leanness of specialized staff in many parks.[71] For example, in 1982, only a few parks—such as Indiana Dunes, Redwood, and Everglades, with special resource problems—had any sizable cadre of scientists.[72] Superintendents have called for more on-site specialists—natural resource managers, historians and curators, planners familiar with the adjacent community, and archaeologists.

This adaptation of the service's generalist tradition to the growing need for specialists has become a major issue in modernizing the park service in recent years. Where are specialists best located—in large centers and in Washington, in each region, or in smaller centers, perhaps with some regions sharing expertise? Should more be located in the parks? Should specialists, such as resource managers, perform their duties as rangers, or as a separate group? If specialists are not classified in the ranger-park management track, what can they look forward to in promotions and good assignments?

Many parks have plenty of work to keep specially trained professionals busy, but, from the system's perspective, detailing specialists to one park may not be the most efficient, or most equitable, allocation of limited expertise.[73] Many persons with specialized training are stationed in the regional offices, the two service centers, or headquarters. Almost half of the architects and engineers in the park service are assigned to the Denver Service Center, for example. About one-quarter of the planners and landscape architects work in the Denver Service Center; one-fifth are in the parks; the rest are assigned to the regional offices and Washington. In contrast, two-thirds of park staff trained in the physical sciences work in the parks. More than one-third of the social scientists, including archaeologists, are assigned to the parks, and a similar number work in the regional offices. (Many of the staff assigned to regional offices with expertise in historic preservation perform "external" functions

## Figure 3.2
## Allocation of National Park Service Personnel, May 1, 1984

| Position | Washington Headquarters | Denver Service Center | Harpers Ferry Center | Rocky Mountain Regional Office | North Atlantic Regional Office | National Capital Regional Office | Mid-Atlantic Regional Office | Southeast Regional Office | Midwest Regional Office | Southwest Regional Office | Western Regional Office | Pacific Northwest Regional Office | Alaska Regional Office | Parks | Cross Total | % of Total Staff |
|---|---|---|---|---|---|---|---|---|---|---|---|---|---|---|---|---|
| Ranger/park manager | 21 | 1 | 7 | 12 | 9 | 24 | 11 | 14 | 9 | 16 | 13 | 6 | 11 | 1,836 | 1,990 | 13.6 |
| Park technician | | | | | | 1 | | | | | | | 2 | 1,897 | 1,900 | 13.0 |
| Landscape architect/planner | 31 | 87 | | 17 | 4 | 4 | 42 | 17 | 10 | 9 | 18 | 13 | 8 | 67 | 327 | 2.2 |
| Construction and development personnel (architects, engineers) | 33 | 237 | 9 | 20 | 11 | 15 | 8 | 17 | 9 | 12 | 7 | 5 | 6 | 148 | 537 | 3.7 |
| Exhibits and publications personnel | 26 | 41 | 68 | 4 | 2 | 4 | 3 | 3 | 8 | 3 | 3 | 2 | 1 | 67 | 235 | 1.6 |
| Physical and biological scientists | 58 | 27 | | 5 | 9 | 2 | 2 | 5 | 5 | 4 | 11 | 7 | 8 | 249 | 392 | 2.7 |
| Historians, social scientists, and museum specialists | 55 | 49 | 28 | 15 | 8 | 4 | 19 | 15 | 48 | 29 | 46 | 9 | 12 | 216 | 553 | 3.8 |
| Acquisitions and concessions personnel | 37 | 11 | | 6 | 4 | 3 | 8 | 9 | 13 | 10 | 12 | 7 | 3 | 43 | 166 | 1.1 |
| Maintenance and labor personnel | 4 | 13 | 13 | | | 4 | | 3 | | 3 | 5 | 1 | | 4,308 | 4,354 | 29.8 |
| Administration personnel | 501 | 113 | 68 | 179 | 87 | 117 | 90 | 102 | 105 | 92 | 139 | 74 | 43 | 1,794 | 3,504 | 24.0 |
| Public relations personnel | 6 | | | 2 | 2 | 1 | 1 | 2 | 1 | 2 | 2 | 1 | 1 | 6 | 27 | 0.2 |
| Security personnel | | | | | | | | | | | | | | 580 | 580 | 4.0 |
| Miscellaneous | 7 | 3 | 1 | | | 2 | | 2 | | | 5 | | | 25 | 48 | 0.3 |
| Total | 779 | 582 | 194 | 260 | 136 | 181 | 184 | 189 | 208 | 180 | 261 | 125 | 95 | 11,236 | 14,610 | 100.0 |

Note: For further explanation of figure, see References section.

Source: Information provided by the National Park Service, Personnel Office, Staffing Branch, 1984

connected to the service's responsibilities—for example, reviewing the eligibility of private developments for preservation tax credits or nominations to the National Register of Historic Places.)

Given the need for specialists, some observers advocate significant new recruitment; others suggest that the basic problem is not the quantity of employees but their more effective deployment. The service does not systematically collect the data needed to analyze these issues. Neither does it have sufficient information about what specialists throughout the system do; what the needs are, especially in relation to size of park, type of park, and regional location; and what strategies have proved effective.

Such usable information is difficult to gather because staff often are not doing the work their classifications suggest or doing it only part of the time. Outdoor recreation planners may clear trails; biologists may work the cash register at a visitor center; sociologists may prepare impact statements. As two rangers, promoted from park technician, said recently, "You can't do a good job if you follow your job description. . . . We're masters of all trades . . . interpreter, law enforcer, fire fighter, maintenance worker, state police, game warden, lifeguard, biologist, host."[74]

Their response—based on the desire for diverse experience to advance their careers and also to do whatever needs to be done— would have pleased Mather.

## The Park Police

In addition to the rangers trained in law enforcement, the Interior Department's crack police unit, the U.S. Park Police, administratively managed by the park service, has special security assignments. The park police, who trace their history to the Park Watchmen assigned in 1791 to patrol federal properties in the nation's capital,[75] numbered about 500 in February 1984. Most are stationed in Washington, D.C., where they may be called out to keep a demonstration orderly, ride alongside the Cherry Blossom Queen in the annual parade, or ensure the safety of hundreds of thousands of persons viewing the Independence Day fireworks on the Mall (a park unit). Park police share responsibility for protecting the president and foreign officials in the Washington, D.C., area. Training is longer and more intensive than for law enforcement rangers, and park police have a separate, higher pay scale and more generous retirement benefits.

Aside from their assignments in the nation's capital, one member of the park police is detailed to each of the ten regional offices for technical assistance. Also, 50 each are assigned to the Golden Gate and Gateway national recreation areas. Officials in these parks claim that the detailing of park police is related to the large numbers of visitors, not the crime rate, which is comparable, per capita, with that of other parks.[76]

*Golden Gate, February 1984. Dave Nettle, a park ranger at work on a historic ship at the Maritime Museum. "I never in my wildest imagination thought I'd wear a uniform and be a ranger. I brought my class here for about six years. When this position opened up, the district ranger called me and asked whether I wanted to be the captain. I came on board and have been here ever since. . . . On a surface level, it teaches these kids firsthand what it is like to be a sailor. Also, the joys of working as a crew. Ships are by their very nature a cooperative situation, so it is a tremendous laboratory and goes far beyond the overnight experience. These children have been training since the first of September. . . . We're putting together a constituency, alerting people to preservation. What we wind up with is a group of people that believes the agency is responsive to them. They see another park uniform, and they know, 'Hey, I'm in a place that belongs to me.' Also, these kids will never look at a historic site quite the same again. They'll go to another site and, because of the personalization that has been built into this experience, they'll look at it."*

## Other Staff

The park service has always employed a large number of "seasonals" to augment the staff during summer vacation peaks. As "shoulder-season" tourism increases and winter visits become more popular in some parks, staffing needs are changing. In Yellowstone, for example, recruitment is now geared to two overlapping groups of seasonals, one starting in spring and working through summer, the other beginning in summer and working through fall, with a few staying through the winter.[77]

The everyday cleanup and repair chores require a sizable maintenance staff. In May 1984, 4,351 persons, 30 percent of the entire staff, worked in the parks as maintenance mechanics, laborers, carpenters, gardeners, custodians, electricians, printers, and auto mechanics (see figure 3.2). The staff is usually recruited locally, paid according to local scale, and less likely to move to different parks. As a result, maintenance people in some parks are paid quite well compared with park-technicians and rangers in the lower grades; similarly, the chief of maintenance may have been in the park much longer than the superintendent. Even though the park service prides itself on being able to "do everything," some maintenance tasks always have been contracted out. (In 1983, in accordance with Reagan administration policies, park personnel throughout the system had to consider expanding the use of competitive bids for maintenance and other park staff functions.)

Finally, of course, the park services hires a large number of persons to perform administrative and clerical functions. About half of them are assigned to the parks, and almost a third work in the regional offices.

## Park Service Jobs for Minorities and Women

The prevailing image of the ranger as a white male is no longer accurate. Statistics show that women particularly are improving their position in the park service, but "It still blows people's minds when they come close and realize I'm a woman," a park technician comments.[78] In 1983, minorities and women filled 9 and 13 percent, respectively, of all the park ranger/management positions. For park technicians, the percentages were 10 for minorities and 42 for women.[79] (There is some overlap in the two groups.) Servicewide, the percentage of all jobs held by minorities in 1982 was 17 percent, with the percentage held by women, 30.[80] Among the highest permanent park management grades, 4 percent were women and 7 percent minorities.[81]

## THE MATHER TRADITION IN A NEW ERA

The role of the National Park Service as steward of America's most treasured lands and sites—together with the tradition of preservation and use that has guided the management of those areas—has created its high standing among the public and a collective pride among its employees. The popular image of the ranger has contributed to this achievement.

Although its public image has remained remarkably constant, the National Park Service so admired by the American public today is the product of almost 70 years of experience. Like the National Park System for which it is responsible, the service has changed continually. The question today is how to retain the strengths in a proud tradition, while simultaneously dealing with expanded and increasingly complex demands. We return to this question in chapter 7 after examining some of these demands.

# Profile
# Fredericksburg and Spotsylvania National Military Park

The serene, dense woods and picturesque rolling pastureland around Fredericksburg, Virginia, give little hint of the fierce battles, cavalry charges, and hand-to-hand combat that wracked the area little more than a hundred years ago.[1] Nor do they speak of the 100,000 casualties that made this the bloodiest acreage in the nation. Fredericksburg and Spotsylvania County Memorial Battlefield National Military Park—called by one of its congressional creators the "cockpit of the Civil War"[2]—is a short one-hour drive down Interstate 95 south from Washington, D.C., just across the Rappahannock River, a historic dividing line between the armies of the Union and the Confederacy. Here on the falls of the Rappahannock sits Fredericksburg—astride the major rail link and shortest path between Washington, D.C., and Richmond, Virginia, the capital of the Confederacy, which lies another hour's drive south.

Much of Fredericksburg, today a quiet, peaceful place of 18,000 people, was leveled, battered, or burned during two major battles that saw General Robert E. Lee rout major Union assaults aimed at Richmond. Just a few miles outside of town at a crossroads called Chancellorsville, Lee scored his most brilliant victory, one that laid the groundwork for his invasion of the North. In that same battle, General Stonewall Jackson executed a daring maneuver that befuddled Union soldiers and secured Lee's victory, but at a terrible cost. Jackson was accidentally shot by his own troops and died eight days later of complications from the wound. Lee lost what he called "my right arm," and many historians maintain that this was the beginning of the end for the South.

Here, too, Clara Barton nursed Union soldiers on wooden floors that still bear the stain of blood. And, in 1864, General Ulysses S. Grant began his inexorable march to victory at Appomattox with two major battles, at a heavily forested, briar-infested area known as the Wilderness and a few days later at the tiny settlement of Spotsylvania Court House. At the Wilderness, hundreds of wounded burned to death as fires swept through woods after an inconclusive fight through underbrush so thick it literally tore the clothes from soldiers' bodies as they charged through it. A few days later, Spotsylvania Court House witnessed savage hand-to-hand combat at the infamous Bloody Angle in what historian Bruce Catton called the most vicious struggle of the Civil War: "Cannon fired at point-blank range and soldiers were stabbed to death . . . with bayonets thrust between the logs in the parapet which separated the combatants."[3] More than 10,000 men were casualties of the daylong battle.

Thousands of dead from these grisly encounters were buried at Fredericksburg National Cemetery soon after the war. In 1927, Congress created a battlefield memorial park encompassing the cemetery and the nearby battlefield sites. There was little debate over the area's historical significance. In fact, if the battlefields had not been so close to one another, there would have been at least four parks, not one. The aim was to commemorate these struggles by preserving the lines of battle, earthworks, and other important features. The War Department was given the authority to administer the park.

Just a few years later, in 1933, this park, along with other battlefields, military sites, and cemeteries administered by the War Department, was transferred by executive order to the National Park Service. The transfer marked a major expansion of the national park concept, which previously had embodied great natural wonders like Yellowstone and ancient archaeological sites like Mesa Verde. Many conservationists of the time questioned the wisdom of this expansion, fearing it would dilute the National Park System's purity.

In the 1930s, the Fredericksburg area was largely rural. The battlefields outside the town sat amid farms and woodlands, scattered with irregular boundaries that followed trenches, march routes, and fields of fire. In many places, the park was only a sliver of land along an old road or cow path where an important troop manuever had taken place. Farmers who sold these slivers to the service often retained the right to cut across park property to reach their fields on the other side.

Land acquisition proceeded slowly until the 1960s when Congress began appropriating substantial sums of money to round out the park. Owners were generally cooperative, with almost all land being obtained on a willing-seller basis. A limit on park acquisition was set for the first time in 1974, with distinct boundaries outside of which no acquisition could take place.

The result is a 10-square-mile area of parkland scattered over four counties and 117 square miles that takes almost eight hours and 110 miles of automobile driving to tour properly. It is all overseen by superintendent Jim Zinck, who was originally a ranger in western parks. Zinck has about 50 people to help him administer the military park, including 8 historians, 6 rangers, and 22 maintenance staff.

*Fredericksburg, November 1984.*

Visitor traffic to the park is fairly heavy—almost 250,000 visits a year—but has remained rather steady since the 1970s.[4] Of those visits, more than 80 percent come from out of state. Over 600,000 people drive through park roads getting to work and pursuing other everyday activities.

Zinck faces many of the same problems that, in varying degrees, are found in other parks. He has to worry about relic hunters who can, with sophisticated metal detectors and a shovel, turn up artifacts at a startling rate. Then there are the tourists who tromp over the old trenches despite signs admonishing them to stay on paths. The wear and tear from thousands of feet is exacerbated by roots from trees that spring up quickly in the moist, humid climate. During the Civilian Conservation Corps's days of the 1930s, the trenches were routinely cleared, but today they are dotted with trees, many as thick as a man's thigh. The park service lacks the money and people to keep the saplings trimmed.

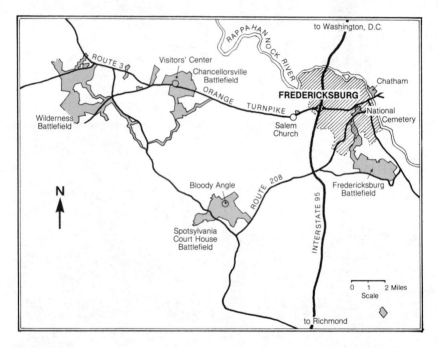

Zinck has made increasing use of volunteers and the local National Guard to get his work done, although he stresses that volunteers require a lot of time and effort to oversee. He has also leased land in the park to farmers whose crops maintain the historical scene on key battle sites and prevent trees from growing, thereby accomplishing park goals and making some money for the park. The farmers operate under carefully worded permits that specify that crops should not be too ''modern''—for example, soybeans are not allowed.

Some special problems arise because of the park's fragmented nature. Visitors are drawn to the Fredericksburg Visitor Center, just off the interstate highway, although park staff encourage them to visit other nearby Civil War units such as the Wilderness and Spotsylvania Court House. The in-town battlefield is surrounded by private land and has little parking. This leads to congestion, especially in the summer when the big tour buses are rolling.

The handsome visitor center at Fredericksburg was built in 1936. The park would like to build a new structure to accommodate summer crowds; in the meantime, the superintendent is trying to encourage visitors to stop at a more spacious center 12 miles away at Chancellorsville. A nearby private camping and recreational facility has spurred visitation at Chancellorsville, but the other two battlefields (Spotsylvania and the Wilderness) remain unknown to many visitors.

The park staff chafe at what they say are outdated interpretative facilities—an old lighted map of the battlefields at the Fredericksburg Visitor Center that is often out of service—but most visitors probably do not notice that much. Most people would agree that the interpretative displays and signs along the automobile tour are excellent, as are maps and descriptive brochures giving the visitor a feel for how the battles played out. Most important, park interpreters, like Chief Historian Bob Krick, exhibit great knowledge about their park as well as a passion for its well-being. But, still, Krick and his colleagues feel much more could be done. Most disappointing to some of his cohorts has been the reduction in visitor hours due to staff cuts. Salem Church, the site of a key skirmish during the Chancellorsville battle, was closed for several years until members of the New Salem Church (home to the Baptist congregation that donated the historic church to the park service) volunteered to open the church on summer weekends.[5]

Despite these problems, a main thrust of the National Park Service in the last few years in Fredericksburg, as through the rest of the system, has been to spend money on maintenance and capital improvements inside the park. No one claims that these tasks have not been necessary. Yet park personnel regret that so little has gone into resource protection. As noted earlier, trenches in the Fredericksburg area need to be cleared of roots, but nothing has been done in many sections for years. Some feel that maintenance funds have been valuable in repairing historic structures, but they add that work was sometimes undertaken by untrained people without proper oversight.

But problems with trees and visitors and lack of qualified personnel seem amenable to the types of solutions superintendents and the park service are most accustomed to handling. One might, in fact, actually conclude that Zinck has an easy time running a park in a scenic, partially rural area where visitation is not overwhelming, there are no concessioners to worry about, and no grizzly bears or other exotic wildlife to manage. Most days, particularly in spring and fall, the meadows and dogwood trees of the Bloody Angle area are so serene that it is hard to imagine any serious problems. But the Bloody Angle is the only spot in any of the four battlefields where the visitor is not peering out over land owned by private individuals. The park's unusual configuration makes it extraordinarily vulnerable to the "third invasion" of Fredericksburg, which has crept down the interstate highway and out into the countryside along major state roads: an invasion of bulldozers. This is the kind of threat that superintendents rarely have the training or power to deal with—growth outside the park in the form of new residential subdivisions, new industrial plants, or new commercial development.

Spotsylvania County, where the Chancellorsville and Spotsylvania Court House battlefields are located, is one of the fastest-growing counties in Virginia. It doubled its population from 17,000 in 1970 to 34,000 in 1980 and continues to grow at a rapid pace. Much of

Fredericksburg, November 1984.

the new growth is along two highways radiating like spokes on a wheel from Fredericksburg. Route 208, a country lane just a few years ago, runs next to Spotsylvania Court House and is being widened to four lanes. Route 3, the old Orange Turnpike, runs four lanes right through Chancellorsville Battlefield; the Virginia Department of Highways and Transportation wants to expand Route 3 to six lanes.

Already Salem Church has been engulfed by housing developments, fast-food restaurants, health spas, and the like along the old Orange Turnpike. Here a small band of Confederate soldiers won what has been called one of the most brilliant and important minor skirmishes of the war, throwing back a superior Union force that had crossed the Rappahannock River and taken Fredericksburg while Lee fought at Chancellorsville. Lee might have been caught in a deadly pincer if the Union advance had succeeded. But the price was terrible. An eyewitness recorded the scene within the church after the battle:

> The sight inside the building, for horror, was, perhaps, never equalled within so limited a space; every available foot of space was crowded with wounded and bleeding soldiers. The floors, the benches, even the chancel and pulpit were all packed almost to suffocation with them. The amputated limbs were piled up in every corner almost as high as a man could reach; blood flowed in streams along the aisles and out the open doors.[6]

Today, the scene in and around Salem Church is far different. The visitor trying to recreate the past is jarred by a self-service gas station just across the road. The local government's idea of compatibility was to have the owner put up a colonial station sign and stick four rows of cedar shingles on the roof of the structure covering the self-service pumps. Local park service officials wanted to buy the land in 1977, but the Washington office thought the $277,000 asking price for five acres was too high. The die was cast in 1981 when the landowner started bulldozing. The land had increased in value to $500,000, not at all unusual in an area just a mile or so from an exit off busy Interstate 95; the Reagan administration had imposed a moratorium on land acquisition.

This story is being repeated at Spotsylvania Court House, where a convenience store already graces a site not far outside the park along Route 208, and the state is currently widening the road to four lanes. While the Wilderness Battlefield's remoteness—20 miles from Fredericksburg—seems to offer protection for the time being,

*Fredericksburg, November 1984. Salem Church (right) and as seen through a nearby gas station (above).*

that is what people once thought about Chancellorsville's 13-mile distance.

What does all this growth mean for park resources? Visual intrusions such as the gas station may become commonplace. Already a supermarket is being planned for a commercial development within a stone's throw of the park's administrative headquarters at Chatham Manor, just north of Fredericksburg on the heights occupied by federal troops when they massed to cross the Rappahannock. Lincoln reviewed troops here during the Civil War. With the atmosphere of battlefield parks and views over fields of honor especially critical, the special quality of Fredericksburg-Spotsylvania is being whittled away.

In addition, Superintendent Zinck says there is increasing local traffic on park roads, no small part of it from new subdivisions that gain access through the old rights-of-way guaranteed to farmers who sold their lands or negotiated easements with the park service years ago. Moreover, increasing recreational use of the parks (to fly kites, wash cars, and the like) detracts from the park scene and the story the park service is trying to tell.

Because of its unusual configuration and broken boundaries, the Fredericksburg National Military Park resembles newer parks—for example, Cape Cod National Seashore and Santa Monica Mountains National Recreation Area (see profiles elsewhere)—where all the land is not owned by the system, and the service must rely on local land-use controls and techniques other than conventional purchase to protect privately owned properties within park boundaries. The park does not have the tools that some newer parks have, such as indirect regulatory power, however, and it even lacks legal authority to accept donations of land or scenic easements on key properties *outside* park boundaries. Remoteness has always been the park's ace-in-the-hole: No one ever dreamed people would be commuting daily from Fredericksburg to Washington, D.C. Today, however, hundreds of van pools and dozens of buses make the trip each workday. The 1974 boundary was meant to secure the park's landscape once and for all as the surrounding area developed, but the growth spurt was far stronger than anticipated.

Park employees have tried to stem the tide in a variety of ways. They have worked with local governments, not to stop growth, but to provide buffer zones around key park parcels. The reception has not been particularly sympathetic, which is not surprising in a formerly poor rural area with local governments run by land- and business-owners. Although Spotsylvania County has enacted a new land-use plan, it, like many other rural jurisdictions, has a tiny land-use planning staff to administer it. And, while much of the land around the park has been zoned for agriculture, rezonings are not hard to come by.

The magnitude of growth and skyrocketing land costs make a large-scale purchase of land by the park service unrealistic. Former Secretary Watt's declaration of a moratorium on park land acquisition signaled the beginning of an era in which acquisition funds have been exeedingly difficult to obtain, although it is unclear whether a change in policies would mean that money would be made available here.

Park service staff have been in the middle of efforts to organize a nonprofit group, called Friends of the Virginia Civil War Parks, which could lend political support to all of these historic units. To deal with development adjacent to park boundaries, they are also exploring methods that do not rely on regulation, such as private land trusts that would use the lure of federal tax deductions to secure donated scenic easements on land around the parks. In return for the federal tax benefits, the landowner would agree to keep the land in agricultural production. Zinck would also like to trade several parcels of excess land outside the park (remnants of tracts that straddled the boundary) for important tracts still in private ownership.

What is being done now does not quite seem to be enough. Visitors 50 years hence may wonder why no one saved a few acres around these historic sites. And they may do their wondering in a car sitting at the "drive-thru" window of a fast-food restaurant just outside one of the park's boundaries.

# Chapter 4
# Stewardship of
# Park Resources

**V**isitors to our national parks expect well-conserved resources, competent staff, informative guided walks, adequately maintained roads and trails. National parks transmit an unspoken statement of good management. Visitor expectations, and the park service's record of success in fulfilling them, are the result of policies and practices dating from the creation of the park system and service.

Park stewardship, however, has become increasingly complicated. Growing knowledge, changing values, and shifting visions of the parks as well as serious pressures on resources today require a reexamination of the purposes of protecting resources, the standards for managing them, and the kinds of experiences these resources permit. Management techniques once unhesitatingly accepted are now controversial or abandoned. Promising initiatives are being taken by the park service. More far-reaching ones have been proposed.

Will measures being developed to manage resources live up to the National Park Service's tradition of success? In the years to come, success will depend not only on park service determination, capability, and action, but also on the willingness of others—visitors, adjacent landowners, politicians—to recognize their own influences on the parks and to address them. This chapter identifies new and intensifying threats to the parks and looks at some of the measures the park service will have to take, at times beyond park boundaries and traditions, to control them.

*Cape Cod, September 1983. Sharon Pittman, seasonal park technician.
"When you tell people that this is National Park Service land . . . they begin
to realize that we have a lot more to offer than just the ocean and the beach
and that we also offer programs and take people out in canoes on the salt
pond and into the salt marsh and do bird walks and things like that. People
have been learning . . . that there is a whole community of things living right
out in the salt marsh and right here along the Nauset Marsh Trail—and that
there's a lot of cultural history as well, with the whaling industry and the
salt works industry. . . . It's really neat when you can share something with
someone and know that they've taken a little bit better concept of the natural
environment away with them."*

## THE GROWING COMPLEXITY OF STEWARDSHIP

In the early days of national parks, deciding what to do with a grizzly bear that mauled a visitor, a raging fire caused by lightning, or a rotting 75-year-old building was easy. The superintendent and park staff quickly killed the bear, suppressed the fire, razed the building. Similar decisions today become the subject of consultations with regional directors and Washington staff, organized interests, and outside experts. New knowledge and changing values and conditions mean these decisions are no longer "simple."

## Natural Resources

The park service's attitudes toward the natural forces that shape park resources illustrate this complexity. In the early days of the park system, little was known about ecology. A resource specialist sums up early practices as "fairytale management, attempting to preserve 'good' species and rid parks of 'bad' species. Mountain lions and wolves were eliminated whenever possible, native forest insects were sprayed if they were perceived to be damaging the forests. Elk were fed hay in the wintertime."[1] If superintendents thought hooved animals were damaging vegetation, the service "reduced" their numbers. Rangers routinely and vigorously extinguished fires. Workers introduced exotic trees* and plowed pastures.[2]

Scientific awareness glimmered in the late 1920s and early 1930s, when George M. Wright's pioneering biological research unit began studying the condition of wildlife in the national parks. Wright's central concern was that the human "hand of interference" be exercised as little as possible so that "every species [is] left to carry on its struggle for existence unaided."[3] For Wright, a glimpse of animals in a "wholly natural" setting defined the unique visitor experience parks are to provide. He urged that natural predators not be killed and that they be reintroduced where they had been extirpated. He advocated eliminating exotic species where feasible.[4]

Yet Wright knew that the presence of humans inevitably altered wildlife so he urged "constructive wildlife management": trained professional staff to intervene with restraint to combat the harmful effects of human influence. Unfortunately, Wright's early death muted the impact of his research.

Until well after World War II, according to a park service biologist, the National Park Service lacked both a substantive resource policy and professional scientists and resource managers:

---

*Exotic species, by definition, are those found in an area to which they are not native. Many are introduced into parks by humans; others are carried in by wind, water, and animals.

[I]n the parklands themselves, biological time-bombs had gone on tick-
ing through all the years of inattention. Now giant sequoias were lean-
ing and falling . . . fears were being expressed that DDT was becoming
an ever greater biological hazard, that the saguaros of Saguaro National
Monument were vanishing, that Yosemite Valley was becoming choked
beyond recognition by an unnatural . . . invasion of trees, that feral goats
threatened the survival of unique vegetation in the national parks of
Hawaii, and that Everglades National Park was dying of thirst.[5]

The situation came to a head in the early 1960s, when the park
service shot over 4,000 elk in Yellowstone. The elk herd's size had
grown after the park's wolves had been eliminated, and the service
believed that Yellowstone's aspens were being destroyed by the elks'
overgrazing.[6] But photographs of piles of bloody elk carcasses in
the newspapers and on television triggered such a public outcry
that a special advisory board on wildlife management was named,
chaired by A. Starker Leopold, zoologist and son of the famed Aldo
Leopold. "Although he didn't realize it would have this effect,"
says Yellowstone's Superintendent Robert D. Barbee, Leopold's
report "became a philosophic manifesto for managing wildlife in
national parks based on the principles of ecology."[7]

Leopold's report criticized many prevailing park management policies: the use of pesticides, the suppression of fire, the killing of
predators, and the failure to remove nonnative species. "In the same
category," the report said, "is artificial feeding of wildlife. Fed bears
become bums, and dangerous. Fed elk deplete natural ranges. Forage relationships in wild animals should be natural."[8]

A leap forward in ecological thinking for the park service in its
time, Leopold's report is often seen today as the charter for "letting
nature manage nature." In fact, the report did not call simply for
letting nature take its course. Parks were to be stabilized at a "desired
state" to look like "a vignette of primitive America." The "primary
goal" in managing national parks, it stated, was that "biotic associations within each park be maintained, or where necessary recreated,
as nearly as possible in the condition that prevailed when the area
was first visited by the white man." Yet parks were also recognized
as "biotic communities [that] change through natural stages of succession." Its goal was naturalness, but the report acknowledged
this could only be achieved through active management: "Management may at times call for the use of the tractor, chain-saw, rifle,
or flame-thrower but the signs and sounds of such activity should
be hidden from visitors insofar as possible."[9]

The report demanded authenticity but accepted "illusion," since naturalness had been grossly and often irreversibly disturbed:

> Restoring the primitive scene is not easily done nor can it be done completely. . . . A reasonable illusion of primitive America could be recreated, using the utmost in skill, judgment, and ecological sensitivity. . . . A visitor entering Grand Teton National Park from the south drives across Antelope Flats. But there are no antelope. . . . If the mountain men who gathered here in rendezvous fed their squaws on antelope, a 20th century tourist at least should be able to see a band of these animals. . . . The goal, we repeat, is to maintain or create the mood of wild America.[10]

The desired scene was romantic; it included, for example, changes wrought by certain humans, the American Indians, but not by others, the first white settlers.

The Leopold report and other efforts reflecting scientific thinking at the time, notably a privately funded reconnaissance of parks by Dr. F. Fraser Darling (an ecologist and vice-president of The Conservation Foundation) and Noel D. Eichhorn (a zoologist),[11] were embraced by the growing conservation community and soon became important influences on park policies.

Over the next two decades, the new approach—of understanding and encouraging natural processes—was applied with varying consistency and success.* Beginning in the mid-1970s, national parks adopted fire management plans that allowed naturally caused fires to burn and called for limited use of prescribed or controlled burning. Protecting forests from lightning-caused fires was, according to the Leopold report, as "unnatural" as indiscriminate burning.[13] By clearing out old and diseased trees and shrubs, accelerating the return of nutrients to the soil, killing insect pests, and stimulating the growth of young vegetation, fires maintain vigor and diversity in the forest.

---

*In 1964, new policy guidelines of the park service stated that: "Management [of natural areas] shall be directed toward maintaining, and where necessary reestablishing, indigenous plant and animal life, in keeping with the . . . recommendations of the Advisory Board on Wildlife Management." Park management policies in 1978 specifically stated that: "The concept of perpetuation of a total natural environment or ecosystem, as compared with the protection of individual features or species, is a distinguishing aspect of the service's management of natural lands."[12]

Protection from fires, ironically, makes forests more vulnerable
to them; because fuel has been allowed to accumulate, fires tend
to be more devastating and more difficult and costly to control. Management policies permitting fires to burn can be highly controversial,
even though park managers take into account nearby development
(such as visitor facilities and historic buildings) and problems from
resulting air pollution. Because of lack of knowledge about the beneficial role of forest fires, public reaction may range from fear to dis-
appointment over the look of charred areas.[14]

Coastal barrier beaches are another complex challenge to natural
system management. Barrier beaches protect the mainland from
oceanic storms and play a critical role in the lives of nesting and
migratory coastal birds. They make possible the continued existence
of wetlands and estuaries.[15] But wind and sea constantly reshape
barrier beaches.

The accessibility of many barrier beaches to the public makes them
prime recreational sites. Many such islands contain communities
of residents and tourist industries and have been altered by jetties,
large parking lots, and shore development that accelerate the natural
forces of erosion. When Cape Hatteras became part of the park system,* the federal government promised to stabilize the barrier
islands and protect residents from inundation and overwash.[20]
When other barrier beaches entered the system in the 1960s and
1970s, similar protection, if not promised, was often assumed.

Barrier island policies illustrate the tension between the park service's mission to both preserve resources and make them accessible.
As experts realized that the constant reshaping of barrier beaches
was a natural phenomenon with many important benefits, the park
service tried to back off expensive beach replenishment policies.
Its 1978 guidelines state that "shoreline processes . . . will be allowed to take place naturally, except [emphasis added] where control measures, required by law or Service commitment, are necessary
to protect life and property in neighboring areas."[17]

In Cape Cod, Indiana Dunes, and Gateway, controversies over
the "commitment" continue. Efforts to replenish beaches at Indiana
Dunes require substantial costs. The decision about whether to fight
erosion of the "hook" at Sandy Hook in Gateway, which gives ac-

---

*Authorized in 1937, Cape Hatteras National Seashore was the service's
first unit with a barrier coastline.

cess to the barrier island beach, has yet to be made. In Cape Cod, a compromise was finally reached after the park service balked at rebuilding a storm-damaged parking lot believed to contribute to beach drift (see the Cape Cod profile).[18]

Perhaps the most widely aired challenge facing the park service in natural process management is the grizzly bears' fate at Yellowstone (see the Yellowstone profile). Threats to the grizzly's future derive from many sources: the pressures of civilization, which have drastically reduced habitat inside and outside the park; weak laws and inconsistent enforcement of laws in the region with respect to hunting and poaching; and former policies of the park service, which tragically allowed the grizzly to get hooked on human garbage, fostering contacts with people that endangered bears *and* people.

Today, the park service is attempting to reduce contact between bears and visitors inside the park. Working with a special Interagency Grizzly Bear Committee representing federal and state agencies that control the bear's habitat, it is trying to establish a self-regulating equilibrium between Yellowstone's remaining bear population and reduced habitat in the Yellowstone ecosystem.[19]

As scientists from George Wright on have understood, maintaining and restoring natural processes in parks that accommodate people calls for knowledge and, inevitably, compromise. Because most parks are no longer pristine, and all are designed to accommodate some presence of people, active management is paradoxically needed to maintain the aura of naturalness. In many instances, there is no unqualified agreement about why a particular resource is under stress, or what to do about it. Human-caused alterations may be combined with natural forces, especially when parks enter the system with resources already degraded and manipulated. (See box on the Everglades.)

Growing scientific understanding has helped to transform yesterday's "fairytale management" of natural resources to today's respect for natural processes. Yet, given the altered state of park resources and the continued influence of humans, management is inevitably more of a philosophy than a science—and one fraught with controversy at that: "The natural scientist cannot . . . solve the political problems that may result from the implementation of his or her recommendations. . . . Nor can science address aesthetic or emotional conflicts, as opposed to ecological ones."

## The Everglades

Early in this century, Florida Governor Napoleon Bonaparte Broward began zealously fulfilling a campaign pledge to drain the Everglades.[1] At that time, the grassy marshland—actually a slow-moving sheet of water—covered most of the Florida peninsula south of Lake Okeechobee.[2] The efforts of Broward and his successors to reclaim the land for agriculture, towns, and industry altered this natural sheet flow, a key element for the continued survival of the Everglades ecosystem. The vision of productive lands was more than fulfilled, but the reclamation had other unanticipated effects.

A long-time visitor to Florida's Everglades recalls when "you could hear the panthers scream at night. In the morning, the birds were so thick you would have to shoo them away."[3] The panther was once plentiful throughout the Southeast, but increased urbanization has reduced its numbers to an estimated 30 in the Everglades region.[4] The plight of the panther is indicative of resource problems confronting other wildlife in the south Florida wetlands. Over a dozen other Everglades animals are listed under the Endangered Species Act.[5] For some, like the West Indian manatee, decline is associated with stress from increased recreational boating activities along the coast. For others, such as the snail kite, decline is linked directly to the loss of suitable habitat from the alteration of the Everglades ecosystem. During the last 40 years, the population of freshwater wading birds in the park has declined by 90 percent.[6]

To be sure, the Everglades even after a century of draining still present a striking and varied system of marshes, sloughs, prairies, pinelands, hardwood hammocks, and mangrove islands. Some of the inhabitants, particularly birds, seem to be recovering, thanks to cooperative efforts of federal, state, local, and private organizations and other influences, such as the ban on DDT in the early 1970s. But beneath the surface is an ecological time bomb.

The Everglades begin at Lake Okeechobee, where 750 square miles of water surface are fed by the Kissimmee River and a complex chain of lakes and streams just south of Orlando, Florida.[7] Before the ecosystem was altered, water overflowed Lake Okeechobee and fanned slowly southward a hundred miles to the Gulf of Mexico. Over the years, in a series of increasingly complex endeavors, Lake Okeechobee was diked, and a series of levees and canals channeled the flow. In the late 1940s, after water inundated farmland and flooded streets in suburban Miami, the U.S. Army Corps of Engineers initiated the Central and Southern Florida Flood Control Project. This $1-billion-dollar program included construction and improvement of 1,400 miles of canals and levees and the installation of tide gates, floodgates, and huge pumps to drain potential farmland.[8] East-West highways through the Everglades further blocked the southward flow of water.

However, it was the channelization of the Kissimmee River in the 1950s and 1960s that most severely affected the Everglades system. A 200-foot wide canal rerouted the once-meandering river into a fast-flowing, 52-mile channel running parallel to its original course. Over 80 percent of its marshlands were lost.[9] As one journalist has written: "[N]o single drainage scheme may have had a more devastating effect on Florida's water, its wildlife, its vegetation, and probably its climate than the channelization of the Kissimmee River."[10]

The hard-fought effort to create the Everglades National Park was intended to protect a portion of this unique, pristine wilderness. However, the boundaries, which include nearly 1.4 million acres, were drawn by politics, not ecology, and water flow to the park could not be isolated from the manipulated ecosystem around it. The Everglades park lies virtually at the mouth of a water supply restricted by the complex maze of levees and dikes.

The park's water needs, until recently, were given low priority in the region's web of conflicting federal, state, and regional land management policies and interests. During dry years, nearly all the water was diverted to farmlands and cities before reaching the park. At other times, abnormally high quantities were sluiced through the park to prevent flooding to the north.[11] Federal legislation ensures minimum flows in the park—adequate to prevent fires, though not necessarily sufficient for wildlife—but sets no maximum limits.[12] During a high-water period in 1983, for example, more than 5 billion gallons a day were flushed through Shark River Slough, an amount far greater than normal and at the height of the dry season.[13]

A scientific study team working inside Everglades National Park since 1976 has gathered extensive data on the extent and effects of the radically changed environment in the Everglades region and its implications for resource management problems in the park. The disrupted terrain has affected the health of indigenous species and made them less able to withstand the rapid invasion of exotic plants and animals.[14] Prolonged reductions in waterflow to the park have converted some wetlands into upland ecosystems. At the other extreme, sudden large discharges destroy the nests of wading birds and alligators. Fish populations in the Florida Bay have declined sharply—some say up to 50 percent—as a result of unnaturally high salinity and virtually unregulated commercial and sports fishing.[15] Nathaniel Reed, former assistant secretary of the interior for fish and wildlife and parks, says the park is "on the brink of death."[16]

Programs are under way to undo some of the damage and to try to manage water flows so that they simulate natural conditions more closely. In 1983, the South Florida Water Management District agreed to a park service plan for releasing water into the park to simulate seasonal flows.[17] In November 1983, Congress enacted legislation requiring an experimental two-year water delivery program for the Everglades, to be monitored by the corps.[17] The corps has modified levees and canals to reduce the large and sudden volumes of discharge in certain park locations.

In August 1983, Governor Bob Graham initiated a seven-point "Save Our Everglades" emergency program, which includes a demonstration restoration of a portion of the Kissimmee River and state acquisition and reflooding of a 95-square-mile area between Lake Okeechobee and Big Cypress National Preserve. One appealing aspect of this program is its comprehensive orientation: the whole Everglades drainage basin is being regarded as an integrated system rather than as an assortment of separate streams, marshes, and lakes. Former U.S. Fish and Wildlife Service biologist and Everglades expert Arthur R. Marshall has developed an even more ambitious plan (Florida's "Marshall Plan"), which calls for repair of the entire Kissimmee/Okeechobee/Everglades system. He believes that draining marshland and rerouting Okeechobee's natural flow has interrupted Florida's "rain machine." His repair plan would dechannelize the Kissimmee, remove blocking spillways and levees south of Lake Okeechobee, install culverts under the roadways, and generally provide for a relatively natural flow from Lake Okeechobee to and through the national park and preserve.[19]

Graham hopes that, as a result of his program, in the year 2000 the Everglades "will look and function more as it did in 1900 than it does today."[20] Says Park Superintendent Jack Moorhead, "We can improve it now if we act soon, but we can never get it back to what it once was."[21]

### Historical and Cultural Resources

The park system collection of historical and cultural resources is enormous, among the largest in the world. Given the rising public interest in historic preservation, the collection deserves, but has not traditionally received, prominence among the park service's responsibilities.

Of the 334 units in the National Park System, 194, or 57 percent (although only a very small percentage of the land area), are managed specifically as cultural and historical units.[21] In addition, many of the other units, including Yellowstone, Yosemite, and Mount Rainier, along with recently added units near urban areas, contain major cultural and historical resources. The service's List of Classified Structures, which identifies historic structures within the system, includes over 10,000 entries, and the official estimate of "museum objects and artifacts of historical significance" comes to 10 million.[22]

The responsibilities of the park service for cultural and historical resources date back to its beginning. The purpose of the parks, as set forth in the 1916 act, was not only to conserve scenery, natural objects, and wildlife, but also "historic objects."[23] This has been reiterated and expanded in key legislation that makes the agency the focal point of federal leadership in "preserving, restoring, and maintaining the historic and cultural environment of the Nation," both inside the parks (its "internal" responsibilities) and throughout the country (its "external" responsibilities).[24] The park service, for example, administers the National Register of Historic Places, the National Historic Landmarks Program, the Historic American Buildings Survey, and the investment tax credit program, under which

*Fredericksburg, November 1984. Ranger cataloging Civil War artifacts.*

historic preservation projects throughout the country have attracted some $7 billion of private investment.[25]

In the 1930s, the park service began acquiring historic properties and building a small professional staff in Washington. It has since rescued a number of the nation's significant buildings and other cultural resources. In Boston, Philadelphia, and the nation's capital, especially, park service presence measurably enhanced the condition, management, and interpretation of treasured buildings. The service is comfortable in the role as steward of historic resources with undisputed national significance, using the highest professional standards to guide physical restoration.

Within the service, however, the perceived core responsibility has always been natural areas.[26] The service's central mission is associated with the great western parks, not military battlefields; with Old Faithful, not the Liberty Bell.

The second-class status of cultural and historical resource management has manifested itself in several ways. Typically, park service staff with responsibility for historical and cultural units, especially in the "cannonball" parks, have complained of being out of the mainstream and of not faring well in the competition for funds and staff. In units not set aside specifically as historical, park staff have tended to regard old buildings—forts, settlements, ranches, taverns, foundries, outbuildings, and the like—as "intrusions" on the landscape and to assume that these intrusions ultimately would be razed in favor of returning the land to a more natural state. As recently as the early 1970s, a high park service official frankly acknowledged, he tried whenever possible "to get rid of old buildings" in the parks.

The service's view of historic preservation has been changing during the last two decades, creating new demands on park managers. The potential significance of many buildings is being recognized as public interest in historic preservation expands. And the park system units added in the 1960s and 1970s have more preexisting development to contend with than older parks. Golden Gate National Recreation Area, for example, had more historic buildings within its boundaries than did all the other parks in the western region combined.[27] However, park managers have until recently been given little technical assistance or staff support for determining which buildings were historically significant, for repairing and renovating them, or for finding uses for them.

The legacy of neglect is costly. Despite the Park Restoration and Improvement Program (PRIP)—the $1 billion crash program to improve park infrastructure that benefited some historic buildings— many historical structures are in disrepair for want of maintenance. The examples range from El Morro, the 16th-century fort guarding San Juan Harbor, crumbling from water damage, to President Taft's home, a national historic site since 1969, but until 1982 without restoration funds, to the W'pama, a historic ship that belongs to the Golden Gate National Recreation Area.[28] Moreover, moldering unclassified papers, records, and objects are often stacked in basements, back rooms, and warehouses without adequate climate, dust, and humidity control. Rich archaeological information in many parks has not been sampled adequately, much less surveyed.[29]

In many respects, protecting cultural and historical properties within the parks raises issues akin to those of natural resources: increased awareness of the problem and respect for the resources does not easily translate into effective management decisions. More information and experts are needed. Cultural resources are threatened by what happens both inside and outside the parks. The park service needs more staff trained in the complex issues of cultural resource management. And improvements must be made not only in obtaining compliance with in-place procedures—such as the consultation requirements of the National Historic Preservation Act[30] and the preparation of adequate resource management plans linked to project proposals and budgets—but also in fashioning new responses to which park personnel may not be accustomed—such as leasing of historic properties and adaptive reuse.

Managing historic buildings presents unique problems. Time, an ally in managing nature, is more of an enemy and less of a healer with historical resources. Fires, including those caused by lightning, burn down settlers' cabins; waves along the shore threaten to wash away historic dwellings; and tornadoes, earthquakes, and severe fluctuations in temperature may severely damage structures. Without regular maintenance, buildings fall into disrepair, and fixing them becomes more expensive. Using buildings is often the best way to ensure upkeep and to protect the landscape—but today the park service is steward of many empty buildings, including some bought from occupants.

Managing these resources requires people with special skills and attitudes. Moreover, cultural resource protection requires distinctive tools. A number of park managers have, until recently, been unfamiliar with or reluctant to use some of the very programs the park service administers—the National Register of Historic Places, for example—or to follow, with regularity, established procedures for consulting with state historic preservation officers when modifying historically significant buildings. Park managers sometimes view a building's designation as historic as a problem—a constraint to their freedom of management.

Perhaps the greatest difference between natural and cultural resources is that no one questions whether stewardship of natural resources is central to the park service's mission. A system to correct shortcomings in managing natural resources is usually debated in terms of costs, means, and priorities, but the basic premise—that the service is supposed to protect natural resources—is not usually questioned. At times, there has been no such consensus about cultural resources. "We've got to win the minds and hearts of park managers," said Jerry Rogers, associate director for cultural resources, in 1983.

In 1979, after surveys by conservation groups culminated in strong congressional pressure, the park service undertook a survey to identify problems that "have the potential to cause significant damage to park resources or to seriously degrade important park values or park visitor experiences."[31] Superintendents in over 300 units responded to the questionnaire and identified more than 4,300 threats to resources. The publication *State of the Parks 1980: Report to the Congress* reported survey responses ranging from the effects of heavy visitor use and vandalism inside to air pollution and destruction of wildlife habitat from activities outside the parks.

Cultural resource issues, preservationists charged, were given short shrift in the 1980 report. Despite some examples of threats to cultural resources, the report emphasized natural resources.* Charging that reporting on the state of cultural resources was "deficient," Representative John Seiberling's (D.-Ohio) staff review concluded that cultural resources were near the "bottom" of priorities in terms of service policies, programs, and personnel.[33]

A separate park service report on *Threats to Cultural Resources*, published in 1982, concurred, emphasizing that "poor communication, lack of training, ignorance of management policies, or misguided intentions" were the major threats to cultural resources. (The report also made clear, however, that cultural resources face such problems as inadequate boundaries, intrusive development, and air pollution—especially acid rain.[34])

The park service has taken various steps to improve its management of cultural resources. Directives now require that park managers obtain permission from higher authorities before demolishing any building listed, or eligible for listing, on the National Register; in the case of listed buildings over 50 years old, this approval must be obtained from the director. Cultural resources have been given new prominence within the park service hierarchy with the creation of a chief curator and an associate director for cultural resources.[35]

The service must also grapple with differences among experts on historical and cultural preservation. Professionals differ about the standards determining a building's or district's significance. The nomination of Nike missile sites, obsolete airfields, and early visitor cabins as historic districts makes some wince. Decisions about which cultural resources to include in the system, and what to do about them once in it, are often heavily influenced by local sentiment and politics.

---

*Some officials believe the park service cultural resources staff shares some responsibility for this outcome, because it did not press for a stronger role when the *State of the Parks* report was being prepared.

Differences also exist over "treatment." Given that every building should not have a "Cadillac" restoration, what standards should guide choices to stabilize, renovate, or restore? What should be done with ruins (reconstruct, create a "ghost structure," leave "as is")? What should be done about damage by natural forces? The park service's justified reputation for quality has sometimes meant a choice between high-quality restoration or demolition. As a historic preservationist commented during a meeting convened for this study, "Too often, the National Park Service has aimed for the best and in falling short . . . may not have been sufficiently energetic . . . to define what is the good, the acceptable, and reasonable."[36] Experts also differ about the appropriateness, in federal parks, of some types of interpretative programs, such as "living history," where actors dress in period costumes and role-play.

The service has trouble responding to newer historic preservation trends that move beyond the "feature" to an entire setting, offering insights into the distinctive human and economic forces that shaped our cities and countryside. Conserving and maintaining such special places requires respect for lesser buildings that make up the "historic fabric" or "cultural landscape" and different management responses to retain residents and encourage appropriate uses. Lowell National Historical Park, Cape Cod National Seashore, and the Olema Valley in Golden Gate National Recreation Area are but a few of the park service's models.

Cultural resource management issues arise from distinct needs in an agency geared to natural resource values and from contrasting professional opinions. Park service involvement in its private or "external" historic preservation activities enriches park service management of its own properties, since it fosters dialogue with professional peers, private organizations, developers, and state preservation officials outside the service.

**Threats to Park Resources**

The continuing growth of threats to park resources is another source of complexity in park stewardship. The 1980 *State of the Parks* survey uncovered diverse pressures on park resources. The problems reported in the survey varied in scale and magnitude from park to park. Aesthetic degradation was the most frequently reported threat, followed by air pollution, logging and mining, the encroachment of exotic plants and animals, visitor impacts and pollution, and inadequate water supply. A notable concern raised by superintendents was the paucity of data to docum  t and corroborate the reported pressures.[37] Moreover, the source of more than half of the reported pressures was outside park boundaries. Following release of *State of the Parks 1980*, Robert Cahn wrote that these "threats to the national park resources and values are the most serious they have ever been."[38]

## Pressures from Inside

Of all the pressures reported by superintendents, visitor use and abuse are the most familiar as well as the most intertwined with the National Park Service's fundamental mission. In the broadest sense, every visitor is a threat to park resources. "The very presence of park visitors necessitates vehicle use and . . . facilities . . . [p]ark roads, trails, concession accommodations, utilities, access routes, sewage lagoons, [and] landfills," the report notes.[39]

Even activities most compatible with park resources—picnicking, camping, hiking, and backpacking—leave a mark. Over time, campers can virtually eliminate the understory vegetation around a campsite. Archaeological and historical sites suffer from daily wear and

*Yellowstone, August 1984.*

tear as well. Human activities can unintentionally disturb the natural behavior of animals, the very presence of visitors may exclude wildlife from limited water sources or prime feeding grounds. Insensitive visitors cause more damage by breaking off branches or chopping down or uprooting small, young trees for firewood.* Careless hikers hasten dune erosion by their trampling and create "informal" trails by walking across delicate alpine vegetation. They build campfires in the wrong places. They litter.

Such visitor-related problems are inevitable if resources are to remain accessible. "To fence the people out would surely preserve the parks, in an abstract sense," Norman Newton, a noted landscape architect and author, observes. "But the parks are for people to enjoy; their justification is in their human values. Again and again one feels the insistence of that ultimate calculus."[40] Despite introducing, in the 1970s, more sophisticated techniques for handling crowds—limiting stays in some popular or fragile camping and backcountry areas and educating visitors about their unintentional disruptive effects—the service still faces a challenge dealing with the effects of visitors, even those whose activities seem most compatible with both resource protection and park accessibility.

Visitor impacts sometimes entail clear-cut abuse. Vandalism and theft are ongoing problems, particularly in historical and cultural parks. Petersburg National Battlefield exhibits have been toppled and cannons rolled down hills. At Gettysburg, vandals have stolen or damaged monuments and battlefield markers. At San Antonio Missions, church artifacts have been defaced and graffiti scrawled on walls and religious sculptures. Arson has caused the loss of hardwood hammocks in the Everglades and cultural resources at Knife River Indian Villages.[41]

In between the extremes of compatible and incompatible are a range of visitor activities on which the park service—drawing on tradition, the legislation establishing a specific park, and its judgments about the effects on resources—must decide about appropriateness. Preestablished patterns of recreation are difficult to disestablish, for example, as in the case of off-road vehicle (ORV) use. Uses based on one set of values often remain when values change—

---

*Even the use of downed timber, long an accepted practice in national parks, has its ecological impacts, since downed wood provides habitat for small animals and ultimately returns nutrients to the soil.

hotels or full-service recreational vehicle campgrounds in sensitive natural areas, for example.

When limits are proposed, either by the park service or by conservationists, sound data linking use to adverse effect are needed. In 1977, for example, ORV use that caused considerable damage to vegetation, wildlife habitats, and other resources was banned by executive order.[42] Nevertheless, pressures to allow ORVs are strong, especially at some national recreation and national seashore areas. Restricted to zones, ORV use continues in some units as park personnel struggle to document damage, curb violations, and mitigate effects.[43]

Historical parks such as Kennesaw Mountain and Valley Forge, carved from once-rural areas, are now subject to more urban and suburban recreational demands—for example, people flying kites or repairing cars.[44] The park service finds it difficult to restrict recreation to activities that do not threaten the historical integrity of the parks.

As new recreational interests develop—for example, snowmobiling and hang gliding—the service must respond. Some managers are ambivalent about the growing winter use of parks, questioning the effects on wildlife and the difficulty of adequately policing snowmobilers. The service decided, however, that spreading visitation throughout the year makes more sense than not and, in 1982, in cooperation with *Snow Goer* magazine, published a *National Parks Winter Fun Guide*, which encouraged readers to snowmobile in 24 park units, including Bryce Canyon and Yellowstone.[45]

Hunting and trapping are a source of continuing controversy. Department of the Interior regulations forbid hunting and trapping in most national park units. However, hunting is specifically authorized in 45 units, mainly national recreation areas, scenic rivers, and national seashores. Trapping is explicitly permitted in 20 of these units, prohibited in 14, and has occurred in the remaining 11 because those park managers interpreted hunting to include trapping.[46] In 1984, the service issued new regulations prohibiting trapping as of January 15, 1985, unless specifically authorized in a park's enabling legislation.[47] The National Rifle Association filed suit, claiming that hunting and trapping are historical uses of the parks and conform to the 1916 National Park Service Act in that they are legitimate activities for enjoying the parks.[48]* The National Parks and Conservation Association, on the other hand, worries that hunting might be allowed in virtually every national park, since very few have legislative language specifically forbidding these activities.[49]

Sometimes the real issue is less the physical damage to resources caused by visitors than the effect they have in diminishing for others an experience rarely possible outside national parks. Crowds around the most popular natural or cultural features trample ground cover; yet strategies to reduce resource damage may be aesthetically offensive. Bleacher seats make it more convenient for people to see Old Faithful, but crowds inevitably affect the experience of the natural phenomenon. The Liberty Bell now hangs in a modern vandal-proof structure;† making the Liberty Bell accessible and protecting Independence Hall have had to take precedence over the "authentic" experience of viewing the bell in its original place. (See box on Independence National Historical Park.)

Some areas can reconcile authenticity and accessibility more gracefully, although imperfectly. In Yellowstone, a little way from Old Faithful, lie miles of quite untouched areas. "The crowds are one of Yellowstone's big problems," a reporter writes of a 1983 visit, "and it is sad to think they may be the chief impression many visitors take home. Nevertheless, even when you are fighting the throngs, the park provides unending spectacles; and the quiet places, after you take a look around, are easily found."

*Inholdings*

People think of national parks as places with "entrances," fixed boundaries that divide the area inside the park from that outside.

---

*At present, under interim regulations, trapping is allowed to continue in 4 of the 11 units in question: Delaware Water Gap National Recreation Area, Buffalo National River, St. Croix National Scenic Riverway, and Ozark National Scenic Riverway.

†The bell originally hung in the tower of Independence Hall. During the 1800s, it was moved to Independence Hall's lobby and then in 1976, across the street to its present 24-hour-accessible location.

## Independence National Historical Park

On a quiet Sunday morning, you can ride a horse-drawn carriage along Chestnut Street in Philadelphia. Stopping between Fifth and Sixth streets, you begin a visit to one of the most historic square miles in America. Independence National Historical Park, consisting of some 40 historic buildings scattered throughout 17 city blocks,[1] is an architectural collage evoking the events and personalities significant in America's formative years.

The most well-known building is Independence Hall, the handsome Georgian structure where the Declaration of Independence was signed and the U.S. Constitution was drafted. Dwarfed today by modern towers nearby, Independence Hall was, in its time, one of the largest buildings in the colonies.[2] One city block away is the Second Bank of the United States,

a Greek revival structure inspired by the Parthenon. Another city block away is the First Bank of the United States, the oldest bank building in America and an impressive example of Federal architecture.[3] At several sites, the story of Ben Franklin's immensely productive life unfolds.

If you returned on Monday, you would experience Independence Square as a living, pulsing part of downtown Philadelphia, with thousands of people moving about. This national park is in the midst of a metropolitan area with a population of about four million people.

The building, grounds, and museum collections at Independence National Historical Park are continually battered by the press of people and an urban environment with air-borne pollutants, traffic vibrations, and noise. The buildings were not struc-

Although many parks have entrances and all have fixed boundaries, from the park manager's perspective the boundaries are not hard and fast. Many parks—even Yellowstone, the prototype reserve carved from public lands—have, within their boundaries, some lands that either are owned by private individuals or businesses, other federal agencies, or state and local governments or are encumbered by some form of private rights to mine, graze cattle, or otherwise gain access to parklands.*

The growing number of private and public inholders, together with the lack of money for land acquisition (the traditional response by the park service to private landholders within park boundaries), exposes a gray area in managing park resources: How much control

---

*These diverse holdings inside park boundaries are referred to as inholdings in this discussion, although this use of the term differs from that used either by the National Park Service or the National Inholders Association, an advocacy group created in 1978 (see box on Inholdings).

turally designed for the weight and wear of over a million visitors a year. The marble columns of the First Bank of the United States were not made to withstand the corrosive effects of rain- and dust-borne acids. The deteriorating effects of heat and cold, humidity and dryness, especially affect museum collections inside buildings.

The tower at Independence Hall, just one part of one important building in the National Park System, has not had the maintenance and periodic care needed to ensure its preservation. Between the mid-1960s and 1982, no major work was done on the tower. In 1982, an estimated $175,000 was spent, an amount difficult to target to a single project while hundreds of lesser projects in the region needed funding.[4] Funds for carpentry and repainting are now programmed for a regular five-year cycle.

Yet Independence National Historical Park is in a fortunate position compared to other park units of historical significance. As one of the true gems of the National Park System, its staff of cultural resources professionals is the largest in the system. There are two historical architects on the staff, three historians, and a curatorial staff of five.[5] Many of the other historical parks in the system lack staff in at least one, if not all, of these disciplines.

Independence National Historical Park is a product of urban history too, and its rebirth as a federal park was accompanied by complex state, city, and federal negotiations, exchanges of agreements and funds, and a mix of urban renewal and historic preservation. Although sometimes criticized for extensive clearance of buildings in the areas, the park helped catalyze a wave of residential renovation in the adjacent Society Hill neighborhood and, thus, represents a landmark in the nation's change of perspective about the value of old city neighborhoods.

should the park service have over lands that lie within park boundaries but are owned by others? The service has been accused by the National Inholders Association of meddling with private property[50] and by conservationists of excessive timidity.

While some inholdings have long been a fact of life for park managers, inholders and concerns about them have increased significantly since the 1960s, when a number of parks near settled urban areas were added to the system. Inholders are now more diverse and their activities within park boundaries more troublesome. A business inside Cuyahoga Valley National Recreation Area removed topsoil for commercial sale. In mid-1984, the private owners of 160 acres inside Grand Teton National Park sought to develop their property. At Harpers Ferry National Historical Park, a landowner clear-cut his land and erected a prefabricated house on a highly visible hill at the entrance to the park.[51]

Long-standing mining and grazing rights inside parks also place pressure on park resources and managers. Mineral entry rights and

## Inholdings

Interior Secretary Franklin Lane's letter to Stephen Mather in 1918, often considered the Magna Carta of the National Park Service, established the concept of inholdings and park service policy toward them: "There are many private holdings in the national parks, and many of these seriously hamper the administration of these reservations. All of them should be eliminated as far as is practicable to accomplish this purpose in the course of time, either through Congressional appropriation or by acceptance of donation of these lands. Isolated tracts in important scenic areas should be given first consideration, of course, in the purchase of private property."[1] Essentially the same language was repeated in the more formal statement of national park policies published in 1925.[2]

Officially, this was the servicewide view of inholdings until 1979.[3] When Lane wrote his letter, parks were overwhelmingly designated from publicly held land. Practice and legal authority, however, changed as parks with more private holdings came into the system; bargains were struck that involved a variety of encumbrances on parklands, including mining and grazing rights and forms of access. Congress did not, as a rule, appropriate funds to buy lands that were privately owned but acquired them by donations, either from the owners or from states and local governments that had first bought them.

When Cape Cod National Seashore was established in 1961, for the first time an explicit framework was formed under which hundreds of owner-occupied homes would remain in private ownership, indefinitely, inside park boundaries.[4] Modifications of this model, which depended on the appropriate local government passing compatible zoning, were adopted as other new parks were authorized in or near built-up areas. Ultimate acquisition-in-fee of private lands within parks authorized before 1959 remained official policy, however.[5]

A revised land acquisition policy issued by the park service in 1979 provided that land be acquired on a willing-seller basis (that is, lands would not be acquired unless the owner wanted to sell) in parks established before July 1959, unless there was a threat of incompatible use; in parks authorized after that date, acquisition policy was to be determined on a park-by-park basis according to the unit's particular authorizing legislation.[6]

Under the 1979 policy, the term *inholding* was restricted officially to parks designated before July 1, 1959; all other units were called "newly-authorized areas."[7] The Reagan administration in 1983 revoked the 1979 land acquisition policy but did not provide a new definition of inholding.[8] The Park Service Land Acquisitions Office continues to use the 1979 definition of "inholding areas" and "newly-authorized areas."

The National Inholders Association, established in 1978, defines the term more broadly to include anyone "who owns property or any kind of equity interest within the boundary" of any federal, state, or local area "or is impacted by the management, regulation, or access of that area."[9] Thus, an inholder may own a home or property; have a lease for grazing, access, or residence; hold a mining claim; have a permit for use of an area for a residence, grazing, or mining; hold a permit to do business in the park; or own land adjacent to a federal or state land boundary. The National Inholders Association limits its constituency to private property interests.

leasing of federally owned minerals exist in about 11 units.[52] More-over, the energy crisis exposed the vulnerability of national parks to the possibility of thousands of claims by individuals, businesses, and states to explore for natural gas, oil, and coal. In the 1960s and 1970s, several units were established, such as Padre Island National Seashore and Jean Lafitte National Historic Park, in which only the surface estate was acquired by the park service, and Congress authorized the extraction of gas and oil by subsurface owners.[53] Coal mining could also have a great impact on park resources. Information provided by the park service indicates that there are 25 units where the U.S. Geological Survey has determined that coal definitely underlies all or part of the park; within these, there are some 963,000 acres of private holdings or split estates that may qualify as valid existing rights.*[54] While a system for regulating various mining activities associated with legitimate claims to ensure that the primary resources of each unit are protected may be in place as envisioned by Congress, the problem is often one of inadequate staffing and funding to maintain surveillance over mining activities. In Alaska, for example, where there are over 3,000 claims and only a small staff with few trained in minerals management, two experts have called attention to the service's "critical manpower shortage" in dealing with this "burgeoning problem area."[56]

Cattle grazing is another example of preexisting rights expressly protected when public and private lands were assembled into park system units. About two million acres of parklands are grazed under a variety of permit arrangements from the park service.[57]

Side by side with growing pressures by inholders is the growing recognition that new concepts in park creation depend on nurturing compatible economic and other activities on lands not owned outright by the park service. Expectations about the future of some inholdings, or lands within park boundaries not owned by the park service, changed significantly after 1961, as variations of the ap-

---

*These figures may overstate the problem, since coal may not be found under all of the privately held land and not all of it would be economically feasible to mine. Under the Surface Mining Act of 1977, subject to "valid existing rights," no coal mining is allowed within the borders of any national park; the act also prohibits any mining activity outside parkland that would adversely affect the park.[55] Recent changes, which loosened the definition of valid existing rights, were overturned by a federal court in early 1985.

proach used in the Cape Cod National Seashore were applied in creating other parks. Management to promote compatibility between the parks and activities within them on land not owned by the park service is a matter of increasing importance and will pose serious challenges to park resources and managers in the years ahead.

### Threats from Outside

For all the attention given to the dilemma of preservation versus use inside parks, neither increased pressures by visitors nor incompatible activities by inholders necessarily present the most difficult problems in maintaining the long-term integrity of the park system. As noted earlier, the State of the Parks 1980 report found that more than half of the reported threats—water and air pollution, water supply and quality problems, visual and aesthetic intrusions—either originated entirely or largely outside park boundaries.

"Problems associated with sources located outside the park boundaries," according to National Park Service officials who prepared a follow-up study to the State of the Parks report, "are considerably more complex and much more difficult to deal with.[58]

One of the park system's fundamental mandates is to maintain and conserve wildlife. Yet few national parks encompass within their boundaries the entire ecosystems necessary to maintain natural balance for certain species.[59] The size of a park is particularly crucial for large mammals, whose ranges or migration routes often encompass hundreds of square miles and seasonally extend outside park boundaries. Experts claim that the serious—perhaps fatal—decline of the grizzly bear in Yellowstone National Park is primarily the result of habitat destruction throughout the bear's enormous range.[60] Inadequate acreage also may reduce genetic diversity, resulting in long-term species decline. Extensive development around park boundaries disrupts the natural migration of wildlife in and out of the park, resulting in population isolation and the loss of the genetic exchange that keeps wildlife populations healthy.[61]

Other factors besides park size are linked to species decline. The dramatic decline in peregrine falcons by the mid-1960s, for example, was found to be caused by pesticide residues that altered the birds' breeding physiology. Increased commercial tourism and private boating in southeastern Alaskan waters, particularly around Glacier Bay National Park and Preserve, seem to be the reason why so few humpback whales are being sighted in this area.[62] In many instances, the park service is working with other agencies in trying to shield the young from the hostile forces in the environment, attempting to address long-range solutions to the underlying cause of their decline and thus, to the extent possible, reduce the level of threat.[63]

Deteriorating air quality can seriously diminish the aesthetic and physical experience in the parks. With a few exceptions (automobile exhaust and campfire smoke in Yosemite Valley, for example), air pollution in the parks is carried from outside by prevailing winds. The Grand Canyon's magnificent colors have sometimes been blurred by haze for a third of the year.[64] Some effects of air pollution are not visible. Emissions from smelters and generating plants, for example, contain acids and other chemicals brought to the parks in rain and dust, polluting streams and lakes or the atmosphere. Evidence of damage to park waters and biota is well researched and demonstrable, but establishing a direct link to the origin is difficult. The same is true of the effects of acid rain on cultural resources in parks throughout the country.[65]

Although concerns about water ranked low among those reported in the State of the Parks survey, the essential roles that water quality and quantity play in maintaining natural ecosystems impart a special urgency to the problem. Streams that flow through some parks carry a cargo of sewage, agricultural pesticides, industrial chemicals, and sediment that can prevent human use of the waters, threaten human health, poison fish and waterfowl, and kill aquatic vegetation. Surface pollutants leach into streams flowing into Mammoth Cave National Park, for example, threatening human health and rare shrimp and mussel species.*[66]

Pollution, serious as it is, may not be the most significant water problem the parks face. Given the competing demands by urban development, agriculture, and industry, some parks—particularly in the West—find themselves fighting for water to support wildlife, fish, and vegetation, to serve the needs of visitors, and to maintain

---

*External threats are not the only source of water pollution in the parks. Pollution from unknown sources inside the park, for example, is diminishing the clarity of Crater Lake, which has a unique blue color attributed to the filtering out of all but the sun's blue rays by the crystal-clear water.[67] Some parks with communities inside or adjacent to their boundaries, such as Cape Hatteras and New River, have inadequate sewage treatment facilities and growing in-park populations.[68]

popular visitor activities such as swimming and boating. Some rivers
and streams in arid western national parks are sucked dry in the
summer by legal uses upstream.[69]

Intrusive development is an important cause of aesthetic degradation, the most frequently reported threat in the State of the Parks
report.[70] Many pressures reported separately—urban encroachment,
utility infrastructure, mineral exploration, logging—clearly are part
of the same set of problems that degrade scenic vistas and the special
park experience. Intrusive development is often associated with the
gateway facilities around park entrances, such as Gatlinburg, just
outside Great Smoky, where neon signs, strip development, billboards, and the like line the highway. Such development, critics
argue, does not provide the proper introduction to a great national
park. Many otherwise acceptable activities offend the senses in this
context—one does not want to "see" industry or hear machinery
when visiting a national park. The activity may be objectionable
for its physical effects as well: herbicides used in maintaining utility
lines can damage other vegetation and organisms; logging outside
a park can reduce habitat and exacerbate erosion; proposed geothermal operations near Yellowstone could damage the geysers.[71]

Exotic species encroachment presents yet another threat to some
park units. In a 1984 listing of systemwide natural resource protection priorities, 6 of the top 20 dealt with exotics.[72] Exotic species
are often hardier than native flora or fauna. For example, the tama-
risk, or salt cedar, has invaded watercourses in a number of parks
in the arid Southwest. Its rapid growth crowds native vegetation
and consumes large quantities of water, thereby eliminating sources
of water needed by native wildlife.[73] The costs and difficulties of
removing exotics can be formidable and could involve the use of
pesticides detrimental to other park resources.[74]

A final environmental pressure cited in State of the Parks 1980
is noise. It can seriously affect wildlife and ruin the experience of
contrast from everyday life that many people seek in parks. Low-
flying military aircraft disturb the serenity of Craters of the Moon,
while a commercial airport within Grand Teton flies visitors in and
out of the park. Explosions caused by mining and oil exploration
and weapons testing are another source of disturbance. Highway
noise is more than a minor annoyance in many urban parks: it is
hard to appreciate the hallowed grounds of national battlefield parks
as cars go whizzing by.[75]

*Yosemite, February 1984. Skiing facilities at Badger Pass.*

The *State of the Parks 1980* report, and succeeding documentation, although inadequate, leave little doubt that park resources are under tremendous pressure. Indeed, much about the environments in which parks exist is changing; this, in turn, calls for changes in the way resources are managed.

## PRESERVATION '95: A RESPONSE

Congress and the park service have responded in several ways to the pressures on park resources. After the *State of the Parks 1980* report, Congress requested the service to develop short- and long-term plans for preventing or mitigating resource problems.[76] Since then, appropriations for resource management have nearly doubled, from $49 million in 1980 to $93 million in 1983.[77] (In constant dollars, this amounts to an increase of 46 percent.) Additonal increases in budget and staff have been provided under other programs. The National Park Service has identified hundreds of projects to prevent further degradation of natural and cultural resources and to repair or restore those already impaired. Some of these projects are being carried out using the basic funding provided annually by Congress as well as special appropriations. However, available funding has been insufficient to complete even those resource management projects that park staff feel are most urgent.

The park service, moreover, has not developed a comprehensive, systematic program to protect park resources. The resource management plans currently prepared by the service are for individual units, and projects identified in them must wait for each funding cycle. Some plans have not even been completed.[78]

The contrast with initiatives for visitor facilities and park infrastructure is striking. For example, when visitation increased dramatically in the early 1950s, the service responded with Mission '66, a 10-year, $1-billion program to expand existing visitor facilities and build new ones.[79] More recently, concern in the General Accounting Office and Congress over rundown park buildings and facilities, many of which posed health and safety problems, resulted in a crash effort, the Park Restoration and Improvement Program (or PRIP), a $1-billion dollar initiative undertaken between 1981 and 1985 to repair aging park facilities and infrastructure.[80] By focusing on health and safety, several measures under PRIP improved park resources—for example, historic structures and sewage lines were repaired. A subsequent cyclic facility maintenance program may help to ensure that these needs continue to be addressed.

To assure that protection of park resources receives the attention it deserves, a new initiative is necessary: a 10-year program, Preservation '95, a resources counterpart to the facilities-oriented PRIP. For an additional annual expediture of $50 million on resources protection over a 10-year period, Preservation '95 would enable the service to address its most pressing problems in a pragmatic fashion, train a larger cadre of qualified resource specialists, and institutionalize resource management higher among park service priorities. The need for such an effort, which would be roughly half the cost of PRIP and spread over double the time, is beyond question; in less fiscally severe times, a larger program over a shorter period would be easily justifiable. Although even the costs of a more modest program seem high amid current budget constraints, delaying these initiatives would add significantly to the eventual cost—in those instances where delay did not prevent effective response altogether.

Over the years, the park service has responded well to programs addressing urgent problems. Such programs generate a sense of immediacy and collective initiative otherwise difficult to achieve in a highly decentralized system. Preservation '95 will prevent worthy resource protection projects from being lost amid other priorities. The current system, which provides year-by-year funding corresponding to the annual budget cycle, makes it difficult for park superintendents to plan intelligently for efforts that will take several years to design and implement. If park superintendents and regional directors become convinced that a resource project will not receive high priority in Washington, they will not, in the words of one park service official, "waste a slot in it by including it in their budget requests."[81] A long-term program, while not eliminating the influences of politics and changing priorities, would increase the likelihood of commitment to identified groups of projects.

Another benefit of a focused program is the opportunity it provides to address resource needs comprehensively in ways that pay close attention to cost-effectiveness. When there is a large backlog of projects in a particular area, such as there is currently in resource management, priorities need to be set. Waste can result if projects are assessed piecemeal or if increased dollars are spent before planning determines where and how limited public funds can be spent most effectively.

To avoid waste that sometimes results when funding is increased in a crash program, a year-long planning effort should initiate Preservation '95. Because of steps taken by the park service over the last couple of years, notably the identification of numerous projects that are necessary for combating resource pressures and minimizing their future impacts, this period should be sufficient to update previous plans and design new initiatives.

Congress may have to take the lead in inaugurating Preservation '95. Past resource protection efforts have often resulted from congressional pressures rather than from park service initiative. Members of Congress asked the service for the *State of the Parks 1980* report, for example, and, when it was late in arriving, reminded the service about it.[82] Although the park service began assembling information about its most "significant resource problems" in 1981 as a follow-up to the *State of the Parks* report, it did not request funding from Congress to deal with those problems. Instead, Congress, prodded by intensive lobbying from conservation groups, appropriated money on its own in 1983.[83] Similarly, funds for natural and cultural resources management, which have, since 1978,

increased from 11 to 15 percent of the park service's operating budget, were not all appropriated at the service's request. Although
the budget for natural resource management has increased some
$30 million since 1980, $20 million of the increase can be attributed
to the efforts of conservation groups and Congress, not requests from
the park service.[84]

To ensure success beyond its 10-year life span, Preservation '95
should include measures that will more clearly establish resource
protection as a distinct element of park programming and funding.
Most important are measures to evaluate staff performance—particularly, how well the park service staff designs and implements resource protection efforts. The 10-year initiative would thus serve
not only as a catch-up program for the most pressing natural and
cultural resource problems, but also to establish resource protection more prominently among the permanent elements of park
management.

Preservation '95 should also give the public, Congress, and the
park service itself a better idea of how much money and attention

*Yosemite, February 1984. Mike Slater and Vera Vigness (Burbank, Califor-
nia). Mike: "I've been camping here since 1956, but I never come in the summer any more. The changes that I see are in the people. It's a much more
casual kind of approach on the part of the people now. I'm a rock climber
and I come here thinking of this place as a temple, whereas now the younger
climbers seem to see it as a gymnasium."*

are devoted to resource management. At present, it is difficult to get a precise picture of expenditures. Various accounts, such as the natural and cultural resource preservation funds, are used, in addition to the general budget item of resource management, and it is not always clear what funds cover what projects. Moreover, funds are sometimes allocated to resource projects from other park budget categories, such as PRIP. Expenditures for the same projects have, on occasion, shown up in two different categories—resource management and PRIP—making it especially difficult to determine just how much the park service is spending and where exactly the money is going. Preservation '95, as a separate account, should make a more identifiable and accountable resource management program.

Preservation '95 should include four elements: stabilization, repair, and restoration; systemwide reporting and planning; monitoring and research; and staffing and training.

### Stabilization, Repair, and Restoration

Measures to restore and protect damaged resources form the core of Preservation '95. Congress added approximately $7.5 million in both 1983 and 1984 to the park service's annual budget to address the most serious systemwide "significant natural resource problems." A similar amount was added each of these years for cultural resource management as a result of park service requests.[85] This money has funded numerous restoration projects throughout the system. The service built fences to control feral animals in Haleakala and Hawaii Volcanoes. It removed exotic species from Olympic (mountain goats), Death Valley (burros), and the Channel Islands (rabbits).[86] At several battlefield parks, including Shiloh and Fredericksburg, overgrown trenches are being restored to their historic appearance. Ocean-damaged historic structures are being repaired at San Juan and Fort Jefferson, and numerous National Register buildings are being renovated.[87] Funding, however, has been insufficient to deal even with those projects park staff members feel are most urgent. In 1984, only 61 of the 175 highest-priority "significant natural resource problems" identified by regional offices were funded.[88]* Moreover, these 175 projects had been selected from a much

---

*Many of these projects were designed to collect more information about resources; for example, of the 61 natural resource projects funded in 1984, 34 were for action projects, the remaining 27 were for research and monitoring efforts.[89]

## Park Planning

By law, the protection and use of each park unit is guided by a general management plan (GMP). This basic plan —usually prepared by the superintendent in cooperation with the regional director and the Denver Service Center and approved by the park service director—is the public statement of each park's objectives and policies. The plan sets forth information about the unit's distinctive resources and recreational values; special considerations to be taken into account in formulating management policies for park access, resource protection, visitor use, and the like; and the management policies themselves.

In 1984, 265, or 78 percent, of the park units had approved general management plans. Most were prepared during the 1970s. The quality of the plans varies enormously. Some show creativity and innovation, while others barely satisfy the legislated re-

quirements; some are well-written and concise, while others are verbose; some are current, while others are out-of-date.

In addition to general management plans, parks have prepared related planning documents dealing in greater depth with particular aspects of management or with methods for implementing GMPs. Recent years have seen "action plans" for natural and cultural resource management, handicapped access, concessions management, wilderness, and land protection. (Land protection plans set forth priorities for acquisition in fee and less-than-fee as well as plans for protecting nonfederal lands within park boundaries.) As of March 1984, 261 resource management plans had been approved, and, as of January 1985, 125 land protection plans had been cleared by the secretary of the interior.

larger number submitted by park units to regional directors. For cultural resources, a similar situation exists: many identified emergency interventions and rehabilitations are unfunded. Finally, because funds are so limited, restrictive guidelines limit the types of projects funded. Preservation '95 is essential to permit the park service to address this growing backlog of deferred maintenance and repair.

### Systemwide Reporting and Planning

Effective resource management depends on integrating top-down and bottom-up planning so that the assessment of needs, the setting of priorities, and the link to budget funding are part of one process.

Each budget season, parks identify their priority projects for line-item funding. These projects are reviewed by regional offices, which send their recommendations to Washington for final selection. A park's resource management plan (RMP) helps park managers determine needs for resource protection, but regional directors exercise a pivotal role in setting priorities. (See box on park planning.) In essence, each plan is an inventory of resource conditions and problems, an analysis of possible responses to them, and a set of recommended actions. The development of RMPs for each park unit has been stressed as a systemwide priority since the *State of the Parks 1980* report, and efforts have been made to link requests for funding to projects identified in the plans. (By early 1984, 85 percent of the parks had RMPs approved by the regional office. Some parks have separate plans for cultural and natural resources, but, for most, one plan covers both.) Recent guidelines provide that no resource protection project can be funded unless the park has an approved RMP in which the need has been discussed.[90]

To more effectively establish systemwide priorities, to ensure adequate congressional oversight, and to call public attention to resource needs, the park service should prepare a periodic, systemwide report of resource conditions, problems, actions to address them, and future needs. While the *State of the Parks* report was effective as a one-time effort, periodic reports on the state of park resources should be more comprehensive and analytically sound. Several items need to be covered in these reports. For example, resource conditions in individual units, as well as systemwide issues, should be described. The report should contain an analysis both of the effectiveness of measures taken to address the resource issues identified in individual units and of continuing and planned systemwide policies, actions, and commitments. It should also evaluate the adequacy of current funding levels and legal authorities to address resource problems.

A decentralized park system with largely autonomous units works quite well for many purposes but creates problems for gathering information in a systemwide, comprehensive format that can be helpful to the parks and analyzed by policy makers. Regional oversight does help to set priorities based on overall needs. But, generally, the service now has neither complete awareness of systemwide conditions and trends nor the necessary ability to evaluate what approaches are most effective.

RMPs, although useful in understanding resource conditions and needs within individual parks, have several shortcomings from a systemwide perspective. First, the plans are uneven, reflecting disparities among park staff numbers and skills. Second, with some

260 or so different plans approved,[91] of varying detail and length, it is difficult to develop a complete understanding of the pressures, opportunities, and constraints facing the resources of the system. Third, the Washington office sets overall resource policy but does not review plans unless asked to by a regional office. Finally, it is not clear how regularly the basic plans will be updated, as distinct from the list of priority projects established each year.

The service has tried many approaches to obtain more comprehensive, systemwide information about the condition of resources and to increase information transfer among parks. One approach has been to consolidate certain types of resource issues in special natural resource units and regional centers. Since reorganization in 1983, special units for air quality, water quality, and energy and minerals monitor these particular resources. The special units review proposed projects that may affect the resource; conduct research and inventories; and provide technical assistance to individual parks as well as policy guidance to the regions and Washington. In addition, six cultural resource management centers provide technical assistance and project support to the parks. Through agreements with universities throughout the country, the park service has also established 23 so-called cooperative park study units.[92]

Several other recent steps have increased the transfer of information among parks. For example, a fire information retrieval system is being used by many parks, especially those in the Pacific Northwest, to strengthen responses to forest fires. It permits simultaneous entry of data on fire and weather observations for each park to draw on.[93] Glacier National Park has an interagency agreement with an adjacent national forest to develop a digital geographical information system to inventory and monitor common resources and to analyze data.[94]

Besides permitting the service, Congress, and interested citizens to better understand the pressures park resources face and the needs of the system, these efforts, combined with periodic state of the parks reports, should enable individual parks to obtain a systemwide perspective on conditions and opportunities and to help ensure that the RMPs remain up to date. This enhancement of understanding and planning would be one of the principal benefits of Preservation '95.

*Santa Monica Mountains, June 1984. Oak Tree Preservation Workshop sponsored by the National Park Service for the general public.*

## Monitoring and Research

Sound plans depend on adequate, up-to-date information about park resources, the pressures on them, and the impacts of those pressures. As the park service has stated:

> Good knowledge on the identity and location of all park resources and how they function within ecosystems is prerequisite to their wise stewardship. . . . Put simply, you can only develop plans to protect those things that have been identified and located, otherwise their damage, loss or extinction within a park will likely go unnoticed, and you can only manage properly those resources whose functioning within the system is understood.[95]

Following release of the *State of the Parks* report, a variety of data-gathering projects were initiated. These included basic resource inventories, research on a specific problem (for example, the decline of a fishery), monitoring to determine long-term trends, and research to enhance understanding and interpretation of an event or phenomenon.

Despite such initiatives, serious gaps remain in the information needed by park managers. For example, the List of Classified Structures—the park service inventory of its buildings with cultural and historic values—is estimated to be about 25 to 50 percent complete. Notable gaps exist for newer parks and for those older ones not traditionally managed as historical.[96] For fiscal year 1985, the park service has received some funds for the gathering of basic inventory information on cultural resources, where needs are especially acute. Specific cultural resource projects identified for funding include surveying archaeological sites in Waupatki and Bandelier, cataloging several thousand artifacts at San Juan Island, researching the characteristics of the historic landscape at Fort Spokane, and evaluating historical and archaeological resources at Whitman Mission.[97] Newer parks, such as Martin Luther King, with jurisdiction over some 350 historic buildings, have enormous basic inventory and data collection needs.

Similarly, for natural resources, the service has requested funds in 1985 for "basic inventories of park resources and [for] establishing long-term monitoring programs so that adequate early warning systems are developed for the protection of threatened resources."[98] More information about natural resources is the focus of several projects: inventorying cave resources in Ozark, monitoring water quality in North Cascades, monitoring fishery resources at Virgin Islands, and analyzing the effects of canal discharge on marine resources in Biscayne.[99] A National Academy of Sciences study has recommended a near $1 million research effort on the effects of grazing activities in Capitol Reef.[100]

Preliminary indications for fiscal year 1986 are that the service will seek over $5 million for cultural resource projects and approximately $7.7 million for natural resource projects, many of which include research activities. In both instances, this is a far smaller amount than RMPs indicate is needed.

Although the park service has increased its information and research capabilities, more is needed to keep up with intensifying pressures. Projects that allow for better understanding of park resources and the pressures they face, along with continuing support for regional cultural resource centers, special natural resource units, relationships with universities, updating resource management plans, and other initiatives already under way, should be funded under Preservation '95 to improve information about park resources.

## Staffing and Training

Continuing concerns are expressed, both inside and outside the park service, about the adequacy of staff skills and training and personnel allocation in both natural and cultural resource management. For example, the number of full-time natural resource specialists—about 125—has remained fairly constant over the last few years.[101]

Training initiatives—field instruction, manuals of instruction, and education of selected staff to train others, as well as seminars and workshops—have been stepped up since 1980. A natural resource management training program has been established to increase the number of qualified natural resource specialists in the field; the first class of 35 trainees was selected in fiscal year 1983 to be instructed over an 18- to 24-month period.[102] Training programs and workshops on natural resource management were also begun in 1983 for superintendents and mid-level managers. These were funded at $50,000 with plans to increase the amount to about $350,000 for 7 or 8 programs, including classes for rangers and mid-level managers on water resource management, remote area management, and resource-monitoring skills and classes for superintendents on more general issues.[103]

Other positions within the park service directly influence the condition of natural and cultural resources in the parks: improperly performed maintenance work on a building can destroy or detract from its historic features and fabric; landscaping and construction projects can disrupt important cultural and natural resources. Yet personnel with these job classifications, which comprise a large proportion of park service staff, receive little periodic training in resource management, nor are appropriate workshops and training sessions readily available.

The needs are especially acute in cultural resource management, where the relative lack of training opportunities in part reflects previous attitudes. A number of park experts believe that, given the current state of staff expertise, significant new levels of funding for projects to repair historical and cultural resources could be harmful unless professional expertise in historic preservation—architects, historians, skilled craftspeople—is increased. Others suggest that the inadequacy lies not so much in the numbers of present staff but in where they are and what they do. They warn of a lack of trained people at the park level to supervise untrained workers.[104]

Finally, more training and oversight of private sector and volunteer interpretative efforts is needed to ensure that programs offered by these groups, which have been increasing, fulfill their promise. If the service is to respond to the growing pressures on park resources, such training cannot be neglected.

Unfortunately, the array of resource problems confronting the parks will not be solved by a 10-year program alone. It is a necessary start, however. PRIP has been successful in abating the worst of the health and safety problems in park facilities and infrastructure. But because of the different factors involved in pressures on park resources, even a PRIP-type program for park resources—one that brings with it more money and better trained staff to deal with the most serious and generally obvious problems and sets up a comprehensive way of identifying and evaluating them—will not be sufficient to address all the long-range problems.

Many resource management issues are of far greater complexity than those encompassed under PRIP. Tradition, politics, economics, and even philosophy will continue to influence decisions. Scientific research and data collection can be invaluable in providing information about the consequences of different policy options but will not usually determine a clear policy direction or choice among competing values. Preservation '95 initiatives need to be sensitive to these differences between its own objectives and those of a PRIP, and must include actions that strengthen the organization to deal with these issues.

Congress should consider financing some costs of Preservation '95 by earmarking user fees, including revenues from concessioner franchise fees. While not a panacea, user fees could play an important role in providing funds for maintaining and restoring park resources, although a number of important technical issues—cost-effective collection methods, incentives to individual parks to collect the fee—would have to be resolved. Revenues from such fees, amounting to about $30 million a year, currently go to park land acquisition efforts and to the repair of government-owned buildings.[105]

## THE SPECIAL CASE OF EXTERNAL THREATS

The park service's mandate to preserve park resources unimpaired, difficult enough to apply inside the parks, is far more complex when pressures originate outside park boundaries. Although hackles may be raised when an overused area inside a park is shut off to hikers or anglers, no one doubts the service's responsibilities as zealous steward of its domain. When the service combats outside pressures, its base of support is far less solid.

If a superintendent questions a large industrial or residential complex just outside park boundaries, he or she risks being perceived less as a zealous steward than as a meddlesome neighbor. Local governments express resentment over what they see as federal intrusion in local land-use affairs. Even other federal agencies resist attempts to give the service a say in decisions that may affect park resources.

In a few situations, federal law provides the parks with protections against external pressures. For example, the Clean Air Act, as amended in 1977, provides visibility protection for 48 national parks; the National Environmental Policy Act requires that a federally supported or permitted activity consider, in its environmental impact statement, adverse impacts on the environment.[106]

Occasionally, the park service may be able to exert influence through its control of access routes, water sources, or other resources without which nearby development is impossible. For example, the service is authorized to sell water to the gateway community of Tusayan on the Grand Canyon's South Rim, for example if the park has surplus and it would not be detrimental to park resources.[107] Often, however, a park superintendent concerned about outside pressures must rely on measures open to all landowners, such as persuasion and pleading. Superintendents may appear at local zoning board and planning commission hearings to comment on projects that could adversely affect a park. At Fredericksburg and Spotsylvania National Military Park, for example, the superintendent worked with the developer and local government officials to encourage adequate screening of a small shopping center being built adjacent to park headquarters at Chatham Mansion.[108]

Park personnel often are wary of being looked at as unfriendly neighbors. If superintendents identify an outside development—a new coal mine or power plant near their parks, encroaching residential development—and agitate for action, either by another agency or a local government, to control it, they may raise the ire of powerful adversaries who have access to members of Congress and administration officials. Even if a superintendent successfully forces a resolution of the problem, there is a large element of risk. If the issue is one in which, in hindsight, the superintendent's vision is appreciated, this will garner commendations locally, as well as in the service. But, if the issue festers locally, that superintendent may fear, in the words of one park official, "that somewhere in Washington there is a black mark next to his name."

While recognizing the threats posed to park resources from outside activities, the leadership of the park service has resisted recent initiatives of conservation groups and members of Congress to add to the formal extraterritorial powers of the service. In addition, park service directives have restricted participation in local deliberations regarding neighboring lands.[109] The service argues that, if parks come to be seen as meddling neighbors with authority to thwart developments outside boundaries, then (in the words of former Director Russell Dickenson) new powers might "produce an extraordinary backlash against the purposes and ideals of the national parks themselves."[110]

## Needed: Accurate, Authoritative Information

Lack of documented information, a chronic problem in formulating management plans *within* parks, is more serious by far when a case must be made for remedial steps outside. In some situations, although the service may suspect that adverse changes are taking place, it cannot document the extent of the harm. In other cases, the service cannot pinpoint the origin of the harm.

The problem of air pollution in the Southwest is a prime example of the information quandary. Almost everyone agrees that the views in national parks such as Zion, Bryce Canyon, Chaco Canyon, and Grand Canyon, as well as national monuments in the region, are obscured by air pollution.[111] However, the culprit or culprits are not nearly as clear. Some evidence points a finger at local power plants. Other evidence points toward pollution from copper smelters. Still other people believe that long-range transport from distant centers such as Los Angeles is a major factor.[112]

Mesa Verde presents another example of the need for information. Superintendent Bob Heyder says it is clear that air quality has degraded since 1980 from energy development in the region and that magnificent vistas are being impaired. On a smog-free day, a visitor at certain vantage points can get a spectacular view of four states and can see up to 150 miles. Heyder also suspects that the same pollution is eroding the sandstone cliff dwellings themselves. Explaining his efforts to gather solid information, Heyder understandably says, "I have to live with the locals and the people in the state, and I need hard evidence before I'm willing to fight the air quality issue."[113]

Clearly, the information initiatives recommended earlier as part of Preservation '95 are critical in combating external pressures as well. The lack of specially trained staff to provide the needed documentation of effects is also a serious constraint to more effective park service action.

### Needed: Additional Protection Tools

Even when the service does have a good fix on the problem, available tools are often insufficient to protect the parks. The park service concedes that "external threats, though generally the most serious, are receiving little attention . . . because they are considered more complex and much more difficult to deal with."[114] The serious impacts of projects outside the parks indicates that more must be done. Opportunities for effective action vary, depending on the type and location of the activity causing the pressure.

#### Federal Lands Adjacent to Parks

Some pressures on the parks originate on adjacent federal land. For example, the Forest Service or Bureau of Land Management may authorize mineral extraction, timber harvesting, or energy development on land it manages, and these activities may be visible from a park or create noise or pollution within it.

One might think that activities on adjacent federal lands could be dealt with easily, since they are, in a sense, "within the family." This is not the case, however. Each agency—bureaus within the Department of the Interior as well as those in other departments—has its own statutory mandates and constituencies.

Impressive examples of coordination among the park service and other federal and nonfederal public agencies that administer adjoining lands do exist. Federal, state, and local agencies work cooperatively, for example, in Interagency Fire Centers. At Mt. Rainier, clear-cutting of forests bordering the park was creating wind patterns capable of toppling large Douglas-fir trees within park boundaries. To address this problem, areas adjacent to the park were mapped where critical windthrow problems did exist or could be expected to develop. The National Park Service now cooperates with the For-

*West Yellowstone, Montana, August 1984. West Yellowstone is a "gateway" town located just outside the park.*

est Service in reviewing plans for timber sales adjacent to park boundaries. The Forest Service contacts the park before a sale to see if there are any problems, and the park, in turn, reviews the situation and determines any potential problems.[115]

Perhaps the most widely known coordinating group is the Interagency Grizzly Bear Committee. In the face of dwindling bear population levels, the park service helped organize this committee of representatives from federal and state agencies to coordinate actions and review projects around Glacier and Yellowstone parks, where the grizzlies are making their last stand in the lower 48 states. Federal and state agencies work together to identify and track bears; states have established more consistent penalties for poaching; and open garbage pits outside the parks have been closed.[116]

More commonly, cooperation comes in the more limited form of an opportunity for the park service to comment on proposed agency activities that may affect a park. Various federal laws, including most prominently the National Environmental Policy Act, require agencies to give the service an opportunity to comment, although the agencies usually cannot be forced to do what the service recommends, or even to assign park needs a high priority. Most important, the act requires agencies to consider the impacts of their proposed activities on the environment (which includes affected parks) and to explore less-damaging alternatives.

In practice, agencies sometimes fail to take park impacts into account. For example, a preliminary scoping document prepared by the Department of Energy (DOE) in preparation for an environmental impact statement on a nuclear waste repository did not mention that Canyonlands National Park was a mile and a half distant or that the railroad used to haul radioactive waste would be visible from four major park overlooks;[117] similarly, initial studies by the U.S. Army Corps of Engineers for modification of its Bluestone Dam to produce greater power did not address the potential effects on New River Gorge National River immediately downstream.[118] Pressure by various public agencies and individuals led DOE and the corps to consider the effects of such actions on nearby parkland.

To enhance park protection, conservationists have repeatedly called for legislation to strengthen the voice of the park service over activities on adjacent federal lands. Some legislative proposals offered in the past would force other agencies not only to seek the Department of the Interior's advice, but to follow it. Others, such as the Park Protection Act, as passed by the House of Representatives in 1983, would require other federal agencies that are taking an action on adjacent federal lands to notify the secretary of the interior if the action would have a significant adverse effect on park resources and to provide an environmental assessment and opportunity for comment. The actions of other bureaus within the Department of the Interior would be assessed by the secretary.[119] Another bill would bar federal expenditures or permits for activities in federally managed areas adjacent to some national parks if the secretary of the interior determined that such activities would adversely affect designated habitat critical to native fish and wildlife species located within the park.[120]

Not surprisingly, other federal agencies are less than enthusiastic about what, from their perspective, may appear as attempts to expand park boundaries de facto. Mining and energy companies and other users of federal lands have also been critical. A process is needed that will produce thorough consideration of both park needs and conflicting policies—without an either/or approach. This process should include incentives to work out mutually acceptable solutions.

One possible model is the Endangered Species Act (ESA), which gives the U.S. Fish and Wildlife Service a strong say in projects that affect endangered species but sets up a negotiation process that prompts agencies to search for a consensus on ways to reduce adverse impacts. An ESA provision calls for the drafting of a conservation plan that would allow the proposed activity to go forward in exchange for efforts to enhance the environment of the endangered species and to protect certain areas of habitat.[121]

To balance endangered species protection against other considerations, the ESA also establishes a process for exempting a project from the act's requirements. If the Fish and Wildlife Service determines that a federal action may be detrimental to an endangered species, any of the principal agencies involved may apply to the secretary of the interior for an exemption. After a review board determines that an irresolvable conflict exists—development versus species protection—the board prepares a report on the application for the Endangered Species Committee. This bipartisan committee—called the "god squad" because of its life and death powers over a species—makes the final decision on a project.[122] The committee balances competing national priorities and provides a powerful incentive for agencies to work out a compromise before the squad makes its all or nothing decision on a project.* A similar review of projects on federal lands adjacent to the parks could prompt both the service and the conflicting agency to sit down at the table and peacefully resolve their conflicts.

Actions by other agencies within the Interior Department should be controlled by a directive from the secretary that requires consultation with the potentially affected park and moves the decision up to the regional offices of each agency, to the applicable assistant secretaries, and finally to the secretary, if the parties cannot agree.

Review of proposed projects—even the type of cooperative review in the ESA model—does not wholly meet the needs of parks and

---

*This decision, of course, is subject to review by the federal court of appeals.

their federal neighbors. Effective resolution of conflicting needs requires cooperative planning as well, so that goals may be reconciled before projects are proposed. In practice, most federal lands adjacent to the parks are already subject to formal planning requirements that, along with the National Environmental Policy Act, entitle the park service to comment on plans proposed for adjacent lands.

In planning for adjacent lands, however, as in proposing projects on those lands, the initiative lies with the custodial agency, not with the park service. To enhance the effectiveness of the service and ease the task of other agencies in addressing park needs, the park service should, with funding from Congress, and in consultation with affected federal agencies, identify specific areas—areas of critical park concern—outside park boundaries that serve as critical habitat or migration routes for park wildlife, that provide scenic views, or that are otherwise critical to the parks; moreover, the service should propose development policies for the designated areas that would accommodate park needs.

These plans for areas of critical park concern would be focal points for collecting information and identifying what is needed to protect the parks from external threats, as well as a vehicle for consultation among the park service and any affected agencies. In this sense, cooperative planning fits into the inventory and research components recommended as part of Preservation '95.

With the right legislation, however, these plans can do much more. Such legislation should require other federal agencies, in preparing their plans and activities for adjacent lands, to be consistent to the maximum extent practicable with any specific park service policies established for an area of critical park concern. Precedent for a consistency approach can be found in the Coastal Zone Management Act, which requires certain federal actions to be consistent with state coastal zone management plans.[123] As in the case of the coastal zone, there will be arguments over the application of a consistency requirement to adjacent federal lands, and provisions will be needed to resolve those arguments; the details of those provisions will be critical to making the system work. Nevertheless, a consistency requirement and a mechanism for dispute resolution hold great promise for protecting the parks without disregarding other federal agencies' mandates.

The importance of devising workable mechanisms to control

potentially adverse impacts of projects on adjacent federal lands cannot be overestimated. If the federal government cannot take care of pressures originating on its own land, it can hardly expect more of state or local governments or the private sector.

*Activities Funded or Permitted by the Federal Government*

Many activities that affect the parks do not take place on federal land but do have special federal involvement in the form of federal funding or permits. For example, the U.S Department of Housing and Urban Development may be funding a high-rise hotel near a historic monument under its Urban Development Action Grant program. Federal law may require a pollutant discharge permit for a project planned upriver from a national park. The U.S. Environmental Protection Agency may be funding a major sewage treatment plant to serve new development near a historic battlefield.

As with projects on federal land, several existing laws require the agency involved to let the service comment—the National Environmental Policy Act is the major one. When designated historic properties are involved, the National Historic Preservation Act requires additional comment by the Advisory Council on Historic Preservation, providing an opportunity to work out acceptable mitigation plans.[124] The Advisory Council's review process has successfully resolved some important interagency disputes, but its constructive involvement in contentious cases is limited because of the desire of federal agencies to work things out by themselves. Even so, the Council's process is controversial, and the Reagan administration wants to reduce its substantive effect.[125]

By carefully evaluating the impacts of projects it approves or finances, the federal government can significantly enhance park protection. Despite resistance from other federal agencies, state and local governments receiving federal aid, and private interests, more effective measures are needed to ameliorate the impacts that federally funded or permitted projects may have on parks.

The recently enacted coastal barriers legislation is an excellent model of appropriate measures. That law provides for identification of remaining undeveloped coastal barrier beaches and islands. Any new federal financial assistance in identified areas—for projects like bridges and causeways—is prohibited. Thus, the federal government does not subsidize development in flood- and storm-

*Santa Monica Mountains, June 1984. Bill Zimmerman and Joan Andersson, residents of Topanga Canyon in the recreation area.* "One of the things about this place is it's got a low population density; if it gets a high population density, it will become a very different kind of place. The fact that we're part of the California Coastal Commission domain and the Santa Monica Mountains National Recreation Area means that there are limits on how many roads can be built and how many houses can be built and so on. And there is no end of mountainous terrain like this which has been overdeveloped in Los Angeles."

prone areas that may be eligible for federal aid and insurance payments should storm damage occur.[126] This feature was hailed by President Reagan as a wise, money-saving initiative:

This legislation will enhance both wise natural resource conservation and fiscal responsibility. It will save American taxpayers millions of dollars while, at the same time, taking a major step forward in the conservation of our magnificent coastal resources. [This] is precisely the sort of imaginative environmental legislation this Administration encourages—legislation that solves real problems in the stewardship of our natural resources. . . . This Administration is committed to applying the imagination and common sense demonstrated by this legislation to the resolution of other important national environmental concerns.[127]

Similar legislation for parks makes sense. Why should the federal government continue to subsidize or authorize projects that ultimately force it to spend money on repairs?*

As in guarding park resources from activities on adjacent federal lands, one essential step in controlling federally funded and permitted activities is to define the scope of the service's concerns by preparing plans designating critical habitats, migration routes, and scenic viewsheds important to the parks. Here, too, a reconciliation process—again based on the Endangered Species Act and the Coastal Zone Management Act—to balance park protection and competing interests is needed.

Despite potential benefits to the parks and the added attraction of saving federal dollars, extending the park service's influence over permits and subsidies will undoubtedly be resisted. An interim step might be to make this park protection applicable only to projects receiving a federal *subsidy* and to continue to rely only on the National Environmental Policy Act, the national Historic Preservation Act, and other applicable federal laws when *permits* are involved. In the final analysis, however, if the federal government is not willing to prevent itself from damaging the parks, it can hardly justify asking other interests and governments to do more.

## Nearby Private and Nonfederal Public Lands

Many pressures on parks originate on private property under state and local jurisdiction. The service's ability to do anything about impacts from these lands varies from case to case. If the threat is a billboard to be erected just outside a park entrance or an abutting residential subdivision approved by a local zoning board, the service can only rely on cooperation from state and local agencies and private firms. Sometimes such cooperation is forthcoming—the well of good feeling toward the parks is deep—but just as often other goals take precedence.

A particularly thorny issue exists with respect to private lands inside national park boundaries. A park visitor might assume that lands inside designated boundaries have some special protected status. In fact, they do not, unless the federal government owns

---

*The proposed Park Protection Act, as passed by the House of Representatives in 1983, applies to federal agency funding and permits that affect park resources as well as to activities on adjacent federal lands.

them or has taken other steps (such as purchase of an easement) to protect them.

Federal courts, including the U.S. Supreme Court, recognize the power of federal land agencies to constrain the use of nearby property in certain circumstances. Statutes give the park service this power in a few situations. Redwood is perhaps the best example, where the service has, as a measure of last resort, the power to regulate adjacent lands if the activity on them harms or threatens to harm park resources.[128] Also, the park service, like any landowner, has the power to constrain activities by neighboring landowners that are a "nuisance"—that is, those interfering with the use or enjoyment of the property.

Congress has been called on to broaden these powers by statute, giving the service explicit regulatory authority over inholders and adjacent landowners. Noted environmental lawyer Joseph Sax, for example, has urged Congress to give the park service power to exercise a variety of land-use controls over private lands within park boundaries as well as explicit authority to regulate nuisances (relying on a broad definition of the term that includes visual intrusion) originating on lands outside park boundaries.[129] Such laws, Sax and others point out, should be judicially supportable.

At the heart of opposition to park service power over nonfederal land are respect for private property rights and resistance to federal intrusion into what are generally perceived to be purely local affairs. These values, especially when coupled with a lack of data on the in-park effects of adjacent development, can provoke hostility when the service raises its voice against a project.

To address these concerns as well as park needs, protective measures need to be tailor-made, accommodating the diversity of parks and their local jurisdictions. Opportunities as well as needs vary from unit to unit. A zoning control plan might succeed in New Jersey, for example, where the state and local governments and courts often support strong land-use regulations, but not in states where the courts view land-use controls more skeptically. Tax incentives for preserving historical resources have been more successful in Oregon than in many other places. A proposed subdivision outside Great Smoky Mountains may require a different response from a similar development proposed near Point Reyes.

The most promising current opportunity to protect the parks against external threats from private lands lies in diverse cooperative mechanisms involving the park service and park neighbors. These partnerships are needed to provide a forum where activities can be discussed, differences thrashed out, consensus developed.

Often, such partnerships are more effective if they involve an institution; land trusts are the most important example. Park officials have helped form some local land trusts and have sometimes advised local coordinating councils and land-use agencies.

Government need not be the initiator, however. There is precedent for private initiative in establishing such cooperation. For example, through a series of transactions involving the Appalachian Trail Conference and its affiliates, a 66-acre parcel was recently acquired for a trail-right-of-way, scenic protection, and additional public use, including a hostel.[130]

The park service should actively encourage its staff to cooperate in such partnerships and private initiatives. Some present policies that require clearance or set up administrative hurdles before park service personnel can formally participate are counterproductive. Although clearance policies are based on the understandable desire to not unduly interfere with local governments, these policies miss the mark and ought to be replaced by policies encouraging needed cooperation.

In addition, Congress should establish an experimental program in which the park service would take the lead in establishing partnerships at a few specified parks. Part of this program would involve designating formal park protection zones, adjacent to selected units, within which special tools and resources are available, such as technical assistance and grants to pay for local land-use planning. (These techniques and others, along with the importance of monitoring lands within designated zones, are discussed in more detail in chapter 6.) The service should be authorized to accept land donations and easements within these protection zones. In difficult cases, acquisition of full or partial interests of land may be essential; as at present, acquisitions by the park service should remain subject to congressional approval.

The service ought to establish formal ties with local governments as part of these partnerships. Several parks already have improved their relationships with surrounding governments (and other community interests) in this way, sometimes by forming advisory commissions or voluntary coordinating bodies. Continuing contact with local populations will be especially important if formal protection zones are established. Park service policies should support rather than inhibit, as they sometimes have in the past, such contact.

## Regional Activities Affecting Parks

Some practices that put pressure on the parks cannot be handled well by a local superintendent or by drawing a new protective perimeter around a park. Long-range transport of air pollutants falls into this category, as do some activities that divert or pollute the water resources of parks.

In 1977, Congress recognized air pollution problems affecting the parks by amending the Clean Air Act to provide visibility protection for 48 national parks and national monuments in the park system.[131] Areas around the parks can also be regulated to prevent deterioration of air quality in the parks. These requirements do not provide complete protection—for example, industries far from parks do not have to consider park impacts even though their emissions may eventually degrade vistas by long-range transport. In addition, states may in some instances issue a permit for a facility even if the park service determines that it will degrade air quality or important values of the park, such as visibility.

Another section of the Clean Air Act establishes a national goal to remedy existing visibility impairment in Class I areas such as national parks. Overseen by the Environmental Protection Agency (EPA), states are supposed to include visibility protection in their air quality plans; in doing so, the states have considerable discretion to take economic and energy considerations into account. EPA issued regulations governing such plans in December 1980,[132] but challenges to the rules have slowed their implementation. A major controversy has been whether the Clean Air Act requires states to protect "integral vistas"—landmarks and panoramas visible from inside Class I units. In October 1984, as a result of a lawsuit filed by three environmental groups, EPA proposed to disapprove the air quality plans of 34 states for failure to protect visibility, gave the states additional time to develop regulations, and proposed federal regulations to apply in those states that fail to take the required action.[133]

The service has a specialized unit to address air pollution. The air pollution unit provides valuable expertise to superintendents who are coping with long-range air pollution problems and acts as a focal point of concern for an issue that respects no political boundaries. Recently, as noted, the service created similar special units to deal with water pollution and mineral development.

Problems such as long-range transport of air pollutants cannot be effectively addresssed by treating parks in isolation. Special attention to particular parks, desirable as it is, must be supplemented by action addressing the problems of the whole region.

## CONCLUSION

For 15 years, serious alarms have been sounded about the effects of pressures on park resources—pressures from visitors within the parks and from development outside them. Countermeasures of the type proposed here—better planning for resource management, more adequate funding and staffing, careful targeting of funds on priority problems, regular reports to Congress—will help stave off degradation. The measures recommended to counter external threats are also achievable and will significantly increase protection. Putting these measures into place and making them work effectively deserve a top priority on the national agenda.

Yet these countermeasures—which probably go about as far as the present political consensus will permit—will not preserve resources "unimpaired." Within the parks, degradation at the most popular sites could be eliminated only by discarding the central vision of preservation *and* access that is the system's genius. So the parking lots and bleachers at Old Faithful, or something like them, probably must remain. Outside park boundaries, measures to protect park resources conflict with goals of other land users and of states and local governments; compromise with these goals, too, is inevitable. So long as the country relies on internal combustion engines and coal-fired power plants, the haze at some of the western parks is unlikely to disappear.

Despite the country's best efforts, continuing pressures will produce some resource degradation—gradual, barely perceptible in many places, but degradation all the same. Some of this loss is the unavoidable cost of serving successive generations of visitors and of economic development outside park boundaries. The measures proposed here are needed to avoid still greater losses.

Much more can and should be done to protect the parks against resource pressures. The service should aggressively seek better data and information about the impacts of what is going on around the parks. It must better document the impacts of effective remedial action. And it must also show more ingenuity and willingness to embrace a variety of approaches to the problems it faces. Each park must develop a strategy tailored to deal with its particular set of threats, and the regions and Washington must be willing to back up superintendents in carrying out the strategy. But, by and large, the service cannot take care of the threats unless the secretary of the interior, Congress, and ultimately the public is fully committed to doing so. Attaining this backing must be a primary task on the agenda of those who are concerned about our national parks.

In the long run, if conservation is to keep pace with intensifying pressures, the political consensus must itself shift so that protective measures unachievable today will become achievable tomorrow. Increased understanding of resources can help provide the needed political support. So can enhanced awareness of the pressures on resources and of the measures needed to counteract them.

# Profile
# Cape Cod National Seashore

The creation of Cape Cod National Seashore in Massachusetts in 1961 marked a turning point for the National Park System. The park represented much more than New Frontier glamour, although the many photographs of attractive, tousled-hair Kennedys walking its shores undoubtedly helped capture public interest and secure congressional approval.[1]

The Cape Cod seashore unit was the first sizable park unit in which proximity to large numbers of people—in this case, well over 20 million persons within a day's drive—became an important, explicit rationale for creating the park. In signing the bill, President Kennedy said, "we are going to need a good deal more effort like this, particularly in the more highly developed urban areas, where so many millions of people now live."[2]

But the area clearly qualified for national park status on the ground of resource significance alone. It was one of the two "most outstanding areas" on the Atlantic and Gulf coasts identified in a seashore recreation study by the National Park Service in the mid-1950s. The cape, said the study, had the "longest unbroken and undeveloped sweep of beach in New England, combined with a picturesque and fascinating hinterland."[3] The study drew attention to changes in recreational demand that were leading to rapid development in coastal communities. Public access was assured on almost 7 percent—or 240 miles—of the Atlantic and Gulf coasts.[4]

This relatively small, elbow-shaped extension of Massachusetts has an unusual mix of visual and natural features. Glacial in origin, the cape is constantly shifting. Ever since the ice retreated, the sea level has been rising and the land migrating naturally. Each year,

*Cape Cod, September 1983. Nauset Beach.*

coastal erosion reduces Cape Cod's area by about five acres. If the sea level continues rising at its present rate, in about 1,500 years part of the outer cape will become an island.

This fleeting quality, in geologic time, adds another compelling dimension to the distinctive environment created by the interplay of tide, wind, and water with ponds and beach, cliffs, heathlands, flats, dunes, and forests. Set back from the cape's 30 miles of curving beach are some of the most spectacular banks and cliffs along the Atlantic Coast, up to 175 feet high. This topographical mix gives rise to a marvelous array of plant and animal communities, sea and shore birds, and fish and shellfish, their diversity enhanced by the overlapping influences of northerly glacial flow and southerly warmth, and of bay and sea.

The cape's colorful history reflects the many ways people have influenced, and been influenced by, this setting. Long a magnet for seafarers, the cape saw American Indians, Vikings, European mariners, and English Captain John Smith before the Pilgrims' stopover at Provincetown. Settlement witnessed humans challenging the elements to fish, whale, farm, and sail. Artists, writers, poets, photographers, and lovers of solitude came, seeking inspiration amid the salt and spray of the shores and the clapboard and shake cottages of the fishing villages. Eventually, summer tourists and seasonal residents became the cape's major industry. By 1960, the all-year population was 22,034 residents; the summer population, 54,652.

A controversial unit at its inception, Cape Cod National Seashore today no longer seems startling or "new." Visitors see a park having much in common with others they have been to: familiar cocoa-brown and white signs; helpful uniformed employees; visitor centers with free maps, orientation films, and exhibits; a full schedule of talks and walks; and abundant educational materials for sale. But, for the residents of the six adjacent cape towns (they now number about 22,000, the cape's entire population in 1960) and the park's 34 permanent and 134 seasonal staff, there are frequent reminders of the differences between the Cape Cod unit and more traditional units in the system.

Park Superintendent Herbert Olsen must deal with less-than-traditional problems, like Provincetown's request for renewing its permit to tap a well inside the seashore unit to augment the town's water supply; residents who want to let their dogs run unrestrained along the shores; shellfishers who want off-road vehicle (ORV) access to oyster beds when winter ice prevents boat travel; and the town of Wellfleet's proposal to develop a landfill within the park's boundaries. Olsen's responses are shaped, not only by the traditions of the National Park System and Service, but also by the innovations of Cape Cod National Seashore.

Cape Cod, unlike most earlier parks, was not carved out of lands already in the public domain. It was, in 1961, no wilderness. In fact, influencing the pace and quality of private development was an important objective of those who sought federal protection. Creating a park here involved three major innovations. Congress authorized $16 million to buy land from private owners, an amount that eventually had to be doubled.[5] Although private lands had been purchased before by the federal government to create a park, purchase on this scale was precedent-shattering for the system. That innovation aside, once the private lands were bought by the federal government, their status, so far as park managers were concerned, was the same as any other federal parkland.

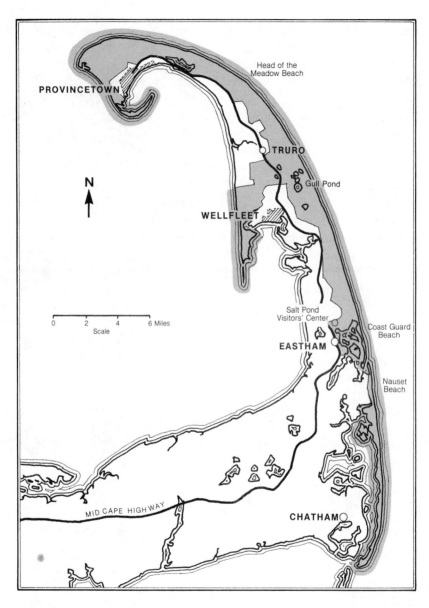

In contrast, two other Cape Cod innovations have ongoing management implications. Large chunks of towns were enclosed within
the park's boundaries. This meant the loss of property taxes to towns
when private lands were sold to the park service; moreover, towns
owning recreational lands, such as beaches, were to think about
donating them to the park. In any case, the location of a sizable

park in the thick of settled communities entailed a closer and more complex ongoing park-and-town relationship than was the case with most other parks in the system.

And, finally, under the "Cape Cod formula," hundreds of owner-occupied homes inside park boundaries were, under certain conditions, assured that they could remain under private ownership indefinitely. This arrangement was more than a compromise with owners. From the start, people recognized that the Cape Cod they wanted to preserve included the picturesque homes and villages and other remains of earlier settlers and ways of life in the distinctive landscape. If development would ruin these visual qualities, so would disrepair and vacancy. The idea was to retain a "living landscape." To reconcile resource protection with private ownership, the park's enabling legislation suspended the secretary of the interior's power to condemn homes within park boundaries if the towns in which the properties were located passed zoning regulations compatible with the park. The towns complied, and about 600 homes, many fronting the ocean or sited near scenic vistas, became permanently part of the park. Most visitors probably do not know where the park begins or ends, although they may be taken aback by occasional "Private Property—Keep Out" signs.

As a result of these innovations, ownership of the 43,500 acres in the Cape Cod unit is mixed: the federal government owns more

*Cape Cod, September 1983.*

Cape Cod, September 1983. Jean and Jim Nies (Shelton, Connecticut). "It's
a beautiful spot to be, and, because it is a national seashore, you don't have
to worry about being on someone's beach. It's our beach. If areas like this
are left open to private development, as we've seen in so many other places,
there is little question that very soon they would have limited access, become
virtually private, and really would not be something that is part of our
national asset that everyone can enjoy. . . . I think there should be an
increasing number of national parks made available if they can be. I guess
they really are those places where you can retain the things that you want
your kids to see. We've taken our children and grandchildren to them, and
I think it's part of our national heritage that's good for them to see."

than half, approximately 27,000 acres; the commonwealth of Massachusetts, some 12,000 acres of tidal land; the towns, more than
2,500 acres; and private citizens, over 1,800 acres.[6] The nine popular
freshwater "great ponds" are owned by the commonwealth and
are surrounded by park service, private, and town lands. About as
many people annually visit Cape Cod National Seashore as visit
Yosemite and Yellowstone combined. Visitation in 1983 climbed
to almost 5 million, after a drop in 1982. By far, the largest proportion of visitors come from the region—New England, New York,
and New Jersey—during the peak months of July and August. The
busy season is stretching into the spring and fall, however. Surveys
show off-peak tourists are older and better educated and travel from
farther away. Motel keepers and merchants offer discounts to
encourage visits by senior citizens.

Superintendent Olsen, who came to Cape Cod in 1979 from earlier assignments at historic and urban parks, is increasing the management emphasis on natural resource protection. At the time Cape Cod National Seashore was created, park system policies specified that new national recreation areas (including the seashore and lakeshore units) were to be managed differently from historic and natural areas, emphasizing recreational use over resource protection. Olsen believes that management of newer parks such as Cape Cod has tilted too far in this recreational direction. In 1982 a resource management specialist, one of three such positions allotted to the North Atlantic region that year, was assigned to Cape Cod.

Raising the standards of natural resource management here can be controversial, even if the issue seems relatively simple. When rangers stop visitors from picking up wood or walking their dogs unrestrained inside the park, for example, the offenders may march into park headquarters and complain that such policies are appropriate in western parks, but not in Cape Cod.

Most of the resource protection issues—water quantity and quality, mosquito control, beach migration or erosion, acid rain—are far more complex. The cape's prized dunes are a case in point. Over the years, heavy use of the dunes—by people driving ORVs, walking, and sliding—has damaged vegetation and accelerated the natural processes of sand migration. The general management plan, prepared in 1970, anticipated ORV use in certain parts of the seashore unit. In 1977, however, an executive order mandated closing public lands to ORVs wherever soil, vegetation, wildlife, or other park values suffered adversely. A study by the University of Massachusetts was commissioned to document how resources were affected by ORV use, and park officials used the findings to close off a highly popular section of the Province Lands dunes. ORV use is permitted year round along the nine miles of beach between Hatches Harbor and Head of the Meadow Beach and during the winter from Head of the Meadow Beach to Coast Guard Beach.[7]

The park's plan for managing ORVs upset drivers, on one hand, and many environmentalists, on the other; the latter wanted the ORVs banned completely. In contrast, Provincetown Selectman Mary Jo Avellar has complained: "This is supposed to be a recreational park, yet people are denied access to it."[8] The Conservation Law Foundation of New England, joined by the Sierra Club and the Massachusetts Audubon Society, filed a suit against the plan, contending that the extensive ORV use permitted by the park damages the ecosystem and conflicts with other recreational uses.*

For many years, the park had little in funds or staff to implement its responsibility to protect the area's distinctive cultural and historical landscape. When the exterior of the Penniman House, a handsome whaler's mansion, was restored over a decade ago, some local preservationists questioned the authenticity of the color of the paint. Today, the park has a staff historian, and experts from the regional office and the Denver Service Center are called in for restoration consultation. Seven buildings and sites are listed on the National Register of Historic Places. ("They receive the same care here they would in an historic park," says the superintendent.) Under special agreements, the Truro and Wellfleet historical societies inform visitors about the significance of several historic buildings in the park.[11]

About 80 interpretative programs a week are offered by the park from June to Labor Day, attracting some 2 percent of the visitors. Most visitors "grow into the educational aspects of the park program after they exhaust the possibilities of sunbathing," says the park's chief of interpretation, G. Franklin Ackerman. He contrasts this with western parks, where the novice visitor "turns to the interpretive programs for guidance, and then becomes independent."[12]

Ackerman points out that the national seashore's enabling legislation is unusually explicit about the park's mission to provide for public "understanding" as well as "enjoyment."[13] Many visitors have specific interests—watching birds or whales, visiting historic homes, hiking. Major park educational themes—the distinctive fragility of the cape in the face of natural phenomena and human-induced threats (for example, acid rain) and the inspirational effect nature has had on human courage, innovation, and artistic endeavor—are often communicated in programs related to these recreational pursuits.

---

*In a June 1984 decision, a federal district court in Massachusetts decided that the park service's plan was "effectively protecting the ecology. . .from the impact of ORVs," but that the secretary of the interior had not adequately considered "whether motor vehicle use of the Seashore in general constitutes a legitimate recreational use under the Seashore Act."[9] As of the summer of 1984, the park was conducting a survey concerning visitor attitudes about ORV use as part of determining its continued appropriateness in the park.[10]

The program to help interpret the park for visitors continues to benefit from special money made available in the late 1970s: four new films produced for the visitor center, 45 wayside exhibits, and a complete set of new museum exhibits for the Salt Pond Visitor Center. Ackerman calls this a "last hurrah." Such activities now seem low in national priorities, he says, and newer parks, such as Voyageurs in Minnesota, where he served earlier, suffer especially. At Cape Cod, there have been slight cuts in interpretative activities in the spring and fall, even though the number of interested visitors during these seasons is increasing.

The operating budget of Cape Cod National Seashore has been relatively stable in recent years, allowing only for pay increases. However, the park attracts some volunteers who help out with maintenance, educational, and visitor management activities. In addition, the 1983 Jobs Act funded almost $200,000 worth of labor for repair and rehabilitation projects, and the Youth Conservation Corps program enabled high school students to spend some summer weeks maintaining and improving trails.

The Reagan administration's emphasis on rehabilitating and rebuilding park facilities (the Park Restoration and Improvement Program, PRIP) resulted in some additional construction funds for Cape Cod. As a relatively new park, it has less of a problem with deteriorating facilities than many parks have: still, the $200,000 from PRIP in 1982 was useful in repairing ramps and stairways, reshingling roofs, and installing a new septic system, for instance. "This replaces the cyclical funds we used to receive, but I don't care what they call it," says Superintendent Olsen.[14]

In 1983, PRIP funds will be used to restore the interior of the Penniman House and to rebuild the parking areas at Coast Guard Beach and Nauset Beach. Interest in the Penniman House was sparked when the Barbara Johnson collection of whaling artifacts, including some possessions of the Penniman family, turned up at a Sotheby Parke Bernet auction. Some 20 local benefactors helped the park buy several of the collection's Penniman objects.

As time goes by, Cape Cod's innovations are still being tested. How can the integrity of the cultural landscape of cabins, farmhouses, cottages, and occasional merchant houses be retained as owners and tastes change and people want to add bedrooms, boathouses, or decks, or to just build grander houses? (Homeowners allowed to remain within the national seashore pay local taxes and can sell their properties.)

Owners who wish to modify their homes must request building permits and variances from the towns. The towns, in turn, inform the park's chief of environmental planning, Jim Killian, who has been in the Cape Cod unit for more than 10 years and is said to have a prodigious ability to keep track of the status of all properties. If the park service does not object to the town's proposed approval, the permits are granted. Some owners do more than their permits call for—one tripled the size of his house instead of adding a bedroom, for example. The park depends on the town to monitor compliance, but in practice towns may look away if the change is consistent with their zoning.[15]

Those concerned with such practices feel that incremental modifications, even if not significant now, may, over time, reduce the authenticity of the landscape the park is supposed to protect. In 1981, park guidelines officially permitted homes to expand by 50 percent. "When you try to perpetuate the number of houses as we do," the superintendent concedes, "then you have to permit some replacement and new building—but within limits."

Cape Cod National Seashore has some remaining acquisition problems. In response to recent initiatives in Washington, D.C., all condemnation suits but one were settled in 1983. The park is developing a land protection plan, emphasizing alternatives to acquisition-in-fee for the remaining private and town-owned parcels in the park.[16] Faced with stepped-up demand for retirement and vacation homes in recent years, towns look at the lands they own within the park as places to site public facilities, arguing that they need lands outside the park to accommodate new development. In the past, through land swaps, sites within the park were made available for a fire station and a school, but the present superintendent is less disposed to such arrangements.

Virtually all of these issues have come, at one time or another, before the 10-member advisory commission that represents the six cape towns, the county, the commonwealth (two members), and the secretary of the interior. This kind of commission, a park system "first" at Cape Cod, has since been established in a number of the newer parks—for example, Indiana Dunes in Indiana, Golden Gate in California, and Lowell in Massachusetts. The commission was created in recognition of Cape Cod National Seashore's difference

*Cape Cod, September 1983. Marsh in township of Wellfleet.*

from more remote parks, and of policies that would benefit from ongoing consultation with adjacent public and private interests. The commission's value as a sounding board for friends, skeptics, and foes is widely recognized, and its life, originally set for 10 years, has been extended. Members in 1984 included a marine biologist, a former president of the Massachusetts Beach Buggy Association, and a faculty member of Harvard University's John F. Kennedy School of Government.[17]

The commission, for example, supported the superintendent's decision in 1983 to close down a motel that had been operated by a concessioner since the park was established. Given the numbers of new motels in the area, commission members thought that visitors had a wide choice of privately run accommodations. From the beginning, local businesses outside the park were expected to provide most of the tourist services. (The Cape Cod unit has only three concessioners.)

Meeting bimonthly in public sessions, the commission has been a voice for constraining new recreational activities, such as hang-gliding and blocking a state-requested boat ramp. The commission and the former park superintendent worked together to support federal legislation providing temporary payments to compensate cape towns for taxes lost on lands acquired by the national seashore. Some argued that the towns were benefiting sufficiently from increased tourism to offset such losses, but town officials countered that the costs of providing some services increased. Arrangements were worked out to reimburse towns for providing emergency fire and rescue services; police services are not reimbursed, however.

Both town police and park rangers patrol within the seashore boundaries. Up to 30 law enforcement rangers are on duty during the summer, enforcing federal regulations dealing with offenses that damage park resources and traffic laws and crimes against persons or property. They work cooperatively with the town police, who are responsible for compliance with local and state laws within seashore boundaries.

When Cape Cod National Seashore was established, sentiment in the towns was strong, in favor and against. Many believed the federal government could help protect the cape they knew and loved and were willing to accept some restrictions on use of their property to accomplish this objective. But others were convinced that the park would reduce the economic benefits of tourism or objected to what they saw as unwarranted federal intrusion in cape affairs.

Certainly no one who visits the cape today can seriously argue that tourism has been adversely affected. Even those who have at times complained of inappropriate federal influence concede that the park has been a tremendous asset. "The park is here to stay. It has caused a marked appreciation in value," says Joshua Nickerson, the owner of a sizable lumber business on the cape and an advisory commission member for over a decade.[18] "Most of the people have come to think the park is a good thing. This is a small peninsula. If it had been allowed to develop, there wouldn't be a square inch left," the late Wellfleet Selectman Wilbur Rockwell concluded.

# Chapter 5
# The Private Sector
# in the Parks

The private sector has been involved in national parks from their earliest days. The act designating Yellowstone authorized the secretary of the interior to lease small parcels of parkland where accommodations for visitors could be built and operated.[1] By 1880, eight years after Yellowstone was created, it contained seven frontier-type log cabins, a small hotel, riding-horse and pack-train facilities, guides, and stage lines.[2]

Although participation varies from park to park, private organizations today take part in nearly every aspect of park activity—from food, lodging, maintenance, and interpretative services to assisting in the acquisition of parkland. The diverse network of participating organizations includes large corporations, family-owned businesses, volunteers, contractors, and nonprofit cooperating associations.

Major concession operations have been the most visible component of private sector activity in the parks. Visitors are likely to remember the facilities owned and operated by major corporations in a few of the most revered parks: Grand Canyon, Yellowstone, and Yosemite, among others. The clusters of buildings and commerce in some of these places on crowded summer days are reminiscent of suburban shopping malls or small towns.

Particularly as a result of changes during the past 20 years, the private sector's role is, in fact, more diverse. In some of the new units added to the system, local initiatives that led to the park's creation have been transformed into continuing participation. Volunteers and nonprofit organizations are now significant providers of services and support in several parks, old as well as new,

171

sometimes through formal arrangements such as cooperative agreements and leases of historic buildings. Some private sector activities
enrich park visitors' experiences in ways not otherwise achievable.
Others represent a cost-effective way of providing services. If
structured properly, additional private sector involvement can
benefit parks in the future.

The benefits of private sector involvement must be weighed, however, against the costs, some of which are substantial. Inevitably,
participating organizations influence use of the parks, yet few of
them—even the nonprofits—bring the same mix of concern for resources and visitor experience that informs the park service. Commercial facilities can impair resources or diminish visitors'
experiences; at some point, commercialism destroys the contrast
from the commonplace that national parks are specially suited to
provide. There is also long-standing concern that the terms of concession contracts may be too generous, enabling some concessioners to profiteer at the expense of visitors or taxpayers.

During the 1970s, debates over private sector activity in the parks
focused on concessioners. Conservation groups, including The Conservation Foundation, called for reducing the number of facilities
and replacing large concessioners with nonprofit or quasi-public
corporations.[3]

Controversy in the 1980s was provoked by former Secretary of
the Interior James G. Watt, who aggressively sought greater private
sector involvement in the parks. At the start of his term, Secretary
Watt made these remarks to a gathering of national park concessioners:

> It is time for a new beginning and the private enterprise system must
> be looked to for rejuvenation and enthusiasm as we try to make the parks
> more accessible and usable for the people. . . . You folks are going to
> play a tremendously important role and a growing role in the
> administration of our national parks and we are going to reach out to
> involve you in some areas that you haven't been asked to be involved
> in before.[4]

In keeping with Reagan administration directives, Mr. Watt proposed that private companies provide services traditionally undertaken by park service staff. This kind of reorientation, some feared,
would switch the role of the park service from that of the primary
provider of services to that of policeman and bureaucrat, with conse-
quent loss of some of the parks' special qualities.

Questions over private sector involvement promise to remain in the forefront of public debates over how parks should be used and managed. This chapter looks at how the private sector—not only for-profit organizations but also nonprofits and volunteers—should be involved in the parks and what changes should be made in their roles and park service management.

## CONCESSIONS IN THE PARKS

Short and narrow Yosemite Valley, the main attraction in Yosemite National Park, is an often-cited example of intense concessioner development. As of 1974, the valley's concession facilities, almost all owned and operated by one concessioner, included 1,498 lodging units and

> 3 restaurants; 2 cafeterias; 1 hotel dining room; 4 sandwich centers; 1 seven-lift garage; 2 service stations with a total of 15 pumps; 7 gift shops; 2 grocery stores; 1 delicatessen; 1 bank; 1 skating rink; 3 swimming pools; 1 pitch-and-putt golf course; 2 tennis courts; 33 kennels; 114 horse and mule stalls; 1 barber shop; 1 beauty shop; and 13 facilities for the sale of liquor.[5]

One of the largest developments in the valley is Yosemite Village, a moderate-size shopping mall adjacent to park service headquarters and the visitors' center. Today a complex with modern-looking wood and stone architecture, the shopping center 15 to 20 years ago was a collection of old stone buildings that stocked some basic provisions for visitors and year-round residents. A large combination market/department store now dominates one building. In the market, the selection comes reasonably close to that of a typical supermarket. The department store sells the conventional souvenirs—sweatshirts and teeshirts with Yosemite logos and slogans, bear statues, ashtrays—as well as western clothes and items such as toothpaste and film. A bank and barbershop are also located in the complex.[6]

Yosemite Village is hardly typical. Only 111 of the 334 park system units have any concessions at all; food service is provided by concessioners in 70 units, lodging in 36. Operations in 5 parks—Glen Canyon, Grand Canyon, Lake Mead, Yellowstone, and Yosemite—account for nearly 60 percent of total concession sales.[7]

Lodging, food service, souvenirs, and general merchandise together account for 67 percent of concessioners' gross receipts throughout the park system, with food service the largest at 22 percent.[8] A visitor to *all* units would find, in various places, restaurants, cafeterias, fast-food stands; grocery markets, camping goods stores, souvenir shops; primitive cabins, hostels, exquisite old hotels. Transportation services include shuttle-buses, ferries, and bicycle rentals. Gas stations are a familiar sight in the larger units, as are coin-operated laundromats. Concessioners also provide interpretative services to visitors and sell books and maps, bus and boat tours, rafting and canoeing trips, and burro rides.

Often concessions are specifically related to a particular unit or type of unit. There might be beach equipment rental and sales; boat and boat slip rentals; tennis and golf facilities. For winter sport enthusiasts, cross-country skis can be rented in an increasing number of units, as can snowmobiles; privately run downhill ski operations have existed for some time in three parks (Lassen Volcanic, Rocky Mountain, and Yosemite).[9] Some of the larger, more heavily used natural units contain privately operated hospitals and clinics under concession agreements. There are bathhouses and massages at Hot Springs National Park, a baseball batting range in Gateway National Recreation Area.

Concession facilities and operations not only serve a variety of tastes but reflect a variety of styles of park development—from the primitive and virtually unnoticeable to the elegant and grandiose, from the latest technology to rustic simplicity. Primitive cabins in Yellowstone contain only cots and go for $13.50 per night. The widely acclaimed Ahwahnee Hotel in Yosemite, built in 1927, has rooms that start at $117.00 per night.[10] Electronic games are now a concessioner-provided feature at some parks, while concessioner-operated stagecoach rides and cookouts date back to the earliest days of the parks.

The organizations providing these varied services run the gamut from large conglomerates to small, local businesses. Although some concessioners are nonprofit groups, most are profit-making companies. The largest concessioners are the ones that have drawn the most public attention. TW Services, which has concessions in five units (Bryce Canyon, Grand Canyon, Yellowstone, Zion, and Death Valley),* employed more than 2,800 people and had estimated gross

---

*In late 1984, TW Services acquired the rights to operate the concessions in Everglades National Park.

receipts in excess of $27 million in 1983.[11]   Subsidiaries of large corporations such as MCA, Inc., ARA Services, Greyhound, AMFAC, and Del Webb operate concessions in 16 parks.[12] National Park Concessions, Inc., which was chartered by the park service in 1941 to develop facilities and provide services "solely in the interest of public welfare," has a contract covering operations in Olympic, Big Bend, Mammoth Cave, Isle Royale, and the Blue Ridge Parkway.[13]

Most concessions are small. Out of more than 500 concession contracts, only 113 had gross sales of as much as $250,000 in 1983; the largest 55 generated about 86 percent of the business.[14] (See appendix C.) At Grand Canyon some 20 river-rafting concessioners generally employ between 10 and 30 people each and have estimated gross receipts that average around $300,000 a year (the range being from just over $100,000 to $1.6 million). At Great Sand Dunes National Monument, the only concessioner services are firewood sales and four-wheel-drive guided tours. Together, the two concessioners there employ fewer than 10 people.[15]

## POLICY FRAMEWORK FOR CONCESSIONS

When the first parks were created, it was simply assumed that private companies and individuals would operate within them. If the parks were going to be used and enjoyed, facilities and services had to be provided to accommodate visitors. Proposals for the federal government to step into the concession business were not advanced.[16]

Private operators were also looked on as a primary source of revenue for the parks. During Yellowstone's first five years, Congress did not appropriate any park funding; it expected that rents paid by the park's private operators would yield adequate revenues to administer and protect the area.[17]

Concession operators in the parks were generally granted either contracts or less formal operating permits, depending on such factors as the extent of services to be provided, the size of the operation, and the duration of the agreement. Operating permits were short-term agreements administered on a park-by-park basis, usually with conditions attached to protect access to resources and ensure that investments in park facilities were made. Concession contracts were awarded to those who were expected to make much larger investments and, in return, granted more security to the investments made. These distinctions continue to the present.*

On assuming his position as the first director of the park service, Stephen Mather found the private operations in the parks unsatisfactory. He thought that competition among private operators was abhorrent to park goals. He favored monopolies within the parks both as an effective management tool and as an inducement for additional private investment. Under the broad authority of the 1916 act establishing the National Park Service, Mather advanced a number of policies that proved effective in stimulating new private investment.[19] By 1924, the concession business in Yellowstone was operating as a regulated monopoly, and visitor accommodations were improved and expanded.[20]

The Concessions Policy Act of 1965 formalized many policies dating from Stephen Mather's time.[21] At the heart of the act is the requirement that the secretary of the interior exercise authority "in a manner consistent with a reasonable opportunity for the concessioner to realize a profit."[22] The act also expressly authorizes—but does not require—continuation of the following practices:

- allowing monopolies and granting existing concessioners a preferential right to provide new or additional facilities;
- recognizing concessioners' equity—known as a possessory interest—in the facilities or improvements provided by them so that a right to compensation exists if contracts are terminated or not renewed;
- subordinating franchise fees to the objectives of preserving the areas and providing adequate and appropriate services at reasonable rates; and
- extending or renewing contracts or permits before their expiration date to promote additional investment and continuity of operation.[23]

The secretary of the interior also may include provisions in contracts that compensate or otherwise protect the concessioner against loss of investment (but not of anticipated profits) caused by discretionary acts of the secretary. Moreover, franchise fees are negotiable

---

*About 35 percent of the concessioners operating in 1984 were under contracts (which currently can be for as long as 30 years). The remainder were under permits (granted for a maximum of 5 years).[18]

at the time of contract renewal and can be reduced in exchange for a concessioner's promise to construct additional facilities.

Although intended to provide an atmosphere conducive to private investment, the act also spells out safeguards against inappropriate use of park resources:

> The preservation of park values requires that such public accommodations, facilities, and services as have to be provided within those areas should be provided only under carefully controlled safeguards against unregulated and indiscriminate use, so that the heavy visitation will not unduly impair these values and so that development of such facilities can best be limited to locations where the least damage to park values will be caused.[24]

Accordingly, the act directs that "such development shall be limited to those that are necessary and appropriate for public use and enjoyment of the national park area . . . and that are consistent to the highest practicable degree with preservation and conservation of the areas."[25] This "necessary and appropriate" standard for determining what facilities belong in the parks has not been easy to apply. In practice, tradition and the asserted need to ensure profitability as well as provide visitor services have not dictated a stringent interpretation; witness the beauty shops, souvenir stores, and cocktail lounges that operate in some of the great western parks.

Simultaneously ensuring that national parks are economically attractive to concessioners and that the parks' distinctive characters are retained has been at the heart of much of the recent controversy surrounding concessions.

## Today's Concerns about Concessions

Mather's concern over monopoly versus competition has shifted to current questions over the need for some of the incentives provided to concessioners, the influence of concessioners in establishing park policies, and the compatibility of some of their operations with the needs of resource management and the types of experiences parks provide.

### Profitability

Many of the concessioners' contracts in force today, most of which were negotiated in the 1970s, grant concessioners the traditional investor protections authorized by the Concessions Policy Act. Monopoly rights, possessory interests in facilities, and preferential rights to provide additional services have been granted to most major concessioners.

So long as concessioners' investment is wanted, the need for some investment protection is clear. Private operators will only enter into or renew concession agreements if their contract terms guarantee

*Yellowstone, August 1984. Marina at Yellowstone Lake.*

them a reasonable chance to get a return from their operations. Contract terms also must take into account the complications that influenced traditional park service policy and that still face some concessioners: for example, short operating seasons; a labor force that generally cannot commute; higher costs for supplies transported to faraway places; and complete governmental regulation of locations, goods, and prices.

Some critics—fiscal conservatives and others, as well as conservationists—however, charge that traditional incentive provisions of concession contracts create an imbalance among the interests of the concessioner, the government, and the public in favor of the concessioner.[26] Investor protection, some contend, is sufficiently ensured by subsidies resulting from other governmental policies: the federal government provides roads in the parks, it provides advertising to encourage park visitation, it grants monopolies, and it has a statutory mandate to set rates and franchise fees at levels that give the concessioners a "reasonable opportunity" for a profit. Accordingly, critics question the need to let contracts without competitive bids and to grant preferential rights for new or additional services.

The most widely criticized practice is the granting of market value possessory interests in facilities that concessioners erect on federally owned parkland.[27] This, some maintain, allows concessioners to realize windfall profits on their investments, in addition to profits from their services. If the government terminates a contract that includes a possessory interest, the concessioner receives compensation equal to the "sound value," or reconstruction costs, of the structure (not to exceed fair market value), less physical depreciation. Thus, a concessioner that in 1920 invested $100,000 in a facility worth $500,000 today generally receives $500,000, less physical depreciation, even though it may have recovered long ago its $100,000. Some critics propose instead that the government should pay the concessioner only the unamortized book value of the facilities.

Some of the problems posed by possessory interests are illustrated by the dilemma the park service faced in Yellowstone in the late 1970s. A 1966 contract with Yellowstone Park Company required the concessioner to invest $10 million in facilities by 1975.[28] By the time the mandated investment period ended, the company, after several years of declining profits and deteriorating facilities and service, had come under new ownership (soon thereafter it became a part of General Host). In August 1975, the park service extended the investment deadline an additional two years.

In 1976, the park service assembled a Yellowstone Concessions Study Team, composed of representatives from the park's two principal concessioners, the service's Denver Service Center, its regional office, and the park's management itself, to examine the situation.[29] After eight months of investigation, the study team concluded that, while the park service had taken steps to provide General Host with a profitable enterprise and incentives for investment, "the company's management cannot respond to visitor needs because the company is not oriented to service to the public, but only to the generation of profit dollars." The team found the problems with General Host's operation to be "major in nature," requiring "a major overhaul of Company attitudes and policies to solve them."[30] It made several specific recommendations about reorganizing the company and changes in its lodging, merchandising, transportation, and food services.

By 1978 after receiving another contract extension, General Host had invested only about 59 percent of the funds required by its contract. Because no progress had been made by the concessioner to implement the study team's recommendations, meet its contractual obligations, or improve service to the public, the park service started to terminate the contract for unsatisfactory performance. The parties then negotiated an agreement for the park service to buy out the contract.*

The service ran into difficulties in negotiating agreement on the concessioner's possessory interest in the facilities. The service wanted to pay compensation equal to the book value of the facilities but determined that the contract and precedent required payment of fair market value. The government was convinced that it could exercise sufficient control over subsequent concessioners only if it bought General Host's interest. Congress, in 1979, appropriated $19.9 million to purchase the possessory interest and thus terminate General Host's contract.†[32]

*Influence*

The influence that concessioners have over park policy decisions has provided another focus for concern. Early in the 1970s, in Crater Lake National Park, the park service allowed the construction of several concessioner facilities, including an employees' dormitory, a gift shop, and a cafeteria addition, while a new master plan was being drafted for the park. When the plan was completed, delineating future development of the park, the assistant secretary of the interior for fish and wildlife and parks, Nathaniel Reed, rejected

---

*In the meantime, the park service spent over $1.2 million buying General Host's Everglades contract because the company similarly failed to commit sufficient resources to operate in that park.[31]

†Some park officials, who were not directly involved in the Yellowstone buyout, believe that the fair market value of General Host's possessory interest was actually close to $4.5 million, not $19.9 million.

it and ordered it redone. He found that the plan lacked supportable reasons for recommending additional concessioner development and appeared to have been dictated by the terms of the concessioner's contract, rather than park purposes.[33] A few years later, in Yosemite, a draft master plan was again rejected by the assistant secretary, who remarked that it appeared to have been written by the concessioner, MCA.[34]

Those events and others prompted a congressional committee to hold hearings on park service planning and concessioners' operations. Its report, issued in 1976, concluded that the role of the concessioners in planning had been disproportionately greater than the public's. The report claimed that concession contracts had protected the government's interest inadequately and that some typical provisions—for example, the granting of monopolies, preferential rights, and possessory interests—were "creating windfalls no longer necessary for the large businesses operating concessions."[35]

Efforts to move a concessioner's facilities out of a prime area in Zion National Park illustrate the political clout large concessioners can sometimes muster. In the early 1970s, park officials at Zion determined that several of the concessioner's facilities, including cabins inside the park's majestic canyon area, were no longer compatible with park purposes. Moreover, because the town of Springdale, Utah, just outside the park and less than 10 miles from the canyon, could accommodate more facilities and would welcome the opportunity to do so, the service concluded that some facilities inside the park were no longer necessary.

Unlike concessioners in many other great western parks, the concessioner at Zion had no possessory interests in the buildings it operated; the park service owned them. Because the concessioner's contract had expired and nearby towns needed time to accommodate visitors, park staff in Zion awarded the concessioner, TWA Services (now TW Services), an interim, five-year contract to operate the facilities in the park. Zion park officials and the neighboring towns intended to use that time to get ready for change, but TWA used the time to garner political support among Utah officials and business executives to keep the facilities in the park and have its contract extended. The controversy reached the U.S. Senate, where some vocal, powerful members agreed with TWA Services; the concessioner's facilities in Zion still stand and, in fact, have recently been renovated.[36]

*Compatibility*

Finally, critics question whether some concessioners' activities belong in the parks at all. Often, questions over concessions are the focal point of debates about the appropriate level and kinds of facilities and services in the parks. People have genuinely different visions of the parks and of the facilities that belong in them, and these differences tend to be magnified when a facility or service is supplied by the private sector. The major concession operations have sparked the most controversy.

Heightened concern about the compatibility of concession activities sprung in large part from several changes during the 1960s and 1970s: increasing concessioner involvement and investment in many of the great western parks as part of Mission '66; growing visitation and user pressures in many of the same areas; the dawning of environmentalism with its concern for natural systems; and the takeover of several major park concessioners' operations by some of the country's leading corporations.

Problems during the 1970s at a few parks, principally Yellowstone and Yosemite, brought concessions to the forefront of public debate. The use of some concessioners' facilities for conventions and business meetings was questioned. A 1974 study of seven western parks by the General Accounting Office (GAO) revealed that 143 conventions or group meetings were held in these parks, 53 of them during the peak visitation season.[37] In 1974, during Yosemite's peak season of May through September, 19 percent of the total room nights were scheduled for conventions and other group meetings.[38]

Congressional hearings on concessioners' activities in the mid-1970s resulted in a report that concluded that the park service had not been discouraging conventions during peak or near-peak seasons and that some of the facilities and services in Yosemite were inconsistent with the natural surroundings.[39]

To preservationists, the sheer extent of facilities and concessioners' operations in such prime locations as Old Faithful, Yosemite Valley, the Grand Canyon, Zion Canyon, and a few other areas—not to mention some of the services offered—has become incompatible with park preservation and the park experience. The National Parks and Conservation Association (NPCA) recommended in 1974:

> All new concessions belong outside the boundaries of the parks where tourist traffic may boost small town revenues. Further, to the extent possible, the Park Service should phase out current concession opera-

tions to locations outside of parks. . . . How can parks be preserved in an unimpaired state for present citizens or future generations when bulldozers are busy carving out new sites for gift shops at the behest of powerful concessioner firms?[40]

Similarly, The Conservation Foundation's 1972 report, National Parks for the Future, observed that concessioners "too often bring the people to the parks for the wrong reasons" and recommended

> that a long-term program of concessioner replacement be started on a pilot basis and proceed according to an equitable timetable until the parks are free of major private entrepreneurs and the public has regained full control of facilities planning and operations.[41]

What most concerns critics is what they see as the concessioners' continual drive for more facilities and urbanlike services in the parks.* A leading environmentalist critic of park policies, Michael Frome, wrote in 1983 that:

> It would be one thing if park concessioners over the years had demonstrated concern and responsibility for park resources. But the concern of the most vocal and powerful of them has been for the protection of their vested interests—of the public subsidy they receive for private profit. . . . They have allowed park visitors to stay overnight in buildings that constitute fire hazards and have marketed the worst kinds of trashy trinket souvenirs at exorbitant profit.[42]

Along similar lines, Destry Jarvis of NPCA complains that park service oversight is too lax, allowing "concessioners' profits . . . to be more important than protection of park resources."[43] Commenting on Fortune 500 and similar companies becoming concessioners, Joseph Sax observes that:

> The acquisition of park concessions by large recreation industry corporations presents a novel problem. More than a century's experience demonstrates that without supplementary, high-profit amusement facilities, traditional hotels and restaurants are not very remunerative. There is little evidence to suggest that the new breed of industrial concessionaires wants anything less than maximum profits.[44]

Major concessioners and their supporters respond to these criticisms in a variety of ways. Some complain that environmentalists only want the parks for themselves. "The Park Service is cutting

---

*These concerns, and others over policies that promote concessioners' investment and the effects those investments have on park preservation and use, were intensified by former Secretary Watt's previously noted initiatives to increase concessioners' participation.

back the concessioner methodically so that we have less and less security. . . . It's all because of intense pressure from environmentalists who want to keep the parks pristine and only allow young people who can backpack to use them," says Don Hummel, former head of the Conference of National Park Concessioners and Glacier Park Company.[45]

Major concessioners also point to their need for revenues, contending that certain levels or particular types of services are provided to allow operators a sufficient return on investment. They complain that critics lump all concessions together even though some operations are in poor financial condition. The costs of providing, for example, only one medium to inexpensively priced hotel and restaurant in certain areas cannot be made up, they maintain, unless some services that entail lower costs and higher returns (such as souvenir sales) are allowed to offset the losses.

Most frequently, though, concessioners base their arguments for permission to provide more services on the grounds that they provide what visitors want. In recent years, this had led to debates over the purposes of the parks and the role the market should play in determining what goes on inside them. Critics claim that concessioners' developments tend to create a market for the services they provide. As Joseph Sax asserts, "The building of elaborate hotels, shops and modern campgrounds attracts more and more people in search of the kind of recreation those facilities promote."[46] Moreover, concessioners put continual pressure on the park service for permission to provide more. To quote Sax again, "the commercial imperative is to develop, to find new markets, and exploit them. . . . What concessioners want most is the opportunity for additional development—the chance to build more facilities and sell more services."[47]

Even if major concessioners are satisfying demand rather than creating it, however, the question remains whether the parks should supply the full range of market demands. In 1974, then park service Deputy Director Russell Dickenson (he later served as director of the service) answered that it should. Responding to congressional questioning regarding the appropriateness of liquor sales by concessioners inside national parks, Dickenson said:

> Our position as administrators of public parkland is to reflect the appropriate requests and views and needs of public services, and it is our view that the public has sought and has wanted the sale of alcoholic beverages where the public accommodations are.[48]

Preservationists, not surprisingly, see the issue differently: only those demands consistent with park purposes—use and enjoyment of park resources, not urbanlike services—should be satisfied inside the parks. In the provision of goods and services, no less than in other management decisions, the park service is expected to lead rather than follow consumer demands. As Sax notes: "People get the recreation that imaginative leadership gives them. No one wanted Disneyland any more than they wanted Yosemite National Park. The question is whether there is a legitimate place in this society for recreation that is not likely to be sufficiently profitable for private entrepreneurs."[49]

## Park Service Responses to the Concerns: Concessioners as Public Utilities

In recent years, the park service has moved toward a public utility model in managing concessioners.* As one recent study of park concessioners notes:

> They are highly regulated by the NPS [National Park Service], which can cap prices and go so far as to inflict unprofitable lines of business on concessioners to ensure balanced service to the public. Conversely, the concessioner has an almost guaranteed access to a protected market.[51]

Virtually every aspect of a concessioner's business is regulated by the service. The food served, the service provided, the facility built, the souvenir sold, the rafts floated down the river—all of these and more come under the careful scrutiny of the park service. Even the amount of beef put into a hamburger is evaluated to approve the price charged to the public.[52]

Based on economic feasibility studies and examination of a unit's characteristics, the park service determines the facilities and services to be provided by concessioners. It establishes the rates charged, basing them on factors that vary from park to park, prices charged by vendors outside the parks, the size of the concessioner's

---

*Things were more rough-and-ready in the early days. When the Great Northern Railroad had finished a hotel in Glacier, Stephen Mather reminded the company that its sawmill must leave the park. At the company's request, Mather granted it more time. The deadline expired and the railroad company again asked for additional time, although the hotel was already receiving guests. Mather, who was in the park at the time, rounded up park service trail crews that afternoon and had the sawmill blown up.[50]

*Yellowstone, August 1984. Kitchen in hotel.*

investment, the length of season, and the cost of labor and materials.[53]

The service also sets the franchise fees a concessioner pays for the privilege of operating in a national park. These fees are based on the concessioner's opportunity to make a profit, the rate of return required to encourage further investment by that concessioner in the park, whether an improvement program has been or is under way, and the objectives of the contract.[54] In 1983, figures from concessioners showed that, on average, they paid 1.8 percent of their gross receipts as franchise fees.[55] Franchise fees paid by individual concessioners in 1983 ranged from a high of $723,480 to a low of $50.[56] (Figure 5.1 shows aggregate concessioners' gross receipts, income before taxes, and franchise fees since 1977.)

In the wake of problems in Yosemite, Yellowstone, and elsewhere, and other influences in the 1970s, the service has increased its ability to oversee concessions. One of the most important changes has been a commitment to increasing staff and funding for concession management. In 1971, for example, concession management in the service was centralized in 20 full-time positions, 16 of them in Washington. The budget was $386,000. By 1985, the service had a concession management budget totaling about $3.5 million and had 87 full-time-equivalent positions concerned with concessions, most of them in regional offices and in those parks having the largest concession operations.[57]

**Figure 5.1**
**Total Concessioner Receipts, Income, and Fees, 1977–1983**
**(in million dollars)**

|      | Gross receipts | Income before taxes | Franchise fees |
|------|----------------|---------------------|----------------|
| 1977 | $189.4         | $18.5               | $3.7           |
| 1978 | 220.9          | 21.1                | 4.2            |
| 1979 | 233.0          | 19.2                | 4.4            |
| 1980 | 266.2          | 20.6                | 4.9            |
| 1981 | 309.0          | 28.7                | 5.7            |
| 1982 | 318.8          | 30.9                | 5.8            |
| 1983 | 340.0          | 30.6                | 6.2            |

Source: National Park Service, Concessions Division, 1985.

Responsibilities for concession management are divided among Washington headquarters, the regional offices, and the parks. The parks have authority to administer concession authorizations, approve rates, implement capital improvement projects, and ensure that the operations are well managed on a day-to-day basis. The regions ensure that the policies of the park service director are implemented, that the contracts are negotiated and executed in a timely fashion, and that the contracts protect the interests of the park and public. The Washington concessions office develops policies and procedures. As one of the originators of this arrangement noted, "it recognizes that Washington could never know enough about a park to get directly involved in the contracting."[58] The Denver Service Center, which has a concessions branch, acts as a consultant to the regions, providing economic analysis and feasibility studies on various projects.

The beefing-up of staff has occurred qualitatively as well as quantitatively. Back in 1974, then park service Director Ron Walker testified, in response to congressional questioning on concessions management, that

> We have not been tough with them. They, in turn, have been able to cut deals, and to confuse or to hoodwink a superintendent because he is not knowledgeable in hotel management, in food management, in

the sales of curios and souvenirs. . . . [W]e expect the poor superintendent, who came out of park recreation management, a zoologist or
botanist to be a businessman and handle these programs involving large
sums of money and assets.[59]

Today, the chief of the concessions division notes that the service
can "deal with concessioners more on a business-like basis, rather
than on just an environmental basis as we used to in the past."[60]
Accountants, financial analysts, and persons with experience in
the food, hotel, and general merchandise industries are among those
who have been been gradually added to the concession management staff. In addition, a program of periodic seminars and training
sessions for service personnel, including superintendents, has been
initiated to improve their knowledge of the food and lodging industries and contracting issues.

A detailed concessioner inspection and evaluation program has
been instituted; every facet of an operation is inspected and, in
essence, rated by park personnel. This inspection also forms the
basis for determining whether there is annual compliance with the
contract—and whether a concessioner is entitled to a preferential
right to contract renewal. Training sessions are held on contract
and rate approval. Standard contract language has been devised
with provisions inserted to take account of past problems, consistent
with the Concessions Policy Act.[61]

The park service also requires an annual financial report from
each concessioner. Concessioners with sales of $250,000 to $1
million a year must have their financial statements reviewed by independent accountants, and those with sales in excess of $1 million
a year are required to have their financial statements independently
audited. These annual reports are reviewed by the appropriate park
and region and then analyzed by the concessions division in Washington. One park service concessions official notes that "the annual
financial reports are used in everything we do; they are one of the
best management tools we have."[62]

## Future Needs and Opportunities

Four kinds of measures deserve consideration as possible responses
to continuing concerns about the role of concessions in the parks.
Releasing financial data on individual concessioners, to permit informed public scrutiny of the park service's oversight process and
evaluation of possible changes in that process, is one essential step.
The other opportunities are buy-outs, revision of the terms of conces-

sion contracts as opportunities arise, and strengthening of the oversight process.

### Release of Information on Profitability

Under the Concessions Policy Act, the park service has broad discretion to determine what services concessioners provide, what rates they charge, and what franchise fees they pay. The service must consider each concessioner's opportunities to make a profit, so it requires each one to submit financial data. Public efforts to obtain the data, however, have been unavailing; the service releases some aggregate data for concessioners as a whole, but does not provide the data on individual concessioners that would allow public scrutiny of dealings between the concessioners and the park service. Operating on public land, often under contracts that confer a long-term right to operate with little or no competition, concessioners are subject to a regulatory process that resembles that of a public utility regulatory commission—yet that process is not fully open to public accountability.

Both concessioners and the park service contend that information on the gross receipts and net profits of these operations must be kept confidential to protect the competitive position of concessioners. Such information is beyond the reach of the Freedom of Information Act, they claim, citing a court ruling in the mid-1970s on a request by the National Parks and Conservation Association for detailed financial information far beyond that involving profitability.[63]

As a result, public efforts to evaluate the oversight process must rely on estimates and inferences. Systemwide data reveal, for example, that 71 percent of current concessions show a profit,[64] although the public cannot determine what goes into these calculations or what the profit margins are. Discussions with concessioners and park service personnel indicate that some concessioners—particularly small, one-park businesses—make very little profit but that a few do quite well.

That businesses continually bid for concession contracts is evidence of their belief that operations are or could be profitable. Another factor suggesting profitability is the takeover of some concessions by major corporations including those that already operate concessions in other parks. Four of the six bids for the major concession at Yellowstone in 1981 came from such companies.[65]

Reliance on inferences such as these is not an acceptable substitute for evaluating the data that the service is withholding. The service should reexamine its finding that such information is exempt from the Freedom of Information Act. If necessary, Congress should enact legislation to make this information available. Disclosure would permit more effective public scrutiny of the rates set and activities permitted by the park service as well as reduce opportunities for favoritism in establishing and administering contracts. It would also enlarge the opportunity for informed dialogue between concessioners and other park interests, with less of the stridency that must be expected when the facts are kept secret.

### Buy-outs: Separating Ownership from Operation

Several possible reasons can exist for considering a public buy-out of a concessioner's interest. One, exemplified by the Yellowstone buy-out, is to remove a concessioner that is not complying with contractual requirements. Another is to get rid of facilities that are no longer compatible with park needs. Still another is to reduce the concessioner's investment and thus enable it to make a profit or alter operations to fit changing conditions.

During the 1970s, the park service purchased possessory interests, many of them quite small, at about 10 parks.[66] Some interests were bought because the concessioner was having difficulty making ends meet. In a few cases, the acquisitions allowed the concessioner to continue operations and turn the business around. In recent years, however, possessory interests have not been purchased.

In the near future, too, tight budgets are likely to permit few, if any, buy-outs, especially of the larger concessions. Purchase of possessory interests under typical contracts requires the park service to pay fair market value and is thus very expensive. In addition, congressional appropriations may be difficult to justify compared with other park needs, especially if a buy-out is desired for some reason other than nonperformance.

Recent changes, however, do make certain types of buy-outs less costly. In cases of unsatisfactory performance, statutory and policy changes in the wake of the Yellowstone buy-out reduce the price that the service must pay. One year of unsatisfactory performance or two consecutive years of marginal performance are grounds for terminating a concession contract. If this happens, the park service no longer has to pay fair market value for a possessory interest in park facilities; instead, it must pay only the book value of the facilities, less depreciation.[67]

Moreover, as a result of a recent change in park service policy, concession contracts are to provide only book-value compensation for structures that are damaging to the park environment and are to be removed completely from the park. (Facilities simply relocated within a park are still to be given fair market value.) It is unclear whether this new policy will be applied to renewals of existing concession contracts; with many major contracts coming up for renewal over the next decade, this will be an important issue.

There may also be opportunities to secure funding for buy-outs from heretofore untapped sources. Suggestions include, for example, creating "quasi-public benefit corporations" to finance buy-outs and having philanthropic arms of major corporations underwrite concession facilities much as they sponsor public television programs.[68]

### Reducing Protections as Opportunities Arise

Some concessioners maintain that traditional contract terms, notably the granting of possessory interests equal to the fair market value of the concessioner's investment, are essential for continued investment. Although an absence of information makes it difficult to evaluate such claims, the terms of a few recent contracts at least make clear that some traditional protections are not always needed.

For example, one of the contracts for Yellowstone's major concessioner, TW Services, contains an innovative provision designed to rehabilitate, replace, and in a few cases relocate facilities, consistent with the park's management plan, without granting a possessory interest. Negotiated in 1981, the five-year contract imposed no franchise fees. Instead, the concessioner agreed to invest 22 percent of its annual gross receipts in a Capital Improvement and Maintenance Program. Only improvements beyond that commitment give TW a possessory interest (to the extent of additional investment), and this interest will be the unamortized book value of the improvements, not the fair market value traditionally granted.[69]

In a similar arrangement, when the park service contracted in 1982 with National Park Concessions, Inc., to operate facilities at five parks, the concessioner committed over $2.3 million to improve

*Yellowstone, August 1984. Original Hamilton's Store, with Terry Povah (inset), store manager and grandson of the store's founder. "We started in 1915; the park service started in 1916. We're one of the few family-owned, long-established concessioners in the park system. My grandfather was a very enterprising guy who recognized a need. He fulfilled that need and was willing to reinvest all of his profits or a tremendous amount of his profits back into the facility to keep the plant going. . . . A lot of the problems that have gone on historically, not just at Yellowstone but at some of the other parks, have been that they are very seasonal, very expensive to maintain and operate. As a result, you get people in here that skim the summer business and don't put money back into the facility and then sell it. You have a turnover of concessioners and management, and you don't have the personal vested interest that you do with a privately held corporation. That is true in a lot of the parks. . . . We have a good working relationship with the park service, and, when they make inspections, anything less than a "98" is unacceptable as far as our own in-house management is concerned."*

public facilities. An additional 1.5 percent of gross receipts is to go toward upgrading and constructing visitor facilities.[70] In some cases, book-value possessory interests are given, and in others the higher fair market or sound value is granted.

Contracts containing such provisions have been entered into or are being negotiated for several other parks. The park service has been seeking a $200 million commitment from concessioners over the next few years to rehabilitate visitor facilities in the parks. In recent years, the park service has identified rehabilitation needs and has sought concessioner investment by entering into longer term contracts in return for the reinvestment commitment. Although the service has started to examine each case individually, in most a corresponding enlargement of the concessioner's market-value possessory interest has been granted.[71]

It sometimes has been assumed that the Concessions Policy Act requires the service to grant all the traditional protections in new concession contracts. In fact, as the experience with innovative contracts at Yellowstone and other parks makes clear, the act gives the service substantial discretion. The act does not require the granting of preferential rights to provide new or additional services, nor does it require the park service to grant monopolies to concessioners. In addition, the act gives possessory interests to a concessioner for any improvement acquired or constructed, at a valuation not to exceed fair market value, "unless otherwise provided by agreement."[72] Thus, even in dealing with possessory interests, the park service is free to negotiate the formula for compensation when new contracts are drafted.

The situation is less clear when an existing contract expires and is renewed or extended. By law, a previous possessory interest does not expire when a contract expires. In negotiating a new contract, however, there may be situations in which concessioners are willing to modify those interests as part of a contractual arrangement that confers other benefits.

Given its flexibility, the Concessions Policy Act can be more compatible with park interests than some have previously thought. Although statutory revision could remove the service's authority to grant some incentives, the service could do a good deal of tightening up under present law.

Two principal protections are required by the act. One is the requirement that the secretary of the interior (on behalf of the park service) exercise authority so that concessioners can realize a profit. This probably should be retained in any revision. The other is the requirement that concessioners who have performed satisfactorily be given a preferential right to contract renewal.* Intended as an incentive for good performance—a concessioner who can earn the preferential right will presumably strive harder to get it—the preferential renewal right gives concessioners a great deal of influence and an almost guaranteed right to continue operations indefinitely.

Continuity of service may indeed be preferable to the results of periodic competitive bidding. In the past, however, some concessioners, while maintaining that such a right was essential to obtaining needed capital to build and upgrade facilities, have used it to increase the value of the operation in negotiating its sale. The Concessions Policy Act should be amended to make the preferential right to contract renewal discretionary rather than mandatory, giving the park service more flexibility to determine and negotiate in individual situations.

Park service policy should also seek to ensure that another preferential right—the right to provide additional services—is granted rarely, if at all. When routinely granted, the right seems to perpetuate the service's inability to respond to changing conditions and inspire high-quality performance. The right increases the influence and negotiating position of concessioners; it does little to motivate high-quality performance or assure the best arrangement for the public.

Possessory interests will continue to stand in the way of the park service's efforts to compel responses by concessioners to changing conditions.† Based on the information currently available, as a long-term goal, the park service should use every opportunity to move toward a situation in which possessory interests are valued at un-

---

*This right, guaranteed by the Concessions Policy Act, allows an existing concessioner to meet any bid offered that is more favorable than its own and therefore retain its contract. In fact, if the present concessioner comes close to meeting the bid, it generally receives the contract because the park service must also give weight to prior satisfactory service and favors continuity of operations.

†In reviewing the arrangements under which concessioners operate, a U.S. court of appeals found that "This compensable possessory interest, where it has been incorporated into a current concession contract, poses a considerable, even insuperable barrier to competition at the contract renewal stage."[73]

amortized book value rather than fair market or sound value. If the service cannot move in this direction on its own, Congress should take the necessary steps to support such an objective.

## Strengthening Park Service Oversight

Oversight of concessioners will continue to be a formidable challenge for the park service. Despite park service control over virtually all aspects of a concessioner's operation, concessioners, especially the larger ones, have powerful tools at their disposal that require the service, in essence, to coexist as equals with the concessioner.

For example, with 10 years left to go on a contract plus a preferential right to renewal and to provide additional services, a concessioner has considerable leverage in responding to requests from the park service. If a park superintendent asks a concessioner to operate a tour and shuttle-bus system, the concessioner may respond that it will consider the request only if the park allows it to raise its rates at a nearby hotel, include more souvenirs or other gift items in its store, or do something else to increase its profits. In one park recently, the opportunity to have a small lodging facility turned into a youth hostel was not pursued because the major concessioner's contract gave right of first refusal to provide additional accommodations in the park.[74] Even where the contract permits the superintendent to dictate terms to the concessioner, the practical considerations in conducting a day-to-day relationship may lead the superintendent to side with the concessioner.

A 1982 study of franchise fee policies by an independent accounting firm stated that:

> Concessioners enjoy a security of continuity unknown in the private or public sector. . . . The preferential right of renewal (assisted by the practical effect of possessory interest) essentially guarantees that the competent concessioner has perpetual enjoyment of a monopolistic environment. . . . As a result of these privileges . . . the negotiations between the two parties cannot be considered to be at full arms length. They are more akin to partners bound together, who, while bargaining to increase their individual positions, must consider the positions of both parties as a whole to maximize the returns of both parties.[75]

Although the park service has made several significant advances in responding to this difficult situation, additional strengthening of its concession management capabilities could increase the contributions made by major concession operations and reduce their

impact on park resources. Periodic training programs for concessions branch personnel should continue and be expanded. Information and experience in dealing with the private sector should be
systematically exchanged with other federal and state land agencies.
(Other federal agencies, for example, typically do not grant
possessory interests to concessioners.[76]) Programs should also be
instituted for concessioners' employees—at the concessioners'
expense—so they are aware of the changing needs of the parks and
visitors. Dealing with increasing numbers of park users who do not
speak English is one area in which the park service and concessioners could improve.

In general, the park service's oversight should reward concessioners for doing what is best for park visitors, consistent with park
values. For the most part, concessioners' services meet minimum
standards of quality, but they often fail to show creativity or regional
distinctiveness. Greater use of financial incentives and penalties,
such as fee reductions and increases, might encourage creativity
if fashioned in ways that correspond to the diversity of operators
and service needs in the parks.

Virtually every type of private sector arrangement—concessioners,
nonprofit cooperating associations, contractors, volunteers—comes
under the purview of a different office within the park service. Some
of these arrangements present similar problems, but there seems
to be little communication and exchange of information among different park service branches. So that each office may learn from
the others, routine coordination and exchange of activities and information are essential. There might also be some value in consolidating some of the service's offices.

Although the service's regulatory approach appears to be a realistic response to current needs, more cost-effective ways of administering concession regulations need to be explored so that both the
service and the private operators are not overwhelmed by costly
administrative burdens. Regulatory requirements should take better
account of the differences in concessioners' sizes, services, and investments in the parks.

### The Need for Continual Reassessment

Growing pressures on parks' resources, coupled with increasing
demands for authenticity in visitors' experiences, create a continual
need to reassess the place of concession facilities and services in

the parks. Changes will not come rapidly. In thinking about concessions, as in thinking about the parks generally, it is important to
consider the long term. Park service policy is already clear about
dealing with proposed new concessioners. New commercial services
are to be provided outside the parks when possible, not within them:

> If adequate facilities exist or can feasibly be developed by private enter-
> prise to serve the park visitors' needs for commercial services outside
> of park boundaries, such facilities shall not be expanded or developed
> within park areas. The service shall cooperate with state and local gov-
> ernments to develop the recreational region around major parks in a
> manner designed to meet the visitors' needs without degradation of the
> non-park environment or loss of quality of the visitor experience through
> uncontrolled and unregulated growth.[77]

This policy, if carried out, will benefit the parks, the public, and
most providers of commercial services. Although facilities inside
the parks could be a source of federal revenues and, if sensitively
located, might be less obtrusive than some commercial establishments in gateway communities, those benefits are more than out-
weighed by the likelihood that new commercial installations would
harm park resources and diminish the visitors' experience. In the
infrequent cases in which new concessioners are needed to provide services, the park service should insist on terms that retain
its power to compel adaptation to changing circumstances.

Much as in the case of new concessions, there appears to be an
emerging consensus against significant expansion of major existing facilities. Former park service Director Russell Dickenson observed that:

> We don't have to try to double the existing accommodations at the Grand
> Canyon or Yellowstone or any place else. I see that plant as essentially
> fixed. Any increase in visitations that cannot be properly accommodated
> within the existing facilities will have to be absorbed by gateway com-
> munities—by the private sector. Most of the big national parks should
> not be further developed for overnight accommodations and the kinds
> of amenities that are associated with public visitations.[78]

Translating this sentiment into action will be an ongoing test of
the park service's commitment to sensitive integration of major concessioners. The service's policies officially recognize the importance
of locating concession operations "where the least damage to park
values will occur." The opening of major new facilities in Yellowstone's Grant Village, an area now considered by many to be important grizzly bear habitat (see the profile of Yellowstone), creates

doubt, however, about park service sensitivity in applying the policy.

Management of the older, major facilities will continue to challenge evolving sensibilities. Although concessioners' facilities that resemble small communities almost certainly would not be permitted today, there is little likelihood that they will soon be removed. A few facilities have become historic structures in their own right. Others are protected by long-term contractual guarantees that make buy-outs expensive. All serve large numbers of visitors, some of whom are likely to join with the concessioners in appealing to politics and custom in resisting removal. The public utility approach of the park service establishes a realistic framework for the unavoidable coexistence of established major facilities and some of the most magnificent park resources. The service should, of course, continue to reduce the effects of the facilities on park resources and visitors' experiences—for example, by continuing recent efforts to relocate or remove structures from particularly unsuitable locations. As opportunities arise, the service also should use provisions of the Concessions Policy Act to modify concession contract terms to enhance quality, appropriateness, and responsiveness to changing conditions.

In addition, more sensitive, informed public participation in the formulation and application of concession policy is needed. Views on concessioners tend to be polarized, and constructive dialogue among interested parties—the park service, concessioners, and conservation groups—has, unfortunately, not been a significant part of arriving at policy. Release of information on profitability is essential for including the public in this dialogue.

One result of the traditional stridency is that, as viewpoints are aired about concession policy, the diversity of concessioner and private sector activity is often overlooked. The focus in debates is on the dozen or so largest operations in the great western parks. These operators get lumped together in both perceptions and policies with the hundreds of other concessioners, many of which are small, local, one-park businesses that have not found the parks to be a gold mine for their investment and hard work. Despite their significantly smaller staffs and less substantial profits, small concessioners, like larger ones, must contend with massive amounts of regulation and paperwork and occasionally drawn-out processes for making decisions. As a result, generalizations too often tend to oversimplify the issues that surround various concessioners' involvement.

Also overlooked at times are some of the valuable contributions that concessioners—big as well as small—have made and continue to make in the parks. Some operators and their employees have worked in a particular park longer, and feel more attached to it, than park service staff who have moved from park to park throughout their careers.[79] Some concessioners have long been involved with interpretative programs that enrich visits. And, in some areas, concessioners offer access and facilities to many visitors who otherwise might not be able to enjoy a national park. It is up to these operations, the park service that regulates them, and the conservation groups that monitor both to further this part of the concessioner tradition.

## NEW AND EXPANDING ROLES FOR THE PRIVATE SECTOR

Greater reliance on the private sector has been a key element of the Reagan administration's policy for the parks. "Management efficiency" guidelines issued by the park service require superintendents to more aggressively seek outside financial support, to increase activity by volunteers and cooperating associations, to contract out more services, and to allow concessioners to play a larger role in the parks.[80] They also call for establishing new fees on services to visitors and for raising existing fees. Superintendents are encouraged to seek private donations through fundraising campaigns, gift catalogs, donation boxes, and "adopt-a-park" campaigns. Performance under the guidelines is a factor in evaluating superintendents' performances.

Both revenues and donations have increased in recent years. Yet, because the guidelines only went into effect at the beginning of 1983, it is too early to evaluate performance under them. They have not, however, been without their critics, both within and outside the park service. Some in the service view the guidelines as a major change in direction for the parks that will cheapen the public's image of the system, cause superintendents to spend too much time on matters not within the basic mission of the service, and enable the private sector to have too great a role in the parks. They worry of fostering unnecessary competition among parks and superintendents and spending more money than the parks will receive in return. One superintendent complained that "it costs me about $100 to process every donation of $20."

Conservation groups and citizens active in specific parks also express concern that the guidelines emphasize reducing park costs at the expense of protecting park resources. Perhaps most disturbing to these groups is the notion that park superintendents will be evaluated on the basis of how much money they raise for a park—a more easily quantified standard than the quality of the environment they maintain and the quality of visit their parks provide.

The most controversial aspect of these efforts to increase management efficiency has been the attempt to rely more heavily on outside contractors for work, such as maintenance, normally performed by park service personnel. Under an Office of Management and Budget (OMB) policy (called A-76) that had been around for years, the park service, under former Secretary Watt's command, was required to assess the costs of several service-provided activities and then to put those services out for competitive bid; if a private contractor could save 10 percent, the service was to contract the activity out.[81] This enraged some park service employees (who feared losing their jobs as well as diminishing park quality) and preservationists. The result was a 1984 law that largely exempts the service from the OMB circular.[82]

Without fanfare or controversy, however, the private sector's participation in the parks has been increasing for more than two decades. As the park system expanded and diversified, the contributions of nonprofit organizations and volunteers, in particular, increased too. This dynamism is one of the elements that the management guidelines seek to tap. Other efforts also promise to continue or enlarge the private sector's participation. Based not on ideology but on a desire to address needs that the park service cannot best address alone, these efforts include leasing of historic properties, permitting agriculture in the parks, and stimulating travel to lesser-used parks.

### Nonprofit Organizations and Volunteers

Nonprofit organizations account for much of the increased private sector participation. The groups are diverse—from large cooperating associations and foundations with programs in many parks, to small, volunteer-run, one-park groups. Although the expansion of nonprofit activity has taken place in old and new units alike, it is most

*Yosemite, February 1984. Ron Voss and Janet Olson (San Lorenzo, California) in the Ahwanee Hotel. "We were married here in the valley last year, and now we're returning for our anniversary. This place is never the same; yet it's like coming home. We really value the quiet, especially since she teaches sixth, seventh, and eighth grade. We brought the top layer of our wedding cake back, but it defrosted on the ride over, so it was a mess. The kitchen crew at the Ahwanee completely redecorated it—with whipped cream and strawberries. Everyone's been so nice."*

prominent in parks created within the last two decades. Some of the units established in or adjacent to metropolitan areas are becoming centers of innovative private sector activity. Renovation at the Fort Mason Center in Golden Gate has brought cultural and commercial resurgence; economic revitalization has been a primary park objective at Lowell; and working farms and compatible private businesses have remained within Cuyahoga. Golden Gate alone has roughly 100 nonprofit organizations operating in the park that perform a variety of tasks, including building and trail maintenance, fundraising, interpretation, food service, and classroom education to the community.[83]

Nonprofit organizations promise to hold an increasingly prominent place among private sector activities in the parks. Because their activities are relatively new and unheralded and because no single office in the park service oversees or evaluates their contributions, it is important to look at the spectrum of opportunities that exist

for the private sector, the relationships between these organizations
and the park service, and the policies needed to assure that outside involvement safeguards the parks and enriches visitors' experiences.

## Cooperating Associations

Library, museum, and historical societies support the park service
in many areas. Congress recognized these cooperating associations
in 1946 and authorized the secretary of the interior to assist them.
As of early 1985, 64 associations existed in over 300 units of the
system; two of them—Eastern National Park and Monument Association and Southwest Parks and Monuments Association—operate
in more units than any others.[84]

In general, these nonprofit associations produce interpretative
materials, such as guide leaflets, pictures, crafts, maps, and books;
acquire historic objects and develop displays; install museums and
other facilities; distribute educational and scientific materials produced by the park service; operate book stores and sales counters;
furnish newsletters about park activities to visitors; and conduct
tours in some parks and interpretative lectures and films in others.[85]
At Gettysburg, for example, the Eastern National Park and Monument Association operates the bookstores and publishes pamphlets
about the area's history; it also developed a 30-minute electric map
program that tells the story of the battle there.[86]

Cooperating associations sometimes assist the park service in less
conventional ways. For example, in Crater Lake in 1981, one association printed and set up road signs around the park because park
funds were low and because, according to one service official, "It
would have probably taken months to get formal approval, requisi-
tion, and printing when those signs were needed yesterday." Two
cooperating associations, one at Golden Gate and the other at the
Jefferson National Expansion Memorial, hired directors of development to lead in fundraising and "friend-raising" efforts.[87]

Receipts of cooperating associations in excess of their costs are
turned over to the park service to support interpretative programs
in the park, with a small percentage of total profits generally appor-
tioned to the park service director's fund. In 1983, cooperating
associations had gross sales of $20.9 million and returned $3.3
million to the parks.[88]

The park service has a large say in the organization and activities of the associations. A park service employee (usually the chief park interpreter or historian) works with each cooperating association. Service personnel also advise associations on business matters and conduct training sessions. Similarly, cooperating associations' merchandise and their pricing decisions are subject to the park service's approval. The service has compiled a list of "appropriate" items that associations may sell and has complete editorial and design control over all publications. Cooperative agreements with each association run a maximum of five years, but they sometimes give rights to automatic renewal if performance is satisfactory. All associations must submit an annual financial report; those grossing more than $250,000 must submit audited financial statements.[89]

## Volunteers

Thousands of people donate time each year to help interpret, protect, and maintain the parks. In fiscal year 1984, nearly 27,000 volunteers contributed 1.2 million hours of work in some 265 parks. The value of this volunteer time is conservatively estimated to be $8.5 million.[90]

One of the most prominent vehicles for volunteer activity is the Volunteer in Parks (VIP) program, which Congress created in 1970.[91] Funded at $1 million in 1985 (up from $250,000 in previous years), the program provides unpaid volunteers with worker compensation, coverage for tort liability, and, in some cases, the use of a campsite and reimbursement for out-of-pocket expenses. VIPs cannot supplant park service staff but can fill jobs no longer funded. About 8 percent of the VIP workforce are over 61 years old; 23 percent are under 18. Some 45 percent are women.[92] VIP participants have been involved in living history performances, arts and crafts demonstrations, and resource identification and environmental education projects.

Other vehicles for volunteer activity include national organizations, such as the Sierra Club, and local support groups, such as the Committee to Preserve Assateague Island. In 1982, about 600 high school and college student volunteers worked in nearly 80 park system units through the private Student Conservation Program.[93] The Appalachian Trail Conference, which includes about

60 organizations, performs operation and maintenance tasks on the Appalachian Trail, saving the park service more than $1 million a year.[94]

The park service recently expanded its efforts with volunteers, encouraging their participation in a wider variety of activities, attempting to recruit more highly qualified persons, and paying more attention to their management. As the park service increases its reliance on outsiders, it needs to become even more sophisticated in their recruitment, training, and administration. As a step in this direction, the park service conducted a VIP management training program and clearinghouse for improved recruitment in 1983 and 1984. It also began evaluating volunteer programs more systematically in 1983 and should expand those efforts.[95]

## Fundraising and Support

Fundraising and support from a variety of private sources are gaining momentum in several parks. Private funds often are given for acquiring land, restoring and maintaining parks, compiling historical collections, buying equipment, and upgrading visitors' services. The $115 million raised in fiscal year 1983 for repairing the Statue of Liberty and Ellis Island came from a variety of private sources, including bake sales and door-to-door canvassing by elementary school children, direct mail solicitation, and corporate sponsorship. The Custer Battlefield Preservation Committee formed in 1982 to help acquire 9,000 acres within the authorized boundary of Custer Battlefield, had raised nearly $100,000 by the end of 1984. Funds have also been provided by the National Park Foundation, the National Parks and Conservation Association (NPCA), and others.[96]

Nonprofit organizations have been instrumental in acquiring lands, historic artifacts, and furnishings for park units. Almost 5 percent of the land brought into National Park Service, Forest Service, and Fish and Wildlife Service management between 1965 and 1979 was bought first by nonprofit organizations such as the Nature Conservancy, the National Park Foundation, the Trust for Public Land, and various local groups. Private donations were instrumental in establishing Women's Rights National Historical Park in 1981 and have played a key role in several other areas designated within the last decade.[97]

One organization that provides systemwide support to various park activities is the National Park Foundation, a nonprofit quasi-public corporation chartered by Congress in 1967 to encourage private gifts to the parks and to provide grants for projects of direct benefit to the park service. From 1968 to 1979, the foundation, at the request of the park service, acquired and protected 65 tracts of land, totaling over 27,300 acres with an appraised value of nearly $19 million, for subsequent inclusion in the park system. Some of these tracts were donated outright to the foundation; others were bought with contributions to the foundation.[98]

During this same period, the foundation supported 95 projects through direct grants to the park service for environmental education and park management programs and for visitors' interpretation activities. Since 1983, it has administered the Visitors Facility Fund, which was created by Congress in 1982 to reinvest revenues from concessioners' franchise fees to rehabilitate government-owned buildings in the parks.[99] The secretary of the interior serves as chairman of the foundation's board of directors, which includes the director of the park service and individuals appointed by the interior secretary for six-year terms.

Another way in which private sector support for park activities is manifested is through gift solicitation catalogs for individual parks. Santa Monica Mountains produced the park system's first gift catalog, a stylish document funded by Chevron U.S.A. The catalog suggests donations of all kinds, ranging from rehabilitating a western-town movie set to providing transportation and camping equipment for inner-city residents. Listed prices are from $10 to $30,000. Issued in November 1982, the Santa Monica catalog attracted over $320,000 in gifts to the park by early 1984. (See the Santa Monica Mountains profile.)

Following Santa Monica's lead, 19 other parks have developed gift solicitation catalogs, and 31 more catalogs were in production in early 1985. Admitting that such an approach is not applicable to every park unit, one of the prime movers behind this idea observed there are at least three benefits to producing a gift catalog and soliciting outside funds: "It gets park equipment that it [the park] probably would not be able to secure through the budget process; it gives a park local and national visibility, something that is especially important for the newer units; and, by identifying park needs, it helps crystallize staff thinking."[100]

As another part of this effort, more attention is being paid to setting up collection devices in the parks. As of early 1985, donation boxes had been placed in over 62 parks. Similar to those found in many art museums, the boxes are for voluntary contributions and are located and displayed unobtrusively. A change in Interior Department policy permits individual parks to keep the proceeds from those boxes if a plaque or notice nearby states how the funds will be spent. For example, Hawaii Volcanoes National Park, which has no entrance fee, collected about $20,000 in 1984 through its donation box; the proceeds went directly to the park's interpretative program.[101]

## Leasing Historic Properties

The park service has been negotiating the lease of a lighthouse at Fire Island to a radio station. The proposed lease calls for placing an antenna on the top of the tower, using 200 square feet of storage space in the basement of the keepers' quarters, allowing the lighthouse to be a corporate symbol, and installing a wiring system within the lighthouse. The radio station will pay $300,000, which will offset nearly 40 percent of the costs of total restoration. The keepers' quarters and the lighthouse will remain open to the public.[102] As of early 1985, the lease was awaiting approval by the Federal Communications Commission.

This is but one example of the program under which the park service, in 1982, began leasing historic structures and agricultural lands in parks to individuals and organizations. Authorized by a 1980 amendment to the National Historic Preservation Act, the program is designed to spur rehabilitation and reuse of designated historic structures and land owned by the federal government.[103]* To be eligible, properties must be listed or eligible for listing in the National Register of Historic Places, and the planned reuse of the structure must be compatible with the park unit, although latitude exists in determining appropriate use. By mid-1984, 14 properties had been leased under the program.[104]

Hundreds of historic properties in many units could qualify for leases. The program could also stimulate interest in communities surrounding some of the parks: it creates opportunities for employ-

---

*Antecedents of the program go back over 90 years, when certain Civil War parks were authorized to lease parklands for agricultural uses to retain historical themes. Later legislation authorized a few parks, such as Independence and Golden Gate, to lease land and structures.

ment and investment, and, for historic properties in urban areas, the rehabilitation of park service-owned property could attract other investment in nearby property. Lessees under the program are also eligible for sizable tax credits for rehabilitating buildings when done in conformance with the secretary of the interior's Standards for Rehabilitation and when the property is used commercially. From the standpoint of the park service, another important attraction of the program is that it allows the service to use the proceeds from the leases to maintain and preserve that property or other historic properties within the unit or region. Proceeds from the leases are pooled at the regional level, which then decides how to apportion the money.

The program is being implemented at the park and regional office levels; the Washington office approves leases with an aggregate value of over $1 million or for a term longer than 20 years. According to a directive issued by former park service Director Russell Dickenson, "lease offerings may specify acceptable uses or may be open ended," the latter requiring superintendent approval when a specific use is proposed.[105] Limitations to the leases exist, however, to protect park interests. For example, proposed uses under a lease cannot be inconsistent with park purposes, as set forth in the general management plan for the area; proposed treatments and uses of the property must be compatible with the quality and significance of the historical resource; and the property should not be essential to the significance of the park or otherwise be needed for park service purposes.

To avoid overlap with concession operations, the amendment to the National Historic Preservation Act specifies that the historic property and its proposed use must not be "necessary and appropriate" for public use and enjoyment; if they are, the use comes under the terms of the Concessions Policy Act. This "necessary and appropriate" limitation has been loosely defined over the years, however, so there is some leeway in choosing between the two acts. As a practical matter, park officials considering private sector use of a historic structure may prefer the leasing approach. Unlike concession contracts, historic leases

- allow the proceeds to be returned to the unit that has the property;
- create neither possessory-type interests for improvements made nor preferential rights to renewal;

*Santa Monica Mountains, June 1984. Ron Webster and fellow volunteer from the Sierra Club's Santa Monica Mountains Task Force blazing a trail. "Basically the people working here from the task force are people that like doing this grubby work with their hands. We endure a lot. Lately we've had this rash of horrible bites from some insect on the meadows. We dig out rattlesnakes, we've met every spider, scorpion, biting insect. We've found that there are many things that can poison you besides poison oak. It takes a special kind of person. . . . The trails are very satisfying. Half this crew you see today, maybe more, still lead hikes. I look forward just to going back to trails we've made that I haven't seen for awhile and leading a hike over them and seeing what kind of shape they're in. . . . It's very important to us that people use the trails. We have put trails in rather remote areas, and it's disappointing that the trails won't stand up as well unless they are used. Growth starts back immediately right in the trail tread."*

- permit considerable leeway in what uses can be made of the property;
- do not require the involvement of the park service's Washington headquarters, except for major cases; and
- may last for up to 99 years.[106]

Eventually, the park service expects to lease about 40 to 60 historic properties a year.

A proposed lease for Ellis Island, being considered at the headquarters level, illustrates the opportunities as well as the challenges the program presents. Negotiations have been under way for some

time over the adaptive reuse of the island, the historic entry point
for 17 million immigrants to America. (Forty percent of all Americans can trace their ancestry through Ellis Island.[107]) Various ideas
have been suggested for restoring and interpreting the site. A Statue
of Liberty/Ellis Island Centennial Commission was formed in 1981
to advise the park service on appropriate reuse of the area and to
help raise the necessary funds. Its chairman, Chrysler President Lee
Iacocca, whose parents emigrated to the United States through Ellis
Island, favors noncommercial use of the area, with exhibits and
restoration of the main entry hall as a museum. Funding for this
concept, which would involve 1.5 million square feet of space,
would come largely from private donations. It has been estimated
that the total cost of such an effort would be around $250 million,
of which $40 million has been slated for restoring the Statue of
Liberty.[108]

Another proposal, initiated by a private corporation, involves
developing a portion of Ellis Island under the historic property leasing program for a hotel-conference center. As of mid-1984, the proposal envisaged the developer investing from $50 million to $75
million and rehabilitating, operating, and maintaining the former
hospital buildings under a long-term lease. Under the plan, the
public would retain access to the lobby and the hotel, where park
service staff would provide interpretative services based on the
previous use of the buildings as a hospital. The lease would not
provide funds for restoring the main historic site on the island—
the immigration receiving hall—which alone probably would cost
around $20 million.[109]

## Agriculture in the Parks

More than one-fourth of all park system units include land used
for grazing or farming. There are 56,000 acres of rangelands in Grand
Canyon National Park and 1.5 million acres in Lake Chelan and
Lake Mead national recreation areas; 24,000 acres of beef and dairy
ranches in Golden Gate National Recreation Area and Point Reyes
National Seashore; 400 one- to five-acre sites for row crops in
Natchez Trace Parkway; and over 700 acres of cultivated farmland
at Fredericksburg and Spotsylvania National Military Park.[110] Most
of these agricultural activities are conducted by private citizens and
privately owned businesses under special-use permits from the park
service. The service estimates that there are about 1,000 such per-

mits, although no one apparently knows the exact number or the exact acreage involved.[111]

In the older western national parks, agriculture usually means grazing; there are almost two million acres of rangeland in those parks. However, grazing, which typically was established before public lands were transferred to the park service, has generally been viewed by park service officials as an "encumbrance," an intrusion on natural processes. Grand Teton, Capitol Reef, Dinosaur, and some other parks have specific legislative mandates to phase out grazing and then let natural ecological processes take over. In recent years, range activity in the parks has been declining, but more because of changing economic conditions than because of any park service actions.

At many historic sites and battlefields and in some newer parks, the role of agriculture is very different: it is part of the park scene. "Farming," says a park official, "is one of the most commonly used management tools" to preserve or restore a historical or cultural landscape.[112] A striking example occurred in 1980 in Gettysburg National Military Park when the park service harvested a mixed hardwood pine forest that had grown up since the battle took place and returned the leveled field to crop to restore the areas to what they looked like in July 1863. In some newer parks, whose advocates sought to protect agricultural land from urban development, continued farming is part of the parks' cultural protection purpose. The Marin County ranches in Golden Gate, for example, are often in third-generation ownership and have vivid histories as part of early Mexican-American settlement.

In many historical parks, then, farming under sensitive park service management can be quite compatible with the resource. Special-use permits in the historical parks are short-term, usually from three to five years. This gives the park service some management leverage over environmental impacts and historical authenticity by enabling it to require farmers to adopt adequate protective measures as a condition for permit renewal. For example, in historic areas, the park service may decide to limit the use of modern tools and equipment. At Fredericksburg, farmers are required to submit an annual crop plan describing the types of crops to be planted, the chemicals to be used, and a harvesting schedule; the types of crops planted are strictly controlled to conform to historical authenticity.[113]

For parks in which the primary management concern is natural resources, achieving compatibility is more difficult. Agriculture—despite its scenic, cultural, and historical benefits—can be accompanied by soil erosion, pesticides, contamination of water quality by animal wastes, introduction of exotic species, destruction of wildlife habitat, and so on. The State of the Parks 1980 report by the park service (see chapter 4) described a number of these and other agriculture-related impacts on park resources, particularly from areas outside park boundaries. Little solid information is available about the extent of these impacts, however, or about how much conditions could be improved by better management. According to park officials, oversight of potentially harmful activities associated with agriculture on park service lands has improved since the State of the Parks 1980 report.

The park service, nevertheless, needs to address several issues related to agricultural use. The service has no accurate count of the number of permits it has granted. In some areas, the service and the Bureau of Land Management have not adequately sorted out their respective responsibilities. It is also unclear what changes, if any, the historic properties leasing program, with provisions for competitive bidding and returning revenues to the parks, will have in managing agricultural activities in historical parks.

The park service and Congress should assess opportunities to reduce the incompatibility of longstanding private grazing rights in the parks. The service may be able to tighten the terms of grazing permits, for example. Reducing or withdrawing subsidies for incompatible grazing activities within national parks should also be explored.

A central question is whether the perspective of some newer parks, such as Golden Gate and Cuyahoga, is to be applied to some existing agricultural operations in other parks. In these newer units, the park service recognizes a responsibility to conserve the living landscape, and conservationists support the continuance of agriculture as part of that landscape. When it is consistent with their legislative mandates, park service officials now envision a mix of uses in some newer parks, with commercial agriculture viewed not as a museum demonstration, but as part of the living landscape.*

---

*This vision is not unlike that in the French regional parks where government efforts support local agrarian economies and view them as compatible with, and in fact enhancing, the parks.[114]

## Stimulating Travel to the Parks

Reminiscent of Stephen Mather's attempts to encourage use of the national parks, the park service has been working with travel and recreation industry groups over the last few years to publicize and market the parks. The program, which is led by a special assistant to the director of the park service for tourism, has tapped private organizations—airlines, ski associations, travel agency representatives—to provide publications about the parks, to advise the park service on establishing a central reservation system for its lodging and camping facilities, and to help stimulate use of lesser-known parks.

This cooperation, instigated in part by budget cuts and a 1981 printing moratorium, has contributed to several information and marketing efforts. For example, the Conference of National Park Concessioners produced a guidebook on visitors' facilities and services in the parks. The National Park Foundation published a traveler's guide to all the units in the system.[115] At the 1982 World's Fair in Knoxville, Tennessee, and at the 1984 Olympics in Los Angeles, computerized systems staffed by the park service and volunteers provided up-to-date information on such items as the availability of facilities both inside and adjacent to nearby parks. An exhibit by the NPCA in cooperation with the park service and ARA Leisure Services (a concessioner) at the 1984 Louisiana World Exposition in New Orleans informed visitors about the values of the parks.

In late 1981, the park service established the Travel Industry Working Group, composed largely of travel executives from such organizations as the American Bus Association, American Express, American Ski Federation, American Youth Hostels, and Amtrak as well as representatives from the NPCA, Partners for Livable Places, and the Wilderness Society.[116] The service primarily has tried to learn from the organizations what steps it should be taking to facilitate travel to parks and assure visitors a worthwhile experience. The working group has advised the park service on how to market travel to the parks and has helped in contacting local chambers of commerce and resort owners near parklands to improve travel opportunities.

One motive for this effort is the park service's determination to spread visitors more evenly among the parks and among the seasons. Visitation trends have consistently showed a concentration of visits in a relatively small proportion of parks: 90 percent of all recreational visits in 1981 affected only 35 percent of the parks, and about 95 percent of visits occurred during the short, peak season of summer.[117] Several parks have been little used. Projections indicate that these patterns will continue and are likely to increase in the future, augmented in part by rising numbers of foreign visitors to the parks.

The park service has responded by publishing a guide on "Lesser Known Areas of the National Park System." Former park service Director Russell Dickenson made a practice during his time in office of speaking to major travel-and-tour industry groups, reciting the attractions of national parks, noting the concentration of visitors in a minority of them, and then asking for help in effectively marketing them. The service has also set up booths and displays at travel industry conferences, encouraging attendees to market travel to the parks.

The park service's most aggressive attempt to encourage visitation has been at Voyageurs National Park, on the Minnesota-Canada border. Established in 1975, the park is one of the few large natural area units authorized outside Alaska during the last decade. Although Voyageurs is rich in natural beauty and also has historical importance, it has been relatively little used. By the late 1970s, local support for the park's creation, fueled in part by assurances that the municipalities would prosper from increased visitation to the areas, was turning to skepticism and, in some circles, animosity.

Acting on the initiative of the park's newly arrived superintendent, the park service, in 1982, established a Tourism Development Task Force to work with the park and surrounding communities to stimulate visitation. The task force, which included representatives of a number of private companies and organizations, recommended actions such as developing historical features and working with airlines to develop tour packages.[118]

It remains to be seen how effective the campaigns at Voyageurs and elsewhere will be. Relying on businesses in existing communities to provide needed visitors' services whenever possible—rather than encouraging new commercial facilities within park boundaries—is an adaptation to the conditions of today of the tradition of encouraging visitation. Although it is unlikely that these campaigns will cause many visitors to turn away from Grand Canyon, Yellowstone, or Yosemite, significant increases in visitation to lesser known sites may nevertheless result. Thus, the service might be wise, as part of its cooperative efforts with chambers of commerce and local governments, to make sure that any new facilities outside the parks do not themselves threaten park resources. Moreover, the service needs to ensure that the travel industry remains sensitive to the needs of the parks and that the tour packages offered to the public respect park traditions and are not tailored exclusively for high-priced, quick-stop visits.

## LOOKING TOWARD THE FUTURE

For all the controversy that surrounds its presence in the parks, the private sector makes contributions that are certain to continue and, in some cases, likely to grow. Current activities, including many conducted by nonprofit organizations, enrich visitors' experiences and enhance park management in a remarkable variety of ways. The park service should explore additional ways in which private activities can contribute to the parks and their visitors.

Private sector activities in the parks are not ends in themselves, however; there should be no policy that private involvement either grow or shrink. Rather, responsibility for park activities should be assigned to whoever can, on balance, contribute most effectively to the preservation and enjoyment of park resources.

In deciding on private sector roles in the future, the full range of park values should be considered. Efforts to reduce park costs, important as they are, should not be allowed to overshadow the needs to protect park resources and visitors' opportunities to experience them. The vitality of the park service must also be protected; it would be a particular misfortune to privatize too many of the activities that give the service its traditional distinctiveness, leaving it to focus on law enforcement and bureaucratic responsibilities.

Nor should it ever simply be assumed that private is better, or even cheaper, than park service management. It is important to be sure in each case, for example, that contracting out for service does not impose administrative costs that exceed apparent savings.

Even nonprofit organizations can present costs and headaches. Because of instability, lack of management expertise, and high staff turnover, some of these groups require greater park service oversight than profit-making companies. Recruiting, managing, and training by the service entail costs and resources. Moreover, working with a few groups has proved difficult; one manager characterized such nonprofit concessioners as "unprofessional, unpredictable, and inconsistent; besides, a few of these groups have caused more problems by trying to increase revenues than the profit-making enterprises have.''

In thinking about the future of the private sector in the parks, it is important to look beyond the major concessioners; the principal policy issues lie elsewhere. The likelihood of additional major concession facilities seems small: the availability of visitors' accommodations outside park boundaries within reasonable travel time

*Golden Gate, February 1984. Fort Mason Center, with Andrea Jepson (inset), director of operations, Fort Mason Foundation. ''It would be hard to believe that there would have been anything but some sort of very chic development on the waterfront if the federal government had not signed the agreement with our foundation to manage this center and support nonprofit community-based organizations; we have about 50 of them. . . . The park service takes care of the outside of the buildings, and we take care of everything on the inside. It is the most beneficial, wonderful relationship where we try to have things open for the people. . . . The one drawback about being at Fort Mason is that the facilities are old and, because you can't make any major changes in anything, everything has to be fabricated; they're not making the parts anymore. That part of it is very expensive. Bay District Ranger Maria Burkes and I do a lot a very creative work trying to determine how collectively we can keep something working or something from leaking or something from not blowing in a gale-force wind that might be coming through the Golden Gate Bridge.''*

of many attractions, coupled with more widespread recognition that some of the citylike facilities are indeed incompatible with preservation of park resources, accounts for that. Law and policy already dictate that visitors' needs be satisfied outside the parks whenever possible. Although particular care must be taken in applying these standards to still-remote areas in Alaska, the future of concessioners seems likely to be one of containment, coupled with some expansion to provide recreational services that cannot readily be provided outside the parks.

The existing major concession facilities promise to be around for awhile. Contract terms, notably provisions for market-value possessory interests, can interfere with the necessity of removing some concessioners' structures to more appropriate locations within the parks. Those same terms, paired with the concessioners' influence and the undoubted popularity of some major concessions, make wholesale removal of major facilities a remote prospect. Administrative and legislative measures should encourage renegotiation of contract terms that currently create inflexibility in adapting to changing conditions, but this promises to be a decades-long effort.

After a century of experience in dealing with concessioners, there are lessons to be applied to other private sector activities as well. One lesson is to anticipate the special influence that any private organization, be it for-profit or nonprofit, volunteer or lessee of historic property, can come to have on park decision making. The other is to anticipate the need for flexibility so that today's decisions can be modified tomorrow. Several steps can help avoid some of the problems that concessioners' influence and inflexibility have presented in the past.

- *Open decision making.* Park service decisions about future private sector activities must be open so that all affected interests can participate. A few times in the past, the park service has allowed major concessioners to have greater weight in decisions than the general public has. The service still declines to release information essential to effective public scrutiny of the park service's dealings with concessioners. For the future, both the appearance of fairness and fairness itself are crucial in decision making about all kinds of private sector activity.
- *Reorganization within the National Park Service.* Although there have been impressive improvements, the park service's administration of private sector relationships still reflects an

earlier day in some respects. Virtually every type of private sector concern—concessioners, cooperating associations, volunteers, historic property leases, contractors—is overseen by a different office within the park service or on a park-by-park basis. A stronger organizational framework would allow more information and expertise in dealing with these different groups to be exchanged within the service so that mistakes are not repeated, opportunities are not lost, and consistency is achieved.

- *Legal protections.* Like concessioners, other private sector providers should not be granted excessive legal protections that make removal or change prohibitively expensive. For example, although current park service policy favors lease terms for relatively short durations, the provision allowing historic property leases for as long as 99 years should be reexamined closely.[119]

- *Political obstacles.* Park service policy should take into account the political, as well as legal, difficulty of dislodging established activities that later come to be perceived as contrary to park purposes, either because of a change in the idea of what belongs in the park or because of a change in what a particular group provides. Because the park service can find itself under tremendous political pressure to continue an established activity, it should be cautious when experimenting with private sector activity.

- *Alaska.* Particular attention should be paid to future private sector involvement in parks in Alaska. These parks are so new and unaltered, so remote from national population centers, that they provide a unique opportunity for innovative private sector activity that is responsive to their distinctive needs. However, these parks also present an opportunity to repeat earlier mistakes, so it is critical that the park service apply the lessons learned through its past experience.

In a time when public/private partnerships appear to be a growing trend, national parks stand out as places where the concept of partnership has been a central feature for more than a century. In the past, the park service has looked to the private sector (and especially concessioners) first to create park use and later to accommodate that use. Now the emphasis should be on private forces stimulating visitor awareness of the unique qualities of individual parks.

The challenge for the future is to shape and reshape private sector participation so that it enriches rather than detracts from evolving visions of the parks. Handing over responsibilities to the private sector in the parks should be, not a routine matter, but rather one of giving and receiving something distinctive. With a century of experience and robust private sector participation today, from both the for-profit and nonprofit organizations, there is reason to hope that this challenge can be met successfully.

# Profile
# Santa Monica Mountains National Recreation Area

Santa Monica Mountains National Recreation Area was one of 11 new units created in the National Parks and Recreation Act of 1978. This record-setting omnibus legislation also added almost 2 million acres to wilderness areas in the park system; established segments of eight new rivers in the National Wild and Scenic Rivers System and five new trails in the National Trails System; and authorized rounding out and expanding of boundaries in many existing units.[1]

Some have argued that the Santa Monica Mountains unit in the Los Angeles, California, area was the ill-considered progeny of a congressional steamroller. More than a decade of local advocacy and national debate preceded the park's creation, however. These were years of very rapid growth in the region, and, by 1980, 10.5 million people lived within a 60-mile radius of Los Angeles.

As the suburbs expanded, the idea of using national park status to protect the unusual and complex Santa Monica Mountains' landscape took hold. Some obvious questions were raised: Was there too much development here for a national park? Was the area of national, as well as regional, significance? Why, with so many state and regional players in the land-use game, was the federal government needed? (The area had developed a number of innovations in state and regional land-use management in response to local concerns over rapid growth.) Federal officials were skeptical, and said so. As a result, Santa Monica Mountains National Recreation Area evolved into a new kind of park in which federal acquisition would play an important, but less dominant, role.

The Santa Monica Mountains stretch westward almost 50 miles from Griffith Park in central Los Angeles to Point Mugu, a few miles south and east of the city of Ventura, California. For most of this distance, the mountains skirt close to the Pacific Ocean. North of the mountains lies the heavily urbanized San Fernando Valley; farther west are the growing communities along the Pacific Coast Highway, the Ventura Freeway, and the Oxnard Plain.* Homes perch on ridges and terraces and nestle in canyons. Many of the most expensive are in sizable ranches reached by private roads that put distance between the billboards, motels, restaurants, and closely built homes bordering the freeways.

The continued abundance of natural resources so close to frenzied development provides remarkable contrasts. "It is possible to have a wilderness experience on Boney Mountain . . . while urban dwellers sun on the beaches along Pacific Coast Highway below," the park's resource management chief, David Ochsner, points out.[2]

Nature's contrasts are remarkable as well. Deep gorges cut through ridges threaded by streams that are little more than a trickle in the dry summer months but may become torrents during a winter storm. In the dry heat of summer, the irrigated agricultural lands in the valleys and ribbons of growth along the streams offer relief from the brown vegetation and barren rocks. In other seasons, particularly the winter and spring, the mountains provide hospitable, verdant refuge; temperatures are relatively cool, the hills turn green, and wildflower displays are a major attraction.

The park's Mediterranean climate accounts for its distinctive ecosystem, one that is not well-represented elsewhere in the park system. Gray-green, chaparral-blanketed ridges loom above gently sloping alluvial valleys, while black and white coastal sage highlight California buckwheat and prickly pear cactus. Scrub oak, coast live oak, and valley oak contrast with manzanita, gooseberry, currant, and wild cherry shrubs.

The mountains are home to many species of wildlife and are a seasonal stopover along the Pacific Flyway for migrating birds. Mountain wildlife includes several endangered species (the pere-

---

*The land in Channel Islands National Park is a geological continuation of the Santa Monica Mountains' chain.

*Santa Monica Mountains, June 1984.*

grine falcon, for example) as well as the bobcat, mountain lion, ring-tailed cat, raccoon, California king snake, rattlesnake, mule deer, and coyote.

Rich evidence of human settlement, perhaps going back 7,000 years, complements the natural landscape. A substantial Native American population, possibly the largest concentration in the United States, once lived here. The large fertile ranches are the legacy of Spanish settlement in the 18th and early 19th centuries. The hills offer excellent grazing, and horse breeding is practiced extensively in the Hidden Valley farms. Artifacts of filmmaking—old sets and buildings—remind one that the mountains have been the majestic backdrops for innumerable westerns, *How Green Was My Valley,* and other scenery-rich movies. When the area became the setting as well for homes of celebrities—Bob Hope, Ronald Reagan, and Huntington Hartford—the price of land zoomed.

Conservationist author Robert Cahn attributes the retention of so many natural qualities in the Santa Monica Mountains to the fore-sight of local voters in setting aside state, county, and city parks

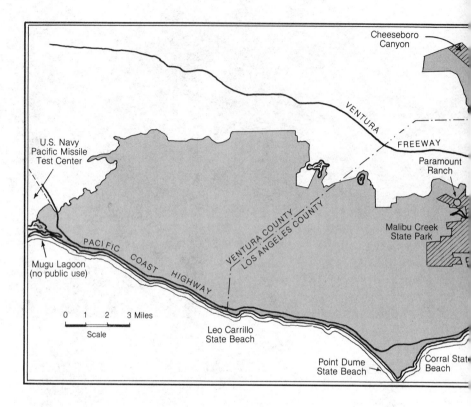

and water districts; the presence of many private camps and recreational facilities; the prevalent landholding pattern of large private ranches; and natural constraints to development—steep topography, with slide-prone slopes, and extreme fire danger.[3]

In establishing the park unit, Congress drew a boundary enclosing 147,465 acres for the national recreation area and around it delineated a larger Santa Monica Mountains' "zone of influence," in all 225,000 acres. This is by far the largest unit created under recent park policies that emphasize creating parks in or near urban areas. The visitor center is less than an hour's drive from downtown Los Angeles.[4]

The land in and around the recreational unit is distinctive in several other respects. Twenty percent was already publicly owned at the time the park was established, including three sizable state

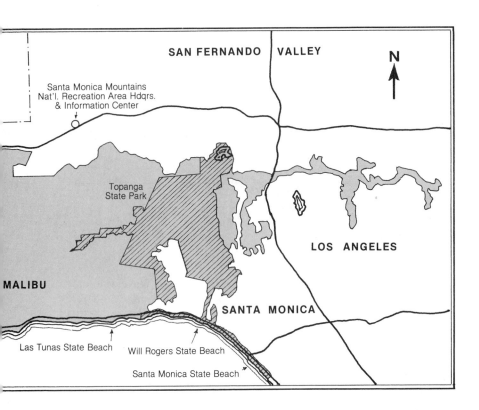

parks—Topanga, Malibu Creek, and Point Mugu—totaling 38 square miles; eight state beaches; a state historical park; four county parks; seven city parks; and lands owned by two water districts.[5] But, in contrast to the situation that existed when urban park units were created in New York City and San Francisco, federal ownership prior to the Santa Monica park's creation was minimal—a 1,500-acre Navy missile test center, 423 acres owned by the Bureau of Land Management, and a 135-acre former Nike Missile site. This federal area included the state's second-largest coastal lagoon, Mugu Lagoon, rich in wildlife habitat.

A second distinctive feature is the extent of private residences, private ownership, and land fever. About 35,000 people live in 15,900 privately owned homes on just under 10 percent of the land inside the recreational unit's boundaries. There are also 80,000

*Santa Monica Mountains, June 1984. Anne Posselt (Van Nuys, California).*
*"I've known and loved these mountains for about 15 years. I came to this*
*country from England in 1961, but I wasn't so aware of these mountains in*
*the early days. At first I hated this landscape, just hated it! But over the years,*
*I've grown to feel very fond of it, and now I really like it—in fact, I really*
*like it. But it's amazing how it took time to become accustomed to it because*
*it is so different. I enjoy the smell of it!"*

undeveloped acres in 3,000 privately owned parcels. As technology
overcomes topographical barriers to development, each year farms
and ranches are converted irrevocably to urban use, and sparsely
developed land is developed more intensively. Increases in land
costs in the region in 1978 and 1979 averaged 36 percent a year.
Even though development slowed somewhat beginning in 1980,
the market for building expensive homes continues to be strong.

Finally, far more than in most other areas where national parks
have been established, in Santa Monica many public agencies have
land-use management or regulatory responsibilties within the boundaries of the national recreation area. In addition to such conventional agencies as the California Department of Parks and Recreation, the Los Angeles County Department of Beaches and Harbors,
and the Los Angeles City Department of Recreation and Parks, there
are more recent, inventive arrangements such as the California
Coastal Commission, a 15-member state coastal planning and man-

agement agency established in 1972 (40 percent of Santa Monica Mountains National Recreation Area lies within the area defined as the commission's responsibility); the State Coastal Conservancy, established in 1976 to develop "creative solutions" to the difficult land-use problems on the coast; and the Santa Monica Mountains Conservancy, a state agency created in 1979 to oversee the implementation of the Santa Monica Mountains Comprehensive Plan.[6]

These distinctions helped shape a novel approach for creating the park. The aim is to stitch together, under the federal umbrella, recreational lands and open space that will continue in state, county, and city ownership; lands that will continue to be privately owned; and a core of land resources to be purchased conventionally in fee by the federal government.

The approach borrows from British "greenline" parks, admired in recent years by American planners and conservationists seeking ways to protect major landscapes, natural systems, and recreational resources without incurring astronomical purchase costs or displacing desirable residential communities and economic activities. The British live, farm, and work in their greenline parks, but private activities are limited through strong local planning controls and agreements with local landowners for land management and public access. An extensive system of "footpaths" enables the public to walk in privately owned rural areas provided that the visitors are unobtrusive and their activity does not adversely affect the resource.

The early years of a park, always critical in setting basic directions, have been especially difficult for Santa Monica. The park, the last spurt in the expansive policies pursued in the late 1970s, was caught by the sharp turn in policy of the Reagan administration: the moratorium, under Secretary Watt, on new acquisitions and an avowed skepticism about urban parks. As estimated costs for completing the park far exceeded the $155 million initially authorized by Congress, its future in the park system seemed in doubt.[8] Acquisition funds plummeted to zero in 1983 and went back up to $15 million in 1984; $6 million was proposed for 1985.[9]

While sizing up the changed climate for implementing Santa Monica's land protection agenda, Robert S. Chandler, the unit's first superintendent, pursued astute strategies that established the Santa Monica unit as an active entity, even though its actual land base was small. A full schedule of walks to observe wildflowers, moonlit hikes, scenic tours for camera bugs, rock-climbing excursions, workshops on outdoor skills, geology talks, whale-watching activities, sea-life explorations, and the like was offered. With funds provided by a grant from the U.S. Department of Transportation,[10] special buses brought school and other groups to the park for environmental and outdoor education programs. The park continued to hold the popular Renaissance Pleasure Faire, a summer weekend festival attracting 300,000 people annually to the 336-acre Paramount Ranch, the unit's first purchase. Numerous cultural events with American Indian and Hispanic groups were scheduled, and Indian organizations were encouraged to build a cultural center.

Today, national park staff conduct programs in the three state parks and often work alongside the state's rangers. Park literature details state, county, and city beaches, parks, and campgrounds in the area. Hikes originating on federal lands cross to state parks and back again. "Interpretation, environmental education, and urban outreach are areas in which the park service has really excelled," Chandler has said. "The states are hungry for our knowledge in these areas." Margot Feuer, a Sierra Club activist instrumental in the park's creation, observes that, "The state has had parks in the Santa Monicas for many years and rarely presented programs."[11]

The park's six-person resource management staff has developed ambitious plans. Their expertise is greater than that usually found in park staff: all have master's degrees, with specialties in geology, ecology, forestry, hydrology, biogeography, and/or land-use planning. They have developed a more complete inventory of plants and wildlife, including data on their condition, "than Yellowstone . . . gathered in its 110 years," drawing on the substantial expertise in the region—10 colleges and universities within a one-hour drive—as well as their own research.[12] Steps have already been taken to monitor acid rain and water quality and quantity; to burn, under controlled conditions, old chaparral to reduce fire risks; and to help property owners with land and fire management problems.

Santa Monica's innovative approaches to attracting private-sector donations attracted attention throughout the park system. Its gift catalogue, a donation from Chevron U.S.A., Inc.,[13] lists specific park needs along with suggested tax-deductible donations: $6,500 to help the park learn more about raptor nesting; $5,000 for a telephotometer for monitoring air quality; $10,000 for a Spanish language information brochure. By March 1984, the park had received $320,000 in contributions, including computers, chain saws, a horse, and cash donations.

The park has recruited many volunteers and nonprofit groups to run programs, an effort helped by its proximity to a large urban population. (There are no for-profit concessioners in this unit.) The William O. Douglas Outdoor Classroom, a group promoting environmental education, and several docent societies provide interpretation and other special programs at various canyon sites. The Sierra Club initiated nature walks in the mountains long before the park was established. Volunteers in the Santa Monica Task Force of the Sierra Club and the Santa Monica Trails Council maintain a large trail system.[14] Under the Adopt-a-Trail program, local schools, the Boy Scouts, and other groups maintain existing trails and build new ones. The Santa Monica Mountains Conservancy has built several wayside overlooks. Such assistance has become especially important as the land base expands. Budget constraints have resulted in cutbacks in staffing for visitor services so that newly acquired areas can be policed and maintained.

Just over 1.5 million recreational visits were recorded on federal land in the Santa Monica Mountains unit between 1979 and 1983. But the park's impact is much greater, park officials argue. Because a park like Santa Monica was purposefully set up to protect the region's resources, regardless of who owns them, officials believe visitation figures, an important weapon in the competition for funds, should somehow reflect the 39 million recreational visits to the beaches and the other public lands within the park's boundary.

Santa Monica, like most other parks in the system, has had to make do with a stable operating budget and staff for the past few years. In 1983, the budget was $1.48 million, and permanent staff totaled 62 persons—35 full-time and 27 less-than-full-time employees. In addition, the park employed 20 seasonal employees and 20 Youth Conservation Corps summer workers. The stagnation in staffing and funding has been especially difficult for a new park faced with demanding, path-breaking decisions. In addition to the visitor services, private, and resource management activities already discussed, Santa Monica staff have had to plan what and how much land to buy, and at what price; decide how and where to use alternative land protection approaches; develop a general management plan and other planning documents; work out cooperative agreements with governments and landowners; and figure out how to pursue the broader mandate to influence development in the rapidly growing area around the park.

Despite the park's other accomplishments at this point, it is still unclear how well the greenline concept will transfer from Britain to the Sunbelt. Will the Santa Monica experiment evolve into a park closer to the traditional model, as a number of advocates would like, or a park in which the acquisition and management policies will help inaugurate a new era of parks, as others have anticipated?

The park's plan for the future envisions that about a quarter of its land, or about 36,000 acres, will be bought and managed by the federal government.[15] This will provide a core of federally owned land identifying the park as a physical place and protecting key resources, as well as a web of federal properties connecting lands protected by state and local governmental ownership, regulation, or agreements negotiated with private owners of remaining lands. Driven by the logic of building a coherent federal land base as a first priority—as well as by budget constraints, uncertain federal policies, and development threats—park officials have so far used acquisition dollars primarily to buy land in fee, rather than to purchase partial interests such as easements that would protect lands from incompatible development without federal ownership and management.

In the first wave of purchases through 1982, $42 million appropriated by Congress bought approximately 6,200 acres. Prices ranged from $500 to $40,000 an acre, with $5,681 as the average.[16] Superintendent Daniel R. Kuehn, who succeeded Chandler in 1983 when the latter became superintendent of Olympic National Park, intends to continue emphasizing fee purchase in spending limited acquisition funds appropriated by Congress.[17] Easements, he says, will be purchased if there are willing sellers—but only if the sales price represents a bargain to the taxpayer.

As of 1983, two conservation easements had been purchased from private owners. One involved the development rights for a second dwelling on 7.11 acres and cost $12,658 an acre; the other involved limiting development on a 10-acre parcel to one single family residence and cost $4,200 per acre.[18] In addition, two right-of-way easements, providing trail access for hikers, have been purchased.[19] Says Margot Feuer, "Easements can be used later to protect vistas around the park and the like, but they don't make sense now when the issue is to establish a park."[20]

In an innovative park like Santa Monica, the question of what lands are purchased is especially important. In earlier parks, it was assumed that everything would eventually be bought, so lands could justifiably be purchased on a "willing-seller" basis. Priorities at Santa Monica are supposed to emphasize resources that are undeveloped, beautiful, or fragile; have ecological, scientific, or recreational value; and connect now-scattered public parklands. Lands threatened by development or those proffered by willing sellers will, in practice, influence the order of these priorities.

Priorities were an issue, for example, when the Trust for Public Land, acting as a middleman between the owner and the park service, offered Cheeseboro Canyon to the park. Because the 1,810-acre site is separated from other park holdings by the Ventura Freeway, some questioned the wisdom of a park service purchase. The park decided to buy the property because of its value in protecting stream drainage and providing wildlife habitat and because the land could be bought at a good price. In another instance, an owner offered to sell a site within the park that he was planning to develop; park officials, however, decided the land was not critical.

By plan, 44 percent of the park, or 64,870 acres, will remain privately owned.[21] Strategies to retain the distinctive mountain and

*Santa Monica Mountains, June 1984. Private development within the national recreation area.*

*Santa Monica Mountains, June 1984.*

rural landscape and to deter undesirable development include purchase of partial interests, such as easements, land-use controls, en-
couragement of private donations, cooperative planning with landholders to raise the standards of private stewardship, and trail
dedications. Compatible private recreational uses will continue.
Easements are proposed for approximately 16,000 acres.[22] Promising initiatives have been undertaken by several land trusts: the
Nature Conservancy, the Trust for Public Land, and two state-created
organizations, the State Coastal Conservancy, and the Santa Monica
Mountains Conservancy. The State Coastal Conservancy is pioneering a transfer-of-development-rights program aimed at reducing the
build-out potential of numerous small vacant lots and redistributing
the unused density elsewhere.

   As in Cape Cod National Seashore, the success of these strategies
for protecting resources on privately owned lands depends a great
deal on the expectations that private owners have with respect to
future development. Unlike Cape Cod, there is no statutory quid
pro quo constraining federal condemnation in exchange for compatible local zoning. The emphasis is on cooperation.

To carry out the mandate to influence resource protection with less federal ownership, park staff spend a good deal of time tracking real estate trends and talking to property owners and local officials, sometimes commenting publicly about how a particular action will affect the recreational unit. In March 1983, for example, Superintendent Chandler wrote a detailed letter to the chairman of the California Coastal Commission outlining his ideas for strengthening the Malibu Land Use Plan, which involves 75,000 acres entirely within the national recreation area.[23]

In another instance, Park Planner Mary Gibson Park testified against a proposed rezoning in Ventura County, arguing that the higher density was not consistent with the regional Santa Monica Mountains Comprehensive Plan or the park's cooperative agreements zone, where the property is located. The developer wrote to Washington headquarters objecting that a park planner testified at a local hearing. The administration defended Ms. Park, however: "Creative techniques . . . can be useful in enabling the protection of a nationally significant resource without . . . acquisition by the Federal government. We do not believe . . . that the managing agency [National Park Service] should be restrained from presenting their opinion of the proper use of land within the park or recreation area."[24]

Park officials are pleased that the 1983 Ventura County coastal land-use plan specifies that the county will provide the park with information about building permits and requests for rezoning. Should the park service object, the county can delay rezoning for a year to give the park time to purchase properties.

The weakest link in regional planning is Los Angeles County, where 65 percent of the park is located. "It is hard to find a county that has fewer concerns about growth," says one park official.[25] The county has given only weak approval to the comprehensive plan for the mountains.[26] Simply by contemplating the rezoning of several sizable parcels within the recreation area, the county can, in effect, raise the asking price if the park can and wants to purchase the properties. A graphic example of the interaction between regulation and land price is a dispute over 275 acres the park wants to buy. The park has offered $1.7 million for the property, recently rezoned for 47 units by the county. The owner claims the property is worth $9 million. Although the coastal commission has so far withheld approval of the rezoning, the owner bases his valuation on the assumption that ultimately the commission will assent.[27]

Arguing the inadequacy of the park service's innovative approaches in this volatile regulatory environment, Santa Monica's
advisory commission in April 1984 recommended that more private
lands be purchased in fee.[28] This 13-member commission includes
a mix of people appointed by the state, local jurisdictions, and the
U.S. Department of the Interior: environmental activists, including
Margot Feuer and Susan Nelson, whose advocacy helped create the
park; local landowners and business interests; representatives of
various governmental institutions; and so on.

The commission has, in its deliberations, discussed a wide range
of park policies in addition to acquisition policies and has made
several recommendations about policies inside and outside the park.
In the summer of 1983, for example, the commission considered
whether the unit should allow hunting, a matter on which feelings
ran strongly for and against. While often allowed in national recreation areas, hunting is not mentioned in the Santa Monica legislation. The California Department of Fish and Game came out in favor
of hunting on the federal lands, although the sport is prohibited
in state parks. Following a lively public meeting, the advisory commission recommended that hunting be prohibited.

The commission was required by Congress to assess how capable
and willing other units of government in the state were to manage
recreational lands in the Santa Monica Mountains. This wording
in the park's enabling legislation reflected ambivalence about
whether the Santa Monica unit should be a permanent part of the
park system. Some of its supporters favored a federal presence, but
only temporarily. After a comprehensive survey of relevant state,
county, and city agencies, the commission in 1983 concluded that
only the federal government has the legal power, expertise, and
willingness to carry out the park's legislative mandate.[29] Superintendent Kuehn agrees that the federal role is not duplicative of other
efforts in the area. "The park service is needed precisely because
of the many interests here, to help produce and manage a common
concept of the recreation area."

As funds are spent to buy more land, Kuehn is trying to impress
on officials in Washington, D.C., the need to increase the park's
staff and budget. "This is a turning point for Santa Monica. It is
time to make the park operational."[30]

# Chapter 6
# Creating the Park System of the Future

In 1981, the curtain fell on the most remarkable period of park creation in the history of the National Park System. In the early days of his tenure, Interior Secretary James Watt declared a moratorium on parkland acquisition. He questioned whether some parks that stood substantially unfinished, like Santa Monica Mountains National Recreation Area, should ever be completed. Some units, he suggested, did not belong in the system at all.[1]

Secretary Watt's actions signaled the end of a two-decade-long trend that saw the number of units in the system increase over 70 percent, from 187 in 1960 to 333 in 1980, and the acreage increase by 196 percent, from 26 million to 77 million (figures 6.1 and 6.2).[2] In Alaska alone, parks carved from the public domain by law in 1980 totaled over 43 million acres, exceeding the combined acreage of all the national parks in the other 49 states.[3]

Driving the decades of expansion were population growth, increasing mobility, and greater affluence, which produced unprecedented visitation levels, putting pressure on a park system that had hardly expanded at all since the 1930s. In the face of these pressures, the influential Outdoor Recreation Resources Review Commission (ORRRC) in 1962 called for a vastly expanded system of parks and recreational sites throughout the nation, and the Land and Water Conservation Fund (LWCF) was created in 1964 to provide funds for parkland acquisition. Urban riots in 1967 and 1968 strengthened calls for more parks near urban areas to serve city dwellers, particularly low-income residents.[5]

**Figure 6.1**
**Number of National Park System Units, 1960–1984**

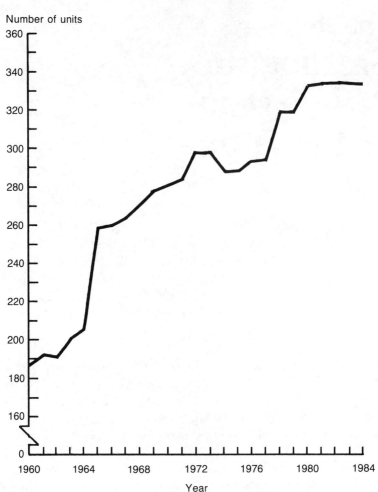

Number of units

The large increase in units in 1965 and the decrease in 1974 reflect administrative changes. Starting in 1965, authorized as well as established units were included in system totals; excluding this change, 16 units were added. In 1974, 10 national cemeteries were included with their associated historic areas, 13 units were switched to a new category of "affiliated areas," and 6 areas of the National Capital Parks received status as individual units; excluding these changes, 8 units were added.

Source: U.S. Department of the Interior, National Park Service, Office of Media Affairs, "60 Years Growth of the National Park System," table, January 29, 1979; and "National Park Statistical Abstract," 1979–1983 (Denver: Denver Service Center, Statistical Office).

**Figure 6.2**
**National Park System Acreage, 1960–1984**

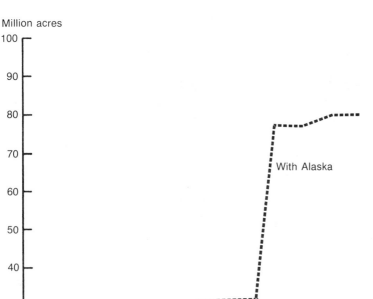

Source: U.S. Department of the Interior, National Park Service, "Summary of Acreages Administered by the National Park Service," tables, 1960–1984.

The units added to the park system in the post-1960 period contained, in addition to land already in public ownership, unprecedented amounts of private property. More than $1.6 billion was spent between 1965 and 1980 to acquire private land for national park use.[6] Even so, the acreage of nonfederal lands within park boundaries rose from fewer than 500,000 acres in 1960 to more than

3 million in 1980.[7]* New kinds of parks like Cape Cod, where some
landowners were allowed to remain and the service was forced to
rely on a variety of measures such as easements and zoning to protect
park resources that it did not own, challenged the service's management capabilities and raised difficult political questions.

In the aftermath of the great expansion, the park system in 1981
entered a period of consolidation. Acquisition funds appropriated
by Congress have been used not to expand the system but to "clean
up the backlog"—that is, to purchase or otherwise protect land in
parks already authorized by law but not yet complete. Funding levels
for land acquisition have been reduced below those of the late 1970s,
although, despite efforts of the Reagan administration, they have
remained significant. Even in 1981, when the administration fought
to cut all park service acquisition funds, Congress appropriated
$65.7 million for acquisition. In succeeding years, the administra-
tion's requests have been substantially increased by a determined
Congress—for example, from $59.8 million to $116.5 million in
1983.[8] Altogether, Congress appropriated $397 million for parkland
acquisition between 1981 and 1984.[9]

Other park initiatives since 1980 have also centered around consolidating rather than expanding park units. Over a million acres
of land within park boundaries have been designated by law as wilderness areas. Some acreage has been added to the system as the
result of boundary adjustments, and the Illinois-Michigan Canal
National Heritage Corridor, in Illinois, has been established by law
as an affiliated unit. Only one new unit, however, the former home
of President Harry S Truman, has been added to the system (through
donation).†

During the cash-short 1980s, there is little likelihood that the
heady expansion of the 1970s will be revived. This is not because
there has been a drop in public visitation; nor is it evidence of a
shortage of additional areas worthy of the protection and public
access that the parks provide—there are plenty of those. What has

---

*In 1980, private lands inside the parks totaled slightly more than 1.1 mil-
lion acres, and other nonfederal acres slightly more than 2 million acres. All
figures exclude Alaska.

†During this period, the Nancy Hanks Tower Center in the Old Post Office
Building in Washington, D.C., was also added to the National Capital Parks.

changed is the public perception of the federal government's capabilities and responsibilities to provide parkland during a time of massive budget deficits. "Cleaning up the backlog" is absorbing all the funds being appropriated for acquisition.

## THE SYSTEM OF THE FUTURE: CLASHING VISIONS

Although park creation on the scale of the late 1970s cannot be expected in the near future, the National Park System is unlikely to stand still. At a minimum, the system of the future is likely to include some additional historic sites (birthplaces of presidents, for example) and a few new carvings from the public domain (although nothing remotely on the scale of the 1980 Alaska parks). Acquisition of some private land inside existing parks will continue. There will also be some protective acquisitions, following boundary adjustments, to defend existing parks against external pressures.

A more expansive vision sees today's parks as only the core of a future system providing preservation and public access to many more of America's special places. Some additional parks of substantial size would be formed, not only from the public domain but also, in at least a few cases, by acquiring private land. In the tradition of the 1960s and 1970s, both experimental parks responding to the priorities of their time and extensive "greenline" or cooperative parks, in which protection and access would be provided in varied ways, would also be established. The role of the park service might also vary considerably from park to park. At some, the service could play its traditional role of principal manager, while at others— perhaps the majority of future units—its principal role might be to provide financial and technical assistance, as it does today at such affiliated units as Pinelands National Reserve and the Illinois-Michigan Canal.

A fundamental issue facing the park system today is whether the system of the future will embrace the larger vision. If not, the nation will still have a splendid park system, with reason to be proud that it carved that system from the public domain and made major additions during a period of creativity that lasted late into the 20th century. By pursuing the larger vision, however, there will be reason for greater pride as the parks heritage is adapted to address an increasingly important need in a mobile, developed country: providing protection and public access to special places.

It is important to pursue the more expansive vision of the future. The United States still has many unprotected special places worthy of preservation in the national park tradition—among them, the Florida Keys, Tallgrass Prairie, Big Sur, and the Columbia River Gorge. In addition, protective acquisitions, to defend existing parks, are needed.

To pursue the larger vision effectively in a time of constrained domestic spending, two obstacles must be overcome. One is a fear that expansion harms the system, straining the funds and skills available for management. The other is the belief that the system is complete, that nothing worthy of it is left to be added.

### Fear of Strains on the System and the Service

No matter who had been chosen president in 1980, expansion of the park system in 1985 would be proceeding more cautiously than it was at the end of the 1970s. Warnings by that time were being voiced by park advocacy groups, federal watchdog agencies, Congress, and some park service officials, all of whom were worried about overly rapid system expansion, neglected facilities, threatened natural and cultural resources, and the rising costs of responding to higher standards in managing national park units. There was a lot of talk about the need to digest recent innovations.

If park creation is to be restored to the national agenda, concerns about the harmful effects of expansion must be carefully considered. Some people worry that expansion harms units already in the system: by siphoning money and personnel away from parks like Yellowstone to more "marginal" sites and by tarnishing the system's reputation for quality.

The park service undoubtedly was taxed by the great expansion of the 1960s and 1970s. Park historian William Everhart has written:

> The parks were in financial trouble in 1976—and are today—partly because there are so many of them. The considerable number of parks added in recent years has inflicted enormous strains on the organization.[10]

How serious were the strains? Did the new parks consume staff and funds that would otherwise have been available to manage older ones? The data are not conclusive. Changes in counting methods and definitions create considerable difficulties in making comparisons among various years. Most of the older parks appear to have at least held their own in personnel and funding. Although Yel-

*Yellowstone, August 1984. Old Faithful.*

lowstone did lose a significant number of full-time employees from 1960 to 1980 (from 114 down to 85), it was one of the few parks that did. Some, like Yosemite, remained fairly constant, while a few, like Grand Canyon, increased substantially (from 68 to 94).[11] Reliance on temporary staff increased considerably in almost all parks during the 1970s, but this seems to be largely due to congressional ceilings on permanent employees.

If the park system had not expanded during the 1960s and 1970s, it is doubtful that the old parks would have garnered all the people and money Congress bestowed on the new units. Instead, expansion, like tourism in the 1920s, may have been a key to the political support for the overall system during this period.

Moreover, the new urban and "greenline" units of the expansion era may be benefiting the older parks by serving as laboratories for new ways to cope with issues—such as crowds, crime, and neighboring local governments—that older parks, too, increasingly face. More than one superintendent from a large western park has noted that even places like Grand Teton face inholder and external development pressures, which are commonplace for personnel in newer units like Cape Cod. Other western superintendents have described their positions as being akin to city managers or people managers.[12]

As for the second concern—that new parks may tarnish the system's reputation for quality—some of the units added during the last two decades are undeniably obscure. Allegheny Portage Railway and Maggie Walker National Historic Site, to name two, are not on anyone's list of world-class wonders.

There is no persuasive evidence, however, that the system's overall reputation for quality has suffered in the public mind. Even some critics of the process used to establish many newer parks recognize the benefits of the end result. One has admitted, "On the credit side, the system, whose historical holdings at one time seemed limited to birthplaces and battlefields, was enhanced by a number of richly varied parks more reflective of the nation's cultural achievements."[13] Another observer stated, "There were clearly deficiencies, but the product was better than the process. Sometimes events pass the debate by and you must act."[14]

Helter-skelter though it sometimes was, the expansion of the 1960s and 1970s protected some magnificent resources that would otherwise have been lost or degraded—Redwood, Lowell, and Voyageurs, to name a few. Although some lesser resources were protected as a means to serve urban populations and achieve other objectives, the expansion was a wise long-term investment, adapted to the needs of a changing country.

## The Myth that the System Is Complete

Another important deterrent to creating more national parks is the notion that the park system is complete, that nothing worthy of it remains to be added. In the words of former Interior Secretary James Watt:

> Most of the truly unique areas of national significance requiring Federal management and funding are already part of the National park, forest, refuge, trails and wild and scenic rivers systems. In an era of budgetary constraint, we should be seeking to round out the Federal estate and manage better the areas that are part of that estate.[15]

The idea of a completed park system has been a recurring issue for the past two decades. Congressman Wayne Aspinall (D.-Colo.), who oversaw the national parks as head of the House Public Lands Committee in the 1960s, is reported to have frequently asked park service officials when the system would be finished.[16] President Johnson proposed in 1966 that the system be completed by 1972, the centennial year of Yellowstone's creation.[17]

Searchers for completeness seem to assume that park sites are in finite supply and that the task is to select the best ones for inclusion in the national system. Lesser sites—those not of "outstanding national significance"—are viewed as more appropriate for state, local, or private parks. This kind of attitude is misconceived, however, overlooking the fact that parks are not simply found but are created for a variety of purposes. It is from this perspective of creativity that the park system carries a message not only about quality resources but also about the evolving values of the country that has preserved and managed these resources in ways sensitive to its people's changing demands and aspirations as well as to the needs of the places themselves.

Throughout the history of the park system, successive generations have defined what they believed worthy of inclusion in it (see chapter 2), and, even during the present period of consolidation, that evolution continues. Examples can be seen in two recent proposals for extending the park idea: the Illinois-Michigan Canal, which was authorized by Congress in 1984, and the Olmsted Historic Landscapes Act, which was under congressional consideration in 1985.[18]

The Illinois-Michigan Canal was constructed in the mid-1800s to link the Great Lakes and the Mississippi River. It was abandoned in 1933 because of railroad competition. The canal itself is of considerable interest today, but the raison d'être of this new unit is far broader—it is to tie together and display the varied landscapes, archaeological and historic sites, and industrial history of the area. Park service personnel will provide technical assistance, but management of the area will remain in state and local hands.[19]

Another recent effort in Congress involves parks and landscapes designed or influenced by Frederick Law Olmsted. Congress held hearings in 1984 on a proposal to protect these sites, not by creating any national park units but by building on existing efforts in the 37 states and District of Columbia where they are found. If the Olmsted Historic Landscapes Act is adopted, the emphasis will be on ensuring protection by improving coordination among existing federal, state, and local programs for parks, recreation, and historic preservation. The park service will take the lead in improving that coordination.[20]

At the time Secretary Watt was saying that the park system was finished, the National Parks and Conservation Association was promoting a list of 17 areas identified as potential greenline parks. These included such varied landscapes as the Big Sur Coast in California, the Great Basin of Nevada, the Tallgrass Prairie of Kansas, and the Hudson River Valley and Thousand Island areas of New York. While some of these areas may fit the traditional park mold, the majority do not. It is important that the park system's unique combination of preservation and access be extended to encompass areas such as these.

## RESTORING PARK CREATION TO THE NATIONAL AGENDA

The question today is how the dynamism that produced the expansion of the 1960s and 1970s can best be rechanneled to create more

*Yosemite, February 1984. Hazel Fredericks (Mineota, Minnesota) on caterpillar ride at Badger Pass. "This is so new to me; I just can't believe what I'm seeing. I came to visit my son in San Jose, and he said, 'You've got to see it.' We walked over the falls last night in the dark. It was so gorgeous, just takes your breath away. And to see this—I know when I get home I'll just wonder, Did I really see it? Was I there?"*

parks in the very different context of the 1980s. The special opportunity represented by the public domain, most recently in Alaska, is largely (though not wholly) gone. Willingness to replace that opportunity by continued commitment of substantial funds for acquisition has not been demonstrated. The opportunity that may prove greatest in the long run—a broadened concept of parks to incorporate human settlements that remain partially under private, local, and state control—is still in the nascent stage.

To create a future system that builds on past successes as well as present realities, initiatives are needed in five areas. First, and most immediate, a strategy must be developed for coping with the backlog. Second, the processes used by the park service to acquire private land must be improved to assure that they are perceived as fair and effective in the eyes of the public. Third, measures are needed to refine and apply the concept of greenline or cooperative parks. Fourth, initiatives are needed to create public confidence in the process used to select new park units. Finally, adequate funding must be provided.

## Coping with the Backlog

A formidable obstacle to creating more parks, especially during a time of constrained domestic spending, is the fact that the United States has not yet come close to buying all the needed land in the parks already established. The backlog amounts to more than 306,000 privately owned and unprotected acres, excluding Alaska* (figure 6.3)

Substantial amounts of backlog land have been purchased in recent years. Although park authorization virtually stopped in 1980, land acquisition has continued (figures 6.4 and 6.5). Between 1981 and 1984, almost all funding from the Land and Water Conserva-

---

*The service's figures for acreage remaining to complete each unit are based on ceilings authorized by Congress and on information provided by regional directors in preparing their FY 1984-85 budget justifications. Discrepancies exist in some cases between acreage estimates released by Washington and those from individual park units. At Jean Lafitte, for example, officials report that 2,600 additional acres are needed to complete the unit, although park service headquarters puts the figure at 997 acres. At New River Gorge, the park shows 62,000 acres needing protection, while headquarters quotes 46,900 acres.

**Figure 6.3**
**National Park Service**
**Land and Water Conservation Fund**
**Federal Portion Backlog after Fiscal Year 1984,**
**Within Existing Authorizations**

| Area | Tracts | Acres | Amount |
|------|--------|-------|--------|
| Inholdings [pre–1959 units] | 2,195 | 34,118 | $127,142,712[1] |
| Alaskan areas | Unknown | Unknown | Unknown |
| Allegheny Portage | 2 | 36 | 333,831 |
| Antietam | 25 | 1,474 | 5,500,000[2] |
| Appalachian | 234 | 20,085 | 30,429,277 |
| Bent's Old Fort | 2 | 39 | 512,607 |
| Big Bend (boundary expansion) | 1 | 21,250 | 1,500,000 |
| Big Cypress | 257 | 7,442 | 0[3] |
| Big Thicket | 220 | 4,683 | 0[3] |
| Biscayne | 5 | 65 | 1,600,000 |
| Chaco Culture | 11 | 4,530 | 10,500,000 |
| Channel Island | 2 | 58,358 | 26,360,000 |
| Chattahoochee River | 58 | 2,071 | 4,980,000 |
| Chesapeake and Ohio Canal | 16 | 200 | 5,337,595 |
| Coronado | 2 | 84 | 472,113 |
| Cumberland Island | 8 | 1,826 | 3,260,000 |
| Cuyahoga Valley | 475 | 3,888 | 0[3] |
| Delaware Water Gap | 162 | 3,810 | 21,556,064[2] |
| Ebey's Landing | 1 | 10 | 79,000 |
| Fire Island | 126 | 153 | 2,736,041 |
| Fort Laramie | 3 | 66 | 362,000[2] |
| Georgia O'Keeffe | 2 | 4 | 36,000 |
| Golden Gate | 85 | 9,254 | 9,336,360 |
| Golden Spike | 16 | 532 | 298,000 |
| Grant-Kohrs Ranch | 4 | 841 | 724,236 |
| Great Sand Dunes | 1 | 1,900 | 265,000 |
| Gulf Islands | 13 | 607 | 0[3] |
| Harpers Ferry | 12 | 10 | 300,000 |
| Jean Lafitte | 30 | 997 | 32,660,570 |
| John Day Fossil Beds | 3 | 490 | 3,054,003 |
| Kalaupapa | 6 | 150 | 2,500,000 |
| Kaloko-Honokohau | 3 | 621 | 24,704,208 |
| Lyndon B. Johnson | 4 | 1,242 | 1,400,000 |
| Lower St. Croix | 41 | 612 | 740,000 |
| Manassas (boundary expansion) | 35 | 873 | 5,700,000 |
| Martin Luther King, Jr. | 54 | 7 | 2,985,000 |

### Figure 6.3 (continued)

| Area | Tracts | Acres | Amount |
|---|---|---|---|
| Monocacy | 13 | 515 | $2,155,617 |
| Mound City Group | 4 | 93 | 1,000,000 |
| New River Gorge | 541 | 46,990 | 14,497,991 |
| North Cascades | 7 | 226 | 0[3] |
| Padre Island | 1 | 275 | 334,100 |
| Palo Alto Battlefield | 1 | 50 | 3,000,000 |
| Petersburg | 7 | 5 | 1,550,000 |
| Point Reyes | 38 | 673 | 4,217,518 |
| Redwood (legislative taking) | — | — | Unknown |
| Redwood (Highway 101 bypass) | 1 | 1,515 | 10,000,000[4] |
| Rio Grande | Unknown | Unknown | 1,650,000 |
| Rocky Mountain | 7 | 559 | 6,036,884[2] |
| St. Croix | 251 | 8,196 | 5,308,450 |
| Salinas | 26 | 412 | 1,140,000 |
| San Antonio Missions | 49 | 151 | 7,651,455 |
| Santa Monica Mountains | 1,119 | 41,623 | 63,489,333 |
| Santa Monica (state grants) | 51 | 5,098 | 25,770,000 |
| Saratoga | 4 | 445 | 400,000 |
| Sequoia (Mineral King) | 41 | 648 | 4,614,589[2] |
| Sleeping Bear Dunes | 76 | 2,563 | 6,648,747 |
| Theodore Roosevelt | 3 | 146 | 83,000 |
| Tuzigoot | 6 | 751 | 1,350,000 |
| Valley Forge | 26 | 207 | 5,078,435 |
| Virgin Islands | 264 | 1,819 | 6,292,000[2] |
| Voyageurs | 99 | 1,537 | 4,500,000 |
| War in the Pacific | 61 | 245 | 15,400,000 |
| Wind Cave | 2 | 232 | 219,500 |
| Transfer to Bureau of Land Management (fiscal year 1983)[5] | 243 | 9,594 | 30,000,000 |
| Total | 7,055 | 306,896 | $549,752,236 |

[1]Based on estimate dated 09/30/83.

[2]No statutory ceiling; amount shown based on estimate at time of authorization.

[3]Requires increase in statutory ceiling authorization.

[4]Based on current estimate.

[5]$30 million was transferred to the Bureau of Land Management during fiscal year 1983. That amount has not yet been specifically identified. When it is identified it will have the effect of increasing the remaining authorizations at those areas from which it is taken.

Source: Table provided by the National Park Service, Land Resources Division, 1984. Georgia O'Keeffe, shown on table, was deauthorized in 1984.

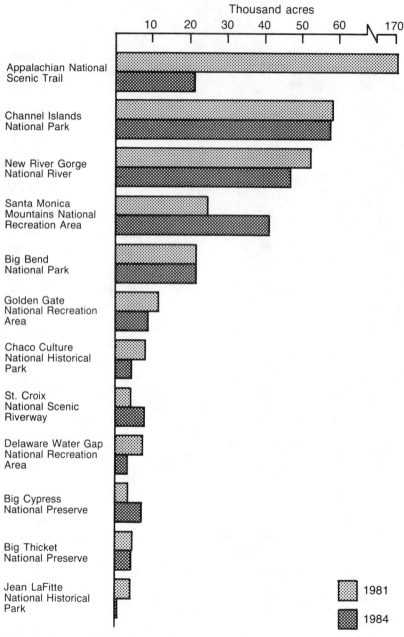

**Figure 6.4**
**Backlog Change at Selected Parks, 1981–1984**

Thousand acres

Appalachian National Scenic Trail

Channel Islands National Park

New River Gorge National River

Santa Monica Mountains National Recreation Area

Big Bend National Park

Golden Gate National Recreation Area

Chaco Culture National Historical Park

St. Croix National Scenic Riverway

Delaware Water Gap National Recreation Area

Big Cypress National Preserve

Big Thicket National Preserve

Jean LaFitte National Historical Park

1981
1984

Note: The increase in backlog acreage for some units in 1984 is the result of boundary changes or re-evaluation of site acquisition with the preparation of Land Protection Plans.

**Figure 6.5**
**Total Parkland Backlog, 1981–1985**

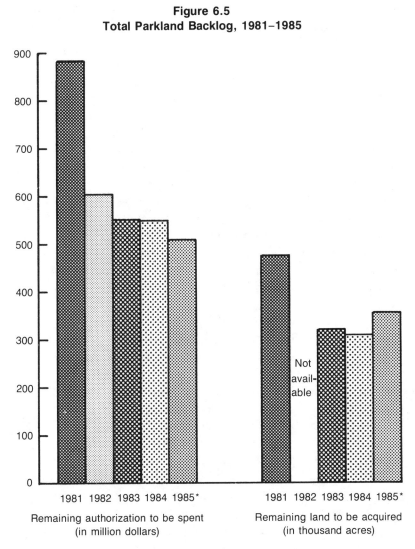

Remaining authorization to be spent
(in million dollars)

Remaining land to be acquired
(in thousand acres)

\* The figures for 1985 are Park Service projections for fiscal year 1985.

Source: U.S. Department of the Interior, National Park Service, "Land and Water Conservation Fund, Federal Portion Backlog After Fiscal Year 1981–1985," tables.

tion Fund (LWCF) that went to the park service—$397 million—
was used to acquire backlog land. Using both fee acquisition and
alternatives such as scenic easements, the service reduced the backlog acreage at Jean Lafitte by 78 percent and along the Appalachian
Trail by 88 percent. In some parks, the backlog declined because
recently completed land protection plans called for reducing the
amount of parkland to be acquired. Nevertheless, in 11 units, unacquired acreage increased during the same period as a result of
new land protection plans or boundary adjustments by Congress.

Compelling reasons exist for reducing this backlog. Most important, acquisition is needed to complete in fact the parks that have
been established by law. Acquisition is also essential to accommodate private landowners, some of whom have been waiting for years
for the service to live up to promises to buy them out. Delaying
acquisition can drive up eventual purchase costs. Although land
values recently have stabilized in many places, the trend in the past
has been steadily upward; from 1969 to 1979, the per acre price
of LWCF land purchased by the U.S. Forest Service increased about
900 percent.[22]

On the other hand, there are compelling reasons to look beyond
the backlog in considering acquisition needs. Creating or expanding a park may present a unique opportunity to protect a threatened
resource, and the opportunity may disappear if action is delayed.
The backlog should not be allowed to prevent systematic evaluation
of the full range of proposals for creating and expanding parks.

To reduce the backlog most effectively and also to remove the
obstacle it creates to further system expansion, there is need for
an analysis by the park service of private lands within existing parks
so that each parcel can be assigned to one of four categories:*

- Top-priority lands that should be acquired rapidly to prevent
  incompatible development, provide essential access or services
  for visitors, or relieve unusual hardship for landowners. (During
  the last few years, Congress has informally given priority to
  lands in this category by focusing acquisition funding on parcels for which acquisition proceedings have already reached
  the courts and threatened parcels at specific parks.)

---

*This analysis is already under way in some units as part of the service's
land protection planning process.[23]

- Remaining lands that should be acquired as expeditiously as possible.
- Remaining lands that require expeditious protection by tools such as easements or local land-use regulations.
- Lands that are not threatened or not essential to park services or access and may never need to be acquired.

In addition, two assessments of backlog costs are needed: First, a thorough assessment must be made of the dollar value of the land in the backlog. The eventual financial cost of cleaning up the backlog is unknown. No one has undertaken the expensive task of appraising the roughly 7,000 parcels of backlog land,[24] and informal estimates are notoriously unreliable, since land costs can rarely be determined precisely and can change rapidly.

In 1984, the park service released figures showing a backlog cost of approximately $550 million (figure 6.3).* The figure was not obtained by estimating land values, however, but rather by totalling the amounts that could be spent without exceeding congressionally authorized funding levels. The actual cost of the land probably will be hundreds of millions of dollars more—without even considering the amount of money needed for Redwood National Park (see box).[25] In many cases, the actual market value of the unacquired land is greater than the funding level authorized by Congress; in other cases, lands still remain to be acquired even though all authorized funds have been spent. For example, no additional spending has been authorized for purchasing lands inside Big Cypress National Preserve in Florida. However, park service headquarters reports that 7,442 acres inside the preserve remain unacquired, and park staff put the figure several times as high.

There is also a need to assess opportunities to reduce anticipated acquisition costs—particularly those in excess of current congressional authorization ceilings. When land acquisition spending bumps against authorization ceilings, Congress typically responds by increasing the ceilings, but, with the prospect of enormous over-

---

*Approximately $127 million of this figure is for obtaining lands in parks designated before 1959. Some of these lands pose no immediate threat to the parks and fall into the low-priority acquisition category. The $550 million figure also includes $30 million for a special funds transfer to the Bureau of Land Management.

## Redwood National Park

Redwood National Park, surely the most expensive national park in history, promises to cost additional millions of dollars. Redwood is usually excluded from backlog calculations, however, because the funds for it are not expected to come from the Land and Water Conservation Fund. Created in 1968 and enlarged in 1978,[1] Redwood includes huge tracts of extraordinarily valuable timber land acquired from private landowners.* Because of imminent threats to several particularly important Redwood groves, the additional land was acquired in 1978 through a legislative taking that immediately vested title in the federal government.[3]

The original acquisitions authorized in 1968 cost $148 million. But the federal government and the three major timber companies involved have yet to agree on the value of the almost 45,000 acres acquired through the 1978 legislative taking. As of 1984, the federal government had deposited $352 million with the U.S. District Court in California to compensate landowners for that taking. The timber companies assert, however, that the land is worth between $752 million and $812 million.[4] In congressional hearings, park service personnel have estimated that the final bill will be in the $550 million range, plus interest.[5]

The debate over the Redwood proposal in 1978 demonstrates that Congress did not intend to fund Redwood out of the Land and Water Conserva-

tion Fund, from which other purchases are funded. Witness this statement by Senator Ted Stevens (R.-Alaska) regarding an amendment he was proposing (and which was ultimately accepted): "I am disturbed that the moneys are earmarked to come from the land and water conservation fund. I believe that a taking of this type, a legislative taking, on a bill that is considered to be an extraordinary approach to a problem concerning the national parks, should not be funded from the land and water conservation fund. . . . What this really means is that acquisitions of this type should be financed by normal appropriations. . . . To encumber the fund is going to put us in the position of having an overdraft."[6]

The legislation itself provides for payment of any Redwood judgment out of a special General Accounting Office permanent judgment appropriation.[7] Normally, this appropriation is not available for land condemnation judgments, but the Comptroller General determined in 1983 that Congress intended that it be used for Redwood.[8]

---

*Making it even more expensive, the Redwood legislation contained a generous package of benefits for loggers who lost their jobs when the park was set aside. As of April 1984, the park estimated that worker compensation benefits had amounted to more than $100 million.[2]

runs, this piecemeal response is unwise. It is time for an informed, systemwide response that includes a search for opportunities to complete the parks in ways less costly than acquisition. Ways to elicit state and local cooperation in completing parks should be included in this assessment.

Because of the sensitivity of these two assessments and the importance of performing them soon, they are appropriate tasks for the Presidential Commission on Outdoor Recreation Resources Review, which was established in early 1985 by President Reagan.

## Improving the Land Acquisition Process

Land acquisition is a critical element in establishing most parks. The park service, like any public agency acquiring land for public use, faces delicate issues as it tries to reconcile park needs with the needs of private landowners. Inholders often face uncertainty about acquisition plans, and, at times, park service personnel have been high-handed.[27]

If handled successfully, the acquisition process can control costs by enabling land to be purchased expeditiously, particularly in situations where land prices are rising rapidly. The treatment of landowners can also influence public perceptions of the park service and thereby enlarge or diminish future opportunities to create new parks.

Until the 1960s, the park service had relatively little direct responsibility for land acquisition; land had most often been transferred to it from some other federal agency. Some parks that included substantial private lands had been created (for example, Shenandoah and Grand Teton), but these lands typically were purchased by a state government or a philanthropist and transferred to the service—what former director Conrad Wirth called the "beg, borrow or steal system."[28] Only occasionally had Congress authorized purchase of a few critical private parcels.

A new approach became necessary in the 1960s when Congress began to carve parks out of private lands. In parks designated before 1959, the service continued, unless resources were threatened, to wait for willing sellers. Private lands in post-1959 parks were to be promptly acquired in accordance with policies established in the enabling legislation for each new unit.[29] The basic working approach for newly authorized areas during the 1960s and early 1970s was to buy land from any willing sellers and then, by way of condemnation, go after other land needed for park use. Typically, the park would quickly acquire as much land as possible, often before a general management plan or a survey to identify significant buildings had been completed.

Even so, the acquisition process often took years. New parks were authorized more rapidly than acquisition funds were appropriated. The resulting delays brought problems that persist today.

One such problem is inflation of land prices. Walter J. Hickel, secretary of the interior under President Nixon, called attention to the problem, citing rampant land inflation at Cape Cod and Point Reyes national seashores:

> A citizen, hearing the announcement that such-and-such a national park has been authorized, believes it has thereby been acquired. Often, only the concept of the park has been approved. No money has been appropriated to pay for it. Once the park is authorized, the land values increase sharply, over a period reaching a point where they are ten and sometimes fifty times as expensive as when the park was initially authorized.[30]

Ninety percent of the park managers responding to a questionnaire sent out for the *State of the Parks 1980* report stated that threatened private lands had doubled in value over the last 5 years. Nearly 85 percent estimated that land values had quintupled over the last decade.[31]

A second problem is the adverse impact of development. Residential communities within older parks (like Wawona in Yosemite) have stirred controversy; preservationists have charged that these communities are incompatible with the parks. The airport in Grand Teton faces similar objections, especially in light of periodic proposals for its expansion. During the 1960s and 1970s, major efforts to develop resources were begun or proposed within several western parks. For example, in 1977 the Phillips Petroleum Company drilled an exploratory geothermal well on an inholding at Lassen Volcanic National Park. Only two years later, after extensive surface damage had occurred, was the park service finally able to condemn the tract.[32]

Preservationists have asserted that the park service's policy of not condemning lands in pre-1959 parks just does not work. Instead, it allows incompatible development and leads to exorbitant acquisition costs when the service finally can purchase the land. In 1972, The Conservation Foundation's report *National Parks for the Future* urged that all inholders be removed from the parks.[33]

A third problem, fair treatment of private landowners, is important not only in itself but also as an influence on public attitudes toward the park service. In some parks, the service acquired a reputation

*Yosemite, February 1984.*

for unfairness during the mid-1970s as it sought to carry out new responsibilities for land acquisition and for other land protection techniques that it had seldom used in the past. Complaints began circulating that the service was sometimes purchasing land, thereby forcing out inholders, even where authorizing legislation allowed private owners to stay put. Some inholders also asserted that the service had too much discretion in selecting what land to take and when and that the service sometimes harassed owners until they sold out.[34] A series of General Accounting Office (GAO) reports charged that the park service bought too much land rather than using alternative protection measures, such as easements and zoning, that would have allowed landowners to stay put.[35]

Events in Cuyahoga in the late 1970s received widespread publicity. Congress's apparent intent there was to protect some occupied land through the use of easements and thus let the occupants stay, yet the park set off on a program of full-fee acquisitions that forced many inholders to leave their lands. Landowners began a campaign of protest, and Representative John Seiberling (a resident of the area and a driving force in the park's creation) complained publicly about the service's tactics with those who would not sell out quietly. Soon thereafter, the park changed course, but, by that time, the damage had been done.[36]

Although the service has, of course, dealt amicably with many landowners, Cuyahoga has provided a convenient soapbox for opponents of park expansion. A film funded by one of the Cuyahoga inholders appeared on public television.[37] Complaints have also been made about the park service in the Upper Delaware River, where one critic has alleged that little effort has been made to understand local sentiment or include citizens in planning efforts.[38] The National Inholders Association thrives, with officers frequently on the spot to warn citizens affected by proposed parks that difficult times lie ahead.[39]

*Past Responses to Acquisition Problems*

In 1979, the Carter administration established a policy requiring all parks to have plans setting forth overall strategies for land acquisition. The new plans were to establish, before any buying started, a general order of priority for acquisitions, to make clear what interests would be acquired—for example, full fee versus scenic easement—and to specify compatible and incompatible uses in inholding areas to help landowners know what they could do on their lands.[40] The new policy was widely commended, although inholders continued to complain that things had not improved enough. Over the next two years, more than 100 plans were finished for existing units.[41]

When Secretary Watt took office in 1981, he further tightened land acquisition policy by replacing those land acquisition plans with land protection plans that were to rely "to the maximum extent practical [on] cost-effective alternatives to direct Federal purchase of private lands."[42] As of January 1985, some 125 land protection plans had been finished and approved, and the Department of the Interior was developing a more methodical process to ensure that funds are spent on the most critical parcels.[43] Nevertheless, some inholders—including some who want to be bought out—have been left in limbo.

*Needed: Further Responses*

Some measures to improve the acquisition process can be taken by the park service itself. Others depend on congressional action before future parks are authorized.

*Completion and Updating of Land Protection Plans.* To ensure that acquisition funds are spent where they are needed most, the park service must complete its land protection plans. These plans should be developed openly in consultation with landowners, local governments, advisory commissions, and local conservation groups. The plans also should be updated periodically in consultation with park interest groups.

*Better Estimation of Acquisition Costs.* Congress and the park service need to establish an improved process for estimating acquisition costs before new parks are authorized. A few highly publicized, sensational cost overruns show why. The original cost estimate for Cuyahoga was $35 million, but that figure later jumped to $70 million. Now the area's chief legislative advocate estimates the total bill will be closer to $90 million, and the park service recently put the figure at $166 million.[44] Similarly, at Santa Monica Mountains, the cost ceiling contained in the authorizing legislation was $155 million; park service officials' estimates of the eventual cost of acquiring lands in that recreation area now range from $250 million to $600 million.[45] Although these huge discrepancies are not typical (acquisition of the Appalachian Trail, for example, has consistently stayed beneath its statutory ceiling),[46] improved procedures are clearly needed so that funds can be realistically allocated.

In deciding whether to authorize a new park and in establishing a spending limit for each unit, Congress generally relies on cost estimates prepared by the service. Often, however, Congress acts with incomplete or inaccurate cost information. Sometimes, Congress does not give the service adequate funds or time to undertake an accurate estimate.[47]*

Occasionally, political considerations lead to low estimates of acquisition costs, with park supporters in Congress winking at the

---

*Federal law requires the park service to prepare a report for Congress that shows the estimated cost of land acquisition for the first five-year period. This applies, however, only to units recommended by the service.[48]

results. The low estimates help get the unit authorized, and then, when the money runs out, supporters can argue that unless the project is finished the past investment will be wasted.

Another major reason cost estimates are often lower than actual costs is that it takes Congress longer to appropriate funds than has been assumed in the estimates. Consequently, as land speculation and inflation take their tolls, the ultimate price tag rises. At Santa Monica Mountains, for example, authorizing legislation established a five-year timetable for appropriation ceilings, with provisions allowing for unappropriated amounts to be available in succeeding years. Although $125 million was authorized through the end of fiscal year 1981, Congress had only appropriated $37 million.[49] During the 1970s, land values in this area rose by as much as 35 percent per year.[50]

The steps required to improve cost estimates have long been obvious: adequate funds and time for the service to prepare estimates; truthful, realistic estimates by congressional proponents of new parks; updating of estimates when acquisition is delayed. Unfortunately, however, none of them are easy to put into practice. One step that could help—the reliance, in proposing new parks, on "park opportunities reports" prepared by the park service—is discussed below under "Improving the Park Selection Process."

*Improvement of Socioeconomic Impact Studies.* To aid in the evaluation of land acquisition proposals—especially when new parks are being suggested—studies of the proposals' social and economic impacts on local governments and residents should be broadened. The service has adopted guidelines requiring such analyses[51]—referred to as sociocultural studies—but the focus appears to be on adverse impacts. The analyses should also reflect potential benefits, such as the projected economic benefits from tourism and expenditures by the service and its employees.

*Establishment of an Emergency Fund.* To permit rapid acquisition in special cases involving either backlog land or new park designation, Congress should create a revolving emergency fund. Both outside threats and opportunities to buy out inholders occasionally warrant rapid acquisition. Sometimes, the availability of acquisition funds is also necessary to get landowners to comply with approved park plans. The Cape Cod formula, under which the park service can, in effect, compel compliance with local land-use regulations by condemning land where violations occur, will not work unless the local residents know that the park service has the money to proceed with comdemnation. An emergency fund could also help the park service to dissuade opportunistic developments, aimed at thwarting park planning efforts or driving up acquisition costs, while park protection plans are being completed.

The park service has a small amount of money (less than $5 million) to draw on for emergency acquisitions in parks established before 1959, but limited size and scope hamper the fund's effectiveness. The park service should be able to draw on a revolving fund quickly, without additional congressional authorization, in three types of situations:

- when a special opportunity arises to purchase a key parcel that has been identified for acquisition in an approved land protection plan, but for which Congress has not yet appropriated funds;
- when proposed development on an inholding threatens park resources and acquiring the land is the only available alternative; or
- when funds are necessary to make credible park service threats to condemn inholdings in the event of failure to comply with approved land-use controls.

The emergency fund should, at least at first, be relatively small—around $20 million. To ensure accountability, the park service should be required to submit to Congress annual reports on acquisition expenditures from the fund. All other acquisitions would continue to be subject to regular appropriations from Congress.

This approach is similar to a technique used by the California Coastal Conservancy. The conservancy was created to restore and enhance coastal resources, provide access to the coast, and preserve valuable lands. Funded by bond issues, it has the power to buy, sell, develop, and restore lands. By sometimes purchasing land that is threatened by development and reselling it with development restrictions, the conservancy has been an important complement to the land-use regulatory program of the California Coastal Commission.[53] One of the conservancy's great assets is its flexibility to act quickly when necessary without waiting for new legislation or approval of some higher level of a bureaucracy.

## Making Greenline or Cooperative Parks Work

The scale of the park system of the future depends in part on the success of greenline or cooperative parks that incorporate private property within park boundaries and sometimes state and local government lands as well.* The success of the greenline approach matters not only because several greenline parks are already in the system but also because that approach is critical to establishing future parks. In many of America's special places—particularly areas where high-quality resources are being subjected to intense development pressures—massive federal land acquisition would be inappropriate or unacceptable, not only because of its cost but also because of its disruption of landowners and their communities. Only greenline parks, by intentionally including human settlements, hold promise of accommodating and protecting these "living landscapes," shaped in part by the continuing choices of private residents.

In several diverse parks, the service has been experimenting with supplements to acquisition—measures such as easements, zoning, and financial incentives. (See box on "Supplementary Measures to Protect Privately Owned Land.") In some units—for example, Cape Cod—the park service has been a primary actor in terms of both land ownership and monitoring supplementary measures such as local zoning regulations. In others, like Pinelands National Reserve, the service's role has been limited to technical and funding assistance to a state agency charged with protecting the area.[54]

Although the service has officially embraced supplementary measures as a way to protect land in major unfinished parks, acceptance outside Washington has been lukewarm at best. Many officials prefer the more secure protection and convenience of management that ownership in fee provides. Reluctance to use scenic easements, for example, dates back to early experiences of the service along the Blue Ridge and Natchez Trace parkways. In both cases, the states through which the parkways ran were given a lump sum of money and told to purchase as many easements as possible. Unfortunately, landowners were not always fully informed of the rights they were relinquishing, and subsequent owners were often not aware of, or

---

*The term greenline is sometimes used more narrowly to apply only to areas protected by state agencies (for example, Adirondack Park in New York and Pinelands National Reserve in New Jersey). However, the concept of mixed land ownership patterns and uses is also applicable to national park areas.

did not feel bound by, the easements. Not surprisingly, the service ran into great difficulties when it tried to manage and enforce the easements.[55] It did not take long before word spread that easements spelled trouble and were a poor alternative to outright full-fee acquisition.

Toward the end of the Carter administration, the park service began providing field personnel with technical aids such as handbooks on how to use supplementary protection measures.[56] Despite signs that the service was starting to purchase more less-than-fee interests in land, it was still apparent that service personnel preferred acquisition. The General Accounting Office concluded in several studies that many agency officials believed nonacquisition alternatives were "costly, ineffective, and administratively burdensome."[57] Today, several superintendents are experimenting with supplementary protection techniques, but wholehearted acceptance is by no means assured.

### Evaluating Greenline Measures

Supplementary land protection measures used in greenline parks are no panacea for solving all the problems associated with full-fee acquisition. Acquisition or other protective measures must be selected case by case, after such factors as costs (both initial and subsequent), level of protection, need for access, state and local cooperation, and complexity of management are given careful consideration.

*Reduced Acquisition Costs.* Often, the principal motive for choosing supplementary protection measures is the desire to reduce or avoid acquisition costs. Acquiring partial interests such as easements tends to be less costly than full-fee purchase. For zoning, no compensation need be paid. Land exchanges, too, generally avoid out-of-pocket expenditures of public funds.

In practice, however, the cost saving often is less clear-cut than it might at first seem. Less-than-fee interests sometimes cost almost as much as the land itself—for example, in cases where an easement prevents construction on property with a market value that has been inflated by development pressures. There are indirect costs, too. Dealing with landowners and local governments requires expenditures not just at the time protection is established but indefinitely thereafter. Financial incentives to landowners, grants in aid to local

## Supplementary Measures
## to Protect
## Privately Owned Land

Supplementary protection measures for privately owned land are diverse. They vary in permanence, public costs and landowner compensation, degree of resource protection, and provision of public access. Some of the most important measures are:

• *Partial ownership (such as easements)*. Instead of acquiring all ownership rights in parkland ("fee-simple" ownership), the park service may acquire partial ("less-than-fee") ownership. Partial ownership often takes the form of an *easement*, although there are variants such as acquisition of *development rights*. Partial ownership is sometimes used in combination with other techniques; for example, land may be acquired and resold subject to deed restrictions that limit future development or use.

Whatever its form, partial ownership typically restricts the use of property for the purpose of achieving scenic, or conservation, objectives or providing limited public access. For example, an easement may prevent a landowner from cutting trees or modifying structures without approval by the park service. Easements can also require an owner to take certain action: for example, to provide reasonable and safe trails for public use or to maintain wildlife habitat.

Easements are used extensively in some units, including the Blue Ridge Parkway and Sawtooth National Recreation Area (managed by the U.S. Forest Service)[1] and with less frequency in a number of others.

Easements may be purchased by the park service or donated by a land-owner, who may then take advantage of federal income tax deductions.

• *Acquisition and lease*. Acquisition and lease can be considered a variant of conventional acquisition since the park service becomes and remains the owner of the land. Instead of managing the land, however, the service leases it to an individual or corporation, sometimes to the former owner in which case it is called acquisition and leaseback. For example, a rancher in a greenline park might sell his ranch to the park service and lease it back for continued ranching; the terms of the lease would determine how the land could be used.

• *Land exchange*. Land exchanges, too, usually involve ownership in fee by the park service. What is distinctive about land exchanges is that the private owner receives another piece of property instead of cash. Federal laws contain detailed procedures and requirements that must be satisfied before an exchange can be accomplished. For this reason, and because the federal government does not have a good inventory of potential trading stock, exchanges are not widely used, although there has been a movement to make them easier to employ.

• *Land-use regulations*. Regulations such as zoning can affect not only the use of private land within park units but also that land's value and thus the price that the park service must pay to acquire it. Since the service itself has no general authority to regulate the use of private land, any land-use regulations governing private land in the parks are adopted by state or local governments.

In several units created since 1960, including Cape Cod and Fire Island, local zoning regulations play a key role in park protection. In these units, the park service cannot condemn specified lands within park boundaries so long as the owners use them in accordance with local regulations that the Department of the Interior has found compatible with park policy.[2]

• *Developer contributions.* Under state or local laws, developers must sometimes make contributions to resource conservation. For example, the California Coastal Commission requires a developer to earmark four acres for preservation or public use for each acre of wetland developed.[3] Such contributions (sometimes called "exactions") can sometimes be used to extend protection of parklands, although the approach raises several legal and administrative issues.

• *Private stewardship.* In a variety of ways short of binding legal agreements, and often as a result of informal consultation with park officials, landowners within national parks have long modified the ways they manage their property in deference to the park. Some parks, for example Santa Monica Mountains National Recreation Area, are taking vigorous initiatives to develop cooperative park service/landowner programs with respect to such activities as planting native species and encouraging compatible residential design and good land planning.

• *Incentives and assistance for landowners.* Incentives and assistance for landowners can be used alone or in combination with measures such as easements, zoning, or reliance on private stewardship. In either case, such "sweeteners" or conflict resolution procedures supplement the regulatory process. They can also be useful to secure positive action by a property owner—for example, the provision of access across private property to a river or the maintenance of a trail.

Federal tax incentives have been important in fostering the donation or bargain sale of important natural areas to private land trusts like the Nature Conservancy and in promoting preservation and rehabilitation of historic buildings. The donor of land or of a restrictive easement can take a charitable tax deduction. In the case of historic buildings, the federal tax code allows developers a 25 percent credit for approved preservation expenditures.[4] Tax and financial incentives can also be an important adjunct to other protection techniques. Although several members of Congress have proposed making federal tax breaks more widely available to landowners in or near parks, budget deficits make the likelihood of such incentives uncertain.

• *Technical assistance and grants-in-aid to governments.* Many local governments, particularly in semideveloped rural areas, do not have the financial resources or expertise to deal with complex land-use planning issues. Yet the success of a greenline effort usually depends on a cooperative and knowledgeable local partner to park service efforts.

In a few instances, notably at Pictured Rocks and Sleeping Bear Dunes national lakeshores, Congress has authorized federal land managing agencies to provide grants to local regulatory and planning agencies.[5] At Sleeping Bear Dunes, the park service helped fund economic impact studies for two counties soon after the park was established a decade ago.[6] Other economic impact studies have been performed at Cape Cod and Redwood. These techniques have not been used extensively, however, and seem to be triggered by local tension over a park's creation rather than as an integral part of the planning process for a new park.

Perhaps the most ambitious use of incentives to stimulate local planning occurs in New York State's Adirondack Park, where the Adirondack Park Agency pays up to 87 percent of a local government's cost of preparing local land-use plans.[7] The agency also develops model ordinances and helps train local zoning officers.[8] Between 1973 and 1982, the agency provided assistance to 84 communities in the park at a cost of more than $1.4 million.[9]

governments, and other "sweeteners," though they can make management easier, add further costs. And, in some cases, acquisition of property may eventually prove unavoidable to provide sufficient protection; in such cases, supplementary measures serve only to postpone acquisition costs, perhaps to a time when land values have sharply appreciated.

Level of Protection. One of the most difficult judgment calls in selecting protection techniques is determining what level of protection is needed against possible future incompatible uses of a property. At one extreme are unprotected inholdings that have coexisted with federal parklands for decades, so far without apparent damage to park resources. At the opposite extreme are parcels subject to intensive development pressures where delays of a few months have dramatically increased the costs of full or even partial acquisition. Properties that seem to need little protection today may require it in the future, at which time protection may have become prohibitively expensive.

The various supplementary measures offer significantly different levels of protection. Acquisition and leaseback, for example, can provide virtually complete protection. Partial acquisition also gives the park service an ownership interest that (depending on its terms) can permanently bar incompatible development. Zoning provides far less secure long-term protection, since the park service has no ownership interest and local governments can change zoning regulations. (However, the park service may have substantial leverage over those governments if it has backup condemnation authority like that at Cape Cod.) Financial and tax incentives, when used alone, provide still less protection.

*Need for Access.* To remain consistent with park tradition, public access must be a key attribute of every park system unit. Even if most of the lands in a unit are protected by easements or zoning, the park service or some other public agency should own a core area of the unit to provide access and space for interpretative facilities. In many cases, this core area may be stitched together out of land already owned by state and local governments or other federal agencies. In other cases, however, acquisition of some land in fee is essential. In Santa Monica and Cuyahoga, for example, one of the most critical undertakings for the service has been to assemble such a core area quickly so that each place "feels" like a park.

*State and Local Cooperation.* Close cooperation among public land managers is needed in greenline parks, where lands may be owned and managed by other federal agencies or state and local governments. Numerous opportunities exist for integrating management of resources and visitor service to reduce duplication, improve resource protection, and enhance the visitor experience. However, in units where public and private property are intermingled, park objectives can often be thwarted by local governments, which may, for example, extend utility lines for housing projects or grant rezonings for inappropriate development. Local cooperation can be critical in evaluating the feasibility of attaining park objectives. To assure long-term local cooperation and consistency, the park service has used various carrot-and-stick approaches. Voluntary efforts, such as those used at Santa Monica Mountains (see profile), have also been tried.

*Complexity of Management.* Greenline land protection techniques depend on sophisticated management, including continuous day-to-day attention after they have been put in place. Attention must constantly be paid to monitoring and enforcement, intergovernmental coordination, and sometimes also the use of incentives to encourage landowner cooperation and land stewardship. These supplementary techniques create indefinitely the sort of relationship that already troubles the park service in dealing with inholders: a relationship with someone inside the park who is there on terms not set entirely by the service. In cases where regulations or easements

Yosemite, February 1984.

vary significantly from one property to the next, or where owners are unaware of the exact nature of the restrictions on their land, management is particularly difficult. Consistent and fair enforcement can also be a problem; a landowner who feels he or she is being policed more stringently than a neighbor naturally resents it.

Experience outside the park service suggests possible responses to these problems. The U.S. Forest Service, for example, has compiled an excellent track record in managing Sawtooth National Recreation Area. The historic preservation field offers other useful precedents. Local preservation groups often assist local governments in monitoring facade easements on landmark buildings, in effect acting as the "eyes" of the administering agency. In some instances, the volunteer organizations actually own the easement and assume full responsibility for monitoring and enforcement.

Park service officials administering less-than-fee techniques must maintain continuing relationships not only with affected landowners but also with affected state and local governments. For example, at Cuyahoga, the service deals with no fewer than 25 jurisdictions ranging from 2 regional councils of governments (in the Cleveland and Akron metropolitan areas) to 7 counties concerned about the impact of the park on tax revenues.[58] At Santa Monica Mountains, the service cooperates with 6 local jurisdictions, 11 state agencies, and an assortment of sanitation, water, transit, and air quality management agencies. In addition, the California Coastal Commission has regulatory power over the coastal zone, which extends as much as five miles inland in the Santa Monica Mountains.[59]

Working relationships with local governments are important. At Cape Cod, the individual effort of one park official to work with local leaders, monitor development, and review permits is widely credited with making land-use arrangements there work to the extent they have. In the past, park personnel in some units have attended local zoning meetings and maintained informal contacts with local officials.

In a few parks—Cape Cod, Indiana Dunes, and Golden Gate, for example—advisory commissions are established by statute. In several other areas, voluntary coordinating bodies have been established to improve communication among affected governments. The Cuyahoga Valley Communities Council, for one, was organized to provide a forum for local governments and park service representatives to discuss park issues of mutual interest. The council has provided information to area residents about federal tax credits for historic preservation and about federal payments in lieu of taxes to local governments, for example.[61]

## Improving Greenline Measures

Greenlines will succeed only if protective measures (easements, zoning, incentives, assistance) can be established and then managed effectively over the long term. This requires continuing relationships with landowners and governments as well as sophisticated management methods. The park service must broaden its experience with, for example, monitoring and enforcement of land-use restrictions, cooperation with state and local governments through such mechanisms as voluntary coordinating councils, and the application of incentives and technical assistance to encourage cooperation and land stewardship.

While park service experiments in managing greenline units are encouraging, they are so diverse and often so new that it is not yet possible to define the best models for such parks or to declare the approach an unqualified success. At Cape Cod, most of the land is owned by the federal government, while, in Lowell, federal ownership is minuscule. In other greenline units, the appropriate mix of federal, state and local, and private ownership and management is still being worked out. One of the most promising future avenues—exemplified by the Pinelands National Reserve in New Jersey—may be park service cooperation with a state government acting as a pivotal partner in the arrangement.

If greenline parks and supplementary land protection techniques are to live up to their promise, not only for the creation of future parks but also to assure the success of present greenline units and to protect those more traditional parks facing external threats, the park service should take several steps:

*Continual Evaluation.* The service needs to continue current efforts to evaluate supplementary protection techniques in varying situations. A recently completed series of case studies of eight existing national parks offers an excellent model for future efforts. These studies weighed the pros and cons of various land protection techniques that might be appropriate in the eight parks. In a few, supplementary measures appeared feasible, while in many, land purchase was the preferred technique.[62]

Future studies of greenline techniques should not be conducted with financial savings as their sole concern; an acceptable level of resource protection must also be assured. The studies should also consider that, though alternative approaches may be cheaper at the outset, they may cost more in the long run because of the complex management they require.

*Staff Training and Expertise.* Supplementary approaches to land protection require experienced staff to implement them—people who have detailed knowledge of the tools they are using and who can work with the public effectively on a day-to-day basis. Staffs at many units lack these skills, having focused their attention on managing publicly owned lands.

Some experts in administering less-than-fee measures can be found in the park service, other federal and state agencies, and private organizations, but they are scattered throughout the country. To deal with this problem, the Department of the Interior could organize "expert assistance teams" of those specialists to advise staff members at individual park units on how to implement land protection plans. Separate teams might also be organized within each administrative region of the service to provide information and advice on less-than-fee techniques, successful approaches and pitfalls, and legal developments.

Even more important in the long run would be the establishment of park service personnel policies that reward specialization in the use of less-than-fee techniques. A separate job classification in the application of such techniques and the management of areas in which they are used—comparable to the classification established for resource management specialists—should be considered.

*Involvement of Land Trusts.* Over the last decade, private nonprofit land conservation groups—known generally as land trusts—have emerged as important players in the land protection picture. Generally speaking, these organizations seek to conserve natural, agricultural, and historical resources by acquiring property interests in areas threatened with development. Land trusts use their nonprofit status to obtain below-market-value sales of property or donations. Trusts usually can act very quickly, and often they can work with landowners who refuse to deal with government agencies.[63] Approximately 500 private land trusts in the United States have preserved close to three million acres—an amount of land nearly the size of Connecticut.[64]

*Santa Monica Mountains, June 1984.*

In many instances, the trusts acquire easements that allow a land-owner to continue using the property in some fashion, while preventing the land from being further developed. The landowners may get a reduced property tax assessment and, in cases of clear public benefit, may take a charitable-donation deduction on their income tax. If a trust does acquire full title to some land, it often resells the property to a public agency such as the park service. Such a "rollover" purchase can sometimes result in substantial savings to government, and the trust can use funds from rollover transactions to purchase, or acquire easements on, additional threatened property.

The park service already has worked closely with land trusts in several areas to protect threatened parcels before Congress appropriated funds for their acquisition by the government. Despite these efforts, however, the full potential of land trusts has yet to be realized by the park service. Several parks are now considering the use of private land trusts as part of their land protection initiatives,[65] a trend that should be encouraged through experiments at several units. The service might also stimulate the creation of land trusts and support their work—for example, by offering them technical assistance. And park service staff might sit on the advisory boards of groups working near parklands or encourage "Friends of . . ." organizations to expand their roles to encompass land acquisition.

*Exploration of Tax Incentives.* Incentives, in the form of preferential property tax assessments or federal income tax credits or deductions, could become an important protection tool in the future, although (as noted above) they offer little long-term assurance of protection unless they are combined with other techniques. Many state and local governments already offer property tax breaks for some farmers, for example, and owners of historic properties, and some jurisdictions are tailoring tax incentives specifically for land conservation purposes.[66]

Within the service, studies are currently under way to examine an expanded role in land conservation for tax incentives.[67] Several members of Congress have also introduced legislation to make conservation tax incentives more widely available.[68]

Because tax incentives entail revenue losses and administrative costs, they must be carefully tailored to public needs to be cost effective. Only identified critical parcels should be entitled to incentives, and the potential for abuse should be scrutinized. The National Trust for Historic Preservation recently called attention to abuse of preservation tax incentives. As the trust noted, "A few well-publicized 'fleecings' can kill a well-intentioned program—even one that is applied honestly and thoughtfully, as are the preservation incentives, more than 99 percent of the time."[69]

*Consideration of Supplementary Techniques with Future Park Proposals.* Congress should assure that less-than-fee options are explored before future parks are authorized. Park legislation should direct the park service to explore a range of alternatives so that purchase does not occur when alternatives are preferable. There may be cases in which legislation should specify that only a certain amount of land be purchased in fee, but even in those cases the service should be given sufficient latitude to construct the best protection plan based on a mix of techniques.

In some future parks, cooperation by state or local governments may need to be required as a *quid pro quo* for federal involvement and funding. A park's authorization legislation might, for example, specify the type of local zoning cooperation used at Cape Cod. In other units, law might call for review by the park service of local cooperation and progress (as is being done in various ways at Pinelands and Lowell); failure to win certification could cause withdrawal of federal funds for acquisition or even a complete pullout by the service.[70]

If state and local governments are not willing to agree to a Cape Cod-type formula or to a certification process, then future park proposals should proceed only if acquisition is the main protection tool. As one astute commentator observed almost 10 years ago, as the park service and other federal agencies "consider investing limited funds available for park acquisition, they cannot help but be deterred from investing in areas which do not have legal authority to protect the park resource. Under the best of circumstances,

## Politics and Park Selection

The process of creating parks has never been tidy. Even when the great western parks were being carved out of the huge public domain, few entered the system without debates and compromises.

For example, the idea for a national park centering on the Grand Canyon surfaced as early as 1882,[1] little more than a decade after Major John Wesley Powell explored the lower reaches of the Colorado River and returned with tales of this wild and spectacular gorge. That legislation languished, and, while the area was subsequently designated a national forest (1893), a national game preserve (1906), and a national monument (1908), the park idea made little headway because of opposition from local politicians and economic interests.[2] In the meantime, tourism at the canyon was beginning to boom. In 1901, the Santa Fe Railroad completed a spur line to the South Rim, and a few years later the grand El Tovar Hotel was erected.[3] There was also great interest in the area from miners, and schemes were afoot for dams and irrigation projects.

In 1918, the breakthrough came when the Senate Committee on Public Lands and Surveys reported favorably on Senator Ashurst's Grand Canyon park bill.[4] Opponents were quieted with a provision that stated valid existing land claims were not to be affected and another that permitted power and reclamation projects and prospecting and mining in the park when allowed by the secretary of the interior. Another section prohibited building any structure that might block the view from land owned by powerful newspaper magnate William Randolph Hearst.[5] In the House, before the Committee on Public Lands, Representative Carl Hayden steered further compromises by inserting provisions to protect property rights of the Havasupai Indians and to allow the

mixed private/public parks are a gamble with the federal recreation budget."[71] In the future, the park service should use greenline or supplementary land protection techniques only if it can be fairly certain it will win the gamble.

## Improving the Park Selection Process

The willingness of the United States to create more parks will be influenced not only by acquisition costs and land-protection practices but also by public confidence in the quality of the resources added to the system. To provide this confidence, measures are needed to improve the process used to select and establish new parks.

Since the earliest days of the parks, the selection process has been highly political. (See box on Politics and Park Selection.) There is

secretary to grant railroad rights-of-way across the park.[6] The legislation was signed into law in 1919, and the land was transferred to the park service.[7]

Over the next few years, the service was plagued with problems stemming from mining claims—many fraudulent—and lack of control over critical parcels such as the Bright Angel Trail, a favorite route to the canyon floor.[8] Subsequent selective purchases and legislation helped ameliorate these difficulties, although plans for dams affecting the canyon seem to surface periodically, the latest one being in the early 1980s.

Park historians like John Ise and Alfred Runte have documented other bitter battles over setting aside public land for the great early natural parks.[9] In some instances—for example, Grand Teton—parks were created only through complicated land transactions and generous private donations.

Then, like today, there were pressures for "political" parks. Horace Albright, second director of the service, recounted how, in 1922, Interior Secretary Albert B. Fall pressed hard for what Fall termed "The All-Year National Park" in New Mexico. Others pinned the derogatory name of "Mexican Freckles" on the proposed park because of its disconnected pattern on a map. The proposed area just happened to form a great crescent around a ranch Fall owned. While the park did have some significant natural features, Mather knew it lacked national park quality. Yet he dutifully studied the area personally and made an adverse report on it to the secretary. Then, according to Albright, Mather was so worried his action might mean his dismissal or some other disaster for the fledgling service that he suffered a nervous breakdown. The park made it through the Senate by unanimous vote but foundered in the House, where it never reached the floor.[10]

also a history, however, of efforts to devise standards, plans, and procedures to help the political process reach more sound decisions. During the 1970s, some of these efforts sought to rein in a Congress bent on expanding the system. Today, they are needed to strengthen the case for park creation during a time of federal retrenchment.

Experience suggests the difficulty of making the park selection process more analytical. Standards, plans, procedures all present some opportunities, yet all have shown limitations.

An informal standard of quality for new park units is even now in place, at least in theory. Units are widely expected to meet a standard of "national significance"; thus, resources of merely "regional significance" do not belong in the system.[72] In practice, however, this standard can at best provide only quite general guidance in selecting sites. Any broad standard applied to such a diverse system will often function more as a rationalization to explain decisions than as a useful guide in making them.

Plans depicting the future system have also been prepared, notably the 1972 National Park Service Plan. Although intended to help complete the park system by identifying "gaps" in its representation of ecological and historical themes, the plan made its greatest contribution by spurring imaginations about what the park system might be—serving not as a limit on expansion but as an inventory of opportunities. Even as an inventory, though, the plan was not broad enough to address the full range of park goals. (To illustrate, it nowhere considered the role the system might play in providing resource-based recreational opportunities close to urban areas, although that was a burning issue of its day. Nor did it mesh well with nascent greenline park initiatives, which had goals such as landscape and open space protection rather than the protection of ecological or geological diversity.)

As a tool for establishing priorities for deciding what was worthy of the park system, the 1972 plan was also flawed. Not only were its goals narrower than the historical goals of the system itself, but the plan viewed the system separately from other elements of the nationwide network of conservation lands. Largely as as result, the plan did not dominate the process for identification or authorization of new areas in the 1970s. In the future, too, there is little likelihood that any plan can successfully prescribe an end-state picture of the system of the future; the problems faced by the 1972 plan are unlikely to be overcome.

Finally, administrative procedures have been established from time to time to try to improve the park selection process. Under the "Section 8" process established in 1976 legislation, for example, the park service was obligated to review prospective additions to the system and annually make detailed reports to Congress on at least 12 of them.[73] That process, somewhat more analytical than past approaches, was just beginning to be applied when the efforts of Representative Phil Burton (D.-Calif.) culminated in the Omnibus Park acts of 1978 and 1980. The study process did not prove influential during that period. (As one ex-official from the Office of Management and Budget put it, "There was no constituency for hard analysis.")[74] The process was dismantled in the early 1980s for lack of funding.

*Measures Needed Now*

Any renewed effort at park creation will face the continuing issues of selectivity and quality that gave rise to the "national significance" standard, the 1972 plan, and the Section 8 process. In the very differ-

*Santa Monica Mountains, June 1984.*

ent context of the 1980s, it is more important than ever to find an approach more successful than those proved to be.

Despite the difficulty of applying formal quality standards, a prudent evaluation process for the 1980s should be explicitly focused on the quality of resources and management that are the core traditions of the park system and the park service. The founders of the system focused their attention on the quality of its resources; to retain quality, they were willing to sacrifice size. It is this conviction that the resources included in the system are indeed the nation's "crown jewels" that underlies the pride that millions of Americans feel for their parks. In the future, other goals—to provide a playground, rescue a local park system, or revitalize a struggling local economy—may be served secondarily, but preserving quality resources should remain paramount.

Conservation groups have a critical role to play in providing a constituency for a high standard of quality—as they have historically, dating back to the early years of the system. With limited choices before them, in any quality/quantity dilemma conservationists must continue to insist on quality.*

Benefiting from the strengths as well as the weaknesses of the 1972 plan and the Section 8 process, evaluating candidates for national parks in the 1980s should involve both identifying many potential park sites and then winnowing out the smaller number that should be part of the National Park System. The park service staff and the public have important roles in this process. Specifically, a new process for selecting future parks needs three basic elements: (a) a register, (b) inventories, and (c) periodic reports evaluating park opportunities:

Register. One key element of the process should be a register of a broad spectrum of natural and cultural resources, comparable to the National Register of Historic Places, which the park service already maintains. Like the historic register, the new register should include sites worthy of special management by somebody, somehow. It should list potential national park sites, of course, but it should also call attention to places that might be better suited for

---

*This was not always the role conservationists played in the 1970s. They were often too hesitant to criticize individual units or to raise questions about costs. As one noted, "No one wanted to be perceived as anti-park. Conservationists must go with a package that sells."[75]

management by one of the many other agencies, governments, and institutions that provide protection. Although such a list would be likely to include more sites than could possibly be protected, a broad-based nomination process is nonetheless worthwhile. Nominations should be made and evaluated much as they are for the National Register. An additional benefit is that this could establish, for example, a firmer basis for the tax deductibility of easements donated to land trusts.

*Inventories.* To supplement the register in bringing potential park sites to public attention, the park service should reinstitute targeted inventories of the kinds that have been prepared from time to time in the past. The precedent for targeted inventories is distinguished. The park service prepared an inventory of potential national seashores in the 1930s, decades before these seashores were actually designated.[76] The 1972 National Park System Plan identified various types of ecosystems, landforms, sites, and buildings that merited protection.[77] The Heritage Conservation and Recreation Service completed an excellent survey in the late 1970s of potential additions to the wild and scenic river system,[78] and the National Oceanic and Atmospheric Administration and the Fish and Wildlife Service have prepared complementary surveys of areas of critical environmental concern along the East Coast.[79] Inventories undertaken by the Nature Conservancy gather and manage information on natural ecological diversity; as of 1984, the Nature Conservancy had helped start programs for 35 states, 2 regions, 1 Indian Reservation, and the Tennessee Valley Authority.[80]

To be effective, inventories need a focus far more specific than "nationally significant resources." The selection of the seashore focus by the park service survey in the 1930s provided direction to future efforts. Effective inventories for the future must also focus on appropriate themes.*

Two themes appear particularly worthy of immediate exploration through a targeted inventorying process:

- *External threats and critical habitats*—an inventory of cases in which park boundaries need to be expanded to protect the

---

*In 1984, the park service was involved in two noteworthy historic landmark studies: the "Man in Space" program sites—areas important to the space program—and the "War in the Pacific" study.[81]

parks from external activities, including threats to outlying
areas that are critical habitat for park wildlife. A recent case
in which such expansion was necessary involved Chaco Culture
National Historical Park, where potential strip mining was
severely threatening the unique Pueblo ruins in the park; legislation in 1980 expanded park boundaries and added the protection of many outlying sites under the jurisdiction of other agencies.[82] Similarly, at Black Canyon of the Gunnison National
Monument, a recent law added some 7,000 acres to protect
the north rim of the canyon from "view-destroying development."[83] A systemwide examination of such needs in other
areas will lead to more effective protection.

- Greenline or cooperative parks—a focused inventory of potential sites at which the greenline park concept could be applied
  and refined. The inventory should include areas, like Pinelands
  National Reserve and the Illinois-Michigan Canal, that could
  perhaps benefit from greater federal recognition and assistance,
  even if formal park designation were politically or financially
  impractical.

To supplement inventories of external threats and cooperative
parks, the park service should seek funds for updating and completing several natural and cultural resource inventories started in
the 1960s and 1970s by federal agencies, state and local governments, and private conservation groups. Many remain unfinished.
The National Register of Historic Places contains only a fraction
of eligible structures, and the Historic American Buildings Survey
isn't close to completion even with respect to federally managed
areas. The same is true of various inventories begun at the state
and local levels.

With modest funding, the park service could play an important
catalytic role in several ways. First, to provide a model for other
entities, it could complete and update surveys of its own holdings
according to sound professional standards. Second, following the
example of the Nature Conservancy's inventory effort, it could com-
puterize inventory data, making it readily accessible inside and outside the service.* Third, the service could provide seed money for

---

*The only accessible list of structures on the National Register of Historic
Places—published in the *Federal Register*—is out-of-date shortly after it is
printed. The List of Classified Structures, which is the service's own inventory of structures eligible for the National Register, has recently been
computerized.

inventories undertaken by state and local governments and private groups, which can produce impressive results for only a few thousand dollars by relying on donated expertise.

*Periodic Reports Evaluating Park Opportunities.* The park service should report to Congress regularly, perhaps every two years, its current view of opportunities to create parks. Such reports would call congressional and public attention to needs and opportunities that are not now being systematically examined. Preparing the reports should also cause the park service to synthesize the results of the inventory process.

The reports should include the latest available information on the backlog of unacquired land for already designated parks, together with recommended priorities for its reduction. This information will be essential to provide a realistic context for the evaluation of park opportunities.

A report of this kind might produce several park proposals, and this "batching" of proposals could invite problems reminiscent of the "park-barrel" era, especially if consideration is not given to the system as a whole. Nevertheless, this seems preferable to evaluating sites in isolation. Political tradeoffs will occur in any event; grouping proposals together could help to focus attention on opportunities for the park system as a whole.

### Deciding Who Should Protect What

In choosing among possible future national park sites, it is important to consider whether some institution other than the park service could protect individual areas as well as or better than the park service.

*Additions to the Park System in the Context of the Nationwide Network of Conservation Lands.* The 334 units of the National Park System can be envisioned as somewhat random patches in a much larger quilt of natural and cultural sites administered by federal, state, and local agencies and by the private sector. The 79.4 million acres in the park system constitute only 10.7 percent of the 709 million acres of federal lands and waters managed primarily for resource conservation and use (figure 6.6).[84] Millions of acres of national forests and Bureau of Land Management (BLM) lands are available for hiking, camping, fishing, and other activities that also take place in the parks. (In terms of visitation, the park service ranks third among the major federal land holding agencies; the U.S. Forest Service ranks first.[85])

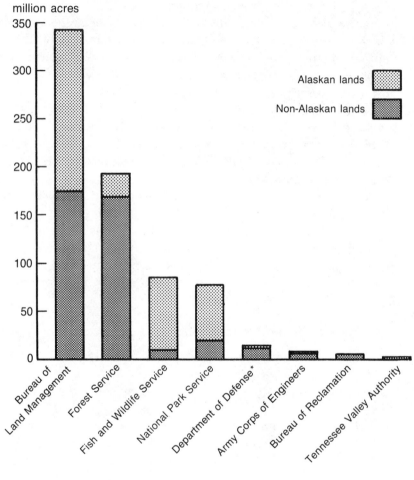

**Figure 6.6**
**Acreage of Federally Owned Lands**
**by Managing Agency, 1983**

* Excluding the Corps of Engineers

Source: U.S. Department of the Interior, Bureau of Land Management, "Public Land Statistics 1983" (Washington, D.C.: U.S. Government Printing Office, 1984).

State and local governments have expanded their park systems significantly in the past two decades. Between 1960 and 1979, the number of state parks increased 44.6 percent, while their acreage increased 68 percent.[86] Although these parks have approximately one-quarter of the acreage of national parks in the contiguous 48 states, they have almost twice as many visitors.[87] Many states contain protected forests, fish and wildlife reserves, and historic sites in addition to parks.

Similarly, the private sector is an important ally both in recreation and preservation. Of the nation's 1.3 billion privately owned acres, almost 740 million are forest and range lands.[88] A 1977 survey found that almost one-third of these lands were open for public recreational use.[89] Hunting is the most common activity on private recreation lands with hiking, picnicking, fishing, and snowmobiling allowed in some areas. The private sector also provides many of the nation's campsites, golf courses, tennis courts, and ski areas.

Private nonprofit organizations play a critical role in preserving resources and providing for visitor use. The Nature Conservancy, for example, has 500,000 acres of ecologically diverse lands,[90] and the National Trust for Historic Preservation owns several notable historic properties open for public use. Mount Vernon, the home of George Washington, and Monticello, the home of Thomas Jefferson, are both owned and maintained by private nonprofit organizations.

Resources in the national parks sometimes resemble those in other systems. The national forests contain wilderness areas—such as Bob Marshall, Selway-Bitterroot, and Golden Trout—that encompass lands equal in their grandeur to many of the great western parks. Samplings show that visitors to the beautiful White Mountains National Forest in New Hampshire often think they are in a national park. Some state coastal parks contain resources identical to those at national seashores and lakeshores. In some areas—Redwood, Indiana Dunes, Santa Monica Mountains, and Assateague, to name a few—state parks adjoin federal units.

Formal management categories, too, often blur. The 88.8-million-acre National Wilderness System comprises land managed by each of four federal agencies (the park, forest, and fish and wildlife services and BLM).* The National Wild and Scenic Rivers System includes segments of rivers that flow through lands managed by three agencies (the park and forest services and BLM). National Recreational Trails cut across a wide variety of federal, state, and

---

*The forest service manages far more wilderness in the 48 contiguous states than the park service does; all but 4.4 million acres of the park service's 36.7 million acres of wilderness lands are in Alaska.[91]

privately owned lands. The 7 forest service national recreation areas
are managed in ways similar to the 17 park service national recreation areas; the forest service-managed Sawtooth National Recreation
Area in Idaho, for example, resembles a greenline park with its inter-
mixed private and public lands and imaginative use of easements
and other land protection techniques.

Plans for the future of the park system, therefore, should not view
the parks in isolation but in the context of this nationwide network
of conservation lands. Despite legitimate concerns about duplication
of effort and inadequate stewardship by other agencies, about lack
of coordination and even antagonism, the presence of numerous
federal, state, and private conservation agencies adds to the richness of the land estate and spurs innovation and experimentation.
Strategies for the 1980s and beyond can be shaped more realistically
by collaboration mechanisms rather than by wholesale transfers of
acreage from one agency to another or from one level of government
to another (though, to be sure, transfers may sometimes be desirable). For example, instead of noting a "gap" in the National Park
System because it contains no unit reflecting the California Gold
Rush, planning should take account of the fact that Sutter's Fort,
where workmen first found traces of gold, is a California state park,
as are other thematically relevant sites.

What is unique about the national parks is the commitment that
they be dedicated to both preservation and visitor use. Most forest
service and BLM lands, by contrast, are managed for multiple uses
that include timber production, range forage, and mining. In wildlife
refuges, natural processes are often manipulated (diking, flooding,
cutting of trees and grass) to favor particular species. In wilderness
areas, the focus is tilted more toward preservation; buildings and
roads are prohibited. Although the uniqueness of the National Park
System must never be overlooked, the existence of land managed
by other agencies should be weighed in evaluating park creation
and expansion. (This attention is needed also in considering possible
"dedesignations" of present parks; see box on "Dedesignation of
Park Units.")

*The Park Service Role in "Protecting the Rest."* Although the
park system is only one element in a much larger land conservation
network, the park service has—and should continue to have—special responsibilities for conserving land outside its own system.
Indeed, the service can play a central role in shaping the network

## Dedesignation of Park Units

The delicate issue of park dedesignation is best considered in the context of the larger network of conservation lands. The issue was hot during the early days of the Reagan administration as rumors flew about a "hit list" of units that were to be dedesignated.[1] Secretary Watt had made clear that he believed some recently authorized national recreation areas like Santa Monica were of insufficient quality to warrant park service protection and that, by getting rid of them, more time and money could be focused on truly worthy parks. Confidential memos leaked from the Interior Department showed that Secretary Watt was going beyond rhetoric and actually putting the dedesignation wheels in motion.[2]

Nothing came of all this, and nothing should until a sound process is established to provide dispassionate analysis of opportunities to strengthen the system. At some point in the future, however, delisting of some units might be considered—not, however, to make room for the developers but, rather, to consider which public agency should provide future management of some marginal sites.

Some 35 parks have been delisted since 1895, for a variety of reasons.[3] Some sites, particularly smaller ones, were not deemed nationally significant; larger sites generally failed to live up to expectations because of encroaching development, lack of funds for acquisition and management, and the like.

In most instances, arrangements were made for continuing protection and management of delisted sites. Lake Texhoma National Recreation Area in Oklahoma, for example, was transferred to the U.S. Army Corps of Engineers in 1949. Mackinac Island National Park, designated in 1875 and administered by the War Department until 1894, was transferred in 1895 to the state of Michigan. Lake Millerton National Recreation Area was turned over to the state of California in 1957.[4] According to a recent study, "none of the units have lost their integrity as historic, natural, or recreational areas, even under non-NPS administrations."[5]

Delisting is not, however, a potentially significant source either of improvement or cost cutting for the park system. At most, only a few units seem at all likely even to be considered, and the federal government might well find itself having to agree to contribute funds for future management of delisted units, particularly in units accepted by state or local governments.

Until a workable system is established to review new area proposals, no action should be taken to delist any unit. After a process is established for creating new units, the same process might be extended to permit analysis of delistings if appropriate safeguards could be assured for any delisted areas.

as a whole, helping to collect the needed information base for candidate sites and "protecting the rest" in other ways as well.

If the various land conservation systems are to take account of one another, some agency needs to take responsibility for thinking about the entire network. Questions may be raised about the park service's ability and willingness to take such responsibility for lands it does not manage. With some justification, critics can point to hesitancy among top park service officials in tackling tough, politically sensitive resource issues and to a lack of imagination in crafting responses to new challenges. Yet with the hands-on experience it has gained from parks that range from Yellowstone to Cape Cod, from involvement in innovative protection efforts in places like Pinelands, and from running the National Register of Historic Places, the park service appears more qualified than any other agency to provide national resource conservation leadership.

By providing technical assistance and modest funding, the service could have important influence even on land it does not own. One example already cited is the service's work with the Pinelands National Reserve. Another is the work that the service is doing in river conservation. Operating under the mandate of the National Wild and Scenic Rivers Act, the service has supplied invaluable help in the form of technical planning assistance and small grants to a host of state and local governments and citizen groups interested in protecting important river corridors without federal acquisitions.[92] The service's experience in this area, plus the access it has to inventories and other information and the expertise it has developed in interpreting resources for the public, has put it in a unique position to foster conservation on a broad basis.

The park service also is in a good position to help forge links among conservation efforts when the resources at stake go beyond political boundaries or are not amenable to protection by only one agency. For instance, one prime place for broader park service involvement would be the Everglades, where it is becoming increasingly clear that the region's resources cannot be protected by managing only a small part of a large ecosystem.

## Funding: The Future of the Land and Water Conservation Fund

Finally, one must confront the question of funding. For two decades, the Land and Water Conservation Fund (LWCF) has supported land acquisition for national and state parks, the addition of substantial acreage to the nation's wildlife refuge system, and the development of outdoor recreational facilities on state and local parklands. A brief list of accomplishments since the LWCF was established in 1964 shows how important it has been to land conservation in the United States:

- State and local governments have matched in varying proportions over $2.5 billion in LWCF grants to plan, acquire, and develop more than 27,000 parks and outdoor recreation facilities in some 14,000 communities.[93]
- By the end of 1983, the park service had spent $1.9 billion in LWCF money to acquire 1.5 million acres of land for national parks (figure 6.7).[94] Money from the LWCF to the service over the past 20 years has averaged about 25 percent of the park service's total appropriations, reaching as high as 40 percent in some years.[95]
- From 1965 to 1982, some 2.8 million acres of recreational land were purchased by the federal agencies receiving LWCF money.[96]
- The LWCF has paid for pre-acquisition-related work, such as identifying parcels and landowners and searching title, to decrease the time before purchase.[97]

At present, however, the future of the LWCF is uncertain:

- Its legislative authorization expires in 1989.[98]
- There have been cutbacks in acquisition funding since 1980: from a peak of $367.2 million in 1978, the park service share of LWCF money dropped to $65.7 million in 1981 and was $122.5 million for fiscal year 1984.[99]
- The Reagan administration has proposed to shift funds previously used only for land acquisition to support construction and maintenance, thus further limiting the amount available for acquisition and expansion.[100]

Thus, the country faces some of the same problems that prompted creation of the LWCF: a substantial backlog of authorized but unacquired parkland, difficulty in obtaining money for park expansion, and erratic funding levels for state and federal programs.

No other single decision will so fundamentally shape the National Park System of the future as the selection of a successor to the LWCF. No matter what land protection techniques are used by the service, continued funding for land protection will be essential.

*The Track Record of the LWCF*

Congress established the LWCF after the Outdoor Recreation Resources Review Commission (ORRRC) recommended that, to meet

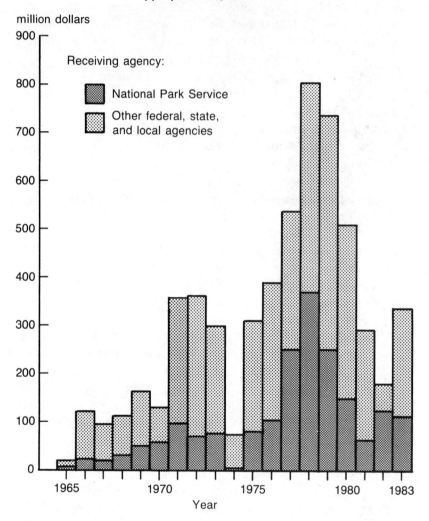

**Figure 6.7**
**Land and Water Conservation Fund**
**Appropriations, 1965–1983**

Source: U.S. Department of the Interior, National Park Service, "Land and Water Conservation Fund—History of Income, Appropriations, and Amounts Available for Appropriations," table, dated January 1985; and "National Park Service Acquisitions by Fiscal Year, Land and Water Conservation Fund (Includes Redwood NP)," table, dated December 30, 1983.

the nation's recreation needs, all levels of government should provide continuing funds at levels substantially greater than were then being spent. Originally, the LWCF received revenues from the sale of surplus federal property, the motorboat fuel tax, and user fees from the federal recreation estate. When these sources proved less bountiful than anticipated, Congress amended the act in 1968 to provide a minimum annual income to the fund of $200 million. The shortfall between revenues from the above sources and the $200 million floor would come from subsequent appropriations from the government's general fund and, if necessary, from oil and gas lease revenues on the Outer Continental Shelf (OCS).[101] (In fact, approximately 90 percent of LWCF receipts now come from OCS revenues.[102]) Congress raised the floor to $300 million annually in 1970 and to $900 million in 1977.[103]

The state share of the LWCF provides matching grants to state governments (and, through states, to local governments) for acquisition and development of recreational facilities. The federal share of the LWCF, however, provides money only for the acquisition of recreation lands administered by the Department of the Interior's National Park Service, Bureau of Land Management, and Fish and Wildlife Service and the Department of Agriculture's Forest Service.[104]

The LWCF was intended to provide for parks and recreation a predictable, sizable flow of earmarked funds that would be insulated from the year-to-year competition for congressional appropriations. Indeed, some members of Congress apparently believed that the LWCF would be a true trust fund—revenues earmarked for the LWCF would flow into a separate account that could not be used for other purposes, although Congress would have to appropriate money from the fund before it could be spent. Thus, the flow of revenues into the LWCF would be removed from the political process, while use of fund money would not.

In practice, the LWCF does not operate, and has never operated, as a true trust fund in the same way as the Highway Trust Fund; income to it may be (and is) used for other purposes and funds cannot be spent for recreation without advance approval from the applicable appropriations committees in Congress. Neither, however, is it simply another authorization, since the "fund" does exist, even if only on paper. Instead, the LWCF lies somewhere in between, and this hybrid character has confused discussion of the fund—even in Congress.[105] Yet the fund's existence has seemingly

Santa Monica Mountains, June 1984. Richard Idler, developer. "I think that
the major concern probably is not so much how the land's to be used—whether
it should be for open space or some form of development—but that, if it's
for open space, then, please somebody, buy it. Somebody take it from me
and compensate me properly for it. And that procedure is lengthy, a year
to five or eight years. . . . As a developer, I have an interest in open space
because I feel that it's a positive force in land use. I think it's a great asset. . . .
It's just that I think we're always getting extremes. Extremes on the part of
the developer who says he wants to do everything. And extremes on the part
of somebody who says, 'We don't want any more growth; we just want to
keep it all open.' Neither one of them is really practical, in the long run,
and they both work against the general objective of trying to obtain some environmental balance and provide open space and still permit use by the public
as well as by private owners of the property."

made it easier for Congress to appropriate money for park service
land acquisition—nearly $2 billion in 18 years (figure 6.7).

The key to understanding the LWCF is that there are essentially
*two* LWCF accounts—a receipts account and an appropriations
account for distributing state grants and moneys for federal land
acquisition programs. The receipts account grows by $900 million
each year, less whatever is appropriated to the appropriations account. The receipts account, however, is merely a bookkeeping
account. Although $1.8 billion was nominally in it at the end of
fiscal year 1982,[106] there is, in fact, no separate fund, no money

lying idle or invested in government securities. Instead, the money "in" the LWCF receipts account is really part of the general treasury and is included in the federal budget as an "offsetting receipt."[107]

A characteristic that makes the LWCF a hybrid between a trust fund and a plain authorization is its "carryover" feature. Unlike most other federal appropriations, once money is transferred to the fund's appropriations account, it is considered a "no-year appropriation" and is available for use indefinitely. This feature is both a cause of and cure for variations in annual appropriations from the LWCF. If the park service accumulates a large reserve of appropriated but unspent LWCF funds, Congress may reduce its LWCF appropriations to use up the surplus. But, at the same time, the carryover feature blunts the destabilizing effect of fluctuations in annual appropriations. Figure 6.7 illustrates this relationship by showing the park service's LWCF appropriations and the amount available for obligation (that is, appropriation plus carryover from the previous year). For example, $23.6 million remained unobligated at the end of fiscal year 1973. Fiscal year 1974 saw widespread budget cuts due to the recession, and Congress appropriated only $910,000 of LWCF money. By fiscal year 1975, carryover funds were down to $3.7 million, and LWCF appropriations rose to nearly $80.2 million.[108]

Despite its successes, the LWCF has not escaped serious criticism. Some say that because the fund is not totally insulated from yearly political squabbles, it is subject to the whims of the political process; one federal study asserted that the fund is unstable because it is too open to politics.[109] Moreover, appropriations from the LWCF have fallen far short of authorized levels and critics point out that the unstable funding level makes it difficult for federal agencies and, especially, states to plan for future recreational needs.[110] A more subtle complaint is that the fund has spurred park creation, but not acquisition, by giving Congress and others a false sense of having a huge pot of money to draw from when, in fact, the LWCF is running out of money.

*Needed: An Assessment of Revenue Sources*
*and Funding Mechanisms*

Various options exist for funding park system acquisitions after the LWCF expires. They can be grouped into two categories, revolving around the two fund accounts. Proposals related to revenue sources include an excise tax on recreation equipment, increased reliance on user fees, revenues from onshore federal resource development, park bonds, and an income tax checkoff. Suggestions for fund distribution mechanisms include a true trust fund, a policy that a new park's full acquisition cost be automatically appropriated when the park is authorized, and a simple reauthorization of the LWCF.

For several reasons, it might be desirable to turn to new sources of revenue. Both user fees and an excise tax are based in part on the "user pays" principle and seem to bear a closer relation to recreation and parkland than do OCS revenues. Such fees and taxes, set low enough so that they added little to the cost of the affected equipment or park unit, could still yield significant revenues. User fees, of course, already contribute to the LWCF (although they did not from 1968 to 1980), but they could be employed more widely. Income tax checkoffs and park bonds have been used successfully in some states[111] and deserve further consideration, although their relationship to parkland use is less direct than user fees and excise taxes.

It has often been proposed that a true trust fund be established as a fund distribution mechanism. One such proposal, introduced in Congress in 1983, envisions a trust aggregating $10 billion, financed from OCS revenues, over a 10-year period. Invested in U.S. Treasury notes at 10 percent interest, this trust would yield $1 billion per year.[112] Such a trust fund would provide more funds annually than have ever been appropriated from the LWCF, and, unlike the LWCF, the money flow would be steady and reliable.

A basic objection to trust funds is that they limit Congress's ability to set annual priorities, particularly in times of fiscal constraint. Why, it is argued, should park acquisition be immune from budgetary cutbacks when aid to the poor and pollution control activities, for example, are not?

If there is a justification for a park and recreation land trust fund, it lies mainly in the source of the revenues. Because general tax revenues have no close relation to parkland, there is little justification for a parkland trust financed by those revenues. But federal resource exploitation diminishes our natural estate and frequently precludes alternative uses of the land or water, at least during exploitation. Often, permanent degradation results. Thus, it makes sense that some of the federal revenues from using the nation's natural resources, including those on the Outer Continental Shelf, should be used to preserve other natural resources.

## Continuing the LWCF: Some Recommendations

To protect important resource land against development, substantial funding for land acquisition must be continued. Even if no new national parks are established, the park service will require a funding level approximating that of the last four years (roughly $100 million annually) to maintain a minimal land acquisition program: continuing acquisition of lands in the backlog (which is unlikely to have been cleaned up by 1989) and purchasing lands essential to protect existing parks from external pressures. A more expansive vision of the future park system, however, warrants a higher level of funding. An annual figure of $200 million for the next 10 years is needed to address the backlog, protect existing parks, and create new ones.

A compelling case has not been made, however, for establishing a true trust fund that would be earmarked for national park purchases and still be funded mainly by OCS revenues. Although there is a nexus between OCS revenues and parkland acquisition, it is not so close that these revenues should automatically be diverted from other programs in tight fiscal times.

Nevertheless, the inherent difficulty in funding land acquisition that was a motivating factor in establishing the LWCF, and the moral logic that some of the revenues derived from natural resource depletion (and, in some cases, degradation) should be invested in the nation's permanent estate, argue for continuing the psychological, though incomplete, insulation from politics that the LWCF has provided. Overall, the LWCF represents a happy medium between a trust fund and the need to seek annual appropriations.

As noted above, user fees and a recreational equipment excise tax both bear a closer relationship to parkland acquisition than do OCS revenues, and there is a correspondingly greater justification for establishing a trust fund from those sources. Such a trust fund (supplemented, perhaps, by revenues from the sale of surplus federal property) might be sufficient for normal acquisition needs. One study estimated that potential excise tax revenue on certain recreation equipment could have amounted to $150 million based on 1972 sales data.[112] At today's prices, the total would likely be much higher. Thus, a trust fund financed in this manner deserves additional study by the new Presidential Commission on Outdoor Recreation Resources Review.

In addition to national parks, other federal agencies, as well as state and local governments, have an important role to play in pre-

*Yellowstone, August 1984.*

serving natural and historic areas and providing recreation. Continued stable support for state and local recreation projects is necessary, especially since many of these programs, like the park service, have a tremendous backlog. Congress should continue to reject any attempts to eliminate the states' share of the LWCF or its successor.[114] To increase the reliability of LWCF grants to states, Congress should consider multiyear appropriations.

All in all, the LWCF has proved workable and successful. Although some fine-tuning is needed, and a trust fund supported by user fees and a recreation excise tax deserves examination, Congress could do far worse than to simply reauthorize the LWCF.

### THE NEXT DECADE

In the aftermath of the era of expansion, the park creation process since 1980 has entered a quiet period; consolidation may continue to be more prevalent than acquisition and expansion for some time to come. Still, there must be a continuing effort to consider selective additions to the park system to take advantage of special opportunities to protect important resources and to protect existing parks. The backlog, though formidable, should not be allowed to prevent systematic evaluation of proposals for creating and expanding parks. There is little hard evidence that the recent expansion damaged the system or that careful additions today would weaken it.

The slower pace of expansion in the 1980s may create opportunities for the park service (with public backing) to play a more influential role in shaping the system than it did during the congressionally led expansion of the 1970s. Because no clear consensus exists about what constitutes a "quality" resource that belongs in tomorrow's system, it will be crucial that the process used to identify park candidates and review their qualifications be respected by the public, Congress, and park service staff. Resource quality should remain the overriding criterion when selecting new areas, but increased emphasis should also be placed on costs, local impacts, public access, and the extent of local cooperation, particularly when a proposed park has greenline characteristics.

The greenline park concept holds particular promise in shaping the system of the future. Opportunities to carve parks out of public lands are fewer than they once were, and the costs of acquiring private land for parks are increasingly daunting. Using only fee acquisition to protect parks would force the country to resign itself to seeing fewer, smaller new parks. The greenline approach offers the prospect of a greater number of larger, less costly units.

While greenline parks appear promising, however, they demand skills and expertise that the park service currently does not have in sufficient supply. Steps must be taken both to meet the administrative challenges of the greenline concept—better state and local cooperation, more monitoring and enforcement, technical assistance, and better trained service personnel—and to resolve other issues like fairness to inholders, public access, and land protection during the planning process.

Greenline parks can help keep the service on the cutting edge of land conservation and protect quality resources that might otherwise be lost, but they should not be thought of as cost-free. There will always be a need to acquire land even in greenline parks to establish at least a core area to provide access and allow development of interpretative facilities. Thus, it is important to consider how this acquisition, albeit modest by 1970s standards, should be financed. The Land and Water Conservation Fund has performed admirably, and, with some fine-tuning, it can meet the needs of a new generation of parks.

The next decade for the park system as far as acquisition and expansion go will be less flamboyant than the latter years of the 1970s, but it should not be an era of do-nothingism. The coming years can be a tremendous opportunity to consolidate and secure the remarkable gains of the park expansion era and, at the same time, to extend the use of creative land protection techniques with the park service at the forefront of land conservation efforts.

# Chapter 7
# The Challenges Ahead

**M**anaging the 79.4 million acres in the National Park System presents an extraordinary set of challenges. Although the challenges demand responses from all Americans involved with the parks as visitors, advocates, policy makers, or partners in providing services, responses by the National Park Service and the conservation community will be crucial in shaping the future of the system. The Presidential Commission on Outdoor Recreation Resources Review, recently established by President Reagan, can also make a great contribution (see box).

## THE NATIONAL PARK SERVICE

To deal with its increasingly complex responsibilities, the park service must respond to a series of internal management deficiencies. Disconcerting reports from outside evaluators as well as from inside the service itself suggest that management is less sophisticated than is necessary to carry out the service's distinctive mission in the 1980s. Among the reported concerns are:

- *The lack of sound information for well-reasoned decision making.* A 1977 report by the management consulting firm of Coopers and Lybrand said that the park service has "a substantial amount of data, but little useable information."[1] Six years later, the service's new Office of Information Management said much the same thing: "Information is inaccessible when we need it and inadequate when we get it."[2] The preceding chapters of this book have stressed the need for improved methods of acquiring, processing, and using information to manage resources more effectively.
- *The lack of integration between planning and budgeting.* This problem, found in other Department of the Interior agencies

293

as well, means that the comprehensive management plans pain-
stakingly produced for most parks have not been used sufficiently as a basis for budget determinations.[3] Members of Congress have repeatedly complained that budget requests are poor-
ly justified.[4] Recent efforts at improvements must be
strengthened.

- *Ad hockery in developing new policies.* Decentralization and
  staff autonomy in the field, although beneficial on balance, undoubtedly contribute to lack of clarity in policy making. As
  Coopers and Lybrand suggested, "When policy is set every-
  where, it is set nowhere."[5]
- *Dissatisfaction in the service over such matters as recognition,
  career tracks, mobility, and a "caste system" between different
  types of parks.* Recent trends inside and outside the park service have undermined some traditional personnel policies.
  Aligning personal lives with a park service career is more difficult today with two-income families and increased interest in
  home ownership. The diversity among park units and greater
  specialization adds to the concerns about career ladders, advancement, and recognition that are present in any bureaucracy.
- *The impending eligibility for retirement of many high level
  officials.* While there is no assurance that officials will retire
  when they become eligible, the service may lose a good many
  of its most experienced staff within 5 to 10 years. The service
  needs to select and groom promising new managers. Hiring
  from outside the agency to bring new perspectives and energy
  is also needed. In a number of instances, staff transferred to
  the service when the Heritage Conservation and Recreation Service was dissolved have been a valuable source of new
  approaches.

In fashioning responses to the challenges, national leadership
must keep in mind the Hippocractic dictum, "First, do no harm."
The National Park Service is enormously popular. Polls show that
a surprisingly large proportion of Americans have visited the national parks and remember them with affection and admiration.
Moreover, the public expresses a higher regard for experiences in
national parks than in other publicly owned recreational areas.[6]

## National Park Service Accomplishments

Over the past 25 years, the park service has displayed innovation
and institutional change, even though that change has not always

## The Presidential Commission on
## Outdoor Recreation Resources Review

In January 1985, President Reagan created, by executive order, the Presidential Commission on Outdoor Recreation Resources Review. With a broad charge encompassing numerous outdoor recreation concerns, the commission is slated to submit its report in early 1986.[1]

A generation ago, in 1962, an earlier Outdoor Recreation Resources Review Commission (ORRRC) documented the need for vastly increased public commitment to outdoor recreation. The central message of rising demand and short supply became the touchstone for two decades of policy initiatives. "An increasingly urban, mobile, and affluent America is seeking the out-of-doors as never before," it warned, and recreation lands were far from many of the people who needed them. It found that most of the recreation acreage was in the West, whereas the people were not.[2] ORRRC recommendations included the creation of a new funding mechanism to purchase federal, state, and local parklands and the establishment of national systems of wilderness, rivers, and trails, all of which became reality.

In 1983, the Outdoor Recreation Policy Review Group, which was chaired by Henry L. Diamond, called for a new ORRRC.[3] Legislation to establish a new commission passed the Senate with support from the Reagan administration but failed in the House in the waning days of the 98th Congress. The president's executive order came shortly thereafter. With a broad charge and limited time to respond to it, the commission faces difficult choices in setting its agenda. Several of the topics that it would be worthwhile for the commission to assess have been suggested in this report, including the dollar cost of cleaning up the backlog, opportunities to complete unfinished parks in less costly ways, ways to improve the land acquisition process, and alternative futures for the Land and Water Conservation Fund. Numerous other topics are set forth in the report of the Outdoor Recreation Policy Review Group.[4]

Although close consultation between the commission and the park service is essential in addressing issues such as these, there is reason to welcome independent analysis by the commission. Some issues, notably the future of the Land and Water Conservation Fund, affect not only the park system but the entire nationwide network of conservation lands and are therefore best addressed from a perspective broader than that of any executive agency. In addressing other issues—such as estimating the dollar values of property in the backlog, where there is every incentive for the service to keep cost estimates low—the commission enjoys a freedom from institutional constraints that might impede objective analysis by others.

Ultimately, the greatest contribution that the commission can make is to assure that there is no fundamental discontinuity in the conservation policies articulated by the original ORRRC. Adaptation to the needs of a new generation is imperative; changes in the country's demography, economy, and values give the commission much to consider. The commission, sensitive to the magnificent precedent established by the original ORRRC, can help to assure that the needed adaptation builds on the successes of the past even as it responds to the needs of the future.

come fast enough or been sufficiently sensitive, or has been imposed by outside influences. Mission '66, the response to crime in the parks, the creation of environmental education programs, the provision of services for the handicapped, and, recently, the rapid construction catch-up efforts under the Park Restoration and Improvement Program are evidence—regardless of differences of opinion about the details of implementation—of systemwide innovation.

At the park level, there has also been considerable innovation. Faced with the wear and tear on park resources caused by numerous visitors, parks have set use limits in sensitive areas and increased educational efforts. Nonprofit groups are working with park service people all over the country, from the multimillion dollar operation at Fort Mason Center in Golden Gate to the Maryland C.A.M.P.E.R. association, which has fixed up the old CCC camps in Catoctin Mountain Park and rents out cabins to visitors.[7]

There is widespread evidence of remarkable individual dedication in the service. In doing research for this book, Conservation Foundation staff saw many examples—an employee who has set up a charming, low-budget military and community museum at Sandy Hook; an outdoor recreation planner at Santa Monica who attends public land-use meetings in the area; rangers who built a greenhouse to raise specimens for transplanting; dozens of ranger-scientists who have set up small laboratories in extra rooms in park buildings to do their own research; and so on. In sum, regardless of its many problems with linking planning to budgets, determining priorities, and gathering data about hundreds of diverse units, the National Park Service works.

## Tradition and Change

The key to minimizing harm is to recognize that the park service is at once a bureaucracy and much more than a bureaucracy. It has a proud institutional tradition and mystique that carries its people beyond day-to-day dissatisfactions and that transcends issues like career tracks. "A paradox of the National Park Service may be that one can be dissatisfied with a job position, a park, a supervisor, or the agency, and still be greatly devoted to its collective tradition and mission."[8]

The value of such an institutional identification cannot be overemphasized. Analysts trying to figure out why certain private corporations are successful have pointed to institutional pride and staff identification with early leaders as key factors. In successful mature corporations, strong links to the values of founders are often part of the corporate culture; in new corporations—the high-technology companies, for example—vital young whizzes set the tone for their employees. Successful corporations often display an unusual dedication to the "customer" and take conscious steps to stay aware of changing levels of satisfaction and dissatisfaction with their product. Paperwork, reporting, evaluations are unavoidable, but they do not dominate the management atmosphere.[9]

The park service shares these characteristics. But one element in the collective tradition of the park service has no parallel in the private sector—the stewardship of a superlative national estate. The service can justly take pride in the fact that its staff has always been dedicated to protecting the system's resources. Although changing values and information today call for major improvements in resource management, the park service's record should not be diminished by applying today's standards to past actions.

The challenge of the future is to make the service function better as a bureaucracy by building on tradition rather than undercutting it. Many possible corrective measures, although desirable from a bureaucratic standpoint, may not be so attractive when seen in this larger context. For example, the quirks and uncertainties of the current hiring system, which may cause a would-be ranger to move from park to park filling temporary jobs in the hope that a regular slot will open up, undoubtedly lose the service many qualified people. Yet a more conventional hiring process might do a less effective job than the present one in weeding out those who are not dedicated to the parks.

Similarly, the service needs forceful central leadership to chart directions and manage the park system as a system. There is danger, however, that the superintendents' freedom to respond to the remarkably wide range of problems that arise throughout the diverse system could be overly curtailed.

Adapting the generalist orientation of the service to today's need for specialists poses yet another danger for the park service tradition. It is clear that adjustments in "the park service way of doing things" are needed to fulfill the stewardship role adequately; yet there is risk that those changes could undercut a highly valuable esprit de corps.

While the previously cited studies of organizational success em-

*Yosemite, February 1984. Superintendent Bob Binnewies. "I hope that I would be remembered for two or three things. One, I would very much like to see wilderness designation of a portion of the park occur while I'm here. It would cover about 90 percent of the park area. Second, I have worked very hard on the theme that a certain level of development has been achieved within the park and that that level should now be held and no additional expansion or development in the park should occur. Instead, we should shift the focus outside the park and begin to move administrative, housing, and commerical things beyond the park boundary into locations that are still convenient but don't dominate the park itself. . . . The third thing is that I would very much like to see the standards of quality within the park itself, everything from foot trails to highways to concession operations to signs . . . be at a level that is recognized as about the best the profession can provide. I think we're working in that direction, too."*

phasize the importance of tradition and shared institutional culture, they also stress the importance of openness to change. Over the years, as new types of units have been added to the park system or organizational innovations have been advanced, critics of change have repeatedly argued that tradition was being eroded. Perhaps. But tradition must be refreshed with invention. The reminder that "we've always done it this way in Yellowstone" is important, but so is recognition that the advocate for change may serve Yellowstone by injecting new dynamism into management.

## Overcoming Strains

The 1960s, 1970s, and early 1980s have witnessed a marked quickening of the pace of change in the nation's environmental sensibilities, domestic priorities, and institutional responses. During this period, the park service has experienced a scale of innovation that has invigorated but also strained it.

Some of the most visible strains arose because of increasing demands, at both established parks and newer ones, that the service deal sensitively with a growing proliferation of interests: not only visitors with conflicting values but also concessioners, inholders, neighboring landowners, and local governments. The mechanisms for systematically incorporating public views into policy deliberations, particularly at the park level, can be further improved. The tradition of remoteness and park-service-knows-best is a constraint to change. While superintendents need latitude in working out mechanisms for public involvement that respond to particular situations, the days are gone when they could run parks as fiefdoms.

The service's stance of "serving the American people" has created a broad base of support; it has also translated in recent years into reacting to changing values more than to leading the way. In the past two decades, the service has too often failed to generate its own policies and has instead—in its responses to urban parks, concessioner policies, deteriorating physical facilities, and external threats—reacted to concerns raised by others. The service has let long-standing friends in advocacy and constituency organizations carry the flag of controversy while it has tried to maintain the image of professional land steward carrying out the job defined by the political process.

The park service is not, of course, free to set its own course. It is subject to congressional appropriations and oversight. As an agency within the Department of the Interior, it comes under the discretion of presidential appointees and must constantly tack to the political winds.

Thus, a distinctive combination of professionalism and political skills is needed for effectiveness as a park service director. Stephen Mather, a consummate politician, served under three presidents and five secretaries of the interior. In the 1970s, partisan politics became more intrusive. The tradition of long tenure that Mather and Horace Albright established in the position was replaced by the "revolving door," as three directors moved in and out of office in rapid succession (the specific cause varied in each instance).

To reestablish its preeminence, park service leadership must advance a vision of the parks that is as broad and dynamic as today's system and the evolving values that have produced it. The service must develop standards by which its accomplishments can be measured and also report more effectively to Congress and the executive branch on what it is doing and what its needs are.

The park service will require outside cooperation in reestablishing its leadership position. The executive branch must recognize the importance of professionalism not only in appointing the director of the service but also in appointing key assistants.

Congress must look again to the service for leadership. This is not to diminish the essential role that Congress has played, either during the 1960s and 1970s in prodding the service to respond to social trends or during the 1980s in adding to administration requests for operating and acquisition funds and fending off politically motivated threats. A price has been paid for the assumption of that role, however. Congressional initiatives, even much needed ones, coupled with the constraints of executive policy, have sometimes hemmed in the service's discretion and diminished its opportunities to exercise leadership and flexibility. If the challenges facing the service are to be addressed in ways that build on—rather than undercut—traditions, the leadership of the service must be expected to function more forcefully and be given the power to do so.

The service is critical to the stewardship of park resources. From time to time, conservationists have advanced ideas for reorganization of the service—for example, calling for transfer of historic sites out of the park service to the Smithsonian Institution, the National Endowment for the Arts, or to a new independent agency. Experience, however, shows a deeper unity and coherence in the natural and cultural missions. Fundamental reorganization would diminish rather than increase the effectiveness of federal stewardship. The unique tradition of the park service would be very difficult to duplicate.

Its legion of friends should ensure that the National Park Service not be undermined by pursuit of short-run objectives, whether to gain access to mineral resources, satisfy inholders, or single-mindedly

*Santa Monica Mountains, June 1984. Superintendent Dan Kuehn. "We have bent over backwards to try to preserve the rights of private property owners and not interfere. We've tried to make the park popular, and by and large I think we are succeeding. In 1980, a land acquisition plan was developed, and that was done with full public involvement. The public meetings were extremely heated—a lot of volatility and hostility and so forth on the part of the landowners. Last year we went through the same process in putting together our new land protection plan, and the amount of controversy just was really down. . . . Through the efforts of my predecessor to show we were not going to try to run roughshod over everybody and were going to be open and honest, I think we've gained a lot of support. The realization on the part of the landowners . . . that the park was here to stay also led to less controversy."*

to cut costs. We have a right to demand quality of the park service, and it has a right to our support in its efforts to achieve it.

## THE CONSERVATION COMMUNITY

The conservation community also must assume new responsibilities to continue its distinguished record of support for the national parks. The Appalachian Mountain Club, the Sierra Club, and the National Geographic Society were shaping the parks decades before the service and the system came into being. The National Parks and Conservation Association (originally the National Park Association) watches over the parks now, as it has since 1919 when Stephen

Mather, convinced that the new park system would need continuous public vigilance, sponsored its establishment. The Wilderness Society has for half a century served the parks as an advocate for the creation and protection of wilderness.

Local and regional groups, sometimes associated with national organizations like the National Audubon Society or the Sierra Club, but often independent, also provide essential support for the parks. In recent years, for example, local advocacy by such groups as the Save-the-Dunes Council, the People for a Golden Gate National Recreation Area, the Gateway Citizens Committee, and the Friends of the Santa Monica Mountains has been critical to the creation of new parks. Some groups have remained active after parks have been established, providing services to parks and park visitors; their members sometimes serve on advisory commissions or work in other useful roles.

## The Conservation Community and the Park Service

The National Park Service must walk a narrow path as it seeks to serve its diverse constituency. Many within the service share the "park values" that have been an integral part of park tradition since the thoughts and writings of John Muir first received acclaim. As a public agency, however, the service is pulled by the desire to serve all its clients—users who have widely different needs and visions of the park experience.

Not surprisingly, conservation groups have sometimes disagreed with the park service. During the earliest days of the agency, Robert Sterling Yard broke with Stephen Mather over the issue of building a larger constituency for the parks by catering to a variety of tastes that Yard considered to be "vulgar."[10] The diversification of the system in the 1930s, the establishment of Everglades National Park, and the movement to create federal parks in or near urban areas in the 1960s and 1970s were among the other issues on which some preservationist-oriented constituencies disagreed with much of the park service leadership.

When the park service is constrained from airing its views publicly, advocacy organizations continue to play an important role by bringing issues to Congress or a broader public. Also, they may openly criticize the service for being too timid or unwilling to pay sufficent attention to some aspects of its complex responsibilities. This has happened repeatedly during the Reagan administration,

Yellowstone, August 1984. The Shinozaki family (Metairie, Louisiana).

Yellowstone, August 1984. The Prince family (Clear Lake, South Dakota).

Yellowstone, August 1984. Jennifer and Richard Donaldson (Columbus, Ohio).

Yellowstone, August 1984. Two brothers.

as lobbying and national publicity by these groups have prodded Congress to add funds to administration budget requests. Conservation groups have also warned of threats to park resources and have supported legislation, opposed by the park service, to strengthen the agency's power over federal land-use decisions that affect national parks.

### Effective Advocacy in a New Era

In the years ahead, the park service will be called on to cooperate with a variety of interests, including neighboring landowners, inholders, and state and local governments, as well as conservation groups. The new era could move park management closer to the conservationist vision of preserved resources—or, quite the opposite, could move the parks closer to commercialism and away from resource consciousness. In this context, the conservation community must participate more actively in the unit planning process, which is critical for effective influence. This will often be difficult to achieve since the parks are far-flung and some of the citizens who benefit from preservation of park resources live far away. The importance of local support groups can hardly be overemphasized.

*Yellowstone, August 1984. The Hurst family (Denver).*

*Yellowstone, August 1984. Walter and Doris Ritter (Naples, Florida).*

*Yellowstone, August 1984. The Alcazar family (Sandy, Utah).*

The fundamental challenge facing the conservation community, however, remains that of communicating its central message
to an increasingly sophisticated public. Ultimately, the conservation community is the guardian of "park values," of a vision of
the special experience that the parks can provide. The "scenes of
sublimity and beauty" of Olmsted, the "holy temples" of Muir,
and the "wild things" of Leopold—despite telling differences among
the terms—were places protected from the encroachment of civiliz-
ing influences. The most frightening vision these writers conjured
up was the prospect that, because these special places influence
us in ways we don't even fully understand, their disappearance
might cause future generations to lose the capacity even to know
what they were missing.

For many, the vision of unspoiled nature exerts a moral claim
that transcends analyses of "user-days" and cost-benefit ratios. For
those who have seen this vision, the ultimate test of success of the
national parks lies not in their wise use of resources or efficient
allocation of benefits, but in "identifying what is best in our world
and trying to preserve it."[11] As Joseph Sax has noted, "[P]ersuasive
or not, the preservationist's claim is that he knows something about
what other people *ought* to want and how they can go about getting it, and he should not back away from, or conceal, that claim."[12]

Parks should be places for "contemplative recreation," Sax
argues, offering relief from the commonplace experiences of urban
life and the "artificial recreation" widely available outside the
parks.[13] To those who take this stance, downhill skiing, business
conventions, golf courses, supermarkets, beauty parlors, and bars
are inappropriate in national parks not necessarily because of their
"impacts" on park resources—although some do irreversibly and
adversely change the parks' natural environment—but because they
detract from the quality of the distinctive experiences possible in
national parks, experiences that the private market is typically
unable to provide.

It is no accident that the definition of wilderness in the 1964
Wilderness Act is, as Sax has commented, "one of the rare flights
of poetic language to be found in the United States Code."[14] Sax,
more than anyone in recent years, has freshened Olmsted's thoughts
in terms that will become increasingly useful to contemporary
preservationists as they seek wider support for their vision of national parks. "A moment's reflection makes it clear that environmen-

tal and scientific principles are rarely decisive . . . in settling . . .
disputes over protection of . . . parks' natural resources," he
observes.[15]

> [T]he presence of motorboats on the Grand Canyon is not really an
> ecological issue, though it was regularly put in those terms. Nor is
> ecological disruption the sole—or even the principal—reason there has
> been so much objection to snowmobiles or [off-road vehicles]. While
> one element of preservationist advocacy is scientific and truly based
> on principles of land management, another . . . is dominated by value
> judgments. . ... The preservationist constituency [for the parks] is
> disturbed not only—and not even most importantly—by the physical
> deterioration of the parks, but by a sense that the style of modern tourism
> is depriving the parks of their central symbolism, their message about
> the relationship between man and nature, and man and industrial
> society.[16]

There are many, of course, who love the parks but do not share
this vision. One visitor, for example, may seek the parks less as
places of reverence and contemplation than as "pleasuring
grounds." He or she may come to the park to go to the beach or
to stay at a comfortable lodge in a magnificent setting. This kind
of visitor, too, may seek contrast with everyday life, but without
the physical exertion, adventure, even fear, that the preservationist's
vision implies.

Other visitors may seek challenges and the ability to recapture
some of the orneriness of the wild frontier. Hiking or mountain
climbing may be the goal, but so may parachute jumping or snowmobiling or speeding up a dune in an off-road vehicle. This visitor
seeks a chance to be freer, perhaps rowdier, than is possible back
home.

### Fostering Authentic Experiences

To enlarge the constituency for its vision of the parks, the conservation community must continue to foster authentic visitor experiences. Important as it is to protect the parks for those already
prepared to "take them on their own terms," so it is important to
enlarge the number who seek those experiences. Democratic ideals
have rightly moved Sax, like Olmsted before him, to argue that parks
should not simply serve visitors' present tastes but rather should
help them develop a taste for new recreational experiences—to lift
their expectations and satisfactions.[17]

Because the National Park System is so large and diverse, there are opportunities to spread awareness of the preservationist vision while competing demands are also being met. Even in the most populous parts of the system, people can begin to appreciate what is different about park resources. To help visitors understand the wilderness, for example, and to encourage them to "take the next step," some parks (and areas within them) can provide the initiating experiences, while others remain wilder, riskier, and more solitary.

It follows that the park service's efforts in interpretation, sometimes mistakenly treated as one of its lesser responsibililties, are of central importance to the future of the system. A visitor's appreciation of natural areas will be enhanced when what is seen is understood better: for example, what is "exotic," how the human presence has modified the environment, how the service has responded to the changes. Cultural resources, too, can mean more to a visitor who knows why a battle happened in a particular place and what the park service has done to preserve the scene.[18]

Advocates of the preservation message must be especially sensitive to diverse audiences. They must guard against the charge of elitism. To sneer (or seem to sneer) at people who enjoy downhill, rather than cross-country skiing, or who prefer motor boats to canoes, or a visit to EPCOT over a hike in the woods, is to miss the point. Americans want—and have—many opportunities to participate in outdoor activities and practice their various skills, thanks to a remarkable surge of recreational activity provided by the market and diverse public lands.[19] Forging a new consensus about the "right" uses of our national parks requires a sorting out in contemporary terms of which activities belong in national parks, and which belong elsewhere.

In the future as in the past, the conservation community can never dismiss the importance of those who take pride in the preservation of resources they will never see, whose support of "public values" has little to do with their "private preferences."[20] The same person who enjoys Jacuzzis, Disneyland, and a drink in the bar overlooking Crater Lake may also believe that all are out of place in the parks. The people who might have enjoyed the downhill runs at the proposed Mineral King ski resort may support the preservation of that area, even if they have no desire to visit it in its natural state. "We must balance what we want as individuals against the goals that collectively we take pride in," Mark Sagoff observes.[21]

*Yosemite, Feburary 1984.*

    Preserving park resources more nearly unimpaired may ultimately depend on more widespread respect, by an increasingly crowded and developed nation, for the visitor experiences that are less and less available outside the national parks. In communicating to a wider audience the experiences of awe, solitude, adventure, communion, repose, and reinvigoration to be found in national parks, the conservation community can aid the continuing evolution of the park ideal to help preserve the parks for this and future generations.

# Appendixes

# Appendix A

## Directory of National Park Units

| Name | Location | Year authorized[a] | Size (acres) Federal[b] | Size (acres) Nonfederal[c] | Size (acres) Total | Annual visitation (as of December 1983)[d] |
|---|---|---|---|---|---|---|
| Abraham Lincoln Birthplace National Historic Site | KY | 1933(T) | 116.50 | — | 116.50 | 256,126 |
| Acadia National Park | ME | 1919(E) | 38,933.78 | 773.13 | 37,706.91 | 4,124,639 |
| Adams National Historic Site | MA | 1946(D) | 9.17 | 0.65 | 9.82 | 26,162 |
| Agate Fossil Beds National Monument | NE | 1965 | 2,737.52 | 317.70 | 3,055.22 | 10,097 |
| Alagnak Wild River | AK | 1980(E) | 24,038.00 | — | 24,038.00 | not reported |
| Alibates Flint Quarries National Monument | TX | 1965 | 1,079.23 | 291.74 | 1,370.97 | 1,919 |
| Allegheny Portage Railroad National Historic Site | PA | 1964 | 845.83 | 289.08 | 1,134.91 | 55,148 |
| Amistad National Recreation Area | TX | 1965(A) | 57,292.44 | — | 57,292.44 | 1,221,445 |
| Andersonville National Historic Site | GA | 1970 | 453.93 | 21.79 | 475.72 | 110,921 |
| Andrew Johnson National Historic Site | TN | 1935 | 16.68 | — | 16.68 | 119,410 |

313

**Directory of National Park Units (continued)**

| Name | Location | Year authorized[a] | Size (acres) Federal[b] | Size (acres) Nonfederal[c] | Size (acres) Total | Annual visitation (as of December 1983)[d] |
|---|---|---|---|---|---|---|
| Aniakchak National Monument and Preserve[1] | AK | 1980(E) | NM–139,500.00[e] PR–470,000.00 | 5,500.00 | 139,500.00 475,500.00 | not reported |
| Antietam National Battlefield[2] | MD | 1933(T) | 1,700.64 | 1,545.80 | 3,246.44 | 433,122 |
| Apostle Islands National Lakeshore | WI | 1970(E) | 41,853.60 | 26,031.24 | 67,884.84 | 130,913 |
| Appalachian National Scenic Trail | ME to GA | 1968(E) | 62,143.53 | 53,719.51 | 115,863.04 | not reported |
| Appomattox Court House National Historical Park | VA | 1933(T) | 1,322.78 | 2.30 | 1,325.08 | 246,277 |
| Arches National Park | UT | 1929(P) | 66,343.51 | 7,035.47 | 73,378.98 | 287,875 |
| Arkansas Post National Memorial | AR | 1960 | 389.18 | — | 389.18 | 55,443 |
| Arlington House, The Robert E. Lee Memorial | VA | 1933(T) | 27.91 | — | 27.91 | 514,863 |
| Assateague Island National Seashore | MD/VA | 1965 | 17,775.09 | 21,855.84 | 39,630.93 | 2,150,285 |
| Aztec Ruins National Monument | NM | 1923(P) | 27.14 | — | 27.14 | 61,693 |
| Badlands National Park | SD | 1929 | 152,689.56 | 90,612.77 | 243,302.33 | 1,026,981 |
| Bandelier National Monument | NM | 1932(T) | 32,682.89 | 4,234.00 | 36,916.89 | 199,775 |
| Bent's Old Fort National Historic Site | CO | 1960 | 713.60 | 86.20 | 799.80 | 40,173 |
| Bering Land Bridge National Preserve[3] | AK | 1980(E) | 2,507,000.00 | 263,000.00 | 2,770,000.00 | not reported |
| Big Bend National Park | TX | 1935 | 708,118.40 | 33,000.00 | 741,118.40 | 164,926 |

| | | | | | | |
|---|---|---|---|---|---|---|
| Big Cypress National Preserve | FL | 1974 | 518,648.80 | 570,000.00 | 51,351.20 | not reported |
| Big Hole National Battlefield | MT | 1933(T) | 655.61 | 655.61 | — | 46,748 |
| Big South Fork National River and Recreation Area | KY/TN | 1974 | 16,860.00 | 122,960.00 | 106,100.00 | not reported |
| Big Thicket National Preserve | TX | 1974 | 79,616.24 | 85,849.55 | 6,233.31 | 33,355 |
| Bighorn Canyon National Recreation Area | MT/WY | 1966(E) | 68,484.59 | 120,277.86 | 51,793.27 | 373,150 |
| Biscayne National Park | FL | 1968 | 95,024.87 | 173,274.37 | 78,249.50 | 369,082 |
| Black Canyon of the Gunnison National Monument | CO | 1933(P) | 13,358.56 | 20,762.70 | 7,404.14 | 291,618 |
| Blue Ridge Parkway | GA/NC/VA | 1936(E) | 78,162.67 | 82,117.37 | 3,954.70 | 15,208,455 |
| Booker T. Washington National Monument | VA | 1956 | 223.92 | 223.92 | — | 23,007 |
| Boston National Historical Park | MA | 1974 | 34.70 | 41.03 | 6.33 | 2,088,259 |
| Brices Cross Roads National Battlefield Site | MS | 1933(T) | 1.00 | 1.00 | — | 2,035 |
| Bryce Canyon National Park[4] | UT | 1929(P) | 35,832.58 | 35,835.08 | 2.50 | 472,633 |
| Buck Island Reef National Monument | VI | 1961(P) | 880.00 | 880.00 | — | 51,641 |
| Buffalo National River | AR | 1972 | 90,112.71 | 94,221.08 | 4,108.37 | 655,774 |
| Cabrillo National Monument | CA | 1933(T) | 143.94 | 143.94 | — | 1,450,605 |
| Canaveral National Seashore | FL | 1975(E) | 41,844.88 | 57,627.07 | 15,782.19 | 1,075,321 |
| Canyon de Chelly National Monument | AZ | 1931 | — | 83,840.00 | 83,840.00 | 385,992 |
| Canyonlands National Park | UT | 1964(E) | 337,570.43 | 337,570.43 | — | 100,022 |
| Cape Cod National Seashore | MA | 1961 | 27,319.39 | 43,526.06 | 16,206.67 | 4,595,071 |

# Directory of National Park Units (continued)

| Name | Location | Year authorized[a] | Size (acres) Federal[b] | Nonfederal[c] | Total | Annual visitation (as of December 1983)[d] |
|---|---|---|---|---|---|---|
| Cape Hatteras National Seashore | NC | 1937 | 30,318.88 | 0.55 | 30,319.43 | 1,685,628 |
| Cape Krusenstern National Monument | AK | 1978(P) | 540,000.00 | 120,000.00 | 660,000.00 | 10,375 |
| Cape Lookout National Seashore | NC | 1966 | 23,270.83 | 5,143.91 | 28,414.74 | 68,000 |
| Capitol Reef National Park[5] | UT | 1937(P) | 222,753.35 | 19,150.91 | 241,904.26 | 331,734 |
| Capulin Mountain National Monument | NM | 1916(P) | 775.38 | — | 775.38 | 39,861 |
| Carl Sandburg Home National Historic Site | NC | 1968 | 263.52 | — | 263.52 | 46,673 |
| Carlsbad Caverns National Park[6] | NM | 1923(P) | 46,435.33 | 320.00 | 46,755.33 | 712,247 |
| Casa Grande National Monument | AZ | 1889 | 472.50 | — | 472.50 | 119,229 |
| Castillo de San Marcos National Monument | FL | 1933(T) | 19.92 | 0.56 | 20.48 | 672,624 |
| Castle Clinton National Monument | NY | 1946 | 1.00 | — | 1.00 | 124,165 |
| Catoctin Mountain Park | MD | 1936(T) | 5,770.22 | — | 5,770.22 | 518,939 |
| Cedar Breaks National Monument | UT | 1933(P) | 6,154.60 | — | 6,154.60 | 329,268 |
| Chaco Culture National Historical Park | NM | 1907(P) | 23,009.03 | 10,968.79 | 33,977.82 | 71,420 |
| Chamizal National Memorial | TX | 1966 | 54.90 | — | 54.90 | 119,639 |
| Channel Islands National Park | CA | 1938(P) | 10,890.62 | 238,463.15 | 249,353.77 | 205,024 |

| | | | | | | |
|---|---|---|---|---|---|---|
| Chattahoochee River National Recreation Area | GA | 1978(E) | 3,627.10 | 5,072.59 | 8,699.69 | 1,081,924 |
| Chesapeake and Ohio Canal National Historical Park[7] | DC/MD/VA | 1938 | 13,980.43 | 6,800.57 | 20,781.00 | 6,175,834 |
| Chickamauga and Chattanooga National Military Park | GA/TN | 1933(T) | 8,085.75 | 16.79 | 8,102.54 | 1,020,953 |
| Chickasaw National Recreation Area | OK | 1902 | 9,494.86 | 27.05 | 9,521.91 | 2,238,456 |
| Chiricahua National Monument | AZ | 1933(T) | 11,132.38 | 2.42 | 11,134.80 | 51,737 |
| Christiansted National Historic Site | VI | 1952(D) | 27.15 | — | 27.15 | 100,936 |
| Clara Barton National Historic Site | MD | 1974 | 8.59 | — | 8.59 | 13,131 |
| Colonial National Historic Park[8] | VA | 1930 | 9,244.87 | 73.50 | 9,316.37 | 2,068,928 |
| Colorado National Monument | CO | 1911(P) | 20,453.93 | — | 20,453.93 | 279,492 |
| Congaree Swamp National Monument | SC | 1976 | 15,138.25 | — | 15,138.25 | not reported |
| Coronado National Memorial | AZ | 1941 | 4,572.60 | 177.87 | 4,750.47 | 33,539 |
| Coulee Dam National Recreation Area | WA | 1946(A) | 100,390.31 | — | 100,390.31 | 666,341 |
| Cowpens National Battlefield | SC | 1933(T) | 788.71 | 52.85 | 841.56 | 57,842 |
| Crater Lake National Park | OR | 1902(E) | 183,226.77 | 0.28 | 183,227.05 | 379,008 |
| Craters of the Moon National Monument | ID | 1924(P) | 53,545.05 | — | 53,545.05 | 273,693 |
| Cumberland Gap National Historical Park | KY/TN/VA | 1940 | 20,270.59 | 3.83 | 20,274.42 | 718,375 |
| Cumberland Island National Seashore | GA | 1972(E) | 18,677.56 | 17,732.72 | 36,410.28 | 32,832 |
| Curecanti National Recreation Area | CO | 1965(A) | 42,114.47 | — | 42,114.47 | 1,050,217 |

## Directory of National Park Units (continued)

| Name | Location | Year authorized[a] | Size (acres) Federal[b] | Size (acres) Nonfederal[c] | Size (acres) Total | Annual visitation (as of December 1983)[d] |
|---|---|---|---|---|---|---|
| Custer Battlefield National Monument | MT | 1940(T) | 765.34 | — | 765.34 | 221,398 |
| Cuyahoga Valley National Recreation Area | OH | 1974 | 14,439.25 | 18,020.94 | 32,460.19 | 939,562 |
| De Soto National Memorial | FL | 1948 | 24.78 | 2.06 | 26.84 | 220,721 |
| Death Valley National Monument | CA/NV | 1933(P) | 2,048,754.81 | 18,872.87 | 2,067,627.68 | 635,582 |
| Delaware National Scenic River | NJ/PA | 1978(E) | — | 1,973.33 | 1,973.33 | not reported |
| Delaware Water Gap National Recreation Area | NJ/PA | 1965 | 53,317.37 | 13,379.60 | 66,696.97 | 2,293,666 |
| Denali National Park and Preserve[g] | AK | 1917(E) | NP–4,700,000.00[e] PR–1,300,000.00 | — 30,000.00 | 4,700,000.00 1,330,000.00 | 346,082 |
| Devils Postpile National Monument | CA | 1933(T) | 798.46 | — | 798.46 | 73,612 |
| Devils Tower National Monument | WY | 1906(P) | 1,346.91 | — | 1,346.91 | 267,276 |
| Dinosaur National Monument | CO/UT | 1915(P) | 204,458.01 | 6,683.68 | 211,141.69 | 427,375 |
| Edgar Allan Poe National Historic Site | PA | 1978 | 0.52 | — | 0.52 | 13,858 |
| Edison National Historic Site | NJ | 1955(D) | 21.25 | — | 21.25 | 39,121 |
| Effigy Mounds National Monument | IA | 1949(P) | 1,475.53 | — | 1,475.53 | 99,562 |
| Eisenhower National Historic Site | PA | 1967(D) | 690.46 | — | 690.46 | 145,351 |
| El Morro National Monument | NM | 1906(P) | 1,039.92 | 238.80 | 1,278.72 | 29,278 |

| | | | | | | |
|---|---|---|---|---|---|---|
| Eleanor Roosevelt National Historic Site | NY | 1977 | 180.50 | — | 180.50 | not reported |
| Eugene O'Neill National Historic Site | CA | 1976 | 13.19 | — | 13.19 | not reported |
| Everglades National Park | FL | 1934 | 1,398,652.59 | 286.00 | 1,398,939.19 | 577,439 |
| Federal Hall National Memorial | NY | 1939(D) | 0.45 | — | 0.45 | 115,358 |
| Fire Island National Seashore | NY | 1964 | 6,095.04 | 13,483.51 | 19,578.55 | 531,183 |
| Florissant Fossil Beds National Monument | CO | 1969 | 5,992.32 | 5.77 | 5,998.09 | 51,309 |
| Ford's Theatre National Historic Site | DC | 1933(T) | 0.29 | — | 0.29 | 704,440 |
| Fort Benton[10] | MT | 1976 | — | — | — | not reported |
| Fort Bowie National Historic Site | AZ | 1964 | 1,000.00 | — | 1,000.00 | 4,912 |
| Fort Caroline National Memorial | FL | 1950 | 133.02 | 5.37 | 138.39 | 140,461 |
| Fort Clatsop National Memorial | OR | 1958 | 124.97 | 0.23 | 125.20 | 147,208 |
| Fort Davis National Historic Site | TX | 1961 | 460.00 | — | 460.00 | 71,334 |
| Fort Donelson National Military Park[11] | TN | 1933(T) | 539.60 | 12.40 | 552.00 | 280,644 |
| Fort Frederica National Monument | GA | 1936 | 210.72 | 5.63 | 216.35 | 254,739 |
| Fort Jefferson National Monument | FL | 1935(P) | 61,480.00 | 3,220.00 | 64,700.00 | 11,004 |
| Fort Laramie National Historic Site | WY | 1938(P) | 763.09 | 69.36 | 832.45 | 97,090 |
| Fort Larned National Historic Site | KS | 1964 | 679.66 | 38.73 | 718.39 | 60,788 |
| Fort Matanzas National Monument | FL | 1933(T) | 227.76 | — | 227.76 | 250,790 |
| Fort McHenry National Monument and Historic Shrine | MD | 1933(T) | 43.26 | — | 43.26 | 723,297 |
| Fort Necessity National Battlefield | PA | 1933(T) | 894.47 | 8.33 | 902.80 | 134,187 |

## Directory of National Park Units (continued)

| Name | Location | Year authorized[a] | Size (acres) Federal[b] | Size (acres) Nonfederal[c] | Size (acres) Total | Annual visitation (as of December 1983)[d] |
|---|---|---|---|---|---|---|
| Fort Point National Historic Site | CA | 1970(E) | 29.00 | — | 29.00 | 961,394 |
| Fort Pulaski National Monument | GA | 1933(T) | 5,365.13 | 257.97 | 5,623.10 | 291,318 |
| Fort Raleigh National Historic Site | NC | 1941(D) | 153.05 | 4.22 | 157.27 | 359,761 |
| Fort Scott National Historic Site | KS | 1978 | 16.69 | — | 16.69 | 73,306 |
| Fort Smith National Historic Site | AR/OK | 1961 | 19.18 | 54.18 | 73.36 | 118,692 |
| Fort Stanwix National Monument | NY | 1935 | 15.52 | — | 15.52 | 63,154 |
| Fort Sumter National Monument | SC | 1948 | 186.87 | 2.45 | 189.32 | 244,374 |
| Fort Union National Monument | NM | 1954(E) | 720.60 | — | 720.60 | 12,413 |
| Fort Union Trading Post National Historic Site | MT/ND | 1966 | 392.16 | 41.88 | 434.04 | 9,917 |
| Fort Vancouver National Historic Site | WA | 1948 | 201.73 | 7.16 | 208.89 | 239,650 |
| Fort Washington Park | MD | 1930(T) | 341.00 | — | 341.00 | 256,219 |
| Fossil Butte National Monument | WY | 1972(E) | 8,198.00 | — | 8,198.00 | 16,402 |
| Frederick Douglass Home | DC | 1962 | 8.08 | — | 8.08 | 30,347 |
| Frederick Law Olmsted National Historic Site | MA | 1979 | 1.75 | — | 1.75 | 3,072 |
| Fredericksburg and Spotsylvania County Memorial Battlefields National Military Park[12] | VA | 1933(T) | 5,262.25 | 646.77 | 5,909.02 | 244,328 |

| | | | | | | |
|---|---|---|---|---|---|---|
| Friendship Hill National Historic Site | PA | 1978 | 661.44 | 13.12 | 674.56 | 9,313 |
| Gates of the Arctic National Park and Preserve[13] | AK | 1980(E) | NP-7,150,000.00[e] PR-940,000.00 | 350,000.00 | 7,500,000.00 940,000.00 | 2,138 |
| Gateway National Recreation Area | NJ/NY | 1972(E) | 20,375.87 | 5,935.06 | 26,310.93 | 10,347,510 |
| General Grant National Memorial | NY | 1959 | 0.76 | — | 0.76 | 82,592 |
| George Rogers Clark National Historical Park | IN | 1966 | 24.30 | | 24.30 | 111,083 |
| George Washington Birthplace National Monument | VA | 1930(E) | 538.23 | | 538.23 | 136,708 |
| George Washington Carver National Monument | MD | 1943 | 210.00 | | 210.00 | 79,202 |
| George Washington Memorial Parkway | MD/VA | 1933(T) | 7,045.24 | 96.39 | 7,141.63 | 8,569,579 |
| Gettysburg National Military Park[14] | PA | 1933(T) | 3,638.62 | 247.00 | 3,885.62 | 1,198,949 |
| Gila Cliff Dwellings National Monument | NM | 1933(T) | 533.13 | — | 533.13 | 37,717 |
| Glacier Bay National Park and Preserve[15] | AK | 1925(P) | NP-3,225,000.00[e] PR-55,000.00 | 197.95 | 3,225,197.95 55,000.00 | 92,057 |
| Glen Canyon National Recreation Area | AZ/UT | 1972(E) | 1,193,671.00 | 43,209.00 | 1,236,880.00 | 1,873,031 |
| Golden Gate National Recreation Area | CA | 1972(E) | 27,197.01 | 45,618.03 | 72,815.04 | 17,604,551 |
| Golden Spike National Historic Site | UT | 1957(D) | 2,203.20 | 532.08 | 2,735.28 | 49,571 |
| Grand Canyon National Park | AZ | 1919(T) | 1,177,228.37 | 41,146.87 | 1,218,375.24 | 2,248,082 |
| Grand Portage National Monument | MN | 1951(D) | 709.97 | — | 709.97 | 36,261 |
| Grand Teton National Park | WY | 1929(E) | 306,864.70 | 3,656.24 | 310,520.94 | 1,532,035 |

## Directory of National Park Units (continued)

| Name | Location | Year authorized[a] | Size (acres) Federal[b] | Size (acres) Nonfederal[c] | Size (acres) Total | Annual visitation (as of December 1983)[d] |
|---|---|---|---|---|---|---|
| Grant-Kohrs Ranch National Historic Site | MT | 1972 | 1,371.51 | 127.14 | 1,498.65 | 34,292 |
| Great Sand Dunes National Monument | CO | 1932(P) | 36,426.16 | 2,236.02 | 38,662.18 | 150,177 |
| Great Smoky Mountains National Park | NC/TN | 1926 | 520,003.78 | 265.66 | 520,269.44 | 8,435,475 |
| Greenbelt Park | MD | 1950(T) | 1,175.99 | — | 1,175.99 | 217,141 |
| Guadalupe Mountains National Park | TX | 1966 | 76,292.07 | 0.99 | 76,293.06 | 142,736 |
| Guilford Courthouse National Military Park | NC | 1933(T) | 220.25 | — | 220.25 | 161,504 |
| Gulf Islands National Seashore | FL/MS | 1971 | 98,913.38 | 40,862.08 | 139,775.46 | 4,060,386 |
| Haleakala National Park | HI | 1916 | 27,456.34 | 1,198.91 | 28,655.25 | 864,289 |
| Hamilton Grange National Memorial | NY | 1962 | — | 0.71 | 0.71 | 2,653 |
| Hampton National Historic Site | MD | 1948(D) | 59.44 | — | 59.44 | 83,064 |
| Harpers Ferry National Historical Park | MD/VA/WV | 1944 | 2,126.23 | 112.14 | 2,238.37 | 600,823 |
| Harry S Truman National Historic Site | MO | 1982(E) | — | 0.78 | 0.78 | not reported |
| Hawaii Volcanoes National Park | HI | 1916(E) | 217,298.05 | 11,878.98 | 229,117.03 | 2,247,974 |
| Herbert Hoover National Historic Site | IA | 1965 | 181.11 | 5.69 | 186.80 | 242,562 |

| | | | | | | |
|---|---|---|---|---|---|---|
| Hohokam Pima National Monument | AZ | 1972 | — | 1,690.00 | 1,690.00 | not reported |
| Home of Franklin D. Roosevelt National Historic Site | NY | 1944(D) | 290.34 | — | 290.34 | 212,494 |
| Homestead National Monument of America | NE | 1936 | 182.11 | 12.46 | 194.57 | 22,608 |
| Hopewell Village National Historic Site | PA | 1938(D) | 848.06 | — | 848.06 | 162,159 |
| Horseshoe Bend National Military Park | AL | 1956 | 2,040.00 | — | 2,040.00 | 62,514 |
| Hot Springs National Park | AR | 1921(D) | 4,786.99 | 1,036.55 | 5,823.54 | 1,160,008 |
| Hovenweep National Monument | CO/UT | 1923(P) | 784.93 | — | 784.93 | 13,837 |
| Hubbell Trading Post National Historic Site | AZ | 1965 | 160.09 | — | 160.09 | 147,318 |
| Independence National Historical Park | PA | 1948 | 41.87 | 2.98 | 44.85 | 4,767,889 |
| Indiana Dunes National Lakeshore | IN | 1966 | 9,540.63 | 3,329.02 | 12,869.65 | 1,510,630 |
| Isle Royale National Park | MI | 1931 | 539,281.87 | 32,508.24 | 571,790.11 | 12,928 |
| James A. Garfield National Historic Site | OH | 1980 | 3.41 | 4.41 | 7.82 | not reported |
| Jean Lafitte National Historical Park and Preserve | LA | 1933(T) | 6,278.56 | 13,721.44 | 20,000.00 | 535,196 |
| Jefferson National Expansion Memorial National Historic Site | MO | 1935(D) | 90.96 | — | 90.96 | 2,948,022 |
| Jewel Cave National Monument | SD | 1933(T) | 1,273.51 | — | 1,273.51 | 89,412 |
| John D. Rockefeller, Jr. Memorial Parkway | WY | 1972 | 23,777.22 | — | 23,777.22 | 1,105,434 |
| John Day Fossil Beds National Monument | OR | 1974 | 10,739.15 | 3,272.75 | 14,011.90 | 109,694 |

## Directory of National Park Units (continued)

| Name | Location | Year authorized[a] | Size (acres) Federal[b] | Nonfederal[c] | Total | Annual visitation (as of December 1983)[d] |
|---|---|---|---|---|---|---|
| John F. Kennedy Center for the Performing Arts | DC | 1958 | 17.50 | — | 17.50 | 3,311,436 |
| John Fitzgerald Kennedy National Historic Site | MA | 1967 | 0.09 | — | 0.09 | 18,269 |
| John Muir National Historic Site | CA | 1964 | 8.90 | — | 8.90 | 28,118 |
| Johnstown Flood National Memorial | PA | 1964 | 155.37 | 8.10 | 163.47 | 38,064 |
| Joshua Tree National Monument | CA | 1936(P) | 549,634.12 | 10,320.38 | 559,954.50 | 671,426 |
| Kalaupapa National Historical Park | HI | 1980 | 23.00 | 10,879.10 | 10,902.10 | not reported |
| Kaloko-Honokohau National Historical Park | HI | 1978(E) | — | 1,160.91 | 1,160.91 | not reported |
| Katmai National Park and Preserve[16] | AK | 1918(P) | NP–3,575,000.00[e] PR–374,000.00 | 141,000.00 — | 3,716,000.00 374,000.00 | 11,182 |
| Kenai Fjords National Park[17] | AK | 1980(E) | 580,000.00 | 90,000.00 | 670,000.00 | 24,048 |
| Kennesaw Mountain National Battlefield Park | GA | 1933(T) | 2,882.37 | 2.01 | 2,884.38 | 946,672 |
| Kings Canyon National Park | CA | 1890(E) | 461,580.02 | 56.18 | 461,636.20 | 765,755 |
| Kings Mountain National Military Park | SC | 1933(T) | 3,945.29 | — | 3,945.29 | 224,512 |
| Klondike Gold Rush National Historical Park | AK/WA | 1976(E) | 2,721.33 | 10,470.02 | 13,191.35 | 104,706 |
| Knife River Indian Village National Historic Site | ND | 1974 | 1,293.35 | — | 1,293.35 | 8,373 |

| | State | Date | | | | |
|---|---|---|---|---|---|---|
| Kobuk Valley National Park[17] | AK | 1980(E) | 1,702,000.00 | 48,000.00 | 1,750,000.00 | 2,365 |
| Lake Chelan National Recreation Area[18] | WA | 1968(E) | 61,134.69 | 755.38 | 61,890.07 | — |
| Lake Clark National Park and Preserve[13] | AK | 1980(E) | NP–2,490,000.00[e] PR–1,171,000.00 | 384,000.00 — | 2,874,000.00 1,171,000.00 | 12,332 |
| Lake Mead National Recreation Area | AZ/NV | 1964(E) | 1,468,388.64 | 28,211.88 | 1,496,600.52 | 5,913,768 |
| Lake Meredith National Recreation Area[19] | TX | 1965(A) | 44,977.63 | — | 44,977.63 | 1,844,870 |
| Lassen Volcanic National Park | CA | 1907(P) | 106,366.47 | 5.89 | 106,372.36 | 429,867 |
| Lava Beds National Monument | CA | 1933(T) | 46,559.87 | — | 46,559.87 | 68,737 |
| Lehman Caves National Monument | NV | 1933(T) | 640.00 | — | 640.00 | 30,335 |
| Lincoln Boyhood National Memorial | IN | 1962 | 184.08 | 7.90 | 191.98 | 216,252 |
| Lincoln Home National Historic Site | IL | 1971 | 12.03 | 0.21 | 12.24 | 448,078 |
| Lincoln Memorial | DC | 1933(T) | 163.63 | — | 163.63 | 3,352,825 |
| Longfellow National Historic Site | MA | 1972 | 1.98 | — | 1.98 | 18,566 |
| Lowell National Historical Park | MA | 1978 | 3.54 | 133.54 | 137.08 | 437,999 |
| Lower St. Croix National Scenic Riverway | MN/WI | 1972 | 7,049.37 | 2,415.77 | 9,465.14 | not reported |
| Lyndon Baines Johnson Memorial Grove on the Potomac[20] | DC | 1973 | 17.00 | — | 17.00 | — |
| Lyndon B. Johnson National Historical Park | TX | 1969 | 235.78 | 1,242.00 | 1,477.78 | 299,460 |
| Maggie L. Walker National Historic Site | VA | 1978 | 0.36 | 0.93 | 1.29 | not reported |
| Mammoth Cave National Park | KY | 1926 | 51,567.99 | 826.95 | 52,394.94 | 1,498,503 |
| Manassas National Battlefield Park | VA | 1940(D) | 3,038.50 | 1,474.89 | 4,513.39 | 720,745 |

## Directory of National Park Units (continued)

| Name | Location | Year authorized[a] | Size (acres) Federal[b] | Nonfederal[c] | Total | Annual visitation (as of December 1983)[d] |
|---|---|---|---|---|---|---|
| Martin Luther King, Jr. National Historic Site | GA | 1980(E) | 4.13 | 19.03 | 23.16 | 174,841 |
| Martin Van Buren National Historic Site | NY | 1974 | 38.50 | 1.08 | 39.58 | 6,888 |
| Mesa Verde National Park | CO | 1906(E) | 51,890.65 | 194.49 | 52,085.14 | 604,115 |
| Minute Man National Historical Park | MA | 1959(D) | 655.51 | 93.30 | 748.81 | 1,015,027 |
| Monocacy National Battlefield | MD | 1934 | 425.88 | 1,233.16 | 1,659.04 | not reported |
| Montezuma Castle National Monument | AZ | 1906(P) | 840.86 | 16.83 | 857.69 | 479,722 |
| Moores Creek National Battlefield | NC | 1933(T) | 86.52 | — | 86.52 | 39,532 |
| Morristown National Historical Park | NJ | 1933 | 1,673.89 | 2.05 | 1,675.94 | 626,327 |
| Mound City Group National Monument | OH | 1933(T) | 120.20 | 97.30 | 217.50 | 43,013 |
| Mount Rainier National Park | WA | 1899(E) | 235,404.00 | — | 235,404.00 | 1,106,306 |
| Mount Rushmore National Memorial | SD | 1925 | 1,238.45 | 40.00 | 1,278.45 | 1,562,559 |
| Muir Woods National Monument | CA | 1908(P) | 522.98 | 30.57 | 553.55 | 1,167,337 |
| Natchez Trace Parkway | AL/MS/TN | 1938(E) | 50,132.71 | 56.62 | 50,189.33 | 12,796,122 |
| National Capital Parks[21] | DC/MD/VA | 1933(T) | 6,465.85 | — | 6,465.85 | 6,335,269 |
| National Mall | DC | 1933(T) | 146.35 | — | 146.35 | not reported |

| | | | | | | |
|---|---|---|---|---|---|---|
| Natural Bridges National Monument | UT | 1908(P) | 7,791.00 | — | 7,791.00 | 56,368 |
| Navajo National Monument | AZ | 1909(P) | 360.00 | — | 360.00 | 46,792 |
| New River Gorge National River | WV | 1978 | 597.90 | 61,426.10 | 62,024.00 | not reported |
| Nez Perce National Historical Park | ID | 1965 | 1,833.20 | 275.69 | 2,108.89 | 207,746 |
| Ninety Six National Historic Site | SC | 1976 | 989.14 | — | 989.14 | not reported |
| Noatak National Preserve[3] | AK | 1980(E) | 6,550,000.00 | 10,000.00 | 6,560,000.00 | 4,605 |
| North Cascades National Park | WA | 1968(E) | 504,554.79 | 226.15 | 504,780.94 | 858,041 |
| Obed Wild and Scenic River | TN | 1976 | 1,172.50 | 3,927.34 | 5,099.84 | not reported |
| Ocmulgee National Monument | GA | 1934 | 683.48 | — | 683.48 | 111,014 |
| Olympic National Park | WA | 1933(T) | 904,015.79 | 10,560.67 | 914,576.46 | 2,410,722 |
| Oregon Caves National Monument | OR | 1933(T) | 484.03 | 3.95 | 487.98 | 114,160 |
| Organ Pipe Cactus National Monument | AZ | 1937(P) | 329,199.10 | 1,489.76 | 330,688.86 | 205,090 |
| Ozark National Scenic Riverways | MO | 1964 | 60,642.75 | 20,145.59 | 80,788.34 | 1,408,642 |
| Padre Island National Seashore | TX | 1962 | 130,355.46 | 341.37 | 130,696.83 | 630,165 |
| Palo Alto Battlefield National Historic Site | TX | 1978 | — | 50.00 | 50.00 | not reported |
| Pea Ridge National Military Park | AR | 1956 | 4,278.75 | 21.60 | 4,300.35 | 113,930 |
| Pecos National Monument | NM | 1965 | 364.80 | — | 364.80 | 39,371 |
| Perry's Victory and International Peace Memorial | OH | 1936(E) | 24.97 | 0.41 | 25.38 | 156,293 |
| Petersburg National Battlefield[22] | VA | 1933(T) | 1,523.71 | 1,211.67 | 2,735.38 | 553,208 |
| Petrified Forest National Park | AZ | 1906(P) | 93,492.57 | — | 93,492.57 | 708,512 |
| Pictured Rocks National Lakeshore | MI | 1966 | 35,375.43 | 37,523.43 | 72,898.86 | 441,271 |
| Pinnacles National Monument | CA | 1908(P) | 16,207.71 | 14.06 | 16,221.77 | 170,631 |

## Directory of National Park Units (continued)

| Name | Location | Year authorized[a] | Size (acres) Federal[b] | Nonfederal[c] | Total | Annual visitation (as of December 1983)[d] |
|---|---|---|---|---|---|---|
| Pipe Spring National Monument | AZ | 1923(P) | 40.00 | — | 40.00 | 28,237 |
| Pipestone National Monument | MN | 1937(E) | 281.78 | — | 281.78 | 133,831 |
| Piscataway Park | MD | 1961 | 4,216.03 | 46.49 | 4,262.52 | 69,712 |
| Point Reyes National Seashore | CA | 1962 | 64,164.03 | 6,882.04 | 71,046.07 | 1,424,751 |
| Prince William Forest Park | VA | 1936(T) | 17,410.34 | 1,161.21 | 18,571.55 | 419,793 |
| Pu'uhonua o Honaunau National Historical Park | HI | 1955 | 181.80 | — | 181.80 | 347,840 |
| Puukohola Heiau National Historic Site | HI | 1972 | 34.38 | 43.33 | 77.71 | 40,719 |
| Rainbow Bridge National Monument | UT | 1910(P) | 160.00 | — | 160.00 | 161,551 |
| Redwood National Park | CA | 1968(E) | 75,324.96 | 34,853.07 | 110,178.03 | 473,711 |
| Richmond National Battlefield Park | VA | 1936 | 771.41 | — | 771.41 | 312,786 |
| Rio Grande Wild and Scenic River | TX | 1978 | — | 9,600.00 | 9,600.00 | not reported |
| Rock Creek Park | DC | 1933 | 1,754.37 | — | 1,754.37 | 2,360,791 |
| Rocky Mountain National Park | CO | 1915(E) | 264,166.87 | 1,025.99 | 265,192.86 | 2,599,006 |
| Roger Williams National Memorial | RI | 1965 | 4.56 | — | 4.56 | 15,664 |
| Ross Lake National Recreation Area[18] | WA | 1968(E) | 105,132.37 | 12,441.72 | 117,574.09 | — |
| Russell Cave National Monument | AL | 1961(P) | 310.45 | — | 310.45 | 22,136 |

| | | | | | | |
|---|---|---|---|---|---|---|
| Sagamore Hill National Historic Site | NY | 1962 | 78.00 | — | 78.00 | 123,487 |
| Saguaro National Monument | AZ | 1933(T) | 81,958.17 | 1,615.71 | 83,573.88 | 634,688 |
| Saint Croix Island National Monument | ME | 1949 | 22.19 | 13.20 | 35.39 | not reported |
| St. Croix National Scenic Riverway | MN/WI | 1969 | 23,785.92 | 45,007.41 | 68,793.33 | 440,016 |
| Saint-Gaudens National Historic Site | NH | 1964 | 141.20 | 7.03 | 148.23 | 38,682 |
| Salem Maritime National Historic Site | MA | 1938(D) | 8.80 | 0.15 | 8.95 | 565,898 |
| Salinas National Monument | NM | 1909(P) | 647.19 | 429.75 | 1,076.94 | 35,968 |
| San Antonio Missions National Historical Park | TX | 1978 | 178.83 | 298.60 | 477.43 | 134,904 |
| San Juan Island National Historical Park | WA | 1966 | 1,725.45 | 26.54 | 1,751.99 | 122,540 |
| San Juan National Historic Site | PR | 1949(D) | 53.20 | 21.93 | 75.13 | 1,306,178 |
| Santa Monica Mountains National Recreation Area | CA | 1978(E) | 9,703.12 | 140,296.88 | 150,000.00 | 394,100 |
| Saratoga National Historical Park | NY | 1938 | 2,605.68 | 809.40 | 3,415.08 | 123,519 |
| Saugus Iron Works National Historic Site | MA | 1968 | 8.51 | — | 8.51 | 38,549 |
| Scotts Bluff National Monument | NE | 1919(P) | 2,935.95 | 61.13 | 2,997.08 | 151,984 |
| Sequoia National Park | CA | 1890(E) | 401,769.51 | 718.32 | 402,487.83 | 854,233 |
| Sewall-Belmont House National Historic Site | DC | 1974 | — | 0.35 | 0.35 | not reported |
| Shenandoah National Park | VA | 1926 | 195,008.34 | 63.66 | 195,072.00 | 1,768,378 |
| Shiloh National Military Park[23] | TN | 1933(T) | 3,792.55 | 55.00 | 3,847.55 | 272,092 |

## Directory of National Park Units (continued)

| Name | Location | Year authorized[a] | Size (acres) Federal[b] | Size (acres) Nonfederal[c] | Size (acres) Total | Annual visitation (as of December 1983)[d] |
|---|---|---|---|---|---|---|
| Sitka National Historical Park[24] | AK | 1910(P) | 106.17 | 0.66 | 106.83 | 84,830 |
| Sleeping Bear Dunes National Lakeshore | MI | 1970 | 55,571.47 | 15,449.67 | 71,021.14 | 658,208 |
| Springfield Armory National Historic Site | MA | 1974 | 20.60 | 34.33 | 54.93 | 15,626 |
| Statue of Liberty National Monument | NY | 1933(T) | 58.38 | — | 58.38 | 1,598,829 |
| Stones River National Battlefield[25] | TN | 1933(T) | 350.95 | — | 350.95 | 138,605 |
| Sunset Crater National Monument | AZ | 1933(T) | 3,040.00 | — | 3,040.00 | 375,136 |
| Thaddeus Kosciuszko National Memorial | PA | 1972 | 0.02 | — | 0.02 | 7,037 |
| Theodore Roosevelt Birthplace National Historic Site | NY | 1962 | 0.11 | — | 0.11 | 13,163 |
| Theodore Roosevelt Inaugural National Historic Site | NY | 1966 | 1.03 | — | 1.03 | 16,068 |
| Theodore Roosevelt Island | DC | 1933 | 88.50 | — | 88.50 | 55,901 |
| Theodore Roosevelt National Park | ND | 1947(E) | 69,675.88 | 740.51 | 70,416.39 | 415,118 |
| Thomas Jefferson Memorial | DC | 1934 | 18.36 | — | 18.36 | 1,485,531 |
| Thomas Stone National Historic Site | MD | 1978 | 321.97 | 6.28 | 328.25 | not reported |
| Timpanogos Cave National Monument | UT | 1933(T) | 250.00 | — | 250.00 | 98,475 |

| Site | State | Year | | | | |
|---|---|---|---|---|---|---|
| Tonto National Monument | AZ | 1933(T) | 1,120.00 | — | 1,120.00 | 70,039 |
| Tumacacori National Monument | AZ | 1908(P) | 15.88 | 0.64 | 16.52 | 57,922 |
| Tupelo National Battlefield | MS | 1933(T) | 1.00 | — | 1.00 | 614 |
| Tuskegee Institute National Historic Site | AL | 1974 | 24.09 | 50.30 | 74.39 | 76,060 |
| Tuzigoot National Monument | AZ | 1939(P) | 57.78 | 751.52 | 809.30 | 80,541 |
| USS *Arizona* Memorial | HI | 1980(E) | — | — | — | 1,044,752 |
| Upper Delaware Scenic and Recreational River | PA/NY | 1978 | 3.18 | 74,996.82 | 75,000.00 | 223,096 |
| Valley Forge National Historical Park | PA | 1976 | 2,909.97 | 554.92 | 3,464.89 | 3,448.694 |
| Vanderbilt Mansion National Historic Site | NY | 1940(D) | 211.65 | — | 211.65 | 420,104 |
| Vicksburg National Military Park[26] | MS | 1933(T) | 1,729.14 | 6.84 | 1,735.98 | 653,835 |
| Vietnam Veterans Memorial | DC | 1980(E) | 2.00 | — | 2.00 | not reported |
| Virgin Islands National Park | VI | 1956 | 12,909.34 | 1,786.51 | 14,695.85 | 676,800 |
| Voyageurs National Park | MN | 1971 | 130,788.10 | 87,103.91 | 217,892.01 | 146,454 |
| Walnut Canyon National Monument | AZ | 1933(T) | 2,011.62 | 237.84 | 2,249.46 | 88,376 |
| War in the Pacific National Historical Park | GU | 1978 | 844.23 | 1,113.66 | 1,957.89 | not reported |
| Washington Monument | DC | 1933(T) | 106.01 | — | 106.01 | 1,212,736 |
| Whiskeytown-Shasta-Trinity National Recreation Area | CA | 1965 | 42,428.10 | 75.33 | 42,503.43 | 1,082.532 |
| White House | DC | 1933(T) | 18.07 | — | 18.07 | 1,169, 085 |
| White Sands National Monument | NM | 1933(P) | 144,075.25 | 382.99 | 144,458.24 | 492,902 |
| Whitman Mission National Historic Site | WA | 1936 | 98.15 | — | 98.15 | 108,114 |

## Directory of National Park Units (continued)

| Name | Location | Year authorized[a] | Size (acres) Federal[b] | Size (acres) Nonfederal[c] | Size (acres) Total | Annual visitation (as of December 1983)[d] |
|---|---|---|---|---|---|---|
| William Howard Taft National Historic Site | OH | 1969 | 1.62 | 1.45 | 3.07 | 2,964 |
| Wilson's Creek National Battlefield | MO | 1960 | 1,749.41 | 0.50 | 1,749.91 | 93,573 |
| Wind Cave National Park | SD | 1903(E) | 28,060.03 | 232.05 | 28,292.08 | 503,739 |
| Wolf Trap Farm Park for the Performing Arts | VA | 1966 | 130.28 | — | 130.28 | 258,430 |
| Women's Rights National Historical Park | NY | 1980 | 0.82 | 4.17 | 4.99 | 6,759 |
| Wrangell-St. Elias National Park and Preserve[13] | AK | 1980(E) | NP-8,145,000.00[e] PR-4,255,000.00 | 800,000.00 — | 8,945,000.00 4,255,000.00 | 18,760 |
| Wright Brothers National Memorial | NC | 1933(T) | 424.77 | 6.63 | 431.40 | 484,289 |
| Wupatki National Monument | AZ | 1924(P) | 35,253.24 | — | 35,253.24 | 190,938 |
| Yellowstone National Park | ID/MT/WY | 1872(E) | 2,219,803.32 | 19.38 | 2,219,822.70 | 2,347,242 |
| Yosemite National Park | CA | 1890(E) | 759,452.78 | 1,717.40 | 761,170.18 | 2,457,464 |
| Yucca House National Monument | CO | 1919(P) | 10.00 | — | 10.00 | not reported |
| Yukon-Charley Rivers National Preserve[3] | AK | 1980(E) | 2,211,000.00 | 309,000.00 | 2,520,000.00 | 955 |
| Zion National Park | UT | 1909(P) | 142,793.96 | 3,757.14 | 146,551.10 | 1,273,030 |

## Units Affiliated with the National Park System[f]

| Name | Location | Year authorized[a] | Size (acres) Federal[b] | Nonfederal | Total |
|---|---|---|---|---|---|
| American Memorial Park | GU | 1978 | — | — | — |
| Benjamin Franklin National Memorial[27] | PA | 1972(D) | — | — | — |
| Boston African American National Historic Site | MA | 1980 | — | — | — |
| Cherokee Strip Living Museum | KS | 1976 | — | 6.00 | 6.00 |
| Chicago Portage National Historic Site[28] | IL | 1952(D) | — | 91.20 | 91.20 |
| Chimney Rock National Historic Site[29] | NE | 1956(D) | — | 83.36 | 83.36 |
| David Berger National Memorial[30] | OH | 1980 | — | — | — |
| Ebey's Landing National Historical Reserve | WA | 1978 | 587.52 | 7,412.48 | 8,000.00 |
| Father Marquette National Memorial | MI | 1975 | — | 52.00 | 52.00 |
| Gloria Dei (Old Swedes') Church National Historic Site[31] | PA | 1942(D) | 2.08 | 1.63 | 3.71 |
| Green Springs Historic District[32] | VA | 1977 | 5,490.59 | — | 5,490.59 |
| Historic Camden | SC | 1984 | — | — | — |
| Ice Age National Scenic Trail | WI | 1980 | — | — | — |
| Ice Age National Scientific Reserve | WI | 1964 | — | 32,500.00 | 32,500.00 |
| Iditarod National Historic Trail | AK | 1978 | — | — | — |
| International Peace Garden[33] | ND/Canada | 1931(O) | — | 2,330.30 | 2,330.30 |
| Jamestown National Historic Site[34] | VA | 1940(D) | — | 20.63 | 20.63 |

| | | | Federal | Nonfederal | Total |
|---|---|---|---|---|---|
| Lewis and Clark National Historic Trail | IL to OR | 1978 | — | — | — |
| Mary McLeod Bethune Council House National Historic Site | DC | 1982 | — | — | — |
| McLoughlin House National Historic Site[35] | OR | 1941(D) | — | 0.63 | 0.63 |
| Mormon Pioneer National Historic Trail | IL to UT | 1978 | — | — | — |
| National Center for the Study of Afro-American History and Culture | OH | 1980 | — | — | — |
| North Country National Scenic Trail | NY to ND | 1980 | — | — | — |
| Oregon National Historic Trail | MO to OR | 1978 | — | — | — |
| Overmountain Victory National Historic Trail | VA to TN | 1980 | — | — | — |
| Pennsylvania Avenue National Historic Site | DC | 1965(D) | — | — | — |
| Pinelands National Reserve | NJ | 1978 | — | — | — |
| Roosevelt Campobello International Park[36] | ME/Canada | 1964(E) | — | 2,721.50 | 2,721.50 |
| Saint Paul's Church National Historic Site[37] | NY | 1943(D) | 5.97 | 0.15 | 6.12 |
| Touro Synagogue National Historic Site[38] | RI | 1946(D) | — | 0.23 | 0.23 |

## Sources

U.S. Department of the Interior, National Park Service, *Index of the National Park System and Related Areas, 1982* (Washington, D.C.: U.S. Government Printing Office, 1983); Conservation Foundation staff interviews with National Park Service staff, 1985.

## Size

U.S. Department of the Interior, National Park Service, "Summary of Acreages," table, December 31, 1984.

## Annual Visitation

U.S. Department of the Interior, National Park Service, *National Park Statistical Abstract, 1983* (Denver, Colo.: Denver Service Center, Statistical Office, 1983), pp.8–21; *Index of the National Park System and Related Areas, 1982*; and "All NPS Areas—Recreation Visits (1982 and 1983)," table, 6 pp.

## Column Heading Notes

a. Year authorized, unless otherwise noted: A–Administered; D–Designated; E–Established; O–Originated; P–Proclaimed; T–Transferred.

b. Includes both fee and less-than-fee acreage.

c. Includes both private and other public acreage.

d. Recreation visits.

e. Park unit abbreviations: NM–National Monument; NP–National Park; PR–National Preserve.

f. Affiliated areas comprise a variety of properties in the United States and Canada that preserve significant resources outside the National Park Service; all draw on technical and financial assistance from the service.

## Other Notes

[1]Proclaimed as a National Monument in 1978; established as a National Monument and Preserve in 1980.

[2]Includes Antietam National Cemetery, 11.36 acres (federal).

[3]Proclaimed as a National Monument in 1978; established as a National Preserve in 1980.

[4]Proclaimed as a National Monument in 1923; authorized as Utah National Park in 1924; changed to Bryce Canyon National Park in 1928.

[5]Proclaimed as a National Monument in 1937; established as a National Park in 1971.

[6]Proclaimed as a National Monument in 1923; established as a National Park in 1930.

[7]Placed under National Park Service in 1923; proclaimed a National Monument in 1961; changed to National Historical Park in 1971.

[8]Includes Yorktown National Cemetery, 2.91 acres (federal).

[9]Established as Mt. McKinley National Park in 1917; established as Denali National Park and Preserve in 1980.

[10]National Park Service operates visitor facilities at Fort Benton as part of Missouri Breaks Wild and Scenic River, administered by the Bureau of Land Management.

[11]Includes Fort Donelson National Cemetery, 15.34 acres (federal).

[12]Includes Fredericksburg National Cemetery, 12 acres (federal).

[13]Proclaimed as a National Monument in 1978; established as a National Park and Preserve in 1980.

[14]Includes Gettysburg National Cemetery, 20.58 acres (federal).

[15]Proclaimed as a National Monument in 1925; established as a National Park and Preserve in 1980.

[16]Proclaimed as a National Monument in 1918; established as a National Park and Preserve in 1980.

[17]Proclaimed as a National Monument in 1978; established as a National Park in 1980.

[18]Visitation figures for this unit are combined and reported with those of North Cascades National Park; no breakdown is available.

[19]Administered under cooperative agreement with the Bureau of Reclamation, U.S. Department of the Interior.

[20]Visitation figures for this unit are combined and reported with those of George Washington Memorial Parkway; no breakdown is available.

[21]Includes Battleground National Cemetery, 1.03 acres (federal).

[22]Includes Poplar Grove National Cemetery, 8.72 acres (federal).

[23]Includes Shiloh National Cemetery, 10.05 acres (federal).

[24]Proclaimed in 1910; established as a National Historical Park in 1972.

[25]Includes Stones River National Cemetery, 20.09 acres (federal).

[26]Includes Vicksburg National Cemetery, 116.28 acres (federal).

[27]Owned and administered by the Franklin Institute.

[28]Owned and administered by Cook County, Illinois.

[29]Owned by the state of Nebraska; administered by the city of Bayard, the Nebraska State Historical Society, and the National Park Service under a cooperative agreement.

[30]Administered by the Jewish Community Center of Cleveland.

[31]Church site owned and administered by the Corporation of Gloria Dei (Old Swedes') Church.

Appendix A

³²The secretary of the interior accepted 29 easements from the Historic Green Springs, Inc., in December 1977.

³³The state of North Dakota holds the 888-acre U.S. portion for International Peace Garden, Inc., which administers the area for North Dakota and Manitoba.

³⁴Owned and administered by the Association for the Preservation of Virginia Antiquities; remainder of Jamestown site and island is part of Colonial National Historical Park.

³⁵Designated as McLoughlin Home National Historic Site in 1941; name changed to McLoughlin House National Historic Site in 1945; owned and administered by the McLoughlin Memorial Association.

³⁶Owned and administered by a United States-Canadian commission.

³⁷Authorized in 1978.

³⁸Owned by Congregation Shearith Israel, New York City.

# Appendix B
# A Chronology of Major Events in the National Park System

1832    Hot Springs, Arkansas, set aside by Congress as the first "national reservation." (Hot Springs became a national park in 1921.)

1864    Congress cedes Yosemite Valley and the nearby Mariposa Big Tree Grove to California for "public use, resort, and recreation."

1872    Yellowstone National Park—the first true "national park"—established by an act of Congress, directing that it be preserved as a "park and pleasuring ground."

1889    Casa Grande Ruin Reservation (now Casa Grande National Monument) authorized to protect the ruins of a massive 600-year-old Indian structure.

1890    Yosemite (excluding the state-administered valley), General Grant (later merged into King's Canyon), and Sequoia national parks established.

           Chickamauga–Chattanooga becomes the first national military park, administered by the War Department.

1892    The Sierra Club founded by John Muir to promote national park establishment and protection.

1899   Mount Rainier National Park established.

1902   Crater Lake National Park established—one of first parks set aside in recognition of its scientific importance.

1906   Antiquities Act enacted, giving the president authority to set aside by proclamation, as a national monument, any federally owned land with prehistoric, historic, or scientific value. Devil's Tower proclaimed as first national monument.

Mesa Verde National Park—the first national park created to preserve a cultural resource—established.

1910   Glacier National Park established.

1913   Hetch Hetchy Dam in Yosemite authorized by Congress after long battle. Congressional approval of dam stimulates park advocates to seek creation of an agency to manage and protect the parks.

1915   Rocky Mountain National Park established.

Stephen T. Mather accepts position as assistant to Secretary of the Interior Franklin Lane, in charge of parks.

1916   National Park Service Act enacted, creating the National Park System and the National Park Service.

Hawaii Volcanoes and Lassen Volcanic national parks added to the system.

1917   National Park Service assumes jurisdiction over the 14 existing national parks and 21 national monuments. Mather appointed director of the service with Horace Albright as assistant director.

Establishment of Mt. McKinley National Park (now Denali National Park and Preserve), which includes the nation's highest peak.

1919   National Park Association (now National Parks and Conservation Association) organized to promote parks and their protection.

      Acadia National Park becomes the first park system unit in the East.[1]

1921   First National Conference on State Parks convened by Mather to promote development of state park systems to complement the national parks.

1926   Shenandoah, Great Smoky Mountains, and Mammoth Cave national parks authorized.

1928   Mather becomes ill; resigns position as director. Succeeded by Horace Albright, his long time assistant, in 1929.

1932   Construction of Skyline Drive within Shenandoah National Park begun, providing model for future parkways in the system.

      George Wright joins park service as chief of the newly created Wildlife Division and invigorates science component of the service.

1933   Executive order by President Franklin D. Roosevelt transfers military-historical areas and national monuments from the War and Agriculture departments to the park service.

      Arno B. Cammerer succeeds Albright as director.

      Civilian Conservation Corps established; provides manpower for construction of facilities and land rehabilitation in many parks.

1934   Everglades National Park authorized.

1935   Historic Sites Act enacted—the nation's first comprehensive policy on historic preservation; sets up classification of "national historic site."

Wilderness Society founded.

1936   Park, Parkway and Recreation Act provides for park service study of park and recreation needs and permits it to assist states in planning.

Boulder Dam (now Lake Mead) National Recreation Area established, the first park service unit designated as a recreation area.

1937   The first national seashore, Cape Hatteras, authorized, establishing the model for an array of future units protecting areas along the coasts and Great Lakes.

1939   Park Service Wildlife Division transferred to Fish and Wildlife Service.

1940   Newton B. Drury, former executive secretary of the Save-the-Redwoods League, becomes park service director.

1941   U.S. enters World War II, leading to a dramatic drop in park service staffing and funding; service headquarters transferred to Chicago until 1946.

1948   Independence National Historical Park authorized.

1951   Conrad L. Wirth becomes park service director.

1956   Mission '66—a $1-billion, 10-year program—initiated to construct and improve park facilities to accommodate increased park visitation.

1958   Outdoor Recreation Resources Review Commission (ORRRC) established by law to conduct a comprehensive study of the nation's outdoor recreation needs.

1961   Cape Cod National Seashore authorized, with nearly $16 million dollars appropriated for land acquisition. Landowners allowed to retain their property if towns adopt satisfactory zoning regulations.

1962    ORRRC report, *Outdoor Recreation for America*, recommends creation of a fund to be used to acquire federal and state recreation land; establishment of national systems of wilderness, rivers, and trails; and establishment of recreation areas near urban areas.

1963    Following an ORRRC recommendation, Bureau of Outdoor Recreation established by executive order to engage in nationwide outdoor recreation planning and provide grants to states and localities.

Advisory board on wildlife management in the parks (chaired by A. Starker Leopold) recommends management of the parks as natural ecosystems to maintain biotic associations "as nearly as possible in the condition that prevailed when the area was first visited by the white man."

1964    George B. Hartzog, Jr., succeeds Wirth as park service director.

Wilderness Act and Land and Water Conservation Fund Act enacted.

1965    Concessions Policy Act enacted.

1966    National Historic Preservation Act enacted, providing for establishment of the National Register of Historic Places.

Pictured Rocks authorized as first national lakeshore.

1968    Congress enacts legislation establishing National Scenic Trails and National Wild and Scenic Rivers Systems.

Redwood National Park established.

1972    Gateway and Golden Gate national recreation areas established as park system expansion emphasizes units near metropolitan areas.

Ronald Walker replaces Hartzog as park service director.

1974    Congress authorizes the first two national preserves—Big Cypress, to protect water flow into the Everglades, and Big Thicket.

Cuyahoga Valley National Recreation Area authorized.

Controversy in Yosemite over the concessioner's role in drafting the park's master plan and filming a television series in the park.

1975    Gary Everhart replaces Walker as park service director.

1977    William Whalen replaces Everhart.

President Carter transfers the historic preservation responsibilities of the park service to the Bureau of Outdoor Recreation and renames it the Heritage Conservation and Recreation Service (HCRS).

1978    Omnibus parks legislation authorizes 21 new National Park System units, including the Santa Monica Mountains National Recreation Area and Jean Lafitte National Historical Park and Preserve; also establishes Pinelands National Reserve, providing federal acquisition funding and park service technical assistance.

Redwood National Park enlarged.

President Carter doubles the size of the park system by proclaiming 10 national monuments in Alaska and enlarging 3 existing units.

1979    Buyout of major concessioner at Yellowstone.

1980    Russell Dickenson replaces Whalen as park service director.

The Alaska National Interest Lands Conservation Act alters boundaries of units proclaimed by Carter in 1978 and redesignates most as national parks or preserves.

Park service issues report, *State of the Parks 1980*, describing threats to the parks' resources.

National Historic Preservation Act amended, providing for leasing and reuse of historic structures managed by the park service.

Congress enacts a second Omnibus Parks Act.

1981    James Watt appointed secretary of the interior; announces changes in national park policy, including a moratorium on parkland acquisition (lifted later that year), rehabilitation of facilities, and an emphasis on private sector involvement in the parks.

HCRS abolished; its functions and staff transferred to the park service.

1982    Secretary Watt announces program to transfer personnel from the Washington and regional offices to the parks.

1983    William Clark replaces Watt as secretary of the interior.

1984    Renovation work, supported by over $200 million in private contributions, begins on the Statue of Liberty and Ellis Island.

Illinois-Michigan Canal National Heritage Corridor Act enacted, providing for federal funding and park service technical assistance to the newly designated area.

1985    Donald Hodel replaces Clark as secretary of the interior.

William Penn Mott, Jr., replaces Dickenson as park service director.

The Presidential Commission on Outdoor Recreation Resources Review established by executive order to review the nation's recreational resource needs.

# Appendix C

## The 20 Largest Concession Contracts, by Estimated Gross Receipts, 1983

| Concessioner (Park) | Length of Contract (and Expiration Date) | Number of Employees | Franchise Fee | Estimated Gross Receipts* |
|---|---|---|---|---|
| Yosemite Park & Curry Company, a subsidiary of MCA, Inc. (Yosemite) | 30 (1993) | 1,712 | $425,003 | $56,667,067 |
| Fred Harvey, Inc., a subsidiary of AMFAC, Inc. (Grand Canyon) | 30 (1998) | 1,056 | 723,486 | 28,939,400 |
| Wahweap Lodge & Marina, a subsidiary of Del Webb Recreational Properties, Inc. (Glen Canyon) | 30 (1998) | 450 | 364,470 | 16,198,667 |
| Hamilton Stores, Inc. (Yellowstone) | 30 (1999) | 750 | 315,061 | 12,602,440 |
| Grand Teton Lodge Co., a subsidiary of Jackson Hole Preserve, Inc. (Grand Tetons) | 30 (2002) | 810 | 77,534 | 10,337,867 |
| Guest Services, Inc. (National Capital) | 20 (1991) | 250 | 257,527 | 8,584,233 |
| Guest Services, Inc. (Sequoia/Kings Canyon) | 20 (1998) | 300 | 54,162 | 7,221,600 |
| Bullfrog Marina, Inc., a subsidiary of Del Webb Recreational Properties, Inc.[1] (Glen Canyon) | 10 (1985) | 300 | 149,620 | 6,800,909 |
| Babbitt Brothers (Grand Canyon) | 20 (1987) | 107 | 137,215 | 6,098,444 |
| ARA Virginia Sky-Line, a subsidiary of ARA Services, Inc. (Shenandoah) | 30 (1988) | 317 | 117,827 | 5,891,350 |
| Glacier Park, Inc., a subsidiary of Greyhound Corporation, Inc.[2] (Glacier) | 25 (2005) | 488 | 69,675 | 4,978,333 |

## Appendix C (continued)

| Concessioner (Park) | Length of Contract (and Expiration Date) | Number of Employees | Franchise Fee | Estimated Gross Receipts* |
|---|---|---|---|---|
| Halls Crossing Resort and Marina, a subsidiary of Del Webb Recreational Properties, Inc.[1] (Glen Canyon) | 12 (1990) | 125 | 92,674 | 4,633,700 |
| Landmark Services (National Capital) | 12 (1989) | 200 | $69,323 | $4,621,533 |
| Lake Mohave Resort (Lake Mead) | 21 (1978) | 180 | 64,107 | 4,273,800 |
| Circle Line—Statue of Liberty (Statue of Liberty) | 10 (1992) | 75 | 295,359 | 4,219,414 |
| Everglades Park (Everglades) | 15 (1994) | 122 | 60,825 | 3,557,941 |
| Echo Bay Resort (Lake Mead) | 18 (1989) | 130 | 70,341 | 3,517,050 |
| TW Services, Inc., a subsidiary of Canteen Corporation[3] (Grand Canyon) | 10 (1983) | 162 | 67,023 | 3,351,150 |
| Mountain Company, Inc. (Mt. Rushmore) | 19 (1991) | 110 | 129,668 | 3,241,700 |
| Guest Services, Inc. (Mt. Ranier) | 20 (1992) | 198 | 77,597 | 3,103,880 |

[1]Del Webb Recreational Properties, Inc., is a subsidiary of Del E. Webb Corporation.

[2]Greyhound Corporation, Inc. has 80 percent ownership.

[3]Canteen Corporation is a subsidiary of Trans World Corporation.

*Because information on concessioner gross receipts is not publicly available, these figures are estimates based on the franchise fee paid and the percentage of gross receipts used by the park service to calculate the franchise fees. Since the sale of some items is excluded from franchise fees, these figures may be lower than the actual gross receipts and only serve to illustrate the scale of the operation. Concessioners that, because of contract provisions, do not pay franchise fees, such as TW Services in Yellowstone and National Park Concessions, Inc., which operates in five parks, are not listed here.

# References

## Chapter 1. Preservation and Use

1. U.S. Department of the Interior, National Park Service, *Index of the National Park System and Related Areas, 1982* (Washington, D.C.: U.S. Government Printing Office, 1983).
2. U.S. Department of the Interior, National Park Service, "Summary of Acreages," table, dated December 31, 1984.
3. Ibid.
4. Ibid.; National Park Service, *Index of the National Park System and Related Areas, 1982.*
5. Wallace Stegner, "The Best Idea We Ever Had," *Wilderness* Spring 1983, pp. 4-5.
6. National Park Service, *Index of the National Park System and Related Areas, 1982.*
7. William C. Everhart, *The National Park Service* (Boulder, Colo.: Westview Press, 1983), pp. 16, 18.
8. Stegner, "The Best Idea We Ever Had," p. 8.
9. 16 U.S.C.A., §1 (1974).
10. Frederick Law Olmsted, "The Yosemite Valley and the Mariposa Big Trees," with an introductory note by Laura Wood Roper, *Landscape Architecture*, October 1952, p. 13.
11. Ibid., p. 16.
12. Roderick Nash, *Wilderness and the American Mind* (New Haven, Conn.: Yale University Press, 1982).
13. Alfred Runte, *National Parks: The American Experience* (Lincoln, Nebr.: University of Nebraska Press, 1979), pp. 93, 104-105.
14. U.S. Congress, House of Representatives, *Congressional Record-House*, July 1, 1915, p. 10364.
15. Ibid.
16. Everhart, *The National Park Service*, pp. 19-20.
17. John Ise, *Our National Park Policy: A Critical History* (Baltimore: Johns Hopkins University Press, 1961), pp. 585-586.
18. George M. Wright, Joseph S. Dixon and Ben H. Thompson, *A Preliminary Survey of Faunal Relations in National Parks.* Fauna Series No. 1 (Washington, D.C.: U.S. Government Printing Office, 1933), p. 4.
19. Lowell Sumner, "Biological Research and Management in the National Park Service: A History," *The George Wright Forum*, Autumn 1983, p. 6.
20. Joseph L. Sax, *Mountains Without Handrails: Reflections on the National Parks* (Ann Arbor, Mich.: University of Michigan Press, 1980), pp. 64-66.
21. Olmsted, "The Yosemite Valley and the Mariposa Big Tree Grove," pp. 20, 21.

22. Joseph L. Sax, "America's National Parks: Their Principles, Purposes, and Prospects," *Natural History*, October 1976, p. 64.

23. Alfred Runte, "Pragmatic Alliance: Western Railroads and the National Parks," *National Parks and Conservation Magazine*, April 1974, pp. 14-21.

24. Phyllis Myers, "The Park Service as Client I," *Architecture*, December 1984, pp. 42-47.

25. Olmsted, "The Yosemite Valley and the Mariposa Big Trees," p. 22.

26. Runte, *National Parks: The American Experience*, p. 103.

27. Everhart, *The National Park Service*, pp. 13, 19.

28. Peggy Wayburn, "A Sierra Club Quiz," *Sierra*, May-June 1984, pp. 66, 68.

29. Runte, *National Parks: The American Experience*, pp. 132-133, 160-161; Robert Shankland, *Steve Mather of the National Parks* (New York: Alfred A. Knopf, 1970), p. 167.

## Profile. Yellowstone National Park

1. Jim Robbins, "Do Not Feed the Bears?" *Natural History*, January 1984, p. 16.

2. Conservation Foundation staff interview with Joan Anzelmo, Yellowstone NP, Public Information Office, 1983.

3. Roderick Nash, *Wilderness and the American Mind* (New Haven, Connecticut: Yale University Press, 1982), p. 111.

4. John Ise, *Our National Park Policy: A Critical History* (Baltimore: Johns Hopkins University Press, 1961), p. 22.

5. Ibid. p. 25.

6. Ise, *Our National Park Policy*, p. 43; Robert Shankland, *Steve Mather of the National Parks* (New York: Alfred A. Knopf, 1970), pp. 214-217.

7. William S. Ellis, "Yellowstone," in National Geographic Society, *The New America's Wonderlands: Our National Parks* (Washington, D.C.: National Geographic Society, 1980), p. 44.

8. Conservation Foundation staff interviews with National Park Service staff, Concessions Division, 1985.

9. Conservation Foundation staff interviews with National Park Service staff, Yellowstone NP, 1983.

10. U.S. Department of the Interior, National Park Service, Yellowstone Park Brochure (Washington, D.C.: U.S. Government Printing Office, 1982).

11. Robbins, "Do Not Feed the Bears?" p. 14; Conservation Foundation staff interviews with National Park Service staff, Yellowstone NP, 1983.

12. Conservation Foundation staff interview with Joan Anzelmo, Yellowstone NP, Public Information Office, 1983.

13. Conservation Foundation staff interviews with National Park Service staff, Yellowstone NP, 1983.

14. Robert Cahn, "Nation's Oldest Park Fends Off New Incursions," *The Christian Science Monitor*, June 14, 1982, p. 12; Dan Whipple, "Mixing Oil and Woods in the Yellowstone," *High Country News*, June 24, 1983, p. 7. The five national forests that immediately surround Yellow-

stone National Park are Targhee, Bridger-Teton, Custer, Gallatin, and Shoshone. About 44 percent of the 8.8 million acres in these forests have leases for oil and gas exploration.

15. Conservation Foundation staff interview with Robert D. Barbee, superintendent, Yellowstone NP, 1983.

16. Conservation Foundation staff interview with Steve Yost, Yellowstone NP, Concessions Management Division, 1983.

17. See appendix C and accompanying notes.

18. Conservation Foundation staff interviews with National Park Service staff, Yellowstone, NP, 1983.

19. Ibid.

20. Ibid.

21. Robbins, "Do Not Feed the Bears?" p. 18.

22. Conservation Foundation staff interview with Robert D. Barbee, superintendent, Yellowstone NP, 1983.

23. Lewis Regenstein, "The Politics of Extinction," reprinted in U.S. Department of the Interior, National Park Service, Yellowstone National Park, *Final Environmental Impact Statement: Grizzly Bear Management Program*, October 1982, p. E-55.

24. U.S. Department of the Interior, Advisory Board on Wildlife Management (chaired by A.S. Leopold), "Wildlife Management in the National Parks," report, dated March 4, 1963.

25. Robbins, "Do Not Feed the Bears?" p. 21.

26. Alston Chase, "The Last Bears of Yellowstone," *The Atlantic Monthly*, February 1983, pp. 63-73.

27. Conservation Foundation staff interview with Robert D. Barbee, superintendent, Yellowstone NP, 1983.

28. "Bears Are Parks's Grisly Problem," *The Washington Post*, October 11, 1984, p. A3.

29. Conservation Foundation staff interview with Joan Anzelmo, Yellowstone NP, Public Information Office, 1983.

30. Conservation Foundation staff interview with Robert D. Barbee, superintendent, Yellowstone NP, 1983.

31. "Coalition Says Yellowstone Needs Elbow Room," *The New York Times*, October 21, 1984, p. 29.

32. Conservaton Foundation staff interviews with staff of TW Services, Inc., 1983.

## Chapter 2. The Unsystematic System

1. U.S. Department of the Interior, National Park Service, "Summary of Acreages," table, dated December 31, 1984.

2. U.S. Department of the Interior, National Park Service, *Index of the National Park System and Related Areas, 1982* (Washington, D.C.: U.S. Government Printing Office, 1983), p. 10.

3. William C. Everhart, *The National Park Service* (Boulder, Colo.: Westview Press, 1983), p. 31.

4. U.S. Department of the Interior, National Park Service, Office of Media Affairs, "60 Years Growth of the National Park System," table, dated January 29, 1979.

5. Ibid.

6. Ric Davidge, "Trends in the National Park System" (Washington, D.C.: U.S. Department of the Interior, Office of the Assistant Secretary for Fish and Wildlife and Parks, draft, 1983), p. 9.

7. Robin W. Winks, "Upon Reading Sellars and Runte," *Journal of Forest History*, July 1983, p. 142.

8. 16 U.S.C.A. §§431-33 (1974).

9. Alfred Runte, *National Parks: The American Experience* (Lincoln, Nebr.: University of Nebraska Press, 1979), p. 45.

10. National Park Service, *Index of the National Park System and Related Areas, 1982*, p. 18.

11. John Ise, *Our National Park Policy: A Critical History* (Baltimore: Johns Hopkins University Press, 1961), pp. 52-53.

12. Ibid., pp. 101, 103-104.

13. Ibid., p. 126.

14. Ibid., p. 120.

15. Ibid., pp. 129-130.

16. Everhart, *The National Park Service*, p. 14.

17. Robert Shankland, *Steve Mather of the National Parks* (New York: Alfred A. Knopf, 1970), p. 56.

18. Ise, *Our National Park Policy*, pp. 212-213.

19. Shankland, *Steve Mather of the National Parks*, p. 170.

20. Ise, *Our National Park Policy*, p. 223.

21. National Park Service, *Index of the National Park System and Related Areas, 1982*, p. 20.

22. Shankland, *Steve Mather of the National Parks*, pp. 170-171.

23. Runte, *National Parks: The American Experience*, p. 66.

24. Ise, *Our National Park Policy*, pp. 136-142. Mather tried unsuccessfully to remove these units from the system. Sullys Hill was transferred in 1931 as a game preserve to the Department of Agriculture. Platt was enlarged and redesignated as Chickasaw NRA in 1976. Wind Cave remains as a national park.

25. Everhart, *The National Park Service*, p. 18.

26. Conservation Foundation staff interview with Marvin Hershey, retired supervisory ranger, Muir Woods NM, 1984.

27. Runte, *National Parks: The American Experience*, p. 48.

28. A collection of papers on the worthless lands thesis appears in *Journal of Forest History*, July 1983, pp. 130-145.

29. Robert M. Utley, "Commentary on the Worthless Lands Thesis," *Journal of Forest History*, July 1983, p. 142.

30. Norman T. Newton, *Design on the Land: The Development of Landscape Architecture* (Cambridge, Mass.: Belknap Press of Harvard University Press, 1971), pp. 521-522.

31. Conservation Foundation staff interview with Gail Vaillancourt, Staff Planner, New Hampshire State Division of Forests and Lands, 1984.
32. Shankland, *Steve Mather of the National Parks*, p. 171.
33. Louis Schellback, "Grand Canyon," in *The New America's Wonderlands: Our National Parks* (Washington, D.C.: National Geographic Society, 1980), p. 97.
34. Ise, *Our National Park Policy*, p. 231.
35. Ibid., p. 242.
36. Ibid.
37. Ibid., p. 247.
38. Everhart, *The National Park Service*, pp. 80-84; Ise, *Our National Park Policy*, p. 506.
39. Runte, *National Parks: The American Experience*, pp. 106-137.
40. Shankland, *Steve Mather of the National Parks*, p. 168.
41. Runte, *National Parks: The American Experience*, p. 115.
42. Ibid.
43. Ibid., p. 117.
44. Stephanie Gilbert, "Private Sector Spearheads Smokies' Golden Anniversary Celebration," *Courier*, April 1984, p. 2.
45. Ise, *Our National Park Policy*, pp. 258-264.
46. U.S. Department of the Interior, National Park Service, Shenandoah Park Brochure (Washington, D.C.: U.S. Government Printing Office, 1984).
47. Ise, *Our National Park Policy*, p. 265.
48. Runte, *National Parks: The American Experience*, p. 108.
49. Ibid., pp. 128, 131, 134.
50. Ibid., p. 134.
51. Susan Schrepfer, "Conflict in Preservation: The Sierra Club, Save-the-Redwoods League and Redwood National Park," *Journal of Forest History*, April 1980, p. 67.
52. Ibid., p. 68.
53. Ibid., p. 75.
54. Runte, *National Parks: The American Experience*, pp. 152-153.
55. U.S. Congress, House Committee on Interior and Insular Affairs, Subcommittee on National Parks and Insular Affairs, *Legislative History of the Redwood National Park Expansion Act of 1978*, 95th Cong., 2d sess., 1978, p. 93.
56. U.S. Department of the Interior, National Park Service, "Land and Water Conservation Fund, Federal Portion Backlog Within Existing Authorizations," table, dated January 12, 1984; Information provided by Dan Salisbury, assistant director for financial and data systems, National Park Service, 1984.
57. 16 U.S.C.A., §79b (Supp. 1985).
58. J. Michael Norman, "Challenge at Voyageurs," *National Parks and Conservation Magazine*, January 1977, p. 8.
59. Ibid., pp. 8-11.
60. Everhart, *The National Park Service*, pp. 127-132.

61. Roderick Nash, *Wilderness and the American Mind* (New Haven, Conn.: Yale University Press, 1983), p. 272.

62. Congressional Quarterly, Inc., *1980 Congressional Quarterly Almanac*, 96th Cong., 2d Sess., (Washington, D.C.: Congressional Quarterly, Inc., 1981), pp. 575-584.

63. Ibid., p. 575.

64. Ibid., 575-578. ANILCA resulted in the designation of 56.7 million acres of wilderness, including 32.4 million acres within national park units.

65. 16 U.S.C.A., §1280 (1974); Dale Russakoff, "Interior to Expand Mining in Parks," *The Washington Post*, September 29, 1983, p. A1.

66. Congressional Quarterly, Inc., *1980 Congressional Quarterly Almanac*, pp. 576-577.

67. Conservation Foundation staff interview with Randy Biallis, Assistant Chief Historical Architect, National Park Service, 1984.

68. Charles B. Hosmer, Jr., *Preservation Comes of Age* (Charlottesville: University Press of Virginia, 1981), p. 580.

69. Ibid., p. 532.

70. Ibid., p. 472.

71. Ibid., pp. 530-531, 563.

72. Ibid., p. 505.

73. 16 U.S.C.A., §§461-469i (1974).

74. Hosmer, *Preservation Comes of Age*, pp. 596-597.

75. Conservation Foundation interviews with National Park Service staff and former staff members of the Office of Management and Budget, 1983.

76. U.S. Department of the Interior, National Park Service, *Part One of the National Park System Plan: History* (Washington, D.C.: U.S. Government Printing Office, 1972).

77. 16 U.S.C.A., §§431-433 (1974).

78. National Park Service, *Index of the National Park System and Related Areas, 1982*, pp. 15-17, 40-42.

79. Conservation Foundation staff interview with Dave Dutcher, Chief Historian, Independence NHP, 1984.

80. Conservation Foundation staff interview with Edie Shean-Hammond, National Park Service, North Atlantic Regional Office, Public Affairs, 1984.

81. Hosmer, *Preservation Comes of Age*, pp. 640, 647.

82. Ibid., pp. 626, 632.

83. Conservation Foundation staff interview with Duncan Morrow, chief, Division of Media Information, National Park Service, 1984.

84. Shankland, *Steve Mather of Our National Parks*, p. 298.

85. Newton, *Design on the Land*, p. 597.

86. Ise, *Our National Park Policy*, pp. 421-422.

87. National Academy of Sciences, Highway Research Board, "Scenic Easements: Legal, Administrative, and Valuation Problems and Procedures" (Washington, D.C.: National Cooperative Highway Research Program Report No. 56, 1968), p. 10.

88. Ise, *Our National Park Policy*, pp. 467-469.

89. Ibid., p. 368.

90. Ibid.; Newton, *Design on the Land*, p. 589.

91. Newton, *Design on the Land*, pp. 577-595.

92. Ibid., pp. 549, 577-595.

93. Ise, *Our National Park Policy*, pp. 437-439.

94. Ibid., p. 425.

95. Ibid., pp. 519-520.

96. Library of Congress, Congressional Research Service, Environment and Natural Resources Policy Division, *Past Federal Surveys of Shoreline Recreation Potential*, Committee Print, 95th Cong., 2d sess., 1978, pp. 3-4.

97. National Park Service, *Index of the National Park System and Related Areas, 1982*, p. 10.

98. Congressional Research Service, *Past Federal Surveys of Shoreline Recreation Potential*, pp. 3-4.

99. Conservation Foundation staff interview with Bob Nash, Minute Man NHP, 1984.

100. John Hart, *San Francisco's Wilderness Next Door* (San Rafael, California: Presidio Press, 1979), pp. 46-48.

101. Conservation Foundation staff interview with Edie Shean-Hammond.

102. 16 U.S.C.A., §459e-1, §460u-3 (1974).

103. Hart, *San Francisco's Wilderness Next Door*, pp. 68-71.

104. U.S. Department of Commerce, Bureau of the Census, *Statistical Abstract of the United States, 1985* (Washington, D.C.: U.S. Government Printing Office, 1984), pp. 880-881; National Park Service, "Summary of Acreages."

105. Hart, *San Francisco's Wilderness Next Door*, p. 7.

106. 16 U.S.C.A., §2301-06 (Supp. 1985). The National Park Access Act of 1978 set up a three-year pilot program "to make the National Park System more accessible in a manner consistent with the preservation of parks and the conservation of energy." The act provided funds for mass transportation projects in the new urban parks at incresing levels: $1 million for FY79; $2 million for FY80; and $3 million for FY81. Unused money remained available until spent.

107. 16 U.S.C.A., §460bb-3 (Supp. 1985).

108. Information provided by Congressman Seiberling's office, 1984.

109. 16 U.S.C.A., §460ff-1(f) (Supp. 1985).

110. 16 U.S.C.A., §§410cc-31-33 (Supp. 1985).

111. 16 U.S.C.A., §410cc-24 (Supp. 1985).

112. Pinelands Commission, "The Pinelands of New Jersey," brochure, May 1982.

113. Ibid.

114. National Parks and Conservation Association, *Greenline Parks* (Washington, D.C.: National Parks and Conservation Association, 1983), p. 101.

115. National Park Service, "Summary of Acreages," tables, dated 1977-1980.

116. See figure 3.1 and accompanying notes.

117. 16 U.S.C.A., §1131(a) (1974).
118. Conservation Foundation staff interview with Clay Peters, Wilderness Society, 1985.
119. Environmental and Energy Study Institute, "Final Scorecard: Environmental, Energy and Natural Resources Legislation, Second Session, 98th Congress," *Weekly Bulletin*, October 11, 1984, pp. 12-13; Conservation Foundation staff interview with Ed Bloedel, U.S. Forest Service, Wilderness Management, 1984.
120. 16 U.S.C.A., §1133 (1974); National Park Service, *Index of the National Park System and Related Areas, 1982*, pp. 8-9.
121. Nash, *Wilderness and the American Mind*, p. 222.
122. William C. Tweed, "Parkitecture: Rustic Architecture in the National Parks" (unpublished, undated).
123. Everhart, *The National Park Service*, p. 98; Nash, *Wilderness and the American Mind*, p. 226.
124. 16 U.S.C.A., §1241 et seq., §1271 et seq. (1974).
125. Conservation Foundation staff interview with Edward Chidlaw, outdoor recreation planner, National Park Service, 1984.
126. Conservation Foundation staff interview with Bob Karotko, WASO, Trails Coordinator, 1984.
127. Conservation Foundation staff interview with Charles Rinaldi, Land Acquisition Program Director, Appalachian National Scenic Trial, 1984.
128. Conservation Foundation staff interview with Bob Karotko.

**Figure 2.2. National Park Trends, 1960-1983**

*Visitation*. The table shows the total for all park visits and, from 1971 on, a separate figure for "recreational" visits. Until that time, all visits were lumped together, thereby making comparisons over time virtually impossible. The park service initiated this change in reporting to distinguish travel related to recreational enjoyment of the parks from routine travel by inholders who live within park boundaries or by commuters traveling on roads that cross a park.

*Staff*. This index is based on the number of permanent employees. Prior to 1982, when all federal agencies were required to adopt a different system for counting staff, the park service, like other federal agencies, provided information about "permanent" and "other" employees without clearly differentiating among those who were working full- or part-time. In general, permanent staff worked throughout the year, while the number of "other" personnel fluctuated seasonally. Some worked less than a year (hence the term *career seasonal* for these jobs), while a number of the "others" worked almost full-time, especially when, in the mid-1970s, ceilings on permanent jobs imposed by the Office of Management and Budget were especially stringent. The index in this figure is based on the total of "permanent" staff, because data for "other" employees are not available prior to 1970.

*Acreage*. Beginning in the 1960s, Congress has authorized considerably more acreage to be included in the park system than has been actually purchased or otherwise protected and made available as parkland. The chart shows authorized acreage.

## Chapter 3. The National Park Service

1. Robert Shankland, *Steve Mather of the National Parks* (New York: Alfred A. Knopf, 1970), pp. 243, 247.
2. William C. Everhart, *The National Park Service* (New York: Praeger Publishers, 1972), pp. 20-21.
3. William C. Everhart, *The National Park Service* (Boulder, Colo.: Westview Press, 1983), p. 18.
4. Everhart, *The National Park Service*, 1972, p. 21; U.S. Department of the Interior, National Park Service, "Report of the Director of the National Park Service to the Secretary of Interior for the Fiscal Year Ending June 30, 1917" (Washington, D.C.: U.S. Department of the Interior), p. 190.
5. Conservation Foundation staff interview with National Park Service staff, Personnel Office, Staffing Branch, 1984.
6. U.S. Department of the Interior, National Park Service, *National Park Statistical Abstract, 1983* (Denver: Denver Service Center, Statistical Office), p. 2.
7. Everhart, *The National Park Service*, 1983, pp. 19-20; Alfred Runte, *National Parks: The American Experience* (Lincoln, Nebr.: University of Nebraska Press, 1979), pp. 101-102; Norman T. Newton, *Design on the Land: The Development of Landscape Architecture* (Cambridge, Mass.: Belknap Press of Harvard University Press, 1971), pp. 531-534, 536.
8. Shankland, *Steve Mather of the National Parks*, pp. 57-59, 62-63, 73.
9. Ibid., p. 243.
10. Ibid., p. 249.
11. Rick Hydrick, "The Genesis of National Park Management: John Roberts White and Sequoia National Park, 1920-1947," *Journal of Forest History*, April 1984, p. 74.
12. *The Wall Street Journal*, November 18, 1983, p. 1.
13. Gary E. Machlis, Mark E. Van Every, and Donna K. Chickering, *Monitoring NPS Employee Attitudes: A Pilot Program for the Albright Training Center* (Moscow, Idaho: University of Idaho, Cooperative Park Studies Unit, undated), pp. 13, 28-29.
14. Ronald B. Taylor, "Rangers: Morale in Wild Wanes," *Los Angeles Times*, April 10, 1984, pp. 1, 14; Philip Shabecoff, "National Parks Face Threat from Civilization They Serve," *The New York Times*, July 30, 1984, p. 1; Machlis, Van Every and Chickering, *Monitoring NPS Employee Attitudes*, pp. 27-29.
15. This remark was made to Conservation Foundation staff during several different interviews with National Park Service staff.
16. U.S. Department of the Interior, National Park Service, "Potential Working Units," table, compiled by the Realignment Coordinating Committee, dated December 9, 1983.

17. U.S. Congress, House Committee on Appropriations, Subcommittee on the Department of Interior and Related Agencies, *Department of the Interior and Related Agencies Appropriations for 1983: Hearings,* Part II, 97th Cong., 2d sess., 1982, pp. 852-853.

18. Conservation Foundation staff interview with John Shrum, budget analyst, Department of the Interior, Office of the Budget, December 20, 1984. Figures are for total appropriations including operations, construction, acquisition, and maintenance. The park service 1984 appropriations were $994 million; the Department of the Interior 1984 appropriations were $6,624 million.

19. U.S. Department of the Interior, National Park Service, "Summary of Acreages," table, dated September 30, 1983; U.S. Department of the Interior, Bureau of Land Management, *Public Land Statistics, 1983* (Washington, D.C.: U.S. Government Printing Office, 1984).

20. National Park Service, "Potential Working Units."

21. U.S. Department of the Interior, National Park Service, *Departmental Manual, part 145,* cited in U.S. Congress, 98th Cong., 1st sess., U.S. House of Representatives, Committee on Insular and Interior Affairs, Subcommittee on Public Lands and National Parks, *Fiscal Year 1984 Budget Report for the National Park Service,* 98th Cong., 1st sess., 1983, p. 125.

22. Ibid., pp. 137-141.

23. "Park People Move from Central Offices to Parks," *Courier,* September 1983, pp. 14-16.

24. National Park Service, "Potential Working Units."

25. U.S. Department of the Interior, National Park Service, *Budget Justifications, F.Y. 1986* (Washington, D.C.: U.S. Government Printing Office), pp. NPS-109-97.

26. National Park Service, "Potential Working Units."

27. Ibid.

28. U.S. Department of the Interior, National Park Service, National Park Service Realignment Committee, "Realignment— Phase II, Management by Objective: Summary Report," dated January 6, 1984, p. 1.

29. Ibid., p. 4.

30. U.S. Department of the Interior, National Park Service, National Park Service Realignment Committee, "Phase II Report, Review of Cultural Resource Management Program," December 5, 1983, pp. 4, 7.

31. Richard Briceland, "Guest Editorial," *Park Service* Summer 1983, p 2. Reorganization of the Washington Office in 1983 abolished the Office of Science and Technology and created a new office of Natural Resources, under which the Air Quality Division and the Water Resources Division were combined into one office with two field units. In addition, the Energy, Mining and Minerals Division was formed by consolidating the energy, mining, and mineral interests within the service's new field component. Professional staff assigned to these three units consist almost entirely of physical and biological scientists—environmental specialists in air quality, hydrologists, mining engineers, petroleum engineers, and ecologists.

32. U.S. Department of the Interior, National Park Service, "Realignment—Phase II," support material for meeting, December 14-15, 1983.

33. National Park Service, "Realignment—Phase II: Summary Report," p. 25.

34. U.S. Department of Interior, National Park Service, *NPS Training Task Force Report*, undated, p. 23. Task force was appointed in November 1980 by the director.

35. Conservation Foundation staff interviews with National Park Service staff.

36. Coopers & Lybrand, *Management Improvement Project, Phase I Report: Management Review and Assessment*, prepared for U.S. Department of the Interior, National Park Service, November 1977, pp. I-144 to I-500.

37. See, for example, Heritage Foundation, *Mandate for Leadership* (Washington, D.C.: Heritage Foundation, 1981), which helped form much of the early thinking of the Reagan administration.

38. Everhart, *The National Park Service*, 1983, pp. 28-29.

39. Ibid., pp. 150-155.

40. Conservation Foundation staff interviews with National Park Service staff.

41. Ric Davidge, "Trends in the National Park System," (Washington, D.C.: U.S. Department of the Interior, Office of the Assistant Secretary for Fish and Wildlife and Parks, draft, 1983) p. 29; Conservation Foundtion staff interviews with National Park Service staff, Personnel Office, Staffing Branch, 1984.

42. U.S. Congress, *Department of the Interior and Related Agencies Appropriations for 1983: Hearings*, Part II, p. 852.

43. Horace M. Albright and Frank J. Taylor, *Oh Ranger: A Book About the National Parks* (New York: Dodd Mead & Co., 1946), p. 8.

44. U.S. Department of the Interior, National Park Service, "Bureau-Wide Summary of Occupation Codes," tables, as of January 7, 1984, pp. 41, 322.

45. Albright and Taylor, *Oh Ranger*, p. 17.

46. Conservation Foundation staff interview with Maureen Finnerty, president of the National Association of Rangers, and assistant superintendent of Everglades NP, December 11, 1984.

47. Conservation Foundation staff interview with Flip Hagood, chief, National Park Service, Training Division, December 12, 1984.

48. See, for example, U.S. Department of the Interior, National Park Service, Office of Media Affairs, *Courier*, Special Issues: *Training Opportunities*, October 1978, Fall 1981, Fall 1982, and Fall 1983.

49. Roland H. Wauer, "Natural Resources Management—Trend or Fad?" *The George Wright Forum* 4(1) (1984), p. 24.

50. Conservation Foundation staff interviews with National Park Service staff.

51. Wauer, "Natural Resources Management—Trend or Fad?" p. 24.

52. Stanley T. Albright, "Remarks" (Paper delivered at the Association of National Park Rangers, Las Vegas, Nevada, October 1983), p. 17.

53. Ibid., p. 17.

54. John McPhee. "Profiles: George Hartzog," *The New Yorker*, September 11, 1971, p. 62.

55. U.S. Department of the Interior, National Park Service, "Assistant Superintendents and Management Assistants" (Memo produced by the

Realignment Coordinating Committee, March 24, 1983).

56. Conservation Foundation staff interviews with National Park Service staff, Personnel Office, Staffing Branch, 1985.

57. National Park Service, "Assistant Superintendents and Management Assistants."

58. Hydrick, "The Genesis of National Park Management," pp. 74-75.

59. Conservation Foundation staff interview with Lewis Albert, then superintendent of Lowell NHP, 1981.

60. Conservation Foundation staff interview with Robert D. Barbee, then superintendent of Redwood NP, 1983.

61. "Park People Move from Central Offices to Parks," pp. 14-16.

62. Albright, "Remarks," p. 18.

63. National Park Service, "Bureau-Wide Summary of Occupation Codes," pp. 42, 322.

64. Conservation Foundation staff interviews with National Park Service staff.

65. Conservation Foundation staff interviews with National Park Service staff, Personnel Office, Staffing Branch, 1985.

66. National Park Service, "Bureau-Wide Summary of Occupation Codes," pp. 41-42.

67. Conservation Foundation staff interview with Michael Finley, Assateague NS, 1982.

68. Conservation Foundation staff interview with Maureen Finnerty, president of the National Association of Rangers, and assistant superintendent, Everglades NP, 1984.

69. Conservation Foundation staff interviews with Michael Finley, Assateague NS, 1982; Flip Hagood, chief, National Park Service, Training Division, 1984; and Maureen Finnerty, president of National Association of Rangers, and assistant superintendent, Everglades NP, 1984.

70. William Tweed, "Parkitecture: Rustic Architecture in the National Parks" (unpublished, undated), p. 28.

71. See, for example, U.S. Department of the Interior, National Park Service, *State of the Parks 1980: A Report to the Congress* (Washington, D.C.: U.S. Government Printing Office, 1980), p. ix-x; U.S. Department of the Interior, National Park Service, "Threats to Cultural Resources," 1982, pp. 1-2, 22; Wauer, "Natural Resources Management—Trends or Fad?" pp. 26-28.

72. Conservation Foundation staff interview with Mark Ruskin, chief scientist, Indiana Dunes NL, 1982.

73. Conservation Foundation staff interview with Dale Lazone, assistant to the deputy director, National Park Service, 1984.

74. Conservation Foundation staff interview with Robert Sampsell and Harry Trimble, park rangers, Assateague NS, 1982.

75. Captain Robert E. Langston, "U.S. Park Police Meet Urban Challenges," *Trends* 16(4), 1979, pp. 25-27; Major Jack M. Sands, "Background of the U.S. Park Police," *Trends* 16(4), 1979, p. 27.

76. See U.S. Department of the Interior, National Park Service, Division of Ranger Activities and Protection, "Parks Reporting a Minimum of 400 Part II Offenses—1979," table, dated June 5, 1980; U.S. Department of

the Interior, National Park Service, *National Park Statistical Abstract 1980* (Denver: Denver Service Center, Statistical Office).

77. Conservation Foundation staff interview with National Park Service staff, Yellowstone NP, 1983.

78. Conservation Foundation staff interview with Mary Gibson Park, Santa Monica Mountains NRA, 1983.

79. U.S. Department of the Interior, National Park Service, "Occupational Listing (EEO), Servicewide, as of FY 84," dated October 1, 1983.

80. U.S. Department of the Interior, National Park Service. "Workforce Profile by Pay Systems, Bureau Total Employment," dated September 30, 1982, p. 590.

81. U.S. Department of the Interior, National Park Service, "Workforce Profile Occupation Series, Permanent," dated October 1, 1983, p. 482.

## Visitation and the Data Dilemma

1. U.S. Department of the Interior, National Park Service, *National Park Statistical Abstract, 1983* (Denver: Denver Service Center, Statistical Office, 1984), p. 38.

2. A. Galipeau, "Changes in National Park Service Visitation Volume 1971-1981," p. 1.

3. Conservation Foundation staff interview with Kenneth Hornbeck, chief, Denver Statistical Office, National Park Service, 1983. In recent years, the service's Denver Statistical Office has implemented auditing procedures that have attempted to improve and further standardize visitation counting procedures.

4. Some trends are captured by measuring the number of overnight stays in trailer camps, backcountry camping areas, and the like. See, for example, National Park Service, *National Park Statistical Abstract, 1983*, p. 35.

5. "Visitation Census," *Park Service*, Spring 1984, p. 21. The recent approval by the Office of Management and Budget for a park service survey to obtain more information about park visitors may yield better data to assist in park management.

## Figure 3.2. Allocation of National Park Service Personnel, May 1, 1984

1. The totals refer to actual personnel, not full-time equivalents, working for the National Park Service as of May 1, 1984. The Chaco, Midwest, and Southeast archeological centers, the Western Archeology and Conservation Center, the North Atlantic Preservation Center, and the Cooperative Park Studies units are counted in regional totals. Staff assigned to the Energy, Mining and Minerals Field Unit, the Air Quality Field Unit, and the Water Resources Field Unit are counted in WASO totals.

2. Job series have been clustered as follows:

*Ranger/park manager.*

*Ranger/technician.*

*Landscape architect/planners*: landscape architect; outdoor recreation; planner; recreation; recreation planner; recreation technician.

*Construction and development personnel (architects and engineers)*: architect; civil engineering; construction; electrical engineering; electronics engineering; engineer technician; engineering and architecture trainee; engineering drafting; environmental engineering; general engineering; mechanical engineering; safety engineering; survey technician.

*Exhibits and publications personnel*: audio-visual production; cartographic technician; cartography; editorial assistance; education and training technician; education and vocations; exhibits specialist; general arts and information; illustration; language specialist; music specialist; photography; printing management; technical information services; technical writing/editing; theater specialist; visual information; writing and editing.

*Physical scientists*: biological sciences; environmental protection assistant; environmental protection specialist; geology; hydrologic technician; hydrology; general physical science; oceanography; physical science technician; physics.

*Historians, social scientists, and museum specialists*: anthropology; archeology; archivist; archivist technician; economist; geography; historian; librarian; library technician; museum curator; museum specialist/technician; social science; social science aid and technician; social services aid and assistant; sociology.

*Acquisitions and concessions personnel*: appraising and assessing; general business and industry; housing management; land surveying; property disposal clerical and technician; realty.

*Maintenance and labor personnel*: ammunition, explosives, and toxic materials work; electrical installation and maintenance; electronic equipment installation and maintenance; fabric and leather work; facility management; food preparation and serving; general equipment maintenance; general facilities and equipment; general maintenance and operations work; general services and support work; industrial equipment maintenance; industrial equipment operation; instrument work; laundry, drycleaning, pressing; lens and crystal work; machine tool work; metal processing; metal work; motion picture, radio, television and sound equipment operation; ornamental work; packing and processing; painting and paperhanging; personal services; plant and animal work; pliable materials work; plumbing and pipefitting; printing; structural and finishing work; transportation/mobile equipment maintenance; transportation/mobile equipment operation; warehousing and stock handling; woodwork; miscellaneous occupations.

*Administration personnel*: accounting and budget; civil rights analysis; contract and procurement; distribution facilities and storage management; financial analysis; general administrative, clerical, and office services; general supply; inventory management; operations research; personnel management and industrial relations; procurement clerical and assistance; property disposal; purchasing; safety and occupational health management; safety technician; statistician; statistical assistant; supply clearial and technician; supply program management; transportation.

*Public relations personnel*: public affairs; public information.

*Security personnel*: guard; fire protection and prevention; police.

*Miscellaneous*: desk officer; investigation; legal; medical, hospital, dental, and public health; seaman; trade specialist.

3. Included in this group are approximately 80 historical architects. Of these, about 15 are assigned to parks, 25 to regional offices, 35 to the Denver Service Center, and 5 to WASO. A number of historical architects in the regions and WASO also have "external" responsiblities for historic preservation—that is, they administer programs such as the National Register of Historic Places, the Historic American Buildings Survey, the preservation tax credit programs, and the section-106 review process, which involves historic properties owned by federal agencies (other than the park service), state and local governments, and private persons.

4. Fourteen additional people were working on the park staff as of May 1984, but they were not classified.

Source: U.S. Department of the Interior, National Park Service, Branch of Employee Evaluation and Staffing.

## Profile. Fredericksburg and Spotsylvania National Military Park

1. Conservation Foundation staff interview with National Park Service staff, Fredericksburg and Spotsylvania County Battlefields Memorial NMP, 1983.

2. Information provided by Larry James, Fredericksburg and Spotsylvania County Battlefields Memorial NMP, 1985; quote attributed to Schulyler O. Bland, in a hearing before the 69th Congress, February 28, 1926.

3. Information provided by Larry James; quote from General L.A. Grant in "Wilderness Campaign," *Papers of the Military Historical Society of Massachusetts* 4 (1905).

4. U.S. Department of the Interior, National Park Service, *Public Use of the National Parks: A Statistical Report 1971-1980*; and *National Park Statistical Abstract, 1983* (Denver: Denver Service Center, Statistical Office), p. 2.

5. Conservation Foundation staff interview with Larry James, 1985.

6. U.S. Department of the Interior, National Park Service,   brochure entitled "Old Salem Church"; quote is from an eyewitness account of Salem Church as a field hospital.

## Chapter 4. Stewardship of Park Resources

1. Gary R. Gregory, "Natural Resources Management in the Parks—An Explosion of Complexities," *Trends* 19(1), 1982, p. 40.

2. David M. Graber, "Rationalizing Management of Natural Areas in National Parks," *The George Wright Forum*, Autumn 1983, p. 49; Alston Chase, "The Last Bears of Yellowstone," *The Atlantic Monthly* February 1983, p. 65.

3. George M. Wright, Joseph S. Dixon and Ben H. Thompson, *A Preliminary Survey of Faunal Relations in National Parks*. Fauna Series No. 1 (Washington, D.C.: U.S. Government Printing Office, 1933), p. 147.
4. Ibid., pp. 147-48.
5. Lowell Sumner, "Biological Research and Management in the National Park Service: A History," *The George Wright Forum*, Autumn 1983, p. 18.
6. Gary Blonston, "Where Nature Takes Its Course," *Science 83*, November 1983, pp. 45, 48; U.S. Department of the Interior, Advisory Board on Wildlife Management (chaired by A. Starker Leopold), "Wildlife Management in the National Parks," report, dated March 4, 1963, p. 17.
7. Conservation Foundation staff interview with Robert Barbee, superintendent, Yellowstone NP, 1983.
8. Advisory Board on Wildlife Management, "Wildlife Management in the National Parks," p. 9.
9. Ibid., pp. 2,4,9.
10. Ibid., pp. 5-6,9.
11. F. Fraser Darling and Noel D. Eichhorn, *Man and Nature in the National Parks* (Washington, D.C.: The Conservation Foundation, 1971).
12. Memorandum from Stuart L. Udall, secretary of the interior, to George B. Hartzog, Jr., Director of the National Park Service, July 10, 1964, in U.S. Department of the Interior, National Park Service, *Administrative Policies for Historical Areas of the National Park Service* (Washington, D.C.: U.S. Government Printing Office, 1964 (revised 1973), p. 90; U.S. Department of the Interior, National Park Service, *Management Policies* (Washington, D.C.: U.S. Government Printing Office, 1978), p. IV-1.
13. Advisory Board on Wildlife Management, "Wildlife Mangement in the Natural Parks," pp. 5.
14. H.J. Cortner, M.J. Zwolinski, E.H. Carpenter and J.G. Taylor, "Public Support for Fire Management Policies," *Journal of Forestry*, June 1984, pp. 359-361.
15. Paul Godfrey, "Barrier Beaches: Special Management Problems," *The George Wright Forum*, Autumn 1982, p. 12; The Conservation Foundation, *State of the Environment*, (Washington, D.C.: The Conservation Foundation, 1982), p. 306.
16. Godfrey, "Barrier Beaches: Special Management Problems," p. 14.
17. National Park Service, *Management Policies*, p. IV-22.
18. U.S. Department of the Interior, National Park Service, *Indiana Dunes National Lakeshore Resources Management Plan and Environmental Assessment*, 1983; and *Gateway National Recreation Area Resources Management Plan*, 1981; Conservation Foundation staff interview with Larry May, assistant superintendent, Indiana Dunes NL, 1985; Information provided by the National Park Service.
19. Paul Schullery, "Securing the Grizzly's Small Portion," *National Parks*, July-August 1984, p. 29. The December 5, 1983 report of the task force appointed by the Interagency Grizzly Bear Committee recommended against supplemental feeding, pointing out that if human-caused mor-

talitites were kept low bears could maintain their numbers in Yellowstone area as did for hundreds of years before dumps. They felt that supplemental feeding was not a cure-all/substitute for proper managemnt of habitat and human activities inside/outside Yellowstone.

20. Godfrey, "Barrier Beaches: Special Management Problems," p. 16.
21. Louis E. Reid and Donald W. Humphrey, "Planning for Cultural Properties in the National Park System," *Trends* 20(2), 1983, p. 3; Conservation Foundation staff interview with Randy Biallus, Assistant Chief Historical Architect, National Park Service, 1984.
22. Reid and Humphrey, "Planning for Cultural Properties in the National Park System," p. 4; U.S. Department of the Interior, National Park Service, "Threats to Cultural Resources," report, dated January 1982.
23. 16 U.S.C., §1 (1974).
24. Executive Order No. 11593, "Protection and Enhancement of the Cultural Environment," May 13, 1971; see 36 Fed. Reg. 5921 (1971).
25. U.S. Department of the Interior, National Park Service, *Administrative Policies for Historical Areas of the National Park System*, pp. 19-20; Information provided by Jerry Rogers, Associate Director for Cultural Resources, National Park Service, 1985.
26. William C. Everhart, *The National Park Service* (Boulder, Col.: Westview Press, 1983), pp. 21-22.
27. Conservation Foundation staff interview with Doug Nadeau, Chief, Park Planning and Resources Management, Golden Gate National Recreation Area, 1983.
28. U.S. Congress, House Committee on Appropriations, Subcommittee on the Department of the Interior and Related Agencies, *Department of the Interior and Related Agencies Appropriations for 1985: Hearings*, Part 6, 98th Cong., 2d sess., 1984, pp. 247, 463; U.S. Department of the Interior, National Park Service, Budget Division, "Park Restoration and Improvement Program, Fiscal Year 1982 Accomplishment Report," dated December 1982; Conservation Foundation staff interviews with National Park Service staff, Golden Gate National Recreation Area.
29. National Park Service, "Threats to Cultural Resources," pp. 8-9, 15-18.
30. National Park Service, *Administrative Policies for Historical Areas of the National Park System*, p. 25.
31. U.S. Department of the Interior, National Park Service, *State of the Parks 1980: A Report to the Congress* (Washington, D.C.: U.S. Government Printing Office, 1980), p. 3.
32. Ibid., pp. 5-6.
33. U.S. Congress, House Committee on Interior and Insular Affairs, Subcommittee on Public Lands and National Parks, *Public Land Management Policy: Hearings*, Part III, 97th Cong., 2d sess., 1982, p. 3.
34. National Park Service, "Threats to Cultural Resources," pp. 4-6, 17-18.
35. Conservation Foundation staff interview with Ann Hitchock, Chief Curator, Branch of Curatorial Services, National Park Service, 1984; Conservation Foundation staff interview with Jerry Rogers, Associate Director, Cultural Resources, 1983.

36. Ann Webster Smith, "Remarks to National Park Service Supervisors,"
    (Paper presented at meeting of Park Service Supervisors, North Atlan-
    tic Region, Saratoga Springs, New York, November 4, 1982), p. 19.
37. National Park Service, *State of the Parks 1980*, p. 6. Three-fourths of
    the threats reported need research to document them adequately; Robert
    Cahn, "The National Park System: The People, the Parks, the Politics,"
    *Sierra*, May-June 1983, p. 50.
38. Robert Cahn, "The Conservation Challenge of the 80s," p. 11, in Eugenia
    Connally, ed. *National Parks in Crisis* (Washington, D.C.: National Parks
    and Conservation Association, 1982).
39. National Park Service, *State of the Parks 1980*, p. 20.
40. Norman T. Newton, *Design on the Land: The Development of Landscape
    Architecture* (Cambridge, Mass.: Belknap Press of the Harvard Univer-
    sity Press, 1971), p. 554.
41. Conservation Foundation staff interview with Ross Holland, then assis-
    tant director, Cultural Resources, National Park Service, January 22,
    1982; Conservation Foundation field visits to Gettysburg National
    Military Park and San Antonio Missions National Historical Park; and
    U.S. Department of the Interior, National Park Service, "State of the
    Parks: A Report to the Congress on a Servicewide Strategy for Preven-
    tion and Mitigation of Natural and Cultural Resources Management Prob-
    lems," 1981, p. 78.
42. Executive Order No. 11989, an amendment to Executive Order No. 11644,
    "Use of Off-Road Vehicles on Public Lands," May 24, 1977; see 42 Fed.
    Reg. 26959 (1977).
43. See, for example, U.S. Department of the Interior, National Park Ser-
    vice, "Summary of Natural Resource SRP [Significant Resource Prob-
    lems] Priorities," memo dated 1981. SRP A-7: ORV Plan Implementa-
    tion at CCNS. *Conservation Law Foundation v. Clark*, No. 81-1004-N
    (D. Mass. June 27, 1984).
44. Cahn, "The National Park System: The People, the Parks, the Politics,"
    p. 54.
45. "Snow Goer's National Parks Winter Fun Guide," *Snow Goer*, September
    1982, pp. 29-36.
46. Jim Moody, "The Snag in Park Trapping," *National Parks*, March-April
    1984, p. 17.
47. *Federal Parks and Recreation*, May 3, 1984, pp. 1-2; U.S. Department
    of the Interior, National Park Service, "News Release," May 1, 1984.
    These regulations impose a prohibition on trapping in 11 areas of NPS
    where it had been a traditional activity but not one specifically authorized
    in laws establishing the unit.
48. *Land Use Planning Report*, May 7, 1984, p. 144; *Federal Parks and
    Recreation*, January 17, 1985, p. 7.
49. *Land Use Planning Report*, May 7, 1984, p. 144.
50. Chuck Williams, "The Park Rebellion," *Not Man Apart*, June 1982, p.
    4; Cahn, "The National Park System: The People, the Parks, the
    Politics," p. 49.

51. Conservation Foundation staff field visit to Cuyahoga Valley NRA, 1984; U.S. Congress, House Committee on Interior and Insular Affairs, Subcommittee on Public Lands and National Parks, *Land Acquisition Policy and Program of the National Park Service*, Committee Print No. 7, 98th Cong., 2d sess., 1984, p. 21; "The Land and Water Conservation Fund: The Conservation Alternative for Fiscal Year 1985," jointly produced by the American Rivers Conservation Council, Defenders of Wildlife, Friends of the Earth, Izaak Walton League, National Audubon Society, National Parks and Conservation Association, National Recreation and Parks Association, National Wildlife Federation, Sierra Club, Trust for Public Land and The Wilderness Society, undated, p. 13.

52. Thomas Lucke, "Letter to the Editor," *Journal of Forestry History*, January 1984, p. 45.

53. Ibid.

54. U.S. Congress, House Committee on Appropriations, Subcommittee on the Department of the Interior and Related Agencies, *Department of the Interior and Related Agencies Appropriations for 1984: Hearings*, Part 6, 98th Cong., 1st sess., 1983, p. 39.

55. 30 U.S.C.A., §1272 (Supp. 1985).

56. Charles W. Wood and Daniel Hamson, "Minerals Management," *Trends* 19(1), 1982, p. 31.

57. Conservation Foundation staff interview with William Supernaugh, Wildlife Biologist, National Park Service, 1983.

58. National Park Service, "State of the Parks: A Report to the Congress on a Servicewide Strategy for Prevention and Mitigation of Natural and Cultural Resources Management Problems," p. 13.

59. Advisory Board on Wildlife Management, "Wildlife Management in the National Parks," p. 3; Jim Robbins, "Do Not Feed the Bears?" *Natural History*, January 1984, p. 16.

60. Candace Garry, "Bats to Bighorns, Salamanders to Sea Turtles," *National Parks*, July 1983, p. 11.

61. Christine Schonewald-Cox, "Guidelines to Management: A Beginning Attempt," p. 420, in Christine Schonewald-Cox et. al., ed., *Genetics and Conservation: A Reference for Managing Wild Animal and Plant Populations* (Menlo Park, California: Benjamin/Cummings Publishing Company, 1983); Garry, "Bats to Bighorns, Salamanders to Sea Turtles," p. 10; Christine Schonewald-Cox, "Wildlife Population Management," *Trends* 19(1), 1982, pp. 22-23.

62. A.R. Weisbrod, "On the Biology and Management of Species Threatened with Extinction," *Trends*, 19(1), 1982, pp. 17, 19; Kim Heacox, "Contested Waters," *National Parks*, July-August 1984, pp. 25-26; U.S. Department of the Interior, National Park Service, "Summary of Natural Resource SRP Priorities," SRP B-1: Humpback Whales at Glacier Bay National Monument.

63. Weisbrod, "On the Biology and Management of Species Threatened with Extinction," p. 20.

64. Cahn, "The Conservation Challenge of the 80s," p. 14.

65. Mary Maruca, "Acid Rain: The Unknown Ingredient," Trends 20(2), 1983, p. 32.

66. U.S. Department of the Interior, National Park Service, Mammoth Cave National Park Resource Management Plan and Environmental Assessment, Natural and Cultural Resources, 1982, pp. I-2 - I-3.

67. National Park Service, "Summary of Natural Resource SRP Priorities," SRP C-9: Lake Water Quality at Crater Lake National Park.

68. Ibid., SRP C-1: Water Quality at Cape Hatteras National Seashore; SRP C-16: Water Quality at New River Gorge National Park.

69. National Park Service, "State of the Parks: A Report to the Congress on a Servicewide Strategy for Prevention and Mitigation of Natural and Cultural Resources Management Problems," p. 51.

70. National Park Service, State of the Parks 1980, p. 9.

71. U.S. Department of the Interior, National Park Service, "State of the Parks: A Report to the Congress on a Servicewide Strategy for Prevention and Mitigation of Natural and Cultural Resources Management Problems," pp. 57, 71; Joseph Priest, "Attacking the National Parks from Within," National Parks and Conservation Magazine, September 1980, p. 9; Bruce Hamilton, "Geothermal Energy: Trouble Brews for the National Parks," Sierra, July-August 1983, p. 21. An interesting twist to the issue of intrusive development threatening park values occurs at Glacier Bay in Alaska. The Park Service wants to move its administrative facilities outside park boundaries, but the neighboring community of Gustavus objects that this will interfere with their desire to maintan a traditional lifestyle.

72. U.S. Department of the Interior, National Park Service, "PRIP Natural Resources Monies FY84," undated.

73. Monica Goigel and Susan Bratton, "Exotics in the Parks," National Parks, January-February 1983, p. 26; National Park Service, "State of the Parks: A Report to the Congress on a Servicewide Strategy for Prevention and Mitigation of Natural and Cultural Resources Management Problems," p. 75.

74. Even as far back as the 1960s, questions were being raised about the management of exotics. See, for example, Darling and Eichhorn, Man and Nature in the National Parks.

75. Federal Parks and Recreation, January 31, 1985, pp. 9-10; National Parks and Conservation Association, "Adjacent Lands Survey: No Park Is an Island," National Parks and Conservation Magazine, March 1979, pp. 4-9; U.S. Department of the Interior, National Park Service, Craters of the Moon National Monument Resources Management Plan and Environmental Assessment, 1982, p. 15; National Park Service, "State of the Parks: A Report to the Congress on a Servicewide Strategy for Prevention and Mitigation of Natural and Cultural Resources Management Problems," pp. 75-76.

76. Philip Burton and Keith Sebelius, Chairman and Ranking Minority Member, Subcommittee on National Parks and Insular Affairs, letter to Russell E. Dickenson, director, National Park Service, July 1, 1980, in

U.S. Congress, *Public Land Management Policy: Hearings*, Part III, pp. 552-554.

77. U.S. Department of the Interior, National Park Service, *Budget Justifications, Fiscal Year 1982*, p. NPS-8; and *Budget Justifications, Fiscal Year 1985*, p. NPS-66. The budget for Resource Management was $48,538,000 in 1980 and $92,987,000 in 1984. In constant dollars this represents a 46 percent increase.

78. U.S. Department of the Interior, National Park Service, "Resource Management Plans Status, as of March 15, 1984."

79. Everhart, *The National Park Service*, p. 27.

80. U.S. Congress, *Department of the Interior and Related Agencies Appropriations for 1985: Hearings*, Part 6, pp. 246-247.

81. Conservation Foundation staff interview with Richard Briceland, associate director, Natural Resources, National Park Service, 1983.

82. Philip Burton and Keith Sebelius, Chairman and Ranking Minority Member, Subcommittee on National Parks and Insular Affairs; letter to William Whalen, director, National Park Service, July 10, 1979, in U.S. Congress, *Public Land Management Policy: Hearings*, Part III, pp. 539-541; Keith Sebelius, Ranking Minority Member, Committee on National Parks and Insular Affairs, letter to William Whalen, director, National Park Service, April 16, 1980, in U.S. Congress, *Public Land Management Policy: Hearings*, Part III, pp. 545-546.

83. Conservation Foundation staff interview with Richard Briceland, Associate Director, Natural Resources, National Park Service, 1983.

84. Ibid.

85. Information provided by Richard Briceland, Associate Director, Natural Resources, National Park Service, 1985.

86. U.S. Department of the Interior, "Summary of Natural Resource SRP Priorities," SRP A-1: Feral Goats/Pigs at Haleakala NP; SRP A-3: Pig control at Hawaii Volcanoes NP; SRP A-5: Burro Removal at Death Valley NM; SRP A-12: Rabbit Eradication at Channel Islands NP; SRP A-4: Goat Management at Olympic ND.

87. National Park Service, *Budget Justifications, Fiscal year 1985*, p. NPS-70; Conservation Foundation staff interviews with National Park Service staff, Cultural Resources Division, 1984; U.S. Department of the Interior, National Park Service, Budget Division, "Park Restoration and Improvement Program Accomplishment Report Fiscal Year 1983," dated January 13, 1984.

88. U.S. Department of the Interior, National Park Service, "Fiscal Year 1984 SRP Funding," dated October 31, 1983.

89. *Ibid.*

90. U.S. Department of the Interior, National Park Service, "Resource Management Program Analysis and Planning Guidelines," dated December 1980, p. 1; and "Natural Resource Budget Formulation Guide," dated February 1984, p. 1.

91. National Park Service, "Resource Management Plans Status, as of March 15, 1984."

92. U.S. Department of the Interior, National Park Service, *National Park Service Realignment—Phase II*, support material for meeting December 14-15, 1983, Washington, D.C.

93. *Park Science*, Spring 1984.

94. Park Science, Spring 1984.

95. National Park Service, "State of the Parks: A Report to the Congress for Prevention and Mitigation of Natural and Cultural Resources Management Problems," p. 15.

96. National Park Service, "Threats to Cultural Resources," pp. 3-4.

97. Conservation Foundation staff interviews with National Park Service staff, Cultural Resources Division, 1984.

98. National Park Service, *Budget Justifications, Fiscal Year 1985*, p. NPS-75.

99. U.S. Department of the Interior, National Park Service, "FY84 SRP Funding," and "Attachment A: List of Significant Natural Resource Problems, by region," dated October 31, 1983.

100. National Academy of Sciences, *Grazing Phaseout at Capitol Reef National Park*, Phase I: *Final Report* (Washington, D.C.: National Academy Press, 1984), pp. 1,38.

101. Information provided by Richard Briceland, Associate Director, Natural Resources, National Park Service, 1985.

102. Ibid.

103. Conservation Foundation staff interviews with Richard Briceland, Associate Director, Natural Resources, 1983, 1985.

104. Conservation Foundation staff interviews with National Park Service staff, 1983.

105. Conservation Foundation staff interviews with National Park Service staff, 1984; see also U.S. Department of the Interior, National Park Service, *Federal Recreation Fee Report, 1983*, 1984.

106. 42 U.S.C.A., §7491 (1983). Section 169A established, as a national goal, the prevention of any future, and the remedying of any existing, impairment of visibility in mandatory class I federal areas where impairment results from manmade air pollution.

107. Conservation Foundation staff interview with David Sharrow, water specialist, Grand Canyon NP, 1984; 16 U.S.C.A., §222 (Supp. 1985).

108. Conservation Foundation staff interview with National Park Service staff, Fredericksburg and Spotsylvania County Battlefields Memorial NMP, 1984.

109. Information provided by Willis Kriz, chief, Land Resources Division, National Park Service, 1985.

110. U.S. Congress, *Public Land Management Policy: Hearings*, Part III, p. 440.

111. Cahn, "The Conservation Challenge of the 80s," p. 14; M.D. Williams and D.H. Nochumson, "Statistical Exploration of the Effects of Copper Smelter Emissions on Visibility in Southwestern National Parks" (Paper delivered at the 77th Annual Meeting of the Air Pollution Control Association, San Francisco, June 24-29, 1984), p. 2.

112. Marga Raskin, "Smog Alert for our Southwestern National Parks," *Na-*

*tional Parks and Conservation Magazine*, July 1975, p. 9; Gus Speth, "The Sisyphus Syndrome: Acid Rain and Public Responsibility," *National Parks and Conservation Magazine*, February 1980, p. 13; Williams and Nochumson, "Statistical Exploration of the Effects of Copper Smelter Emissions on Visibility in Southwestern National Parks," p. 2; Terri Martin, "The Greying of the National Parks," *National Parks*, September-October 1981, p. 23.

113. Conservation Foundation staff interview with Robert Heyder, superintendent, Mesa Verde NP, 1981.

114. Gary Gregory, "State of the Parks 1980: Problems and Plans," p. 89.

115. U.S. Department of the Interior, National Park Service, *Mt. Rainier National Park Resource Management Plan and Environmental Assessment*, 1984, p. 102-3.

116. Robbins, "Do Not Feed the Bears?" p. 19; Blonston, "Where Nature Takes Its Course," p. 54.

117. U.S. Congress, *Public Land Management Policy: Hearings* Part III, p. 440; Conservation Foundation staff interview with Terri Martin, National Parks and Conservation Association, 1984.

118. U.S. Congress, *Public Land Management Policy: Hearings*, Part III, p. 440; Conservation Foundation staff interview with David Reynolds, resource manager, New River Gorge NR, 1984.

119. National Park System Protection and Resources Management Act of 1983," H.R. 2379, 98th Cong., 1st sess., October 6 (legislative day October 3), 1984, pp. 12, 14, 16.

120. "Wildlife and the Parks Act of 1984," Chaffee Amendment No. 2807, *Congressional Record-Senate*, Vol. 130, No. 33, 98th Cong., 2d sess., March 20, 1984.

121. 16 U.S.C.A., §1536 (Supp. 1985); Fred Bosselman, "New Mechanisms for Dissolving Disputes in Federal Environmental Law," *Urban Land*, July 1983, pp. 34-35. This recent amendment to the ESA was based on the process which had been used to resolve a controversy over development of San Bruno Mountain in California, habitat for the endangered Mission Blue Butterfly.

122. Winston Harrington and Anthony Fisher, "Endangered Species," in Paul Portney, ed., *Current Issues in Natural Resources Policy* (Washington, D.C.: Resources for the Future, 1982), pp. 136-137.

123. U.S.C.A., §1456 (1974).

124. 16 U.S.C.A., §470f (1974).

125. 3 PLR 1016, March 1984.

126. 16 U.S.C.A., §3501-10 (Supp. 1985); Ronald Reagan, Press Release on Coastal Barrier Resources Act, October 18, 1982.

127. Reagan, Press Release on Coastal Barrier Resources Act, October 18, 1982.

128. 16 U.S.C.A., §796 (Supp. 1985).

129. Joseph Sax, "Helpless Grants: The National Parks and the Regulation of Private Lands," *Michigan Law Review* 75 (1976):262-263, 265-266.

130. "ATC/TATL Acquire Bears Den," *Trail Lands*, Summer 1984, p. 1.

131. 42 U.S.C.A., §7491 (1983).

132. 45 Fed. Reg. 80084 (1980).
133. 49 Fed. Reg. 42670 (1984).

**The Everglades**

1. Nelson M. Blake, *Land into Water-Water into Land: A History of Water Management in Florida* (Tallahassee, Florida: University Presses of Florida, 1980), pp. 95-100.
2. Kerry Gruson, "Flooding Poses Threat to Everglades Ecology," *The New York Times*, July 25, 1983, p. A10; Steven Yates, "Florida's Broken Rain Machine," *The Amicus Journal*, Fall 1982, p. 48.
3. Bill Belleville, "The Everglades: Headed for Death Before It is Ever Understood," *ENFO*, August 1983, p. 1.
4. "Save Our Everglades, Report Card No. 3," dated August 9, 1984; William R. Mangun, "Wetlands and Wildlife Resource Issues," *National Wetlands Newsletter*, November-December 1983, p. 8.
5. Keith Hansen, "A Trickle of Hope for the Everglades," *Environment*, June 1984, p. 16; Belleville, "The Everglades: Headed for Death Before It is Ever Understood," p. 4.
6. Belleville "The Everglades: Headed for Death Before it is Ever Understood," p. 2; Hansen, "A Trickle of Hope for the Everglades," p. 20.
7. Hansen, "A Trickle of Hope for the Everglades," p. 16.
8. Ibid., p. 17. In 1938, the Army Corps completed the present 38-foot dike around Lake Okeechobee as the first major step in flood control. In 1948, the Corps started the Central and Southern Florida Flood Control Project which entailed construction/improvement of 1400 miles of canal and levees, including the installation of tide gates, flood gates and huge pumps to drain potential farmland. The primary goals of this billion-dollar project were flood control, land development and aquifer protection.
9. Ibid, pp. 17-18.
10. Rose Mary Mechem, "In Florida, the Grass is No Longer Greener," *National Wildlife*, October-November 1982, p. 53.
11. Gruson, "Flooding Poses Threat to Everglades' Ecology," p. A10; Belleville, "The Everglades: Headed for Death Before It is Ever Understood," p. 2.
12. Hansen, "A Trickle of Hope for the Everglades," p. 41; P.C. Rosendahl and P.W. Rose, "Freshwater Flow Rates and Distribution within the Everglades Marsh," in *Proceedings of the National Symposium on Freshwater Inflow to Estuaries*, San Antonio, Texas, September 9-11, 1980. Because of much publicized water quantity problems of the 1960s, the U.S. Congress, through its committee on Public Works, subsequently guaranteed to the park a minimum annual delivery of 315,000 acre-ft/yr.
13. Hansen, "A Trickle of Hope for the Everglades," pp. 19,41.
14. Ibid., p. 18.
15. Belleville, "The Everglades: Headed for Death Before It is Ever Understood," p. 9.

16. Mechem, "In Florida, the Grass is No Longer Greener," p. 55.

17. Belleville, "The Everglades: Headed for Death Before It is Ever Understood," p. 9; Hansen, "A Trickle of Hope for the Everglades," p. 41.

18. Hansen, "A Trickle of Hope for the Everglades," p. 41.

19. Mechem, "In Florida, the Grass is No Longer Greener," p. 55; Yates, "Florida's Broken Rain Machine," p. 53.

20. "Save Our Everglades Report, Card No. 2," dated March 30, 1983.

21. Belleville, "The Everglades: Headed for Death Before It is Ever Understood," p. 3.

## Independence National Historical Park

1. Conservation Foundation staff interviews with National Park Service staff. Independence NHP, 1984.

2. Ibid, 1985.

3. Ibid, 1984.

4. Ibid, 1985.

5. Ibid.

## Inholdings

1. U.S. Department of the Interior, National Park Service, *Administrative Policies for Historic Areas of the National Park Service* (Washington, D.C.: U.S. Government Printing Office, 1964), p. 82.

2. Ibid., p. 86.

3. 43 Fed. Reg. 35752-35754 (1978); 44 Fed. Reg. 24792 (1979).

4. William C. Everhart, *The National Park Service* (Boulder, Colorado: Westview Press, 1983), p. 28.

5. 43 Fed. Reg. 35752-35754 (1978); 44 Fed. Reg. 24792 (1979).

6. 44 Fed. Reg. 24792 (1979).

7. 44 Fed. Reg. 24791 (1979).

8. 49 Fed. Reg. 86 (1983). On January 3, 1983, the park service withdrew its 1979 land acquisition policy and guidelines (44 Fed. Reg. 24790) and began preparation of land protection plans. These are prepared for each unit containing non-Federal land or interest in land within its authorized boundaries. Details of land protection plans can be found at 48 Fed. Reg. 21123 (1983).

9. Chuck Williams, "The Park Rebellion," *Not Man Apart*, June 1982, pp. 3-4.

# Profile. Cape Cod National Seashore

1. For a thorough discussion of the formation of Cape Cod National Seashore see, Francis P. Burling, *The Birth of the Cape Cod National Seashore* (Plymouth, Mass.: Leyden Press, 1978).

2. Ibid., p. 55.

3. Ibid., pp. 6-7.

4. Library of Congress, Congressional Research Service, Environment and

Natural Resources Policy Division, *Past Federal Surveys of Shoreline Recreation Potential*, Committee Print, 95th Cong., 2d sess., 1978, p. 4.

5. Conrad L. Wirth, *Parks, Politics, and the People* (Norman, Okla.: University of Oklahoma Press, 1980), p. 198; Conservation Foundation staff interview with National Park Service staff, Land Resources Division, 1984.

6. Conservation Foundation staff interview with Herbert Olsen, superintendent, Cape Cod NS, 1984.

7. Conservation Foundation staff interview with Peter Hart, chief ranger, Cape Cod NS, 1985.

8. *Sunday Cape Cod Times*, August 8, 1982.

9. *Conservation Law Foundation v. Clark*, No. 81-1004-N (D. Mass. June 27, 1984).

10. Conservation Foundation staff interviews with National Park Service staff, Cape Cod NS, 1984.

11. Ibid.

12. Conservation Foundation staff interviews with G. Franklin Ackerman, Chief of Interpretation, Cape Cod NS, 1983.

13. 16 U.S.C.A., §459b-6(b)(1) (1974).

14. Conservation Foundation staff interview with National Park Service staff, Cape Cod NS, 1983.

15. Charlotte E. Thomas, "The Cape Cod National Seashore: A Case Study of Federal Administrator Control Over Traditionally Local Land Use Decisions," accepted for publication in the *Boston College Environmental Affairs Law Review*; Ann L. Strong, "The Rise and Decline of an Urban Conscience: Urban Environments, Recreation, and Historic Preservation," (Paper delivered at the Conference on the Evolution of American Environmental Politics, Washington, D.C. June 28-29, 1984), pp. 38-40.

16. Conservation Foundation staff interview with Herbert Olsen, superintendent, Cape Cod NS, 1983.

17. Ibid.

18. Conservation Foundation staf interview with Joshua Nickerson, Advisory Commission member, 1982.

## Chapter 5. The Private Sector in the Parks

1. 16 U.S.C.A., §22 (1974).

2. Robert Shankland, *Steve Mather of the National Parks* (New York: Alfred A. Knopf, 1970), p. 115; John Ise, *Our National Park Policy: A Critical History* (Baltimore: John Hopkins Press, 1961), p. 32. Even as far back as the 1890s, nonprofit organizations were providing services to park users. The Sierra Club began leading outings and tours in Yosemite and other California national parks about the time these parks were established. In 1915, it built and operated a back-country lodge in Yosemite. The first park cooperating association, a nonprofit group chartered to help support park service interpretative activities and provide educational materials to users, was established in 1920.

3. The Conservation Foundation, *National Parks for the Future* (Washington, D.C.: The Conservation Foundation, 1972), p. 22.

4. James G. Watt, "Address" (Speech given at the Conference of National Park Concessioners, Washington, D.C., March 9, 1981), pp. 3, 5.

5. U.S. Congress, Joint Hearing before certain House Subcommittees of the Committee on Government Operations and the Permanent Select Committee on Small Business, *National Park Service Planning and Concession Operations*, 93rd Cong., 2d sess., December 20, 1974, p. 120.

6. Based on Conservation Foundation staff field visit to Yosemite NP, 1981.

7. Information provided by the National Park Service, Concessions Division, 1985.

8. Ibid.

9. Ibid., 1983.

10. Ibid., 1984.

11. Conservation Foundation generated data based on information provided by the National Park Service, Concessions Division, 1984.

12. Information provided by the National Park Service, Concessions Division, 1984.

13. Ise, *Our National Park Policy*, pp. 459-460; See also *Concessions Contract* between U.S. Department of the Interior, National Park Service (Big Bend National Park, Isle Royale National Park, Mammoth Cave National Park, Olympic National Park, and Blue Ridge Parkway) and National Park Concessions, Inc., Contract no. CC-0680-2-0001, September 21, 1982, pp. 1, 9.

14. Information provided by the National Park Service, Concessions Division, 1985.

15. Conservation Foundation generated data based on information provided by the National Park Service, Concessions Division, 1984.

16. Since Congress was not spending money on aesthetic or cultural endeavors, such as furthering the fine arts, counting on private sources to support lands withheld from materially productive use appeared to be a logical extension of existing policy. See Hans Huth, *Nature and the American* (Lincoln, Nebraska: University of Nebraska Press, 1972), p. 154.

17. Council on Environmental Quality, *Third Annual Report* (Washington, D.C.: U.S. Government Printing Office, 1972), p. 315.

18. Information provided by the National Park Service, Concessions Division, 1985.

19. See letter from Stewart L. Udall, secretary of the interior, to Wayne N. Aspinall, chairman, House Committee on Interior and Insular Affairs (May 14, 1965), reprinted in H.R. Report No. 591, 89th Cong., 1st sess., 1965, p. 7.

20. Ise, *Our National Park Policy*, p. 211; Donald Swain, *Wilderness Defender: Horace M. Albright and Conservation* (Chicago: University of Chicago Press, 1970), p. 133.

21. 16 U.S.C.A., §§20-20q (1980).

22. 16 U.S.C.A., §20(b) (1980).

23. Concessions Policy Act of 1980, codified in scattered sections of U.S.C.A., Title 16.
24. 16 U.S.C.A., §20 (1980).
25. Ibid., The limitation also applies to "locations where the least damage to park values will be caused."
26. U.S. Congress, House of Representatives, *National Park Service Policies Discourage Competition, Give Concessioners Too Great a Voice in Concession Management*, 94th Cong., 2d sess., 1976, p. 24.
27. U.S. Congress, Congressional Record 111 (1965): 23,624.
28. U.S. Congress, House Appropriations Committee, *FY 1978 House Appropriations: Hearings*, Part 5, 95th Cong., 1st sess., 1977, p. 450.
29. Yellowstone Concessions Study Team, *Yellowstone National Park Concessions Management Review of the Yellowstone Park Company* (Washington, D.C.: National Park Service, 1976), p. 4.
30. U.S. Congress, House Appropriations Committee, *FY 1980 Appropriations: Hearings*, part 7, 96th Cong., 1st sess., 1979, p. 11.
31. Ibid., p. 790.
32. Information provided by the National Park Service, Concessions Division, 1985.
33. Michael Mantell, "Preservation and Use: Concessions in the National Parks," *Ecology Law Quarterly* 8(1): 30-33.
34. Ibid., p. 34.
35. U.S. Congress, House, *National Park Service Policies Discourage Competition, Give Concessioners Too Great a Voice in Concession Management*, H.R. Report no. 869, 94th Cong., 2d sess., 1976, p. 24.
36. William Everhart, *The National Park Service* (Boulder, Colorado: Westview Press, 1983), pp. 66-68.
37. U.S. Comptroller General, *Concession Operations in the National Parks—Improvements Needed in Administration* (Washington, D.C.: U.S. Government Printing Office, 1975), p. 9.
38. Ibid.
39. U.S. Congress, *Policies Discourage Competition*, p. 24.
40. "Concessions: A Continuing Threat to Park Quality," *National Parks and Conservation Magazine*, March 1974, p. 26.
41. The Conservation Foundation, *National Parks for the Future*, p. 22.
42. Michael Frome, "Park Concessions and Concessioners," *National Parks*, June 1981, p. 16.
43. Everhart, *The National Park Service*, pp. 107-108.
44. Joseph L. Sax, "Free Enterprise in the Woods," *Natural History*, June 1982, p. 22.
45. Everhart, *The National Park Service*, p. 107.
46. Joseph L. Sax, "America's National Parks," *Natural History*, October 1976, p. 83.
47. Joseph L. Sax, "Profiting from Parks: None of Watt's Business," *High Country News*, October 16, 1981, p. 13.
48. U.S. Congress, House, Joint Hearing before certain Subcommittees of the Committee on Goverment Operations and the Permanent Select Com-

mittee on Small Business, *National Park Service Planning and Concession Operations*, 93rd Cong., 2d sess., 1974, pp. 120, 125.

49. Sax, "America's National Parks," p. 76.
50. Shankland, *Steve Mather of the National Parks*, p. 209.
51. R. H. Ritchey, *Concessioner Franchise Fee Study* (Washington, D.C.: U.S. Department of the Interior, 1982), p. 1.
52. Information provided by National Park Service, Concessions Division, 1985.
53. Ritchey, *Concessioner Franchise Fee Study*, p. 10.
54. Ibid., p. 11.
55. Ibid., Exhibit iv-4.
56. Information provided by National Park Service, Concessions Division, 1984.
57. Ibid., 1985.
58. Conservation Foundation staff interview with Lloyd "Buddy" Surles, National Park Service, Rocky Mountain Regional Office, 1983.
59. U.S. Congress, House Appropriations Committee, *Appropriations Hearings, Testimony of Ronald Walker, Director, National Park Service*, 94th Cong., 1st sess., 1975, pp. 151-52.
60. Conservation Foundation staff interview with David Gackenbach, chief, Concessions Division, National Park Service, 1983.
61. Information provided by National Park Service, Concessions Division, 1983; See also National Park Service, "Training by Eating," *NPS Newsletter*, July 1981, p. 15.
62. Conservation Foundation staff interview with Andrew B. Dixon, Concessions Division, National Park Service, 1983. The nonprofit American Youth Hostels, which has member affiliates providing lodging in five parks including Golden Gate, Grand Canyon, and Cape Cod, for example, are administered under a special permit that differs considerably from the regular concessioners' contracts and permits. Although rates are approved, the services' permits attempt to encourage hostel use by acknowledging that these are low-cost accommodations (prices range from $5.00 to $7.75 per night) run by nonprofit organizations that provide interpretative programs, encourage nonmotorized transportation, and generally use an existing park service structure. Unlike concessioners that must invest their own capital, the park service undertakes major renovation or provides a new facility when such is required for a hostel.
63. In 1975, the National Parks and Conservation Association (NPCA) filed suit against the park service under the Freedom of Information Act (FOIA) to gain access to the financial records of concessioners. The court denied NPCA access, upholding park service and concessioner claims that such information was exempt from the requirements of FOIA. NPCA v. Kleppe, 7 ELR 20052 (D.C. Ct. 1976).
64. Information provided by National Park Service, Concessions Division, 1985.
65. Information provided by Yellowstone National Park, 1985.

66. U.S. Congress, *FY 1980 Appropriations: Hearings*, pp. 790-91.

67. 16 U.S.C.A., §20b (1980); U.S. Department of the Interior, National Park Service, *Concessions Management Guideline*, Publication no. NPS-48 (Washington, D.C.: U.S. Government Printing Office, June 1984), pp. 11-15, 8.

68. Sax, "Free Enterprise," p. 24.

69. U.S. Department of the Interior, National Park Service, Yellowstone National Park, *Yellowstone Concession Contract*, Contract no. CC 1570-2-0001, February 18, 1982, pp. 8, 12.

70. National Park Service, *Concessions Contract* Contract No. CC-0680-2-0001, September 21, 1982, pp. 1,9.

71. Based on information provided by National Park Service, Concessions Division, 1983.

72. 16 U.S.C.A., §20(e) (1980).

73. NPCA v. Kleppe, 7 ELR 20057.

74. Conservation Foundation staff interview with Robert Johnston, president, American Youth Hostels, 1984.

75. Ritchey, *Concessioner Franchise Fee Study*, pp. 72-73.

76. Bruce Powell, "An Analysis of National Park Service Policies for Concessions Management" (M.S. thesis, Colorado State University, 1984), p. 126.

77. U.S. Department of the Interior, National Park Service, "Special Directive 84-2," *National Park Service Concessions Management Policies*, May 30, 1984, p. viii-2.

78. "Dickenson: On the Job and Other subjects," *High Country News* 13 (24):6.

79. See, for example, Everhart, *National Park Service*, pp. 120-21.

80. Memo from Director, National Park Service, to Regional Directors, "Management Efficiency Planning," December 11, 1982. In explaining the guidelines to regional directors, former park service Director Russell Dickenson noted that "fundraising is friendraising": constituency building is an additional impetus behind many of these guidelines. Former Director Dickenson also chided the service for not being innovative in increasing park revenues and managing the parks more efficiently, saying that state and local parks have been exemplary in these areas over the last 10 years and that it "is clear the direction of the future" for the National Park System.

81. Representative John Seiberling's Office, "OMB Circular A-76 (Contracting)" background information, May 15, 1984.

82. U.S. Congress, *Amendment to Volunteers in the Parks Act of 1969*, 98 Stat. 2718-2719, 98th Cong., 2d sess., 1984.

83. Conservation Foundation staff interview with Brian O'Neill, assistant superintendent, Golden Gate National Recreation Area, 1983.

84. U.S. Department of the Interior, National Park Service, *Cooperating Associations Guidelines*, NPS-32 (Washington, D.C.: U.S. Government Printing Office, 1981); National Park Service, "NPS Cooperating Associations . . . What They Are . . . and What They Do" (Brochure).

85. Ibid.
86. Conservation Foundation staff interview with John Earnst, superintendent, Gettysburg National Military Park and Cemetery, 1982.
87. Conservation Foundation staff interview with James Murfin, director of National Park Service Cooperating Association Programs, National Park Service, 1984.
88. Based on information provided by the National Park Service, 1984.
89. National Park Service, *Cooperating Associations Guidelines, NPS-32,* pp. 6-8.
90. Conservation Foundation staff interview with Roy Graybill, servicewide program manager, Volunteers in Parks, National Park Service, 1984.
91. U.S. Department of the Interior, National Park Service, "Volunteers in Parks, Guideline NPS-7, Release No. 2," Chap. 1, p. 1. See also U.S. Department of the Interior, National Park Service, "Summary Minutes, 86th Meeting, National Park System Advisory Board," March 10-13, 1982.
92. Based on information provided by National Park Service, 1984. See also "Volunteers in the Parks," *National Parks,* January/February 1983, p. 30; NPS, "Summary Minutes, 86th Meeting," p. 70.
93. Student Conservation Association, *"The Student Conservation Program, 1981 Annual Report"* (Charlestown, N.H.: Student Conservation Association, 1982), p. 3.
94. Conservation Foundation staff interview with Dave Startzell, associate director, Appalachian Trail Conference, 1984.
95. Conservation Foundation staff interview with Ray Murray, chief, Park and Recreation Technical Services, Western Region, National Park Service, 1985.
96. Based on information provided by National Park Service, 1984. See also Custer Battlefield Preservation Committee, Inc., "Custer Battlefield" (Hardin, Mont.: Custer Battlefield Preservation Committee, undated brochure); National Park Foundation, *1981 Annual Report,* (Washington, D.C.: National Park Foundation, 1982), pp. 5, 6; and "letter from Russell Dickenson, to NPCA," *National Parks,* January/February 1983, p. 5.
97. "Park Briefs," *Courier,* September 1981, p. 11. As one example of the pivotal positions of private groups in acquiring significant artifacts and displays for the parks, the nonprofit Friends of Independence National Historical Park had, as of 1981, bought 18th century paintings, furnishings, maps, and artifacts for the park valued at over half a million dollars, in addition to furnishing and decorating a reception room. The Friends also secured the site of the historic Slate Roof House for the park.
98. 16 U.S.C.A., §19e (1980). See also *FY 1981 Appropriation Hearings,* 96th Cong., 2d sess., part 11, pp. 498-99, 501, 505.
99. 16 U.S.C.A., §19aa-gg (Supp. 1983). See also, *FY 1981 Appropriation Hearings,* 96 Cong., 2d sess., part 11, p. 502.
100. Conservation Foundation staff interview with Ray Murray, chief, Park and Recreation Technical Services, Western Region, National Park Service, 1985.

101. Ibid.
102. Conservation Foundation staff interview with Randall Biallas, assistant chief historical architect, National Park Service, Washington, D.C., 1983.
103. 16 U.S.C.A., §470h-3 (1981). See also 36 C.F.R., §18 (1983); Mary Manca, "To Let: Buildings with a Past," *National Parks*, November/December, 1984, p. 13.
104. Conservation Foundation staff interview with Randall Biallas, assistant chief historical architect, National Park Service, 1984.
105. Conservation Foundation staff interview with Randall Biallas, assistant chief historical architect, National Park Service, Washington, D.C., 1983. See also, U.S. Department of the Interior, National Park Service, Director, "Special Directive 82-12, Policy on Historic Property Leases and Exchanges," November 26, 1982, p. 4.
106. NPS Director, "Special Directive 82-12", p. 4.
107. Conservation Foundation staff interview with Randall Biallis, 1983; Robert D. McFadden, "Private Help Sought for Restoring Ellis Island," *New York Times*, December 12, 1981; Elliot Willensky, "A Nation Finally Remembers," *Historic Preservation*, July/August 1983, pp. 14-19.
108. Ibid.
109. Ibid.
110. Conservation Foundation staff interviews with National Park Service staff, 1984.
111. Conservation Foundation interview with William Supernaugh, chief wildlife biologist, National Park Service, 1983.
112. Ibid.
113. Conservation Foundation staff interview with William Supernaugh, 1985.
114. Joseph L. Sax, "In Search of Past Harmony," *Natural History* 91(8):42-50.
115. See National Park Foundation, *The Complete Guide to America's National Parks* (New York: The Viking Press, 1981); "*National Parks Visitor Facilities and Services*," (Paper delivered at the Conference of National Park Concessioners, 1983); "Snow Goer's National Parks Winter Fun Guide," *Snow Goer*, September 1982, pp. 29-36.
116. Based on information provided by National Park Service, 1983. See also U.S. Department of the Interior, National Park Service, "Minutes of the Travel Industry Working Group," (Washington, D.C.: U.S. Department of the Interior, September 9, 1981, photocopy).
117. Conservation Foundation staff interview with Priscilla Baker, special assistant to the director of the National Park Service, Washington, D.C., 1983.
118. U.S. Department of the Interior, National Park Service, "Tourism Opportunity Analysis for Voyageurs National Park and Environs" (Draft report of the Tourism Development Task Force, National Park Service, November, 1982).
119. National Park Service, Director, "Special Directive 82-12," p. 3. A 56-year lease of historic property at Antietam was recently negotiated. Myron Struck, "Park Service Rents Historic Real Estate," *Washington Post* April 22, 1985.

## Profile. Santa Monica Mountains National Recreation Area

1. Congressional Quarterly, Inc., *1978 Congressional Quarterly Almanac*, 95th Congress, 2d session (Washington, D.C.: Congressional Quarterly, Inc., 1979), pp. 704-707.
2. Conservation Foundation staff interview with David Ochsner, chief, Resource Management, Santa Monica Mountains NRA, 1983.
3. Robert Cahn, "New Urban Parks Face a Fight to Survive," *The Christian Science Monitor*, June 17, 1982, p. 12.
4. Conservation Foundation staff field visit, Santa Monica Mountains NRA, 1983.
5. U.S. Department of the Interior, National Park Service, *Santa Monica Mountains National Recreation Area General Management Plan* (Denver: Denver Service Center, 1982), pp. 114-119.
6. Santa Monica Mountains National Recreation Area Advisory Commission, "Management of Parklands in the Santa Monica Mountains National Recreation Area," September 1982, p. I-1.
7. See, for example, John Hart, *San Francsico's Wilderness Next Door* (San Rafael, California: Presidio Press, 1979), pp. 147-150; J. William Futrell, "Parks to the People: New Directions for the National Park System," *Emory Law Journal*, 25(2) (1976):299; and U.S. Department of the Interior, Heritage Conservation and Recreation Service, *National Urban Recreation Study, Technical Reports*, vol. 1, *Urban Open Space: Existing Conditions, Opportunities, and Issues*, 1978, pp. 186-187.
8. U.S. Department of the Interior, *Special Review of Land Acquisition Policies and Practices in the National Park Service, Part I. Cost Estimates* (Washington, D.C.: Office of the Inspector General, 1981), pp. 8, 11, 12, 20-21; Conservation Foundation staff interview with Daniel R. Kuehn, superintendent, Santa Monica Mountains NRA, 1984. Authorized ceiling of $155 million included $125 million for direct federal acquisition and $30 million for grants to California for land acquisition and development. The current estimate of $667.5 million was based on the assumption that the full amount would be available in FY82 and that declarations of taking would be used rather than normal condemnation actions to acquire all lands in that fiscal year. These favorable assumptions were offset by other assumptions that would increase acquisition costs including: (1) that all lands identified for fee and less than fee acquisition in the land protection plan would be acquired in fee, (2) that local governments would prohibit development on existing vacant properties and, (3) that there would be no damages against improved properties in easement areas.
9. U.S. Department of the Interior, National Park Service, "Statutory Ceiling," table, undated; "The Land and Water Conservation Fund: The Conservation Alternative for Fiscal Year 1985," jointly produced by the American Rivers Conservation Council, Defenders of Wildlife, Friends of the Earth, Izaak Walton League, National Audubon Society, National Pars and Conservation Association, National Recreation and Park

Association, National Wildlife Federation, Sierra Club, Trust for Public Land and The Wilderness Society, undated.

10. 16 U.S.C.A., §§2301-06 (Supp. 1985). The National Park Access Act of 1978 set up a three-year pilot program "to make the National Park System more accessible in a manner consistent with the preservation of parks and the conservation of energy." The act provided funds for mass transportation projects in the new urban parks at increasing levels: $1 million for FY79; $2 million for FY80; and $3 million for FY81. Any unused funds remained available until spent.

11. Conservation Foundation staff interviews with Robert Chandler, then superintendent, Santa Monica Mountains NRS, 1982 and Margo Feuer, Sierra Club citizen activist, 1983.

12. Robert Cahn, "New Urban Parks Face a Fight to Survive," The Christian Science Monitor, June 17, 1982, p. 12.

13. Conservation Foundation staff interviews with National Park Service staff, Santa Monica Mountains NRA, 1983.

14. Conservation Foundation staff interview with Margo Feuer, Sierra Club citizen activist, 1984.

15. U.S. Department of the Interior, National Park Service, Santa Monica Mountains National Recreation Area Land Protection Plan (Denver: Denver Service Center, 1984), p. i.

16. Conservation Foundation staff interviews with National Park Service staff, Santa Monica Mountains NRA, 1984.

17. Conservation Foundation staff interview with Daniel R. Kuehn, superintendent, Santa Monica Mountains NRA, 1984.

18. Conservation Foundation staff interviews with National Park Service staff, Santa Monica Mountains NRA, 1984.

19. Ibid., 1985.

20. Conservation Foundation staff interview with Margo Feuer, Sierra Club citizen activist, 1983.

21. National Park Service, Santa Monica Mountains National Recreation Area Land Protection Plan, p. i.

22. Ibid.

23. Letter from Robert S. Chandler, then superintendent, Santa Monica Mountains NRA, to Melvin Nutter, Chairman, California Coastal Commission, March 23, 1983.

24. Letter from Ric Davidge, Department of the Interior, Office of the Assistant Secretary for Fish and Wildlife and Parks, to William R. Wolanow, Dayton Realty Company, November 2, 1981.

25. Conservation Foundation staff interviews with National Park Service staff, Santa Monica Mountains NRA, 1983.

26. "Landowner Gets State to Bid for Key Malibu Tract," Los Angeles Times, June 21, 1984, p. I1.

27. Board of Supervisors of the County of Los Angeles, "Resolution Introduced Before the Board of Supervisors by Baxter Ward and Yvonne Burke," October 2, 1979.

28. U.S. Department of the Interior, National Park Service, Santa Monica

Mountains National Recreation Area Advisory Commission, "Resolution Concerning Land Protection Plan," Resolution No. 002-84, adopted April 24, 1984.

29. Santa Monica Mountains National Recreation Area Advisory Commission, "Management of Parklands in the Santa Monica Mountains National Recreation Area," pp. V-1 to V-4.

30. Conservation Foundation staff interview with Daniel R. Kuehn, superintendent, Santa Monica Mountains NRA, 1984.

## Chapter 6. Creating the Park System of the Future

1. U.S. Congress, House Committee on Interior and Insular Affairs, *Land Acquisition Policy and Program of the National Park Service*, Committee Print 7, 98th Cong., 2d sess., 1984, pp. 6-7; See also Statement of James G. Watt, secretary of the Department of the Interior, before the Senate Committee on Energy and Natural Resources, February 24, 1981; Information provided by Willis Kriz, Chief Land Resources Division, National Park Service, 1985. The moratorium was imposed on February 17, 1981 and lifted on June 5, 1981, by the partial rejection by Congress of the administration's proposal to rescind $66 million of the funds then available for land acquisition.

2. U.S. Department of the Interior, National Park Service, "Summary of Acreages," tables, dated 1960-1980.

3. Congressional Quarterly, Inc., *1980 Congressional Quarterly Almanac*, vol. 36, 96th Cong., 2d sess. (Washington, D.C.: Congressional Quarterly, Inc., 1981), p. 575.

4. The Conservation Foundation, *State of the Environment 1982* (Washington, D.C.: The Conservation Foundation, 1982), p. 12; U.S. Department of the Interior, National Park Service, "60 Years Growth of National Park System," table, dated January 29, 1979; William C. Everhart, *The National Park Service* (Boulder, Colo.: Westview Press, 1983), pp. 25-26.; Alfred Runte, *National Parks: The American Experience* (Lincoln, Nebr.: University of Nebraska Press, 1979), pp. 170-171; The Conservation Foundation, *State of the Environment: An Assessment at Mid-Decade* (Washington, D.C.: The Conservation Foundation, 1984), p. 223; The Conservation Foundation, *National Parks for the Future* (Washington, D.C.: The Conservation Foundation, 1972), p. 6.

5. Conrad Wirth, *Parks, Politics and People* (Norman, Oklahoma: University of Okla. Press, 1979), pp. 174-175; Everhart, *The National Park Service*, pp. 69-70.; Outdoor Recreation Resources Review Commission, *Outdoor Recreation for America* (Washington, D.C.: U.S. Government Printing Office, 1962), p. 10.

6. U.S. Department of the Interior, National Park Service, "Purchases by Fiscal Year, Land and Water Conservation Fund," table, dated December 30, 1983.

7. National Park Service, "Summary of Acreages," tables dated January 1, 1961 and September 30, 1980.

8. U.S. Department of the Interior, "Purchases by Fiscal Year, Land and Water Conservation Fund." U.S. Congress, *Land Acquisition Policy and Program of the National Park Service,* p. 6.

9. U.S. Department of the Interior, "Purchases by Fiscal Year, Land and Water Conservation Fund."

10. Everhart, *The National Park Service,* p. 145.

11. U.S. Congress, House Committee on Appropriations, Subcommittee on the Department of the Interior and Related Agencies, *Appropriations for 1977: Hearings,* 94th Cong., 1st sess., 1975, pp. 794-803; U.S. Congress, House Committee on Appropriations, Subcommittee on the Department of the Interior and Related Agencies, *Appropriations for 1982: Hearings,* 97th Cong., 1st sess., 1981, pp. 1237-1255.

12. Conservation Foundation staff interviews with National Park Service staff, 1984.

13. Everhart, *The National Park Service,* p. 148.

14. Conservation Foundation staff interviews with National Park Service staff.

15. Statement by James G. Watt, before Senate Committee on Energy and Environmental Resources, February 24, 1981.

16. Conservation Foundation staff interview with George Siehl (title) and William Duddleson (title), 1982.

17. Conservation Foundation staff interviews with National Park Service staff, 1982.

18. "Illinois and Michigan Canal National Heritage Corridor Act of 1984," Pub. L. No. 98-398, 746, 98 Stat. 1456-1472 (1984); "The Olmsted Heritage Landscapes Act of 1984," H.R. 4356, November 10, 1983.

19. "Seventeen Areas Identified for Greenline Protection," p. 28, in Marjorie Corbett, ed., in *Greenline Parks: Land Conservation Trends for the Eighties and Beyond,* (Washington, D.C.: National Parks and Conservation Association, 1983); "Chicago's Canal Connection," *The Washington Post,* August 12, 1984, p. 1.

20. U.S. Congress, House, "Identifying, Commemorating and Preserving the Legacy of Historic Landscapes of Frederick Law Olmsted, and for other Purposes," Report 98-958, 98th Cong., 2d sess., pp. 5-6.

21. "Seventeen Areas Identified for Greenline Protection," pp. 17-19, 21, 30, 32-33, 34-36.

22. Statement by William K. Reilly, president, The Conservation Foundation, in U.S. Congress, Senate Committee on Energy and Natural Resources, *Workshop on Public Land Acquisition and Alternatives,* Committee Print, 97th Cong., 1st sess., 1981, p. 21.

23. 48 Fed. Reg. 21121-21131 (1983).

24. See Figure 6.3.

25. The figure of hundreds of millions of dollars above NPS estimates to complete the backlog comes from Conservation Foundation staff research and discussions with informed persons inside and outside the service, as well as from service estimates and figures from current condemnation cases.

26. Information provided by National Park Service staff, 1984, 1985.

27. See, for example, Lee Hockstader, "Reagan's Gone and Froze. . .Money," *The Washington Post*, July 27, 1981, pp. B1, B3.; Glenn Pontier, "Impasse on the Upper Delaware," *Planning*, August 1984, pp. 14-20.

28. Runte, *National Parks: The American Experience*, pp. 116-117, 125-126; Wirth, *Parks, Politics, and the People*, p. 260; U.S. Congress, *Land Acquisition Policy and Program of the National Park Service*, p. 3.

29. Joseph Sax, "Buying Scenery: Land Acquisitions for the National Park Service," *Duke Law Journal* 4(1980):714-715; 44 Fed. Reg. 24792, 24794 (1979).

30. Michael Frome, "The Ungreening of Our National Parks," p. 43, in *National Parks in Crisis* (Washington, D.C.: National Parks and Conservation Association, 1982).

31. Sax, "Buying Scenery: Land Acquisitions for the National Park Service,"p2. 720-721.

32. Information provided by Willis Kriz, chief, Land Resources Division, National Park Service, 1985; See also, Sax, "Buying Scenery: Land Acquisitions for the National Park Service," pp. 714-715, 717-718.

33. The Conservation Foundation, *National Parks for the Future*, p. 105.

34. Chuck Williams, "The Park Rebellion; Charles Cushman, James Watt, and the Attack on the National Parks, "*Not Man Apart*, June 1982, p.7.

35. See, for example, U.S. General Accounting Office, *The Federal Drive to Acquire Private Lands Should be Reassessed*, Publication no. CED-80-14 (Washington, D.C.: U.S. General Accounting Office, 1979); U.S. General Accounting Office, *The National Park Service Should Improve Its Land Acquisition and Management At the Fire Island National Seashore*, Publication no. CED-81-78 (Washington, D.C.: U.S. General Accounting Office, CED-81-78, 1981). U.S. General Accounting Office, *Federal Land Acquisition and Management Practices*, Publication no. CED-81-135 (Washington, D.C.: U.S. General Accounting Office, 1981).

36. Conservation Foundation staff interviews with park staff and landowners at Cuyahoga Valley NRA.

37. Ed Wesley, "Public TV's Frontline Attack on the Park Service," *National Parks*, September-October 1984, p. 6.

38. Pontier, "Impasse on the Upper Delaware," pp. 14-20.

39. NIA often on hand to warn citizens about proposed parks: Chuck Williams, "The Park Rebellion," *Not Man Apart*, June 1982.

40. 44 Fed. Reg. 24790-24792 (1979).1

41. General Accounting Office, *Federal Land Acquisition*, p. 13.

42. 47 Fed. Reg. 19785 (1982).

43. Information provided by Warren Brown, National Park Service, 1985; 44 Fed. Reg. 21123 (1983).

44. U.S. Department of the Interior, *Special Review of Land Acquisition Policies and Practices in the National Park Service*, Part I. *Cost Estimates* (Washington, D.C.: Office of the Inspector General, 1981), pp. 22-23, 28; John Seiberling Letter to the Editor, "Acquiring Land for National Parks," *The Wall Street Journal*, June 14, 1982, p. 21.

45. U.S. Department of the Interior, *Cost Estimates*, p. 11.; Conservation

Foundation staff interview with National Park Service staff Santa Monica Mountains NRA, 1984; Information provided by Willis Kriz, chief, Land Resources Division, 1985.

46. Testimony of Ronald J. Tipton, The Wilderness Society,in U.S. Congress, *Workshop on Land Protection and Management,*, Committee Print, 97th Congress, 2d Sess., 1982, p. 420. The circumstances here suggest cooperative landowners which allowed flexibility to use alternative protection strategies, resulting in a low number of adverse condemnation cases.

47. U.S. Department of the Interior, *Cost Estimates*, pp. 7-8.

48. 5 U.S.C.A., §2953 (1977).

49. "National Parks and Recreation Act of 1978," Pub. L. No. 95-625, §507, 92 Stat. 3507 (1978); U.S. Department of the Interior, National Park Service, "Statutory Ceiling," table, undated.

50. Everhart, *The National Park Service*, p. 50.

51. 47 Fed. Reg. 19785 (1982).

52. Information provided by Warren Brown, National Park Service, 1985.

53. Statement of Joseph Petrillo, executive officer, California Coastal Conservancy, in U.S. Congress, *Workshop on Public Land Acquisitions and Alternatives*, pp. 415-416, 418.

54. Jim Jubak, "The People and the Pinelands," *National Parks*, September-October 1984, p. 20.; Jon A. Kusler, *Public/Private Parks and Management of Private Lands for Park Protection*, IES Report 16 (Madison, Wisconsin: University of Wisconsin Press, 1974), pp. 59-63.

55. U.S. Department of the Interior, National Park Service, "Scenic Easements," Memo, dated 1974, p. 3; Donald Sutte, Jr., and Roger A. Cunningham, "Scenic Easements: Legal, Administrative, and Valuation Problems and Procedures," National Cooperative Highway Research Program Report No. 56. (Washington, D.C.: National Academy, 1968), p. 9; John Ise, *Our National Park Policy: A Critical History* (Baltimore: Johns Hopkins University Press, 1961), p. 416.

56. U.S. Department of the Interior, Heritage Conservation and Recreation Service, *Land Conservation and Preservation Techniques* (Washington, D.C.: U.S. Government Printing Office, 1979).

57. U.S. General Accounting Office, *Federal Land Acquisition and Management Practices*, p. 3.

58. Memo from the Cuyahoga Valley Communities Council Inc., "Purpose, Organization and Membership of the Council," March 14, 1980.

59. U.S. Department of the Interior, National Park Service, *Santa Monica Mountains National Recreation Area Land Protection Plan*, June 1984, pp. 3,14. The establishing legislation sets framework for coordination in recreation, resource management and planning among more than 60 jurisdictions.

60. Conservation Foundation staff interviews with National Park Service staff; U.S. Department of the Interior, *New Tools for Land Protection: An Introductory Handbook*, (Washington, D.C.: U.S. Government Printing Office, 1982), p. 68.

61. Cuyahoga Valley Communities Council, Inc., "Purpose, Organization and Membership of the Council," Memo, March 14, 1980; Cuyahoga Valley Communities Council, Inc., *Newsletter* November 1981, pp. 1,3.

62. *Alternatives for Land Protection; A Review of Case Studies in Eight National Parks*, prepared for the U.S. Department of the Interior, National Park Service, 1982; U.S. Congress, *Land Acquisition Policy and Program of the National Park Service*, p. 7.

63. U.S. Department of the Interior, *New Tools for Land Protection*, p. 43; Donald Rubenstein, "Is the Public Local Land Saving Movement Successful?" pp. 18-9 in Lincoln Institute of Land Policy, *Resource Papers: Proceedings of the National Consultation on Local Land Conservation*, October 14-17, 1981, (Cambridge, Mass.: Lincoln Institute of Land Policy, 1982).

64. Philip Metzger, "Public-Private Partners Foster Land Conservation," *Conservation Foundation Newsletter*, July 1983, pp. 1-2.

65. See, for example, U.S. Department of the Interior, National Park Service, "Draft Land Protection Plan, Channel Islands National Park," September 1983, p.37. This explores possible roles for The Natural Conservancy and the Trust for Public Lands; discusses variations on donation involving the formation of a nonprofit corporation/land trust in the vicinity of parks with the sole purpose of raising funds for parkland acquisition; and cites example of The Nature Conservancy trying to raise funds for land purchase of Santa Cruz Island Company.

66. U.S. Department of the Interior, *New Tools for Land Protection*, pp. 45-53.

67. Memo, "Tax Policy as a Management Alterntive for the Conservation of the Natural Resourcs of the Coastal Barrier Resources System," (undated, unreferenced). Letter from G. Ray Arnett to William K. Reilly, August 22, 1984. (Re: tax policy as a possible management alternative for the protection of undeveloped coastal barriers.)

68. See, for example, "Private Wetland and Critical Habitat Enhancement and Protection Act of 1984," H.R. 5900, 98th Cong., 2d sess., 1984.

69. "Self-Policing Is a Must," *Preservation News*, January 1984, p. 4.

70. 16 U.S.C.A., §410cc-24 (Supp. 1985); U.S. Congress, House Committee on Interior and Insular Affairs, Subcommittee on National Parks and Insular Affairs, *Legislative History of the National Parks and Recreation Act of 1978 (Public Law 95-626)*, Committee Print No. 11, 95th Cong., 2d sess., 1978, pp. 920, 922. A different type of certification process is in effect at Sawtooth National Recreation Area. In coordination with other federal agencies, private interest groups, and state and local government, the U.S. Forest Service drafted a comprehensive land use management plan. Private lands within Sawtooth are categorized into one of five land-use categories (agricultural, community, residential, mining and commercial), each of which has certain standards regarding existing use and potential development. Landowners request formal certification from the Forest Service, acknowledging the standards for which their property is zoned. Once certified, the Forest Service withdraws

its right to condemn the private property (U.S. Department of the Interior, *New Tools for Land Protection*, p. 64.)

71. J. William Futrell, "Parks to the People: New Directions for the National Park System," *Emory Law Journal* 25, no. 2 (Spring 1976):312.

72. Conservation Foundation staff interviews with National Park Service staff.

73. 16 U.S.C.A., §1a-5 (1974).

74. Conservation Foundation staff interview with former OMB official, 1983.

75. Conservation Foundation staff interview with Ron Tipton, The Wilderness Society, 1982.

76. Library of Congress, Congressional Research Service, Environment and Natural Resources Policy Division, *Past Federal Surveys of Seashore Recreation Potential*, Committee Print, 95th Cong., 2d sess., 1978, pp. 2-3.

77. U.S. Department of the Interior, National Park Service, *Part One of the National Park System Plan: History* (Washington, D.C.: U.S. Government Printing Office, 1972); U.S. Department of the Interior, National Park Service, *Part Two of the National Park System Plan: Natural History* (Washington, D.C.: U.S. Government Printing Office, 1972).

78. U.S. Department of the Interior, Heritage and Conservation Recreation Service, *Wild and Scenic Rivers System Study: Final List of Potential National Wild and Scenic Rivers* (Philadelphia, Penn.: Northeast Regional Office, 1979).

79. Luther J. Carter, "East Coast Maps to Alert Industry to Ecology Conflicts," *Science*, April 11, 1980, p. 159.

80. Philip M. Hoose, *Building an Ark—Tools for Preservation of Natural Diversity* (Covelo, Calif.: Island Press, 1981); Conservation Foundation staff interview with Carol Hodges, Heritage Operations, The Nature Conservancy, 1984.

81. "Park Advisory Board Puts Landmark Studies on Hold," *National Parks*, January-February 1985, p. 36. In October 1984, the National Park Service Advisory Board recommended that the park service stop work on these two studies. The armed services was apparently "opposed to preserving space launch complexes and World War II sites because of planned development."

82. U.S. Congress, *Land Acquisition Policy and Program of the National Park Service*, p. 19; Pub. L. No. 96-550.

83. 14 *Environmental Law Reporter* 10320, August 1984.

84. National Park Service, "Summary of Acreages," table dated September 30, 1983; U.S. Department of the Interior, Bureau of Land Management, *Public Land Statistics, 1983* (Washington, D.C.: U.S. Government Printing Office, 1984).

85. H. Ken Cordell and John C. Hendee, *Renewable Resources Recreation in the United States: Supply, Demand, and Critical Policy Issues* (Washington, D.C.: American Forestry Association, 1982), p. 45. The methods of measuring visitation vary among federal agencies, and no method is totally reliable, so comparing visitor use of the different federal land systems is difficult. In visits to fee collecting areas and in the

resulting fees collected at these units, the parks outpaced the other systems.

86. U.S. Department of Commerce, Bureau of the Census, *Statistical Abstract of the United States, 1979* (Washington, D.C.: U.S. Government Printing Office, 1980), p. 244.

87. The Conservation Foundation, *State of the Environment: Mid-Decade*, p. 229; U.S. Department of the Interior, National Park Service, *National Park Service Statistical Abstract, 1983* (Denver: Colo.: Denver Service Center, Statistical Office, 1984), p. 2.

88. Outdoor Recreation Policy Review Group, *Outdoor Recreation for America-1983* (Washington, D.C.: Resources for the Future, 1983), p. 24; The Conservation Foundation, *State of the Environment Mid-Decade*, p. 228.

89. Outdoor Recreation Policy Review Group, *Outdoor Recreation for America 1983*, p. 24.

90. The Nature Conservancy, "President's Letter," *The Nature Conservancy News*, July-August 1983, p. 5.

91. Conservation Foundation staff interview with Clay Peters, The Wilderness Society, 1985.

92. Linked to this effort is a Conservation Foundation publication: Rolf Diamant, J. Glenn Evgster, and Christopher J. Duerksen, *A Citizen's Guide to River Conservation* (Washington, D.C.: The Conservation Foundation, 1984).

93. Meg Maguire, "Running on Empty: The Land and Water Conservation Fund at Zero," *National Parks*, July-August 1981, p. 15.

94. National Park Service, "Purchases by Fiscal Year, Land and Water Conservation Fund."

95. Conservation Foundation staff interviews with National Park Service staff, Budget Office, 1983.

96. William Lienesch, "The Slash of '82: LWCF Crippled by Cuts," *National Parks*, January-February 1981, p. 11.

97. 16 U.S.C.A., §4601-9 (Supp. 1985).

98. U.S. Congress, *Land Acquisition Policy and Program of the National Park Service*, p. 32.

99. U.S. Department of the Interior, "National Park Service Purchases, Land and Water Conservation Fund,"; Conservation Foundation staff interview with Howard Miller, Land Resources Division, National Park Service, 1985.

100. U.S. Congress, *Land Acquisition Policy and Program of the National Park Service*, p. 6.

101. Deanne Kloepfer, *The Watt Record* (Washington, D.C.: Wilderness Society, undated), p. 4; 16 U.S.C.A., §§4601-5 (1974).

102. Lienesch, "The Slash of '82: LWCF Crippled by Cuts," p. 11.

103. U.S. Department of Interior, Bureau of Outdoor Recreation, "The Land and Water Conservation Fund: Intent and Accomplishments," in *National Urban Recreation Study*, Technical Reports Series, vol. 1, Report no. 9 (Washington, D.C.: U.S. Department of the Interior, 1979), pp.

251, 253. Note: The 1977 legislation created the "Burton account" to reduce the backlog (16 U.S.C.A., §§4601-7 (Supp. 1985). This money was available for acquisition of "lands, waters, or interests in lands or waters within the exterior boundaries of the national park system, national scenic trails, the national wilderness preservation system, federally administered components of the National Wild and Scenic Rivers System, and national recreation areas administered by the Secretary of Agriculture."

104. Kloepfer, The Watt Record, p. 4; U.S. Congress, Land Acquisition Policy and Program of the National Park Service, p. 4; U.S. Department of the Interior, Heritage Conservation and Recreation Service, "Land and Water Conservation Fund," undated fact sheet. The fund provides grants to states and through them to their political subdivisions—cities, counties, towns, etc. Other federal agencies include recreation resources such as national parks, seashores, lakeshores, forests, wild and scenic rivers, trails, national recreation areas, historic areas, wildlife refuges, and natural and wilderness areas.

105. U.S. Congress, Congressional Record, 94th Cong., 1st sess., October 29, 1975, pp. 34243-34249.

106. U.S. Department of the Interior, National Park Service, Budget Justifications Fiscal Year 1984, p. NPS-280.

107. Conservation Foundatin staff interview with National Park Service staff, 1984.

108. National Park Service, "Purchases by Fiscal Year, Land and Water Conservation Fund."

109. U.S. Department of the Interior, Bureau of Outdoor Recreation, "The Land and Water Conservation Fund: Intent and Accomplishments," p. 225.

110. Ibid.

111. See, for example, "3.3 Million-Checking off for Wildlife," The Environmental Forum, February 1983, p. 5.

112. Meg Maguire, "An Open Letter to Park and Recreation Advocates," Parks and Recreation, November 1982, p. 50; Charles A. Howell, III, "In Support of a Natural Resource Trust Fund" (unpublished, undated paper), p. 2; U.S. Congress, Congressional Record, 98th Cong., 2d sess., March 8, 1984, p. E907.

113. Wildlife Management Institute, Current Investments, Projected Needs, and Potential New Sources of Income for Nongame Fish and Wildlife Programs in the United States (Washington, D.C.: Wildlife Management Institute, 1975), pp. 42-43.

114. Kloepfer, The Watt Record, p. 3; U.S. Congress, Land Acquisition Policy and Program of the National Park Service, p. 6.

## Redwood National Park

1. 16 U.S.C.A, §§79a-j (1974); 16 U.S.C.A., §79b (Supp. 1985).

2. Conservation Foundation staff interview with Sharon Meyerkamp, REPP

coordinator, U.S. Department of Labor Employment and Training Administration, San Francisco, 1984.

3. Conservation Foundation staff interview with Max Findley, Lands Division, Department of Justice, 1984.

4. Ibid; Statement by Willis Kriz, chief, Land Resources Division, National Park Service, in U.S. Congress, House Committee on Appropriations, Subcommittee on the Department of the Interior and Related Agencies, *Appropriations for FY1985: Hearings*, Part 6, 98th Cong., 2d sess., 1984, pp. 376-377.

5. Statement by Willis Kriz in U.S. Congress, *Senate Budget Hearings for 1985*, part 6, 98th Cong., 2d sess., 1984, pp. 376-377.

6. U.S. Congress, House Committee on Interior and Insular Affairs, Subcommittee on National Parks and Insular Affairs, *Legislative History of the Redwood National Park Expansion Act of 1978 (P.L. 95-250)*, Committee Print 11, 95th Cong., 2d sess., 1978, p. 282.

7. 31 U.S.C.A., §1304 (1983); 28 U.S.C.A., §2517 (Supp. 1985).

8. Letter from Milton Socolar for the Comptroller General of the U.S. to the Honorable Vic Fazio, chairman, Subcommittee on Legislative Branch, Committee on House Appropriations, dated September 27, 1983.

## Supplementary Measures to Protect Privately Owned Land

1. U.S. Department of the Interior, *New Tools for Land Protection: An Introductory Handbook* (Washington, D.C.: U.S. Government Printing Office, 1982), pp. 32-33.

2. Francis P. Burling, *The Birth of the Cape Cod National Seashore* (Plymouth, Mass.: Leyden Press, 1978), p. 61; 16 U.S.C.A., §459e-1 (1974).

3. Conservation Foundation staff interview with National Park Service staff, 1984.

4. 26 U.S.C.A., §46 (1984). The Economic Recovery Tax Act of 1981 gives a 25 percent credit for certified historic structures that are either on the National Register or within a registered historic district and certified by the secretary of interior as being of historic significance to the district.

5. 16 U.S.C.A., §460s-11 (1974); William Shands, *Federal Resource Lands and Their Neighbors* (Washington, D.C.: The Conservation Foundation, 1979), p. 53.

6. Shands, *Federal Resource Lands and Their Neighbors*, p. 53.

7. Adirondack Planning Agency, "Evaluation of Adirondack Park Agency Local Planning Assistance Program" (Draft paper, prepared by: Local Planning Staff, Adirondack Planning Agency, New York, July 1979), p. 6.

8. Richard A. Liroff and G. Gordon Davis, *Protecting Open Space: Land Use Control in the Adirondack Park* (Cambridge, Mass.: Ballinger Publishing Co., 1981), pp. 61-63; Adirondack Park Agency, *1980 Annual Report* (Albany: New York Executive Department, 1981), p. 10).

9. Adirondack Park Agency, "Reviewing Park Issues and State Action for

1982," *1982 Annual Report* (Albany: New York Executive Department, March 1983), p. 6.

## Politics and Park Selection

1. John Ise, *Our National Park Policy: A Critical History* (Baltimore: Johns Hopkins University Press, 1961), p. 231.
2. Ibid., pp. 231-232.
3. Ibid., pp. 230-237.
4. Ise, *Our National Park Policy*, p. 232.
5. Ibid.
6. Ibid.
7. Ibid.
8. Ibid., p. 235.
9. Ise, *Our National Park Policy*; Alfred Runte, *National Parks: The American Experience* (Lincoln, Neb.: University of Nebraska Press, 1979); Conrad Wirth, *Parks, Politics and People* (Norman, Okla.: University of Oklahoma Press, 1979); Ronald F. Lee, *Family Tree of the National Park System* (Philadelphia: Eastern National Park and Monument Association, 1972).
10. Shankland, *Steve Mather of the National Parks*, pp. 222-223.

## Designation of Park Units

1. U.S. Congress, House Committee on Interior and Insular Affairs, *Land Acquisition Policy and Program of the National Park Service*, Committee Print 7, 98th Cong., 2d sess., 1984, p. 7.
2. Ibid., pp. 6-7, 40.
3. Alan K. Hogenauer, "Gone, But Not Forgotten: America's Delisted National Park Service Sites" (Paper delivered at the Travel and Tourism Research Association 14th Annual Conference, Banff, Alberta, Canada, June 1983), p. 64. The 34 units delisted include 10 sites that were authorized but never established and 24 units that were established but delisted; does not count proposed sites, established active sites or separately established, but eventually absorbed sites); information provided by Willis Kriz, chief, Land Resources Division, National Park Service, 1985. 4. Hogenauer, "Gone, But Not Forgotten," p. 65. (The exception is the National Visitor Center, which is neither historic nor scenic.)

## Chapter 7. The Challenges Ahead

1. Coopers & Lybrand, *Management Improvement Project, Phase I Report: Management Review and Assessment*, prepared for U.S. Department of the Interior, National Park Service, November 1977, p. I-127.
2. U.S. Department of the Interior, National Park Service, "Info-Plan: A Strategy for Managing the National Park Service Information Resource" (Washington, D.C.: National Park Service, Office of Information Management, 1983), executive summary, p. 1.

3. Coopers & Lybrand, *Management Improvement Project, Phase I Report*, pp. I-72 - I-74; see also, U.S. Comptroller-General, *Budget Formulation: Many Approaches Work But Some Improvements are Needed* (Washington, D.C.: General Accounting Office, 1980), p. 2.

4. U.S. Congress, House Committee on Appropriations, *Department of the Interior and Related Agencies Appropriations for 1979: Hearings*, Part 6, 95th Cong., 2d sess., 1978, pp. 368 et. seq.; U.S. Congress, House Committee on Appropriations, *Department of the Interior and Related Agencies Appropriations Bill, 1983*, 97th Cong., 2d sess., 1982, p. 30; see also, Coopers & Lybrand, *Management Improvement Project—Phase I Report*, p. I-50.

5. Coopers & Lybrand, *Management Improvement Project—Phase I Report*, p. I-50.

6. U.S. Department of the Interior, Heritage Conservation and Recreation Service, *The Third Nationwide Outdoor Recreation Plan* (Washington, D.C.: U.S. Government Printing Office, 1979), p. 46.

7. C.A.M.P.E.R., "Annual Report of Volunteer Activities for Catoctin Mountain Park," 1983.

8. Gary E. Machlis, Mark E. Van Every, and Donna K. Chickering, *Monitoring NPS Employee Attitudes: A Pilot Program for the Albright Training Center* (Moscow, Idaho: University of Idaho, Cooperative Park Studies Unit, undated), p. 29.

9. See, for example, Kenneth A. Gold, "A Comparative Analysis of Successful Organizations" (Washington, D.C.: U.S. Office of Personnel Management, 1981); and Thomas J. Peters and Robert H. Waterman, Jr., *In Search of Excellence: Lessons from America's Best Run Companies* (New York: Harper and Row, 1982).

10. Alfred Runte, *National Parks: The American Experience* (Lincoln, Nebr.: University of Nebraska Press, 1979), pp. 132-133, 160-161; Robert Shankland, *Steve Mather of the National Parks* (New York: Alfred A. Knopf, 1970), p. 167.

11. Mark Sagoff, "We Have Met the Enemy and He is Us or Conflict and Contradiction in Environmental Law," *Environmental Law* 12 (1982): 302.

12. Joseph L. Sax, *Mountains Without Handrails: Reflections on the National Parks* (Ann Arbor, Mich.: University of Michigan Press, 1980), p. 59.

13. Sax, *Mountains Without Handrails*, pp. 42, 45.

14. Joseph L. Sax, "Parks, Wilderness, and Recreation" (Paper delivered at the Conference on the Evolution of American Environmental Politics, Washington, D.C., June 28-29, 1984), p. 21.

15. Joseph L. Sax, "Fashioning a Recreation Policy for Our National Parklands: The Philosophy of Choice and the Choice of Philosophy," *Creighton Law Review* 13, no. 4 (1978-79):974.

16. Sax, *Mountains Without Handrails*, pp. 11, 51.

17. Ibid., p. 61.

18. See Gary E. Machlis, *On Interpretation: Sociology for Interpreters of*

*Natural and Cultural History* (Corvallis, Ore.: Oregon State University Press, 1984).
19. The Conservation Foundation, *State of the Environment: An Assessment at Mid-Decade* (Washington, D.C.: The Conservation Foundation, 1984), p. 223.
20. Sagoff, "We Have Met the Enemy and He is Us," p. 303.
21. Ibid., p. 309.

## The Presidential Commission on Outdoor Recreation Resources Review

1. Executive Order 12503, "Presidential Commission on Outdoor Recreation Resources Review," January 28, 1985; see 50 Fed. Reg. 4991 (1985).
2. Outdoor Recreation Resources Review Commission, *Outdoor Recreation for Americans* (Washington, D.C.: U.S. Government Printing Office, 1962).
3. Outdoor Recreation Policy Review Group, *Outdoor Recreation for America—1983* (Washington, D.C.: Resources for the Future, 1983).
4. Ibid.

# Index